SUCCESSFUL FUNDRAISING

John Baguley

Bibliotek Books

First edition 1996

Second Edition 2000

Grateful thanks are due to many charities who have supported the production of this book by granting us permission to reproduce examples of their campaign literature, in particular, Amnesty International, but also; St Christopher's Fellowship, Shelter, Greenpeace, Oxfam, British Red Cross, the Medical Foundation for the Care of Victims of Torture, the Royal Society for the Prevention of Cruelty to Animals and their advertising agency Abbott Mead Vickers BBDO Ltd. Thanks are also due to Bryan McAllister and *The Guardian* newspaper.

Published by
Bibliotek Books,
19 Warwick Road,
Stafford ST17 4PD, UK
ISBN 1 873017 40 5

*This book is dedicated to
Kitt Baguley, Sam Baguley and Deirdre Morrow.
In apology for the hours I spent at the keyboard.*

Introduction

At the foot of the Potala Palace in Lhasa, I was confronted by the consummate professional fundraiser. Tsering, a young monk, stepped into my path and with a smile as wide as the bright Tibetan sky he said 'Money, please'. His food for that day depended on my generosity, but he was in no way aggressive, and his request did not induce a feeling of guilt. I understood from his demeanour that a refusal would not offend, and he presented his case in the best way possible - a face-to-face, direct, human plea for help. It was obvious from his deep red robes that he was a Buddhist monk, and therefore depended on the kindness of strangers. It was clear the funds he solicited would go to cover his basic needs. January in Lhasa is very cold, and begging in sub-zero temperatures would add a note of desperation to any plea; but he knew that my

Tsering, Lhasa, 2000

gift would add merit to my life as surely as it enriched his, and it was plain that he did not feel demeaned or ashamed by his simple request. I gave him enough to cover his food for a day or so, asked if I could take his picture, and felt good about myself. It was a satisfying encounter for us both.

In the pages of this revised and extended book you will find the lessons of this transaction amplified to cover the fundraising techniques necessary to run both small and large charities, as well as campaigning organisations. In all our sophistication it is easy to forget the situation we are in. No one has any obligation to help us, yet if we have a truly worthwhile cause and approach people in the right way they will give us all the money we need to carry out our work. In our arrogance, we fundraisers have often played on peoples' guilt and pushed our message beyond acceptable boundaries believing we had almost a divine right to demand money. Now we are faced with a new sophisticated public who give not out of duty but out of conviction. In this new environment many fundraisers have seen their efforts fail and their organisations' income fall. Indeed charitable giving by individuals in the UK fell heavily for much of the nineties. The old routines often no longer work and anything less than a highly competent approach will not meet its target.

Indeed, we are now entering an era of 'permission fundraising', spurred by the Data Protection Act and the complaints of our supporters. We are having to ask individuals 'How would you like us to communicate with you?' For many organisations which are now setting up web-based fundraising this comes easily. We ask our supporters if they would like to receive our newsletter and appeals via email instead of through the postal service. Yet, in our ordinary communications we fail at the outset to establish what kind of relationship a simple donation is going to involve. This results in a complex series of 'opt-outs' and 'opt-ins', leaving the supporter confused and apprehensive. Permission fundraising cuts through this confusion and defines the relationship at its first step.

Much of this book is based on the practical consultancy work I have undertaken over the past few years through the International Fundraising Consultancy (IFC) along with my fellow directors Jasvir Kaur and Chris Small. From our website on **http://www.ifc.tc** you can order further copies of this book, read our articles on current fundraising problems, check links to other fundraising sites and learn more about the work of the IFC.

Under the Charities Aid Foundation's broad definition of the voluntary sector, we, in the UK, are in a sector whose income totalled some £9.1 billion in 1991 and £11.8 billion in 1995 (a 29% increase). Further afield, Salamon and Anheier estimate the sector at £400 billion in just seven of the countries they surveyed. It is arguably one of the fastest growing areas of human endeavour, but more importantly it provides the most worthwhile and exciting opportunities for entrepreneurs. These men and women are the real heroes of this millennium, devoting their lives and expertise to the alleviation of human suffering, yet they are undervalued and unrecognised by the conventions of our time. It is my hope, that, within the not too distant future, private satisfaction in our work will be augmented by proper public recognition.

I would like to thank the Open University for its strong support and guidance for this revised edition; my supervisors at the Open University, Chris Cornforth and Geoff Mallory, for their patience whilst I deviated from my research into the global development of NGOs to revise this text; the Institute of Charity Fundraising Managers (ICFM) for their support; and my colleagues at the Medical Foundation for the Care of Victims of Torture for their inspiration for so much of the practical detail.

John Baguley, Lhasa, January 2000

Contents

1   Developing a Fundraising Strategy

How to use this book

Fundraising is like the snow on Mount Fuji - it is often the most visible part of an organisation and the part that people notice first, but below the snow is the structure of the organisation carrying out its work. Holding the whole operation together over time is its strategy. Part and parcel of that overall strategy should be the fundraising strategy. This chapter shows not only the process by which it is created, but also the planning and budgeting that follow closely from a good strategy and ensure that it succeeds.

Setting a strategy

To be efficient in the search for funds it is necessary to plan, and to plan efficiently it is essential to have a strategy. That strategy will consist of selecting the best combination of fundraising techniques for your organisation and deploying them in close combination with the activities of the rest of the organisation, such as promotional or campaigning work. This helps to ensure that the organisation works harmoniously towards its overall goals. Fundraising is often seen as an add-on extra to an organisation's work, or as a necessary evil. Integrating the fundraising strategy into the overall work of the organisation will help change this attitude, reducing stress for the fundraisers and helping to maximise income generation.

An essential part of fundraising strategy is the allocation of resources to

"My administration costs and overheads are absolutely nil. Every penny of your donation will go towards a cup of tea."

Reproduced by kind permission of The Guardian and Bryan McAllister.

fundraising techniques to meet the organisation's need for income over time. Different techniques are needed to meet immediate needs, mid-term (say three- to five-year) needs and long-term (say five- to ten-year) needs. It is essential that short-term needs do not preclude investment in medium- or long-term strategies if income is to be maximised in the medium or long term. An important part of the work of anyone responsible for fundraising strategy is that they communicate the benefits of appropriate investment to those who allocate resources, so that the future needs of the organisation can be met as they occur.

Competitive and collaborative strategies

The technique described below is fine to meet known future financial needs of the organisation but in the real world other factors can play a strong part in strategy development. Your organisation may have strong competitors against whom it may wish to either challenge by competing directly for market share by aggressively fundraising with the same techniques. For example, if their main recruitment technique is direct mail you may compete by producing better direct mail packs (or cover a wider variety of lists), or by being willing to endure smaller returns to ensure that you build a large base of supporters. This process was the one used by Japanese car manufacturers in challenging the US and UK car markets. Alternatively, you could look for a niche they may not be using or even aware of. For example, a cancer charity could steel a march on its competitors by opening up charity shops and buy the expertise necessary by advertising for staff at a higher than usual rate of pay to draw in the best professionals from other organisations.

On the other hand, it could be that as collaborative charities you may choose to avoid fundraising that clashed with others, and in collaboration with another charity you could divide up the market by agreement, each working in a different way to fund complementary work. For example, one charity could look for government funds and fees to open up a new area of health work whereas a sister charity could concentrate on building a donor base of supporters so that it could engage in campaigning to challenge government policy. This could even involve setting up a non-charitable membership organisation to act as a pressure group.

Emergent strategy

Indeed strategy is rarely carried out exactly as planned. This may be due to the external environment causing significant shifts in the situation that governed the formation of the original strategy, or it may be caused by an internal force, such as senior managers who are not happy with the strategy, and subvert the process. If either of these forces is strong enough they can derail a strategy and prevent it reaching its objectives, or corrective action can be taken to stop an emergent strategy from taking place.

In many organisations strategic planning is rarely carried out and strategies emerge from the day to day practical decisions that managers make or by the shifts in policy that the governing body agrees. In rapidly changing circumstances this degree of flexibility can be very effective if deliberately and properly managed but it is more usually a sign of poor management and results in the organisation being blown about one way then another without a clear goal in sight.

Strategic drift

Another danger is that once a strategy is set it is not monitored and corrections are not taken to keep it on course. In these circumstances the objectives can alter subtly and the course of activities drift away from the original target. If this process becomes deliberate then a new emergent strategy may develop along a new path which may or may not be appropriate for the organisation.

Strategic thinking: getting started

If you have just started as a fundraiser in a charity, or if it is time to take stock of where your work is going, a good idea is to borrow a technique for strategic thinking from business management, called 're-engineering'. This has been called the blank page process. Take a blank page and write out where your organisation wants to be in three years time (or five years, or whatever time-span is appropriate) in terms of the income you will be required to generate. From that starting point calculate how you will generate that income as if you were starting from a greenfield site and not from the awful mess you may be confronted with at present. It is surprising what a salutary experience this exercise can be.

Knowing where the organisation would like to be in terms of the work it does, and hence what kind of financial resources will be required, means you can work out how much investment is needed in various areas of fundraising to produce those resources. Naturally, the resources may not be currently available and you may have to trim your investment, thus limiting future income growth. To do all this professionally it is essential to have an overview of the range of fundraising techniques that could be employed to reach your goals. This book will give you that overview. You can read it straight through or just dip in to read about techniques or issues that interest you.

Reviewing the techniques: where the money comes from

Sources of funds are limited in number. They can be roughly grouped into the following categories: funds from individuals, governments, companies, trusts and foundations, the National Lottery (in the UK), trading, interest, dividends and any fees or other earned income. Of course, funds from individuals come via a huge number of routes. As will be explained in detail later, many voluntary organisations' core funding comes in relatively small donations from many supporters (see Fig 1).

In their book *The emerging non-profit sector – an overview* Lester Salamon and Helmut Anheier draw a very wide net around the notion of non-profit organisations. They claim that most non-profit income is from private fees and sales (47% of

1992 Charitable Giving by Source (in $ millions)		
Individuals	101,830	81.9%
Bequests	8,150	6.6%
Foundations	8,330	6.7%
Corporations	6,000	4.8%
Total	124,310	100.0%

Fig. 1 *Statistics from the Chronicle of Philanthropy, USA.*

income) followed by government giving (43% of income). For the purposes of this book that is an unworkably large net, indicating that non-profit business is a vast sector with a revenue of £400 billion in total in the seven countries they surveyed. Here I have concentrated on a more traditional definition which places individual gifts at the heart of charitable and non-profit giving. Even interest and dividends are not usually the responsibility of fundraisers, though just as in the commercial world, the treasury function of charities is increasingly being scrutinised for efficiency as well as safety of investment. If, for example, your organisation receives say, one third of its income from a US sister organisation it would be advisable to 'sell forward' your dollars for an agreed price. Otherwise you are speculating that the price obtained when the dollars arrive will be what you put in your budget for the year or higher. Of course the dollar could move in relation to the pound and if you have not sold forward your organisation could see its income fall heavily below budget. Other considerations include setting an ethical investment policy and the level of reserves that is prudent to hold.

Developing your strategy

The fundraising audit

To determine what techniques and resources you currently have at your disposal and how effective these are, the first thing to do is to undertake a thorough fundraising audit. This should list all the fundraising activities the organisation is now undertaking and critically appraise them. Who is responsible, how much is invested and how much earned?

Comparative figures going back a few years will be essential in order to see if these activities are declining or improving and to make a projection forward. These extrapolations customarily assume that current trends continue unless there are good reasons to think otherwise. To check for such good reasons, it is necessary to look at the external environment as well as your organisation's internal operation.

Check the likely changes that may affect your organisation and its fundraising with regard to social, technological, economic, environmental and political factors - a STEEP analysis. You may find that investment in fundraising could be better deployed over the whole range of techniques to give a higher return on investment (ROI) but remember that some techniques can add synergy to your efforts. For example, national press advertising helps to build profile, and trading often helps local groups to create a feeling of belonging. These latter points are often hotly debated and you will need to form a view perhaps based partly on discussions with supporters. Is ROI everything?

Gap analysis

The next step is to list which areas of fundraising are missing (gap analysis) and the costs and likely benefits of beginning those activities.

This book will form a guide to the range of possibilities available to most fundraisers. Armed with this knowledge, a ranking should be made of all the possible areas of investment in terms of their short- and long-term cost-effectiveness, so that you and the organisation can decide how much of its scarce resources to devote to which areas of fundraising.

Making projections

It must be borne in mind throughout this exercise that maximising income in the long term requires investment at an initial loss (often for one year or eighteen months), so the projections of possible future income from each source should run three to five years into the future.

Income from your donor-base

Essential steps in your strategy are to:

- calculate future projections by estimating how many financial supporters (your donor-base) the organisation will have in each year of the projection. Donors can be called members, supporters, or friends, but their key characteristic is that they pay an annual fee or make a regular donation (usually it is sufficient that they have made one donation in the last two years), and are therefore liable to give again if asked, always providing you have looked after them and built a relationship that met their needs.

- use the average number of donors to indicate future income from appeals, raffles, trading, etc., as the income from these activities is directly related to the number of donors you have (and their giving capacity). Multiply the average donation by the projected number giving in each case.

- reflect on the impact of inflation on your projection, and any other economic indicators agreed with your organisation's treasurer or finance officer.

In using the blank sheet of paper principle to determine where you wish to be in a few years time, it is necessary to:

- estimate the number of supporters you will need in your final year. This tells you the bulk of your income for that year (add likely income from events, grants from trusts, shop income and other non-supporter income).

- work backwards from this estimate to calculate the investment needed each year to 'buy' those supporters. This will be based on the number of new members per thousand pounds invested in each recruitment activity (prospecting) such as direct mail, advertising or leaflets.

- take care not to assume that the market for new supporters is infinite. Amnesty International, for example, has had difficulty recruiting new members through advertisements placed outside the Guardian, Independent and Observer newspapers. Friends of the Earth has undergone a rapid period of growth and almost as rapid a period of decline, as the green movement's media exposure rose and fell dramatically. However, the limits to growth are difficult to estimate, and it is easiest to look at other organisations in your field and determine their level of support as a benchmark or target for your organisation. Support for the Medical Foundation for the Care of Victims of Torture has grown steadily over the last four years with the support base increasing by 25% a year but the lack of a similar organisation to benchmark against makes long-term planning a nightmare.

Working backwards from future needs - an example

If your organisation has 20,000 members in the year 2001, bringing in £200,000 per year, and it will need to spend £550,000 in 2005, then in 2005 you will need 55,000 members, (unless you are absolutely sure of developing alternative sources of income). Can this be achieved?

If 10% of your members leave each year you will need to acquire the following new members each year:

	2002	2003	2004	2005
Start of year	18,000	34,200	48,780	61,902
Add in year	20,000	20,000	20,000	
Total at end	38,000	54,200	68,780	

which will give you a margin of error of better than 10%. Over four years this would be most welcome!

This is a simplified example with no account taken of inflation or other changes in the economy, or increases in membership fees or average donations. I have also ignored new members arriving during 2005, and, for clarity, assumed people all leave at the end of the year.

So the investment now needed is enough to bring in 20,000 new members each year, plus the full costs of servicing those members and appealing to them for extra funds. Is this available?

If a member stays with you for six years on average, and contributes £30 per year on average, in total they are worth (6 x £30) = £180 over their 'lifetime' with you. If the newsletter costs £4 per head per year and all other servicing costs £3 per head per year, then the member would cost (6 x £7) = £42 over their 'lifetime'. So each member is worth (£180 - £42) = £138 to you.

If an advertisement campaign costs £10,000 and brings in 100 members with an average donation of £18 your immediate loss will be £8,200. Over, say, the next six years these members will bring in (100 x £138) = £13,800 showing a long-term profit of £5,600. The question you must now ask is, 'Is this too close for comfort?'

If, instead, 200 people joined, the immediate loss would be (£10,000 - (200 x £18)) = £6,400, but over six years they would bring in (200 x £138) = £27,600 and yield a profit of £21,200. Is this more acceptable?

If, say, 400 people joined, the immediate loss would be (£10,000 - (400 x £18)) = £2,800, but over six years they would bring in (400 x £138) = £55,200 and generate a profit of £52,400. Do you have a more profitable and secure way of raising funds?

Fig. 1a *Planning and investment to meet future needs.*

- work out how much to invest in 'buying' each new donor. For this, you need two vital pieces of information: the average 'lifetime' of a donor with you, and the amount they are likely to give over that lifetime. It is not as easy as it seems to calculate these numbers. The average lifetime of a donor will depend on the drop-out rate, i.e. how many donors cease to support you each year. In a membership organisation you may have this information to hand, but if your organisation is increasing or decreasing rapidly the calculation is still not straightforward.

The average amount a donor is likely to give depends on the total income from all donors (this figure will come from a consideration of all those sources of income that depend directly on the supporters such as raffles, trading, direct mail appeals and legacies), less the total amount you spend on them per person in terms of newsletters, administration, new members' packs, etc., divided by the number of donors.

Income from other sources

If substantial amounts of your income are from other sources such as the government, trusts, shops or events, the future may be more difficult to gauge.

Government policy can change overnight, and the State is in retreat from making provision for the voluntary sector in many Western countries. This process has, perhaps surprisingly, hardly been diminished even by 'Third Way' governments in the UK and elsewhere in Europe. In fact, the current boom in voluntary sector enterprise is largely the result of attempts to replace previous government provision for various social services by charitable activity. During this retreat there have been some legal changes that benefit non-governmental organisations (NGOs), albeit principally those that are registered charities, by improving the range of donations on which a charity can reclaim the tax already paid. Improvements in the law relating to Gift Aid, Covenants and Payroll Giving are examples of this. Pay careful attention to changes in the National Budget which may affect your organisation's income. At the time of writing it looks as if Gift Aid will now be available on all donations if the donor registers in some way for this purpose. This could bring an unexpected dividend to charities or destroy the long term income enjoyed from covenants increasing the volatility in donations that has been a hallmark of the nineties. If your organisation is receiving funds directly from government sources it will know quite accurately the immediate and medium-term prospects for additional income.

Trusts do not usually like to make any long-term commitments which tie up their disposable income for years to come, and prefer to wean charitable organisations into becoming self-supporting. This is often a condition of any trust grant which lasts more than one year. Trust giving is rarely the mainstay of a large, long-lasting organisation. If this is the case with your organisation, it is particularly vulnerable and should be investing in alternative forms of income generation. Small pressure groups with few national supporters are often in this position, and can fold when their trust income dries up. It may be prudent to discuss this with your principal funders.

Shops can generate an excellent income, but you must allow for peaks and troughs. A prudent fundraising strategy will also develop other effective means of raising income as a hedge against the days when shops do badly or there is some unforeseen shift along the product cycle and people will no longer enter 'charity' shops. One such hedge could be the development of e-commerce and fundraising on the Internet.

New Sources

If your gap analysis indicates you should be investing in new areas of fundraising, it will help to discuss these with an experienced fundraiser or consultant to estimate possible income.

Having selected your range of techniques and put these together in a strategy you will need to budget to cover this cost and estimate how much income it will generate over time. Next, plan who does what. This will be essential in turning your strategy into reality. Most of this work will have been done as you selected and marshalled your techniques. You will probably find this to be an iterative process in which you will need to make many adjustments before you come up with an optimum strategy, which will then need to be agreed officially with your organisation before you have the green light to proceed. One practical result of this process is usually to set a new income and expenditure budget.

Testing your strategy

In presenting a new strategy, particularly one involving increased investment or the introduction of new fundraising techniques into your organisation, you may well find that there is a strong tendency to think that it will only work for someone else. 'It won't work here'

It may work in London - but not in Wales, Scotland, or Rutland. It may work for Oxfam, Friends of the Earth and Save the Children - but we are different. It may work in India, Japan and Chile - but it won't work in Canada...

Phrases like these are so familiar to fundraisers that they have developed a stock response - test it! Naturally, there will be some cultural adaptation from country to country or organisation to organisation, but there is also a remarkable level of similarity of response around the globe to fundraising techniques. Schools' sponsored walks work for HelpAge International in India, Africa and Latin America. Direct mail works in Germany, India and Japan. Telemarketing works everywhere there is a phone. This is because consumerism has raced around the world changing the way we all live and creating business structures and ways of doing business which fundraisers can adapt for very positive ends.

Testing everything is a central tenet of good fundraising practice. It is at its most important in direct mail work. Here it is quite possible for you to test even the difference made in the response by a comma in one place or a comma in another place. By splitting the mailing list into two equal, random sets of people and mailing each of these sets with a slightly different letter (coding the reply coupon differently for each) the results can be directly compared.

Of course, more significant things than commas are tested. In fact, so much has been tested so carefully that direct mail letters often bear a frightening similarity to each other.

If your organisation lacks a significant variety of income sources or is neglecting just one important technique, then try out a new idea on as small a scale as possible (always provided the results will be statistically significant) and, if it works, roll it out on a grand scale. It is important to maintain this practice in all your fundraising, as far as possible, as the years go by, and not to get set in your ways.

Testing new techniques, innovating and developing old techniques to keep them working and relevant to the changing market, all take time, research and enthusiasm; but that effort will be repaid by the results. Sometimes the difference will be sufficient to make a whole programme profitable, but though it may be worthwhile as an investment, obtaining resources is much harder if the programme makes even a small loss. In time the response to all ideas and materials runs down, and the best ideas become unprofitable unless renewed; but it often takes very little imaginative thought to revive a programme and regain a healthy return.

Budgeting

The importance of budgeting

I was once offered a fundraising position with a fairly large organisation, which was undertaking some unusual and interesting work on environmental issues, on the basis that, as a fundraiser, I should be able to raise my own salary and quite a bit more. On the face of it that seemed reasonable, but when I enquired how much the annual expenditure budget was to do this they said, 'Oh, what we meant was you must find the money to pay your own salary and then any money you need to spend on fundraising.' I did not accept the position.

Expenditure on fundraising is an essential part of any organisation's outgoings and fundraisers, like any other employees, should have a reasonable and secure income. The lack of proper budgeting for this is quite common, and sadly, this means that organisations do not grow at the rate they should and their charitable work is therefore severely curtailed. It is a false economy in any sector of business to underinvest in marketing the products, or in the research and development of those products.

Making budget adjustments

A proper budget gives you a clear idea of how much to spend on each of the projects that will be undertaken during the year or years ahead, and how much income is expected from each of those projects. Usually these will be on separate lines of the budget, and each month an account will be produced to show how the income and expenditure has gone on each of these lines (the management accounts) so that adjustments can be made to activities if they are over- or under-performing. Most years will see changes taking place with regard to expected income. Expenditure is much easier to predict, and, of course, no-one should overspend their budget without reference to higher authority. A dynamic organisation will immediately respond to this by investing heavily in those aspects of fundraising that are going well and reducing or ceasing expenditure on those areas that are not.

This is a very difficult area in which to take decisions, and mature experience (as well as entrepreneurial flair) is needed to understand exactly why an area of work is not performing as expected, and whether this is a temporary fluctuation or likely to be a permanent state of affairs. Naturally you need much more information than is provided in the management accounts to operate effectively, and this is covered in the 'Planning' sub-section under 'Fundraising reports'.

Budgeting for a single event

Most of your budgeting will be done for activities for which you have a track record. Towards the end of your financial year you may look back and see that you have held a flag day, organised a concert, run a direct mail programme and made four appeals to your organisation's supporters for extra funds. Next year, if things are going well, you will probably want to repeat those activities and organise some new ones. Budgeting for the events you repeat will be done with reference to previous years, and then adding your estimate of any likely increases in expenditure and income - bearing in mind any rate of inflation agreed with your finance officer and/or treasurer. For a new event this calculation will be much more difficult and it is advisable to be conservative.

Example: budgeting for a concert

If you are going to organise a concert, then you will need to look at all aspects of possible expenditure and find a way of estimating the income. The best starting point is to borrow someone else's knowledge and particularly their experience. You will find that most experienced fundraisers will give you quite a lot of information if they have a few minutes free.

- Talk to other fundraisers about their events. Ask about their successes and failures. (This applies, of course, not just to income and expenditure, but also to management of the event.)

- For an event where you are expecting to make money from those taking part, the key is to estimate how many will attend and how much they will give on average. Concert-goers will be attending because they wish to see and hear the star(s) perform. They will not go and sit through a performance they cannot stand because they wish to support your organisation; neither will they pay extra because it is a charity event. So, the previous pulling power of the entertainer will be your guide to the size of venue you can book and the amount to charge.

- As well as the income from tickets, look at as many different ways of making money from the event as you can think of. Sponsorship can help to keep down or eliminate your costs. It also impresses your supporters and others who may naively believe that everything is free to you, including the hall, orchestra, publicity, sound system, after-show party (very important for your key donors and for thanking the celebrities), etc. Discuss the event with companies who have supported you and look at ways they may benefit, e.g. free seats they can give to important customers, or better still the opportunity to meet and socialise with celebrities. This is a key aspect of many events that is often neglected. Much long-term income will result from using your access to celebrities to bring major donors and other key friends into contact with stars. Sponsors usually like to be thanked visibly, usually in the programme but if the event is filmed they may require a presence in the footage and that will need careful negotiation if the film is going to be broadcast.

- You should also make money from selling advertisements in the programme. Ask all the tradespeople who supply you with the goods your organisation uses during the year to buy space in the brochure, and do not forget to invite them to the after-show party.

- Valuable extra funds can come from such things as a bucket collection at the end and T-shirt sales.

- If you are fortunate enough you will actually make more money from sales of 'product' i.e. video, TV, film, cassettes, etc., than from the event. But unless contracts are signed, do not budget for income from that source, as it is notoriously unreliable. Try for the event to be filmed by a keen company in exchange for part of the sales rights and let them undertake the marketing unless you have or wish to gain that professional experience. Remember that performers may not agree to perform if they are to be filmed and may then only do numbers with which they are comfortable. They will need to know upfront and you will need to get written permission which is a nightmare in itself.

- As a rule of thumb, having calculated the income, deduct between 10% and 20% for publicity (posters, adverts, etc.). Be ready to write and phone the media relentlessly to obtain as much editorial coverage as possible and as many listings as you can. Do not rely on your supporters alone.

- Find out how much you need to pay for the hall, how much to fly in your stars and meet their other transport and hotel expenses. Their management will have a standard list of outrageous demands to be met. Do ensure you negotiate to minimise expenses perhaps setting a limit to the amount you are willing to pay.

- Think carefully about the cost of the sound system, stage decoration, rehearsals (hall rental and professional musician costs), the production manager, etc. Be exhaustive in thinking through all the stages of running the show, because extra costs traditionally eat up much more than the expected profits on concerts. Orchestras need rehearsal time and can be very expensive.

- If, at the end of all this, you can still estimate a profit, check the break-even point, that is, how many tickets you need to sell to get your money back. If you can do this on half the sales and still make a healthy profit if only two-thirds of the tickets sell, then you have an event worth running. In practice the margins may be tighter than this and you will need to make a professional judgement (taking as much experienced expert advice as possible) on whether or not to proceed.

Key to success

The actual figures you use should always be conservative. The rule is that your expenditure always happens and the organisation always spends any income you estimate will arrive - so you had better be sure it does!

Be very tough in resisting pressure to pad out your estimated income so that someone's favourite rock concert project can be funded. You will not be thanked later when the expected income does not materialise and the organisation cuts expenditure in the most vulnerable areas, which often means staff costs.

The budget line, then, will simply show the expected income and expenditure for the planned event. If you expect to convert a significant number of people into members as a result of that event, then the consequent income should appear in a membership development line, (not just in the membership subscriptions line), and credited to the event during its evaluation. It is, however, notoriously difficult to convert concert goers to donors – be warned.

Planning

Integrating planning and budgeting

Your master plan can be quite simple; just a sheet of A4 paper with the months of the year across the top, the list of planned fundraising activities down the left-hand side, and a series of crosses in the squares under the months where you plan these activities (see Fig 1b).

It is very useful to indicate on the plan any other activities scheduled by the rest of your organisation that may affect your plans. For example, the dates when any newsletters are issued are important, because you will schedule your appeals to members at suitable intervals between them in such a way as to avoid members feeling that you could have placed your appeal in the newsletter and saved the postage. (The popular press has trained the public to be eagle-eyed about unnecessary expenditure by charities, and to retain their confidence you should be one step ahead.) Incidentally, if you were to place your appeal in the newsletter the sharp fall in response would far outweigh the saving in postage. Or would it? If you are not sure, test!

Naturally, you will also need to work out exactly who is going to undertake each of these activities, when they should start, and the key stages at which you will need to monitor progress. Don't try to do everything yourself.

PLANNED FUNDRAISING ACTIVITIES

	Jan	Feb	Mar	Apr	May	Jun	July	etc.
Advertisements	●		●		●		●	
Direct mail		●		●		●		
Magazine inserts	●			●			●	
Newsletter	●			●			●	
Appeals		●			●			●
Concerts				●				
Art auctions		●						
Etc.								

Fig. 1b *A simple plan of the year's fundraising.*

For the purposes of budgeting you need to be certain that each of these activities really will take place. This is not a wish list. The organisation is about to set out how it will spend the profit from these activities, and it will be your responsibility to see that they occur at the level of profit you say will be generated. Be conservative, but do not simply underestimate to give yourself an easy time. Be prudent, but not pessimistic. Your treasurer should rein in your natural optimism.

Income projections

- For each activity you plan, calculate the expenditure and the income:
  - each category, e.g. advertising, loose-leaf inserts, trading, will probably form a separate budget line.
  - each event will have its own line.
- Before you begin work on the budget, the organisation's financial advisers (usually the treasurer, head of finance and director) will set the basic budget parameters with you. These include the organisation's estimate for inflation next year, the cost of borrowing, etc. The parameters should be conservative, and may give one rate for the increase in prices you will face and another for the percentage increase in donations (the estimated increase in costs possibly being higher than that in income).
- A view should be taken on the effect of any increase in membership or subscription fees. Unless this is dramatic it will have no effect on the overall numbers recruited by any particular means, as the membership fees of most organisations are far less than the average donation - which is a clear indication they are far too low. Many organisations receive, on average, a donation of one third of the fee on top of their membership income. This shows that members themselves recognise that their fee is too low to be properly effective. You may, of course, experience difficulty in convincing your board or council of this.
- For each of your projected activities use historical data from previous years to check for any trends. Increase expenditure by cost inflation, and income by the agreed amount, and you will begin to build up a picture of the financial future.
- Calculate at an early stage the increase in the number of members or donors. This is especially important, as it will affect many of the other budget lines, setting the amount of income from appeals, raffles, trading, and any other activity dependent on membership numbers. For those activities it is essential to multiply the average cost and income (adjusted as before) by the average number of expected members and/or donors in the new financial year. This is where the effect of past and future investment is felt. If you have had the foresight to invest strongly in membership/donor development you will see a correspondingly rapid growth in your income.
- The next area to work out is the expenditure on membership/donor acquisition. This is the key to your future income. Unless your organisation is very popular, this expenditure will be in the form of an investment whereby you lose money in the first year but come into a very healthy profit in year two and each following year for the whole of the member's or donor's 'life' with you. (A slight dip in income as donors retire is usually outweighed by legacy income as your planned

giving programme takes effect. Students often leave the organisation in the early years of their career, but return later if the organisation is still relevant and dynamic.)

The next three years and beyond

The interaction of planning and budgeting

In any one year it is likely that your organisation will have far more activities that it wishes to undertake than it can afford to fund, and it is easy to succumb to the temptation to reduce investment in fundraising.

Often it is only when the draft budgets for future years make it clear that this would drastically reduce future income, and therefore future programme activity, can the temptation be successfully resisted, and your expenditure budget increased by an amount which will ensure adequate growth for the organisation.

It is therefore important for you, along with the organisation's key financial advisers, to plan the draft budgets for a number of years so that the organisation can make a sound decision about investment. This is usually an iterative and time-consuming process, which involves going backwards and forwards, checking what will happen in two or three years time for such and such a level of investment - putting your calculations on a spreadsheet could save your sanity.

To do this accurately it is essential to know how long members and donors stay with your organisation (on average), from each of the different areas of recruitment, and how much they give in additional income. This will both guide the amount of loss you can afford to bear in year one (the more the income over lifetime, the greater the loss that can be borne), and indicate the optimum areas for investment.

Key to success

It would be rash to invest in just the most profitable one or two areas, because the business cycle operates as inexorably with charities as it does with any other commercial activity, and you may experience, for example, a slowing down of the response to direct mail, and an improvement in advertising revenue. It is tempting to think this undermines the budgeting process - but budget estimates are not deadly accurate predictions of what will happen, just the best estimates given the current state of knowledge and without them we could not plan. Waiting for things to happen would be like driving a car looking only in the rear-view mirror.

Naturally, you will take corrective action if things change for the worse, and take advantage if they improve. You will need a degree of flexibility to spend extra money when things go very well (rolling-over the income). If this is not in the budget you may need to go back to your director, treasurer or finance subcommittee, so it is worthwhile discussing this possibility during the budget process.

Planning your cash flow

As part of your planning it is important to know when the organisation may become short of money and how soon this will be made up by future income flows. When this is set out month by month for the next year it forms the cash flow projections. This chart will allow funds to be borrowed and repaid on time or an overdraft to be arranged.

When you have mapped out the total income and expenditure for the whole organisation covering each activity in the year, it is easy to total this up month by month. Bear in mind:

- the time taken to receive and pay bills
- the time taken for income to arrive
  - newspaper advertising revenue will mostly come in during the following week or two
  - direct mail revenue will come in the following month
  - revenue from loose-leaf inserts will come in during the following two months
  - appeals to the donor-base will take a few weeks
  - anything with a monthly giving form will naturally be in twelve monthly instalments.

Ask your head of administration and finance how long it really takes before the tax is reclaimed on covenants, etc. Double that time in your calculations. This cash flow of income, when compared with the flow of expenditure, will reveal the months when you may need to borrow from the bank or dip into reserves. If you do not need to do this you are probably being far too cautious in your investment in fundraising. Though your trustees may set a reserve level of 3 or 4 months of running costs which you will not be able to touch without their permission.

Tax efficient donations

Throughout this book tax efficient donations will be mentioned in several places. A donation made to a registered charity can be simply sent by cheque or put into a collecting box. However, if your donors can be encouraged to give tax effectively, your charity can claim back the tax from the Inland Revenue. Those paying tax at the higher rate can usually claim back, for themselves, the difference between the standard rate (which the charity will reclaim) and the higher rate. Of course, you have to be a tax payer for these schemes to work.

The methods of giving which offer this possibility have been progressively extended in recent years and both the lowest payment threshold and the ceiling for such payments shifted to assist charities. Read each budget statement carefully for changes that apply to charities.

The principal methods of tax effective giving are Gift Aid, Covenants, Payroll Giving, Legacies, where capital gains tax has been incurred on the sale of assets and through the Charities Aid Foundation scheme.

Gift aid

A donor can now gift aid any amount provided they fill out a simple declaration to that effect. Provided they are tax payers the charity can then reclaim the standard rate of tax paid on that donation and into the future though the donor can revoke the declaration in regard to future payments if they so choose.

A deed of covenant

A deed of covenant is a promise to pay a certain amount annually for at least 4 years for no material consideration (i.e. it must be a true gift and as a rule of thumb any incentive, e.g. a newsletter, received in return should be worth less than 2.5% of the gift). Covenants must be made out on an appropriate form - the deed, which, incidentally, does not need an expiry date. N.B. If the forms are to be used in Scotland they will need to be slightly different. Again higher rate tax payers can reclaim the extra 15% they have paid.

Payroll giving

Many companies employ substantial numbers of workers and many professional groups, like legal practices, now run such schemes. The money is deducted via the payroll before tax is taken out and passed to a charity agency (of which there are several, though Give As You Earn run by CAF is probably the best known) which then passes the funds on according to your request. Companies often select a small group of charities to benefit from their schemes. The maximum amount that you can give has in recent years been raised progressively.

Legacies

Gifts to charity from your estate are free of inheritance tax.

Capital gains

This is a useful way of avoiding tax and not passing on the burden. Suppose you have £1000 worth of shares that would incur capital gains tax if they were sold. You can give them to a charity without incurring the capital gains tax yourself and not passing that tax burden on to the charity.

CAF

The Charities Aid Foundation run an ingenious scheme for those donors who wish to make occasional payments to different charities tax effectively. The donor makes tax-efficient payments to CAF and they issue a 'cheque book' from which cheques can be sent to any charity.

International budgeting

Many charities or not-for-profit organisations have a loose international network of sister organisations. Occasionally, these contribute to the centre a percentage of their income, or even all their profits. Often they receive money from the centre to fund their charitable or campaigning activities. Equally often the centre does very little to assist the overseas divisions, though the more dynamic multinationals are beginning to invest heavily in the former second and third world countries. This investment is yielding rich rewards as tried and tested techniques are used on their large, affluent caring classes with little or no competition.

Budgeting for this is difficult the first time around, and it is best to set up an investment fund to be spent in each country whose market you wish to penetrate, rather than budgeting for an early return. The usual careful monitoring will reveal what has gone right and where improvements are needed, which will lead to proper estimates in subsequent years. The returns can be so large that it is tempting to keep ploughing back the profits and go for growth while you are alone in the market - but do not forget that your organisation's public profile and respect for your work are vital factors in fundraising and need to keep pace with your financial investment.

Overseas strategy

A common error is for large charities to consider their overseas operations and overseas branches as financially distinct from each other. This is sometimes to the extent that, although they would like, say, the hospice side of their programme to grow much more rapidly, they will simply not consider using funds available in another sector as seedcorn to accelerate the process. This is particularly noticeable in the case of overseas branches. It may have taken say, the American parent charity forty years to reach its current size but they will puzzle over why the Brazilian branch is taking so long to grow, without giving it any of the experience or funds it needs to improve its income.

Even more serious and prevalent is the mind-set that sees any overseas operation in terms of 'that's where we spend the money we raise over here'. Having invested a large amount of time in ensuring that 85% of all the funds raised go to projects overseas, it is hard to realise that this involves a false distinction: if a reasonable investment of both experience and money were made in fundraising in any country in the world, some funds could be efficiently raised to supplement or replace the grants currently made. It may be more effective in the long term to spend a higher proportion of available funds on fundraising overseas to give greater growth. Multinational companies are beginning to operate in this way, and are becoming multi-domestics (manufacturing and selling in several different countries) with a much greater international spread of all their operations, or are becoming global companies having the head office in one country, manufacturing in several and sales in still more. For those organisations that would like their overseas branches to expand, the current pattern is often as if Henry Ford, having decided Spain was a good place to make and sell Ford cars, had set up a bicycle works there and waited for it to grow into a fully integrated factory.

Of course, the kind of development I'm advocating would alter the earlier equation and complicate the issue of how much is spent on overheads – which has always been a relatively false consideration for many organisations. For example, much of the cost of programme work is the cost of overseas staff and the cost of managing those staff. The overseas development agencies have had a simple answer to criticism of such overhead expenditure, because they could point to the amount going overseas compared with the amount spent in the home country. However, this defence is not available to many organisations which have the onerous task of explaining the nature of their expenditure to an often sceptical and ill-informed audience.

Fundraising reports

You cannot possibly budget, counter changing market conditions, or take full advantage of good fortune if you do not have prompt feedback on how your work is going. Unfortunately, for most finance departments (apart from a few enlightened individuals), letting you know the returns on your work is far from their minds. You may even need to run the department which receives the cheques, as well as the membership department which controls the donor-base - otherwise the time-lag in learning what has happened could be crippling.

In an organisation of, say, 100,000 members with a turnover of £10m principally from those members, the core reports you will need are:

- a weekly report by source code, giving you the number of members, the number of donors and amount of income from each source, such as direct mail, loose-leaf inserts, etc.

- a similar daily report for each advertising code.

- a weekly report for each event (raffles, street collections, concerts, etc.), indicating the number of people giving and the amount received.

- a weekly report of unsolicited donations: number and amount.

- a weekly report of appeals income (number and amount of donations). This will be more sophisticated if you segment your appeals.

- reports on the sale of merchandise. This is both the amount of sales and number of purchases, but also information on individual sales for stock control purposes. (See Chapter 5.)

In addition to these reports you will need to know:

- if your organisation has a non-charitable as well as a charitable wing, how each is performing as a distinct entity.

- by what method people are giving (for example, if a membership drive has brought in the fees in cash only it will not be as valuable as if they are all in direct debits).

- membership by type of member (e.g., single, student, family, platinum, gold, silver, etc.). Lapse rates for each category would also be useful.

This is a far from exhaustive list, but anything less will put a brake on your understanding, and ability to react; so adversely affecting your organisation's income.

Setting up a department

Departments are rarely, if ever, planned. Usually they just grow as the pressure of work overwhelms individuals or the champions and pioneers of various kinds of fundraising have their way in demanding resources for their particular projects.

Starting from scratch

Setting up a department from scratch is the ideal situation, but few of us will ever be that fortunate. The first posts to be established should be those that build the base of the fundraising pyramid, then those that deal with its further development. Later the trading and company posts will emerge, depending on the type of interest that the organisation commands.

Obviously, the basic characteristics of your organisation will influence the development of the fundraising department. The National Trust has excellent properties across the country which can house shops that cater for their visitors. Barnardo's has a very experienced legacy department. Oxfam has grown historically through its charity shops. All these organisations, have the usual range of fundraising employees, but also need specialist staff.

Some organisations will have the government or trusts as their principal source of revenue and this will also require specialist staff. However, such sources do tend by their nature to be rather uncertain providers of long-term finance and it is prudent to diversify your sources of income if you are looking for sustained growth.

The fundraising department should be linked organically with the rest of the organisation and not be considered a very separate or different part.

This helps fundraising to serve the organisation's core aims and objectives as well as raising money. Usually the best fundraising has a strong element of advocacy in it, and can be a powerful tool for advancing the organisation's overall goals.

Planning growth

A planned approach to growth will enable your organisation to anticipate the resources needed ahead of your request, and to budget for that need in advance. If things are working out well, and it becomes necessary to have additional staff or space or computer equipment, it is far easier to acquire the resource if you have made people aware of the reasons for your request ahead of time, so that they can consider it before being faced with the actual decision. Planning also allows you to develop those areas of income generation that will maximise the overall income rather than those that may just be someone's pet project. Not planning growth can lead to huge gaps between potential income and performance as well as a very poor staff income ratio.

You must be careful to consider:

- the profile of the organisation. A high profile is essential for effective fundraising but it may come from an area of fundraising that is not particularly profitable such as advertising or national events. These, then, must be encouraged, not dropped on performance grounds alone. It is usual, however, for a fundraising activity which brings a high profile also to be quite profitable. Profiles rise and fall. A time of high profile is usually a good time to increase investment in membership/donor recruitment.

- in any fundraising department there should be several activities or events which are in the process of being developed into major income earners, but which are not yet very profitable.

Planning events

Typically, it takes 3 years for an event to mature.

• In the first year you will make many mistakes and probably a loss.

• In the second year you can expect a profit, provided you have analysed your mistakes and acted to correct them, as your expertise grows and begins to take effect. You will find out the best pricing policy, the right size and location of venue, the best time of year, etc. Your audience will return and bring their friends, and the stars who give their time for free will know you are capable of putting on a good show, making it easier to recruit their friends and for them to return.

• In the third year all this should all come together to give a large profit; and in subsequent years it can grow until its time passes and a new kind of event is needed to replace it. In this context an event could be the opening of a shop chain, beginning a legacy campaign, starting regional fundraising, etc.

Staffing

The size and shape of a fundraising department varies with the availability of volunteers and the use of consultants. With a freely available supply of volunteers and lots of consultants the actual staffing can be quite low. With all fundraising work done by in-house staff the department can be much larger especially if income processing and recording is also undertaken.

Risk management

All fundraising activity involves risk and good management requires the risk to be recognised and discussed with those approving the strategy. Your trustees may be risk adverse and wish for slow and steady growth or they may wish to take chances in the hope of rapidly developing the organisation. You need to know this in planning your activities.

You should also build into your schedule points at which the risk is assessed and decisions taken to proceed or call off the activity. This will apply equally to a major concert or to a direct mail programme. Obviously, the higher the degree of risk the higher up the organisation the decision to proceed needs to be taken. Your plan needs to state who will be making the decision and at what point in time. Some decisions will go to a charity's trustees who may only meet every four months. If this does not fit in with the fundraising schedule then a contingency needs to be built into the plans. For example, a special meeting may be held just for that one decision. For most fundraising decisions involving risk it is likely that the CEO or director will decide.

In making their decision those responsible will need to have a clear idea of the impact on the organisation of any failure. How that event will affect the reserves or contingency funds will be one question they will need to answer. With ample reserves to cover failure the risk of serious damage to the organisation is reduced.

Do consider the effect of slow moving risk such as relying on a trust that provides a substantial proportion of your income. If you are in that situation then good risk management dictates you move to diversify your sources of income.

Establishing the Case for Support

Before moving from strategy and planing to actually carrying out your fundraising there is a most important step. This is one that a consultant or fundraiser new to the organisation will often carry out in the first instance (even before the activity outlined above) to familiarise themselves with the work and the prospects for success.

This step is to establish a 'case for support'. The case for support as its simplest is the answer to the question. Why should someone give money to help your organisation achieve its objectives? If there is no clear answer then you are in trouble. Communicating the cause in a few simple words or sentences is the first task in asking for funds.

The most successful organisations are those that meet a real and obvious need. That is, one which can be clearly articulated. I do, however, believe that whatever your cause, if it meets a real need, you can raise funds for it. It is often the process of successful funding that makes 'unpopular' causes 'popular'. As the fundraisers solicit funds and so raise the organisation's profile they also increase the number of supporters so, by definition, making it a more popular.

The next step in properly establishing the case for support is to make sure that it has the support of the whole organisation from trustees to volunteers. Otherwise, once to fundraising begins to roll, objections begin to be raised and the programme may be curtailed.

For a full description of the use and development of the case for support see the chapter on capital appeals where the case achieves its most impressive and effective form.

Of course, you can fundraise without having a strategy, or planning or budgeting, in the same way as you can journey up the Amazon without consulting a map or buying provisions, but your chances of returning successfully from your venture are immeasurably increased if you think ahead. We have a duty to exercise what the Quakers call 'good husbandry' over our organisation's resources and this cannot be done without an appropriate strategy.

The following chapters look in detail at the techniques that could be combined into such a strategy and at other relevant issues. Because the bulk of charitable giving comes from individual donations rather than companies or governments this is addressed first.

2 The Fundraising Pyramid

The Pareto principle

The fundraising pyramid, aided and abetted by the Pareto principle, has been the fundraising professional's touchstone for many years now. Pareto was a polymath and, among other professions, a psychologist, who observed that in any group of organisms, 80% of the activity came from only 20% of the participants.

Marketing experts use the same principle, knowing that in general they can obtain 80% of their orders from 20% of their customers. Once fundraisers had considered the Pareto principle in relation to maximising income from an organisation's supporters, the information technology revolution had provided helpful computers with infinite storage and recall systems, and American direct mail gurus had tested every possible variation in appeal letters, there was little to do but sit back and let the money roll in. The majority of successful non-governmental organisations (NGOs) in North America, Europe and Australasia now pursue a fundraising strategy based on the Pareto principle and refined by the common experience of countless NGOs, from Church groups to pressure groups, and from hospitals to political parties.

The central tenet of the strategy is to build up those areas of fundraising that maximise income in the medium to long term, ie. three to five years, the timescale best suited to maximising returns from investment in a donor-base. The key elements in this process are illustrated in Fig. 2a. Of course, any areas of fundraising that look promising in the short-term are not neglected; and you need to vary the mix of fundraising techniques as a defence against the effects of the product cycle (which says that any successful area of business runs down over time unless renewed or replaced).

At each step up the pyramid the numbers giving funds decline, but the amount given increases, and it is only with extensive work at the top levels that the 80/20 ratio can be met.

The five levels of the pyramid

The base of the pyramid

The base of the pyramid consists of supporters who have made an initial donation or paid their first subscription. They are not, however, really supporters until they have

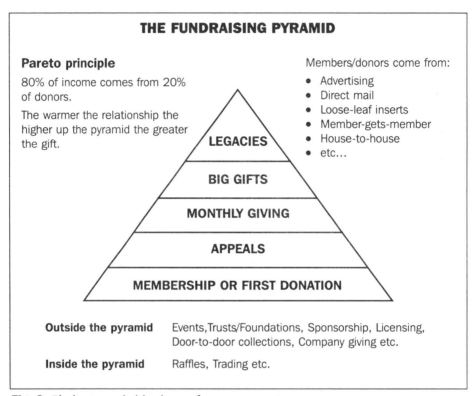

THE FUNDRAISING PYRAMID

Pareto principle

80% of income comes from 20% of donors.

The warmer the relationship the higher up the pyramid the greater the gift.

Members/donors come from:
- Advertising
- Direct mail
- Loose-leaf inserts
- Member-gets-member
- House-to-house
- etc...

LEGACIES

BIG GIFTS

MONTHLY GIVING

APPEALS

MEMBERSHIP OR FIRST DONATION

Outside the pyramid   Events, Trusts/Foundations, Sponsorship, Licensing, Door-to-door collections, Company giving etc.

Inside the pyramid   Raffles, Trading etc.

Fig. 2 *The key to maximising income from your supporters.*

made their second donation or renewed their subscription, as their initial gift may have been just a passing whim, spurred by an effective piece of fundraising. Fortunately, however, the trend among donors is away from impulsive giving and towards making deliberate choices of organisation, to which they remain committed, but only if they find the organisation effective in fulfilling their expectations. Unfortunately for those who like an easy life, these expectations are becoming more significant as donating out of a sense of duty is replaced by the baby-boomers' 'one donation at a time' attitude which is increasing the volatility of donated income. Translating that initial gift into a lifetime's support is therefore crucial, and starts with the organisation's first contact with the donor.

This should make them feel good about their gift, that it is appreciated, and will make a difference. It should be a positive experience, warm and timely, the start of a long-term relationship. Remember, at this point the donor has the highest regard for the organisation, and is very open to suggestions about how to help in future. Many organisations waste this opportunity by sending the annual report, the latest newsletter, any leaflet that comes easily to hand, and a photocopied letter from the director that has not had its date changed for a few decades.

- The first communication should be one of thanks. From the code on the membership form returned by the supporter, you should know if joining or donating is in reply to an advertisement, a loose-leaf insert, or whatever, and the theme and content of the appeal. The letter should mention this: 'Thank you for responding to our recent advertisement concerning ...'.

- If your real need is to develop monthly giving, this is the best time to emphasise and encourage it. Rarely will the donor be as receptive again.

- Set out all the possible options for donors to help you (financially and otherwise), and allow them to choose simply, say, by ticking the appropriate box and returning the form in a reply-paid envelope. It is a good idea to use a brief questionnaire to learn more about your new friends.

- Make sure that you do not put the organisation between the donor and the person they are trying to help. People give to people, not organisations.

The results of split-testing direct mail letters (dividing the mailing list into at least two distinct parts with different codes on each reply device, so that the difference in pulling power between the variations in the pack can be accurately evaluated) indicate that recipients of direct mail letters tend to be very hesitant. They are by nature very shy, need clear, strong guidance about how to respond, and will not act at all if given the least cause for concern. In practice this means that if someone has to look for a stamp, write out their name and address, or buy an envelope, they are far less likely to reply. Hence it pays to make things really easy.

Keys to success
- Offer a form with the donor's name and address clearly printed on it, so that they have very little to fill in, preferably just tick-boxes stating how much they are giving.
- Supply a FREEPOST or pre-paid envelope to return the form in.
- Make matters easier for yourself by using window envelopes in conjunction with the address on the reply form, thus avoiding the need to match two labels in the same pack.

Legal note: the Data Protection Act
For the latest information on the European legislation; which covers the paper files you keep as well as your computer records, and is now in effect, see the Government's website at **http://www.gov.uk**. Under the Data Protection Act, if you intend to hold names and addresses on computer, then you should let people know clearly at the point of joining if you intend to use these for any purpose supporters would not normally associate with membership or the reason why they responded. The information must be as clearly presented as all other information.

According to the Data Protection Register's particular view, this does not include reciprocal mailings from other organisations. These are classified as trading, not direct mail . You must register such activity as trading and ensure people can opt out of such activity at the point of joining. As the European Data Protection legislation comes into force, do check to ensure that people do not need to opt in to such activities. You have been warned!

It is a wise precaution to include this information in the new member's pack as well, mentioning that people can opt out if they wish. Many organisations are now often mentioning reciprocals in their advertising and other first-point-of-contact literature.

The second level of the pyramid

On the second level of the pyramid are donors who have responded to an appeal. (Usually this will have been a direct mail appeal.) Ways of soliciting donations, in descending order of effectiveness, are:

- face-to-face
- telephone call
- personal letter
- impersonal circular.

This order reflects the fact that these methods are progressively more personal and more interactive. The first two methods allow questions about the organisation to be answered immediately.

The most cost-effective approach to ask for additional funds from existing donors, for organisations where the donor-base is in the tens or hundreds of thousands, is usually by direct mail letter. A number of these can be sent each year, provided they have a genuine and persuasive reason for requesting that extra donation. Test to ascertain the point at which an increase in the number of appeals becomes counter-productive. The maximum appears to be twelve per year, largely because most people are paid twelve times in the year, but many organisations limit their appeals to a maximum of six per year, for logistical reasons and because, when appeals have arrived within a month of each other, the results have been far worse than expected. Most organisations seem to average four per year.

Newsletters

In between these appeals members usually receive a newsletter. This serves a very important function for the organisation. The newsletter is the key mechanism whereby your relationship with your supporters is built up and developed. It should

- educate readers regarding the nature of the organisation they have joined, its objectives, how these are achieved, and how effective and efficient the organisation is in achieving them.
- show clearly that the cause is worth supporting, ie. that a very serious problem exists and that the organisation is addressing it effectively.

Through reading the newsletter the supporter should become more knowledgeable about the organisation in a way that leads to a long-term commitment. There is no reason why the supporter should not also be led to become a campaigning activist as well as an active donor, e.g. by writing letters or joining a local group; but the prime purpose of a national membership or donor-base is to secure the financial future of an organisation.

Showing appreciation

The psychology of activists (and staff and volunteers) is very different to that of donors. Activists basically give time, and donors mainly give money. Neither should be made to feel guilty about this, or that their contribution is in some way second best.

Activists are usually brought together in local groups for mutual support. Donating, on the other hand, is often a lone or perhaps a family event.

Acknowledgement of this act is the key to its repetition. The thank-you letter (or phone call) should be prompt, apt and friendly, letting recipients know that the organisation has appreciated their personal generosity and will use the money in the way that was intended, and to good effect.

During their lifetime a person may, however, change from being a student activist to, say, being a young donor, then a local group activist, then a top donor, and later leave a legacy, so make sure your supporters realise you welcome these changes.

The third level of the pyramid

The third level of the pyramid is populated by those who have arranged with their bank to make a regular (usually monthly) donation to the organisation, as well as paying their subscription. Often the inducement for this method of giving is a donor club whose subscription is much larger than the usual fee. In return, club members receive special privileges. Many organisations have several of these clubs with different levels of giving: for example, the WWF had Gold, Silver and Bronze members. The Medical Foundation has their 'Friends of the Foundation' who covenant £30 per month and meet once a year for dinner with a celebrity speaker and their charismatic Director. American zoos have the Chairman's, Keepers' and Friends' Clubs. Often their club members pay substantial fees. This system is possible, firstly, because people are usually paid monthly, and a relatively small monthly donation is much easier than the same sum taken from one month's pay; and, secondly, because the clubs are formed to meet the needs of donors at higher levels of giving.

Often, monthly givers are not approached again with regular appeals. (Sometimes this is used as an inducement to become a monthly giver.) This is a mistake, however, as donors soon miss the involvement of helping by responding to appeals, and receiving their regular thank-you letters, and would begin donating again as well as maintaining their covenants. Many donors cannot even remember with which organisations they have standing orders or covenants. Often they donate to show approval of a particular project, and miss that close involvement with the work of the organisation when they become monthly givers and the opportunity represented by appeals is taken away. Club members are usually among the highest givers to appeals.

Amnesty International in the UK has a club, the 'Partners of Conscience' scheme, whereby members make out a covenant for at least £25 per month. A covenant (or bankers order with gift aid declaration) allows the charity to collect from the government the tax paid by donors on their gifts. More importantly, now that gift aid is available on any gift it allows the organisation to rely on four years of income. Amnesty club members receive a smart but discreet lapel pin in gold and black, bearing Amnesty's logo and the club name.

Segment your donors into groups by dividing them up on the basis of their previous gifts (in total, per annum and by the largest amount given at one time). This analysis should reveal how many clear categories they fall into, and so how many clubs you could create. Think carefully about the appropriate level of giving and rewards for each club. This will usually be a rather messy value judgement, and should involve a testing programme to ascertain what level of annual or monthly gift people are happy with, and which rewards meet their own needs best. These can be needs for recognition, thanks, a feeling of armchair involvement, actual hands-on experience of the work, confirmation of status or real improvement in social status, the opportunity to meet celebrities, etc. It is usually worthwhile to test your ideas by discussing them with small groups of supporters, being very careful not to lead them to tell you just what you want to hear.

Covenants

Covenants are a promise to pay a stipulated amount for at least four years for no material consideration, i.e. any return to the donor must be of very little value. It is worth checking the assumed worth of your newsletter or other club benefits with your VAT inspector. The covenant can, however, run on for the donor's lifetime, so it is not wise to put a finishing date on the covenant form.

Covenants can only be made out to a registered charity, which can then reclaim the tax already paid on sums donated. Incidentally, the Charities Aid Foundation runs an excellent scheme, administering covenants and collecting the tax for those charities which find this an administrative burden. Even many quite large charities become hopelessly behind in reclaiming their tax.

Linking the covenant to a direct debit is sensible, as the bank's administration of banker's orders has become a nightmare. In much of Europe this will take the form of an auto giro payment; which will be paid into a post office along with the monthly utility payments. Check a variety of other organisations' literature to see how covenants are best made out stylistically but always take legal advice on the final form and remember the law is different in Scotland (you will need to have 'signed as a hologram' on the form – honestly).

Despite gift aid now being available for any donation (if your donor fills out a simple gift aid declaration saying they wish that the charity can henceforth, or dated back to 6 April 2000, reclaim the tax they have paid), it is tempting to ignore covenants, but they are still a strong tool for fundraisers because they bind the donor for four years. 'Locked in donors' are invaluable in these days of fickle giving.

The fourth level of the pyramid

The next level of the pyramid is drawn from those who make a special, major gift to the organisation. Usually, these people are researched, located and systematically approached to support special projects requiring large donations. This could be in relation to a capital appeal (say, for a new building) or for an important new area of work, etc. The solicitation can be done in one of several ways.

Research

Potential major donors are often already members of monthly giving clubs, and many organisations do very well merely by creating separate clubs for their top donors which have very high entrance fees and suitable incentives. Often major donors can be found by comparing your donor-base with lists of affluent individuals. The best fundraising consultancies should be able to do this for you electronically. The third key route to discovering major donors is by encouraging your known major donors and influential supporters to use their networks to produce prospects for you.

The approach

The best approach is always face-to-face, whether you are raising a few hundred pounds for a playgroup or a few million for a new University building. The approach should be made by someone in the same peer group as the potential donor, preferably someone who is known to them and who has given a large donation themselves.

Whether the approach is through a personal visit or by phone, letter or email, a persuasive case needs to be developed beforehand, and presented along with a clear statement of the amount being asked for. Research will be needed to ascertain the level at which each person can give. It is important to suggest an amount or range within which the donation may fall otherwise the person being asked is left in the uncomfortable situation of not knowing if they will be thought foolish giving at a one level or mean giving at another. If your director has charm or charisma they may have to be the person to undertake the approaches. Do think long-term. Large donations are raised by such fieldwork over a number of years.

The potential

Big gift clubs and individual solicitations to potential major donors are key techniques in the fundraiser's repertoire. The Pareto principle shows just how important they can be for your organisation. They are more fully explored in Chapter 4 in the 'Monthly giving' and 'Big gift appeals' sections, and in Chapter 8.

The apex of the pyramid

Finally, at the apex of the donor pyramid, sits the legacy or bequest programme or, as it is increasingly called, the 'planned giving' programme. A bequest leaving a percentage of the estate is often called a residuary legacy. There are also pecuniary legacies where a sum of money is left, and specific bequests where an object is left. Always let people know that a valuable object is quite acceptable. Many charities have been left valuable oil paintings, china collections and even houses! Reversionary or life interest wills are those that take care of friends or family by giving them a stated interest in the estate. A member of the family might, for example, be allowed to live in the house during their lifetime, which would afterwards revert to the charity. This is a useful way of securing the interests of the family and still ensuring that a charity benefits.

Sources of legacies

Legacies appear to come from two sources. One source is people who have never made a donation to the organisation and do not appear anywhere in the records; and the other is people who have given regularly through a large part of their lifetime and continue that practice by planning their future and final gift. Interestingly, legacies come equally from both sources.

This means that you should take a broad approach.

- Remind all supporters that it is possible to leave money or goods to the organisation in their will (and, if it is a charity, that it can be done most tax-effectively), after they have taken care of their families. This can be done through your newsletter by an insert of your legacy leaflet and by mentions of large gifts you have received.

- Those who are not known supporters also need to be reached. The main method of doing this is to advertise a free will-making guide in the press and, naturally, to introduce the organisation in that guide.

There are bound to be a number of lawyers on your donorbase who could undertake this for you. (Your donors' research questionnaire will tell you which newspapers and magazines your supporters read.) It is customary, in doing this, to ask the recipient to let the organisation know if they are leaving a legacy to it, offering an incentive to do so in the form of a small but suitable gift such as a pen, badge or book, or putting their name in a remembrance book. A remembrance book may seem a quaint idea but if you are leaving money in your will the thought that your generosity will be recorded permanently is very powerful.

Incentives

Generally, incentives work well and are a useful tool for the fundraiser. In many areas of fundraising, from appeals to the returning of lifestyle questionnaires, the introduction of incentives yields an improved response.

If you use incentives they should be

- appropriate to the organisation. (For example, Amnesty sometimes uses a pen as an incentive because it calls on its members to write letters, and Friends of the Earth will plant a tree in the name of someone leaving a legacy.)

- of good quality, because, to the donor, they reflect the quality of the organisation's work.

- accompanied, when used in an appeal, by a clear indication of the level of giving you would like to see, so that the donor feels comfortable at that level, rather than worrying about being thought foolish for giving so much or mean for giving so little.

In Amnesty's loose-leaf inserts a good quality fountain pen was offered to people who gave £35 or more. Split tests showed that this led to a rise in the number of people giving £35, and an even bigger rise in the number who gave £50. The perceived value of the pens was, of course, much higher than their actual cost, and the increase in income was at least five times greater than the added cost.

The psychology behind incentives used in this way is that they give reassurance, rather than a reason to give. If you give donors an incentive to return a coupon which indicates planned giving, they receive a message that the organisation regards this as an important way of helping. They respond to that message, rather than simply acting to gain the incentive.

Visiting solicitors and bank managers

An interesting method of encouraging legacies is to organise a volunteer team to visit solicitors and bank managers, letting them know all about the organisation and leaving posters and leaflets for them to use if asked by a client to advise on an appropriate charity to which money can be left. Though solicitors will not put forward any particular organisation without being asked, they are often called on to suggest names of organisations in certain categories.

Advertising in the Law Society Gazette or Solicitors' Journal serves a similar purpose, as these are the two main publications shown to clients from which to pick a charity. There is no research to suggest how effective the plethora of other publications might be. (See also Legacy Leaflets and Advocacy, Chapter 4.)

Befriending elderly supporters

In recent years a new approach has grown up which is very close to a much needed social work programme for the elderly. This works extraordinarily well and will become a very large component of most voluntary sector organisations' fundraising, though it is still in its infancy.

The approach is for a full-time member of staff to identify those people who are both elderly and major supporters of the organisation, and to return to them some of the kindness they have shown to the charity during their active lives. This can range from the occasional call, to spending time with the donor, to carrying out errands and assisting with difficulties.

This is always at the donor's complete discretion, and does not involve any approach for funds. This service is often very highly valued by the elderly.

Other techniques for use inside the pyramid

There are several other fairly significant ways of drawing funds from supporters in the pyramid. The most important of these for many organisations are raffles which are covered in Chapter 4. Another key area is trading. Supporters provide a sympathetic niche market and will buy branded goods at a premium. This operation can also be used to provide a springboard for selling outside the pyramid to the general public through licensing deals, the stocking of branded goods in shops and on-pack promotion. Trading is covered thoroughly in Chapter 5.

§

The fundraising pyramid is now a traditional tool but one which has been improved by good practice over the years. Relationship fundraising has codified much of this improvement though how closely our fundraising can match with all our donors' needs and still remain efficient has yet to be determined.

What is certain is that for any organisation that can raise large numbers of supporters, the pyramid provides a simple framework for effectively maximising the income from those supporters over a number of years.

3 Building the Pyramid: Recruiting Members and Donors

Advertising

The best thing about advertising is that it makes your current supporters feel good about their support and introduces thousands of people to your work, who, although they may not give now, will give when they have been asked a few more times. Most people joining or giving through newspaper advertising say that they had intended to give for some time before seeing the advertisement that finally triggered their action.

You are fortunate if you have an advertising budget large enough to warrant employing an advertising agency. Even so, the chances are that you will need to guide your agency carefully in the tough world of charity advertising. Unfortunately, unlike many commercial companies, most charities do not have an extensive series of shops across the country where their products can be bought, and so advertising agencies cannot use their usual techniques to help. If you only have a small budget, you will need to weigh the costs and benefits of using an advertising agency very carefully.

The secret of charity advertising

The secret of advertising for charities is to prevent your advertising agency from trying to enhance your profile or engage in 'prestige' advertising which just boosts your brand awareness, but to have them treat the advertisement just like a piece of direct mail which requires an immediate response. An excellent book on advertising is *Ogilvy on Advertising* by David Ogilvy, who founded the giant advertising agency Ogilvy and Mather. It was published by Guild Publishing in 1985, but I doubt if it is still in print. If you see it, buy it!

Commercial advertising and charity advertising: the crucial difference

Good commercial advertising works long after the advertisement has been seen. It makes sure that when the customer is looking for a product he or she has a favourable impression of the company's brand firmly in mind at decision-making time. It takes a long time (and often much money) to establish this. The advertiser will know what benefits the customer is likely to require from the product - customers are purchasing the benefits of the product not the product itself - and which newspapers, journals and TV spots the customer is likely to watch. This will be established through thorough research. You can use similar techniques to discover where it is best to advertise for new supporters, and who are the most likely kinds of people to support your cause. The crucial difference is, however, that your supporters will be required to respond immediately by filling in a coupon and posting it with their cheque to your organisation. This means that they must stop their perusal of the paper and feel so strongly that something must be done about your cause that they will fill out the coupon there and then.

The way to do this is to create a powerful headline to hold their interest and a dramatic picture that tells a significant part of the story, with just enough text to bring them to the most important part - the coupon. The coupon must be large enough to fill in easily.

The Advertisement

The headline

The headline is often much harder than the rest of the text for an agency copywriter to compose, because they are trained to write a line which tells the story and sticks in your mind for a long while afterwards. This is often done with an intellectual twist, such as a pun or play on words. If the story is told in the headline the reader will 'get the picture' and move on. A good charity headline impels the reader, if he or she has a heart, to read the rest of the text and then to respond. This is not easy for copywriters trained to write commercial advertisements. The headline must be physically large and bold to stand out above the other headlines on the page.

The text

The text can be quite long (but need not be the full page format which Amnesty, almost alone among not-for-profit organisations, has found successful). A succinct statement of the problem, and why joining or giving money will help to solve it, is all that is really needed for most organisations. A large amount of text requires a brilliant copywriter who makes it well worthwhile for the reader to read every word. If one paragraph is boring, unnecessary or irritating, the reader will turn over the page.

Judging advertising copy

Most advertising copy will be short, as the advertisements will only occupy a small space on the page. Legibility is the first requirement. Do not be tempted to cram a large amount of copy, however well written, into such a small space that it is hard to read. People just will not bother to read it and will turn the page. Be ruthless with your copywriter in this regard. Do not reverse out your text, ('reversed out' is white print on a black background). If you really must do this, make sure you see a proof, but beware the newspapers own printing, which is often not up to reversed-out text. Is the text large enough to be read easily? Agency staff often have much better eyesight than your middle aged supporters.

The copy must make a connection between the headline (with supporting picture), and the coupon. It must answer the question, 'Why should I give you my money?' It is not an explanation of your organisation. Resist the temptation to say more than you need to. The main objective is direct response - it is not a funny joke or an attack on your competition. It describes what the problem is, how your organisation can solve it, and how the kind and gentle reader can help.

Brazil has solved the problem of how to keep kids off the streets. Kill them.

Street children who have no-one to look after them help one another. More than one child every day is killed by police death squads.

When Brazilian street children have nightmares, they are not necessarily dreaming.

7,000,000 children live rough in Brazil, some in flimsy shanties, others in city sewers.

They have learned to fear the car that pulls up at night from which heavily armed men jump out. The sound of police boots clattering through the sewers.

The screams as children are caught, the cries and sobs as they are beaten and the flat, final crack of gunshots.

This sounds incredible, but it's true.

Children's corpses, often bearing marks of torture, are turning up at the rate of more than one a day in the streets of Brazil.

A recent study by the Brazilian Institute for Social and Economic Analysis reported that 457 children or adolescents were killed by death squads in just three cities last year.

It came to the conclusion that the squads, many of them run by off-duty policemen, kill "to clean up the streets."

Nor is Brazil the only country in which this happens.

In Guatemala the corpses of street children have been found with their eyes burned out and ears and tongues cut out.

In countries as far apart as Peru and Sri Lanka schoolchildren have "disappeared" after being arrested by security forces.

In Liberia, many children have been arbitrarily killed or mutilated by the government and its opponents.

In South Africa, about 10,000 children were detained without charge or trial between 1985 and 1987.

All over the world, children are imprisoned, tortured and killed by the governments which should be guaranteeing their rights.

In the face of such horror, what can you do to help?

Firstly, become a member of Amnesty, it only costs £12. You can help directly by participating in our letter writing and urgent action campaigns.

We also need donations to enable us to continue our field investigations, to mount campaigns to free prisoners held illegally, to publicise abuses by governments and to give financial help to the families of victims.

Amnesty does get results.

Of the 29,000 prisoners-of-conscience whose cases we have taken up, 26,500 were successfully concluded.

In June, Brazil's President Collor de Mello said that his country should never again be cited by Amnesty International as his government would not tolerate human rights violations.

Sadly, our September newsletter contained many verbatim statements from Brazilian children who had been burned with cigarettes, tortured with scalding water and beaten.

We have to step up the pressure, not just on Brazil but all over the world, and to do this we must have your help.

The task is huge, our resources pitifully small.

Our whole year's advertising budget could not cover filming one 30 second TV commercial, let alone paying for it to be shown on commercial TV.

We can't afford many newspaper advertisements either.

Every pound we've scraped together to run this advertisement has to work hard to help little children who have nobody else to turn to. For their sakes, this advertisement must recruit 1,000 new Amnesty members and raise £100,000.

Please join us. Please be generous. Please give as much as you can. Please do it now.

I wish to be a member of Amnesty International. I enclose £12 Individual ☐
£15 Family ☐   £5 OAP ☐   £5 Student, Under 18, Claimant ☐
I wish to donate £100 ☐   £50 ☐   £25 ☐   £15 ☐   Other ☐

Mr/Ms. _____

Address _____

_____ Postcode _____

To: Amnesty International British Section, FREEPOST, London EC1B 1HE.

AMNESTY INTERNATIONAL

GUARDIAN 2 OCT '90

Fig. 3a *An Amnesty International advertisement heading which forces you to read the text. Once read you cannot avoid filling in the coupon.*

It is human and personal. Good copy is so well written you do not know you have just read it until you are writing out your cheque. It is a call to action for a very good reason. So, the writing flows. It is not stilted and does not talk up or down to its readership. It sounds like a friend. One of us!

The copy must be no longer than it needs to be to obtain a response. A single problem raised in the reader's mind will give an excuse for not giving. More than one and you are in trouble. Go through all copy looking for turn-off points. If in doubt, cut the word or phrase right out rather than trying to find an acceptable substitute.

When composing, your copywriter should think just like your supporters, and should aim to use the same words and mental images that they do. It helps to brief the copywriter on the demographic profile of your supporters. The better the picture you can build up, the more effective the copy will be.

Use focus groups to discuss your advertising. This will enable you to cut across all those unpleasant truths that you have mentally screened out. Did no one respond because a plane crash was first in the news, or because your advertisement did not really make a convincing case for support? You know you have got it right when your existing supporters give to your advertisements. They are saying, 'This is why we joined! This is what we think is important!' Listen to them.

The picture

The picture, with the headline, should clearly convey as much as possible about the problem or the work concerned. Do make sure that you have the copyright for any picture you use. If you are using an agency picture which has featured in the media this can be expensive, but iconographic images that the reader has seen before will convey much more than a picture seen for the first time. Often disasters and problems are encapsulated in one image that comes to stand for the situation with all its complexities. For example, pictures of sick and malnourished prisoners behind barbed wire in Serbian camps once summed up the whole conflict in former Yugoslavia.

Creating an image that does this for your cause will be a very powerful tool in persuading people to help you. You can let the picture state most of your argument, but it need not be shocking.

The ASA code of practice

If your cause is important, then something in your advertisement will probably shock, but it should not offend. Seek advice from the Advertising Standards Authority (ASA) if you are in any doubt. This will help to avoid the situation where you spend time and money creating an advertisement, only to find no one will use it because it contravenes the ASA code of practice. The code of practice is voluntary and, if you do offend, you will just be asked not to use that advertisement again; but being seen to infringe the code will not help to gain you support. Complaints are published, even if they are not upheld. Reply immediately to any enquiry from the ASA, as a delay in response can mean you are infringing the code. Bad publicity is much worse than good or even neutral publicity, and can damage your organisation.

You can obtain a copy of the code of practice from the ASA at Brook House, 2-16 Torrington Place, London WC1E 7HN.

The coupon

The coupon must be preceded by a call to action, such as 'Please join us today'. The customary 'today' is used to give urgency to the message. If the reader thinks they will send off the coupon next week it will languish, tucked into the side of the mantelpiece mirror, or simply never leave the newspaper. Direct mail letters have been used to carefully test different approaches, and have shown that the simple psychology of giving a date by which the reply must be received ('Reply by the 27th and receive a free clock'), or a reason for writing immediately ('Hurry whilst stocks last'), increases the response very significantly. You can think of many ways of adding a note of urgency: 'Any delay means they will ...'

The coupon should make it abundantly clear just what you are asking for.

- If you would like a donation, say so, and suggest the amount. This is not the total amount of the appeal, which would just make an individual contribution look puny, but the amount you desire from each donor.

- It helps to give a variety of amounts with tick-boxes, which gives the donor confidence they are giving an acceptable amount. If, as often happens when you open the envelope, there is no cheque enclosed, it enables you to write back effectively. The tick-boxes really help people not to feel foolish about giving away a lot of money, and not to think you just need £5 (much of which will go in administering the donation).

- Have the highest amount on the left, so that people give the highest they feel comfortable with rather than the lowest. The theory is that, as people read from

Walks R Us

Escape the stresses of modern life by discovering the joys of walking. Our 420 local groups organise regular walks and work to safeguard the many footpaths illegally blocked or under threat.

Why not join us for a walk and help us protect our nation's heritage?

Benefits of membership include:
- an essential Yearbook (worth £4.99)
- a quarterly magazine
- membership of one of our 420 local walking groups
- regular local newsletters
- discounts in many outdoor retailers

The Ramblers

1-5 Wandsworth Road, London SW8 2XX.
Tel: 0171 339 8500
www.ramblers.org.uk

Mr/Mrs/Miss/Ms

Address

Postcode   Date of birth

Tick box for membership type required
☐ Ordinary £20   ☐ Reduced* £11
☐ Family/joint† £26   ☐ Joint† reduced* £14

* Reduced membership is available for the unwaged, retired, disabled, students and under 18s.
† Family/Joint is for two adults at the same address.

Donation £_____ I enclose £_____

☐ We occasionally exchange names (for use once only) with other organisations which may interest you. Tick if you would prefer to be excluded.

Registered Charity No. 306089   XB

Fig. 3b *This simple, striking and direct advertisement has worked wonders for The Ramblers*

left to right, they will work their way along the line of boxes to the amount with which they feel comfortable. If the boxes are the other way around they will feel comfortable much earlier. Interestingly, however, many people seem to give the amount which is in the middle of the range. Circling the 'average' donation in the range can help to upgrade small donors.

- Make sure that the coupon is large enough for everyone to write their name and address clearly. Include 'postcode' in the address space because handwriting is often difficult to decipher, and the postcode is often the most legible part of the address. Use Mr, Ms or your preferred combination. This is very important, as later you could be laser printing these names, addresses and salutation on to an appeal letter. It will be much more personal and effective if you can address people by their name rather than merely as 'Dear friend'.

- A FREEPOST address helps. No one ever has a stamp to hand, and waiting to find or buy one means the urgency goes out of the appeal. If you wish to set up a FREEPOST address, contact your nearest Post Office manager. The address will be the same as your current address, apart from the postcode, and you can alter the rest as you like. The service is quite cheap. The words 'You do not have to use a stamp but it will save us postage' also seem to work for those who do have stamps to hand, and will save you money. About a third of replies respond to this message.

- Remember to put your name and logo on the coupon or elsewhere in large type. The vast majority of people who see your advertisement will not respond but, by associating your organisation with the copy, people will begin both to learn about your work and to think you are an active organisation. Your current members and donors will also gain that impression. In fact, members often return the coupon with a donation to show their support for the part of your work featured in the advertisement. For aesthetic reasons designers always create tiny logos – be decisive about changing this.

It is essential to monitor the results of all your advertising. All your coupons should have a code on them signifying from which advertisement, in which newspaper, on which date, they have come.

Position on the page

The advertisement's position in the newspaper is important. Do not just buy the cheapest space. People read the papers selectively. If you are a third-world development organisation it makes sense to test the foreign news pages. Do not neglect the front page. It may be twice as expensive but nearly everyone reads it, and it has impact and memorability, yielding results that are often more than twice as good as those from other spaces.

Test space rigorously, but remember that this is difficult because the news has a habit of changing each day.

Research questionnaires

The simplest and most effective piece of pre-advertising research is to survey your existing membership. This can be done through a printed questionnaire placed in your newsletter with a letter of explanation and a FREEPOST envelope.

People love questionnaires, and you will continue to receive the replies for years after your closing date (heavily prompted with a note of urgency). You can ask a lot of questions. Thirty questions is not uncommon. Unless you can retain this information against your membership records (without offending the Data Protection Registrar) the survey should be completely anonymous. Expect at least one in five questionnaires back; though sometimes as many as three in five are returned. If you have the computer facilities to keep a mass of information on each member, then you can abandon anonymity and, using a window envelope, send the questionnaires out like direct mail with the name and address already on the form. This may reduce the rate of return, and will mean that your explanation of how you will use the data should be very clear and reasonable, but it will give you an excellent chance to segment and target those who respond. Some organisations waste no time and do this in their new members' pack.

In general your questions will ascertain the demographics of your donor-base. So you will find out:

- how old they are
- their gender
- what kind of education they have had
- what they do at work and play
- how much they earn
- which parts of your work they think are most important
- which newspapers and magazines they read. (A list for them to tick will indicate where you should advertise and place your loose-leaf inserts.)

Testing

Where to place your advertisement in the paper is not the only thing you should test. A key rule in fundraising, if not the key rule, is to test as much as possible. You don't really know anything until you have tested it. So, test concepts as well. Amnesty concentrates on individuals in its advertisements as a way of reaching the public; but it could concentrate on countries or themes like torture or political killing. There are probably many different ways of putting across your organisation's work. With advertising, the difficulty of testing is that the response will vary depending on the paper you use, the position on the page and, most importantly, what else is featured in the press on that day. This means that exact testing is impossible. The willingness of people to support your organisation's work may not appear to be affected by what else is in the news, but be very careful. There could be several other charity advertisements in the same issue and one of them may relate to a news story, which may mean that readers are drawn to support someone else, or your cause appears insignificant by comparison.

Focus groups

Much use has been made of focus groups, and they are easy to arrange through an agency. The idea is that groups of your supporters and others, who have not joined, are brought together, usually in the evening with some food and drink, and asked their opinion of a variety of advertisements. This has to be done very skilfully. Unless you are an expert, the group will miraculously reflect your opinions straight back to you. In theory, focus groups should give you a real idea of why people are attracted to your adverts or put off by them. Your advertising agency should be able to arrange focus groups for you.

Sometimes, we have to take what people say with a bag of salt, as they often act completely differently. Focusgroups told Amnesty that their strong advertisements were a turn-off and that they would never read or respond to them. In practice, however, it is to the stronger advertisements that people have responded by actually joining.

This is not to say that you will learn nothing from focus groups. Amnesty learnt that people respond best if they can identify with just one individual (rather than read about dozens of people suffering), often saying that they felt they had to act to prevent another individual suffering in that way. If you can afford focus groups, try them out, and you will be surprised how informative they can be.

Direct mail

Direct mail is the archetypal gift from marketing to fundraising. It is a simple and easily understood way of raising funds and recruiting members. Its real beauty, however, lies in the ease with which you can test creative ideas in the real world with immediate feedback on how well they are doing. This very process has led, however, to a frightening similarity in most direct mail packages, and it will tax all your innovative powers to devise new formats that work as well as the originals and make your appeal stand out.

Commonly referred to as junk mail, direct mail has a reputation for waste on a large scale. As direct mail agencies and list brokers (who will sell you lists of the names and addresses of thousands of potential prospects), as well as computers, become increasingly sophisticated this is becoming easier to avoid. My first experience of trying to introduce direct mail to an organisation was a curt reply from the director, 'Let me tell you we will never use direct mail here. Now, what else would you like to talk to me about?' It took quite a struggle to get direct mail back on that meeting's agenda, but the organisation went on to triple its membership, principally through the use of well targeted and executed direct mail packages.

The Post Office offers a good discount for bulk mailing, provided that you can put your letters in 'Mailsort order'. This should be discussed in detail with your PO representative, your mailing house and membership department. The only drawback is that you are required to print the ubiquitous Mailsort logo on your envelopes. Junk mail aficionados will treasure these letters, though a lot of other people never open them – but most people really do not notice. There are, however, a lot of other postage stamps and logos that you can use, and for specialist mailings and especially short runs where you are expecting large donations, it does help to make your whole package more attractive by having a real stamp or a smart PO logo on the envelope.

Given the usual low costs of a direct mail pack and a reduced postage rate, it should be possible for you to at least break even if only 2% of those mailed respond. Remember, we are investing in new supporters, not making a profit from them. I have known many fundraisers despair because 95% of the people they mailed did not respond! To be a true fundraiser you must master the art of accepting rejection.

Keeping and using records

Keep as much information on your members as possible (always keeping within the Data Protection Acts), and write differently to as many of them as you can (segmentation). It may not be very cost-effective to write separate letters to many different groups of members, but you can at least try by varying the tick boxes (which set out the amounts you are asking for) on your return coupon, according to the affluence of the people you are mailing or, better still, their past giving record. Why insult them by asking for £15 when they regularly give you £150? Why antagonise them by asking for £1,000 when they have only ever given you £15 at a time? If someone's regular donation is £50, starting the tick-boxes at £50 and working up will often give them the confidence to upgrade their gift.

The direct mail pack

The key elements of a direct mail pack are:
- a carefully designed outer envelope
- an appeal letter requesting help
- a reply coupon
- a FREEPOST envelope
- a leaflet telling the recipient more about the organisation.

The outer envelope

A good direct mail pack has an outer envelope with an intriguing phrase and picture, designed to appeal to those who may be interested in the organisation (and to let everyone else drop it in the bin). A return address (which allows the Post Office to send back to you letters which are not deliverable) is very useful to you, as you can then update your list, taking off those who have 'gone away', etc. This includes the deceased, unknowns and Mr/Ms Very Angry Person.

The appeal letter

Typically these are four pages long, because tests have shown a four-page letter pulls better than fewer pages. In fact, the more pages the better; but remember that each paragraph must be compulsive reading, and that it is hard to write more than four pages keeping your readers with you. Most organisations find it impossible to achieve a satisfactory letter more than one page long - hence the surprising result that they have better returns from shorter appeals. Shorter letters are at a disadvantage because after years of receiving four-page letters it appears to the reader that anything less isn't particularly important. If you ask people in focus groups which they prefer they will say short letters; but in practice they treat the longer letter as more important (provided every word is worthwhile and not just padding).

The format of the letter is simple. You present the problem directly, tell the reader exactly what is happening, so that they know just how appalling the problem is, then tell them how you are going to solve that problem and what they must do for you to succeed in this.

The opening paragraph and the PS are the most-read parts of a letter, so put your important messages there. The best advice I've received on writing is to:

- develop an idea of your target audience (your typical member or donor) and write for them - preferably for an individual reader whose needs you can identify.

- keep your sentences reasonably short and the vocabulary accessible.

- use the active voice: 'The state prosecutor called for the death penalty', rather than 'The death penalty was called for by the state prosecutor' (Amnesty International style book). This is known to help readers and sustain their interest.

- avoid jargon unless you have to use it, and explain it when you must use it.

- allow access to the text by a clearly manifest structure. You will see this done in many direct mail letters by underlining and clear headings. Only underline what really needs emphasis.

Recently, there has been a back-to-basics move linked to the 'relationship' marketing concept. This emphasises writing real letters to people as if they were your friends - not heavily underlined, laser-printed letters with photos mixed in with the text. It seeks to create a relationship by making every contact as personal as possible, rather than considering your donors as a list of names and addresses with no independent needs or will.

The return coupon and FREEPOST envelope

The coupon should be a clear and simple device. A sheet of A5 paper (half A4 size) is usually enough. Do make sure that the return envelope is large enough for the coupon and a cheque to fit inside easily.

- Let the first words repeat the core message of the appeal letter: 'Yes, I would like to help ...' to confirm to the donor and the organisation what the appeal is for. This is now rather a hackneyed phrase and you should find one that is appropriate and true for your own work.

- Either be sure that the money will be used in exactly the way you say it will, or give yourself an opt-out, such as adding '... and for all our other important work'.

- The donor's address will already be on the coupon if you followed the ideas above. If not, lots of room should be left with a clear space for the postcode and Mr/Ms or whichever titles you use, so that you can personalise your letters later.

- The return FREEPOST address should be written out, just in case the FREEPOST envelope is lost or not inserted.

- The size of gift you are asking for should be made clear.

- If it is a prospecting appeal, all the ways for people to join or donate should be laid out, with simple tick-boxes to make the form easy and quick to fill in.

- If you accept credit cards let people know - and don't forget to count the boxes for the credit card number. Many designers get this detail wrong.

- Last, but not least, code every different mailing on the coupon so that you can analyse them.

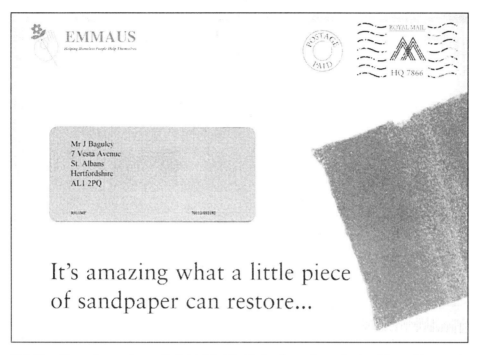

Fig. 3c *The enclosure of a small, light object that helps the reader understand the problem can be intriguing and effective, but it must be clearly relevant.*

The additional leaflet

One useful test you can conduct in prospecting packs, before rolling them out in tens of thousands, is whether it is worthwhile including an extra leaflet or other form of insert. It may well be that your letter is adequate and the extra cost of the leaflet is not worthwhile. Yet it may be that you cannot really say all you need to in the letter (even if it is four pages long!) and need more room without overburdening the letter.

Perhaps, more importantly, you may need to add some pictures to show the situation clearly - both the problem and your solution to it. If enclosing your organisation's standard leaflet, do not forget to remove the usual reply coupon, or you will confuse the prospect and your coding system will not work properly.

If you wish to show horrifying pictures of your work, you may consider putting them in a separate envelope inside the appeal, marked 'This envelope contains distressing pictures which may shock you'. I am told that the device has worked very well for the NSPCA, among others.

A campaigning action, as mentioned above, could also be used. Try testing the insertion of a postcard to send, calling for action to help relieve the problem you are engaged on. The Medical Foundation for the Care of Victims of Torture has found a call to action helps response if used sparingly, i.e. once a year. It has also found the inclusion of an insert requesting supporters to return a Christmas (Season's) greeting to the beneficiaries also greatly improves the response rate.

Addressing direct mail

Last, but a long way from least, is the address. The most common way to handle this is to produce Cheshire labels (a common brand of label which is easy for mailing house machinery to handle) for your mailing house, which they will fix onto your return coupon in such a position that the labels show through the window envelopes. You can also laser print the address onto the coupon, and also, possibly, the letter. This allows you to personalise the appeal; but it is expensive to add the address to the coupon as well - hence the multitude of appeal letters with the coupon attached to the foot of the letter.

Printing the address on the coupon and using a window envelope, then, avoids printing the address twice. You need the address on the reply coupon to build up your records for segmentation, and for measuring the success of each mailing. People will rarely bother to write it on the coupon themselves, and if they are asked to do so it will slow them down (reducing response) and confuse your membership department because people write their addresses differently each and every time. Printing the address also allows your supporters to let you know if you have their name and address recorded incorrectly.

'Gone aways.'

Some organisations remail all the 'gone away' addresses on the grounds that people of a similar nature will have moved into the house. Personally, I'm not convinced by this. If it were true we could mail all the streets where our supporters have lived and double our membership overnight. People have very different psychologies despite living in similar houses. However, as I have never tested the concept I really cannot truly claim to know whether it works or not.

If you have bought a list and more than 3% turn out to be 'gone aways' you should be able to obtain some compensation from the agency that sold you the list. If it is your own list you must ensure that you are paying attention to all the letters that you receive from your supporters. It is very expensive for you, and irritating for your supporters, if you mail 'gone aways' repeatedly. If you are receiving letters that say, 'I've told you three times my husband is deceased,' you have a serious problem in your membership department that requires immediate attention.

Mailing from abroad

There are many fine books on direct mail, so I will not go into exhaustive detail here, but among the ideas you could try is reducing the postage by mailing from an appropriate country abroad. The foreign stamp may help to get your envelope opened. The problems with this are that under the international postal rules you cannot use a UK return address and so the Post Office will not return the 'gone aways'; the cost of shipping your printing abroad could be high; and printing in a foreign country for the first time may not be a rewarding experience. The lower cost of postage from abroad can, however, save you a lot of money, and help turn your appeal into a success by increasing the response rate even a trifle. Postage from the USA, for example, can be much cheaper than posting within the UK!

Varying your appeals

Vary your appeals, so that your members do not get bored with them but believe that you are sending them out because you have a real need, not just because it's time for another appeal. At the same time you must keep the format fairly close to a personal letter. Though beware of becoming too friendly and losing the strength of an appeal.

Advocacy

Advocacy within appeals in not necessarily a bad thing, though if you give someone a list of ways to help, they will probably choose the easiest. Returning a pre-printed postcard is much easier than locating a cheque book. Inviting an action may, however, encourage people to give who have never given before, as the action may draw them into reading the appeal. Test it for yourself. I regret to say I have even lost money on an appeal because it looked too much like a campaigning appeal, asking people to write letters instead of sending in money. Spurred on by some success in adding advocacy to appeal letters I had helped create a pack which suggested several useful actions that could be taken, lost amongst which was the appeal for cash.

One idea is to link an action with a donation. Amnesty has tried split cards which the donor tears in two, sending one half to Amnesty with their donation. This half says, 'I have today sent a letter to such and such a government.' The other half, saying, 'I have today donated, to Amnesty International', is sent to the government concerned, which lets them know the person's depth of feeling. (See also Chapter 4 - 'How effective is advocacy?')

Style

Once you have an established style to your appeals, think about the variations that will make each appeal different.

- Pick a different theme for each appeal - for example, starvation, torture, rain forest destruction; or use geography: Africa, India, Brazil, London.

- Instead of illustrating the problem by reference to individuals, refer to communities; though be careful with this, because focus group tests report that people are very often drawn to support charities through identification with individuals and certainly not through identification with the formal organisation. This is often summed up by fundraisers as 'people give to people not organisations'.

- Vary the person doing the asking, from your director or chairperson to an appropriate celebrity or relevant statesperson. This is sometimes done by adding an additional 'lift' letter from that person, which gives a personal message to strengthen the appeal. Such celebrity endorsement has become so common that it is really only useful if the celebrity really has an appropriate connection and is well known enough to your members to make a difference. Ensure the style of the letter fits the person ostensibly writing it and that they have approved the final text.

- Vary the size of envelope, as well as the enclosures.

- Vary the linking element (which unites all the enclosures and the envelope together). Often this is just a common phrase or campaign logo, but it does help to show you are not just putting the same old appeal out again.

Linking appeals

Linking appeals with each other is useful: 'We asked you for money for a new school bus in June. Now winter has set in, and it has broken down. The children are trudging through the snow.' Making sure that your communications are clearly from one and the same organisation will significantly increase your income in the long term. Write up the results of each appeal in your newsletter and thank your donors. Show how the money was spent and the successes that ensued. Do not be afraid to ask people, 'Look out for the next appeal because its very important'. All too often newsletters and appeals appear to come from different organisations.

Incentivisation

Incentivising appeals work in the same way as other fundraising incentive schemes. The incentive should be appropriate to the organisation (and, if possible, the appeal itself), and used to indicate a higher than usual level of contribution. Its effectiveness will wear off if used constantly.

The World Wide Fund for Nature (WWF) has traditionally sent out car-stickers in all its appeals, and these can be seen advertising the organisation in every traffic jam and car park. Unlike incentives offered in return for a gift, these are freely sent out on the inertia basis, ie. having received a gift the recipient will feel like responding generously in return. They also give free publicity, but only because the scale of WWF mailings is so huge that they will appear over and over again. Can your organisation match this?

Loose-leaf inserts

Loose-leaf inserts are leaflets inserted in the pages of magazines or newspapers. They are not bound in, and often fall out when the periodical is first opened. Some people hold their magazines open over the wastepaper bin to facilitate this process.

Loose-leaf inserts can, however, become a mainstay of your recruitment campaigns. You will find that they have a relatively low response rate, but because they are inexpensive a rate of only 0.25% should be sufficient to break even. A single sheet of A4 paper, folded thrice, is customary, though many other variations are tried. Some even come complete with gummed edges so that the return coupon can be sent back without need of an envelope. You will find this more expensive, but it is easier for the potential member or donor to send it back to you and those few extra returns can be crucial. Do check the glue works!

As in advertising, a striking picture on the front cover helps to capture attention, and a good headline will lead people to read the rest of your text. This must be simple and easy to read, leading straight to the coupon. Like an advertisement, a loose-leaf insert should have a FREEPOST address, making it easy to return.

A topical insert seems to work excellently close to the event but, as magazines have long lead times, you will find this is difficult to arrange.

The ingredients of a good leaflet

The copy needs to move from a clear statement of the problem, to a description of what the organisation will do to solve the problem to how the donor can contribute. Pictures always help. You can use a lift-letter written into a leaflet in the same way as you do in a direct mail appeal but you do have much less space to make your case so it should be succinct and convincing. If you are not using a professional copywriter, carefully read as many inserts as you can manage (I would suggest at least two dozen) and note down the most telling points that really affect you - but do not assume they have all worked well! Think about the 'angle' used to put the points across. Is it an anonymous voice, an authoritative voice, the director, a victim? What do the pictures show - success, the problem, happy faces, suffering people? You should ask yourself, how does the copy lead the reader to respond?

Testing

Apart from being cheap, the best thing about inserts is that they are easily tested. You can insert three different kinds into the same magazine (each with a different code on the coupon, of course) and judge which works best. Though a magazine may only sell you its whole run and not allow you to insert just a few thousand at a time.

Amnesty have run over two million inserts in various magazines for a few years now, and still tests out new ideas and concepts to keep a fresh look in front of the public.

If you do not already know what works best for you (and to really know you must have proved it by proper testing of alternatives), then you must test each concept for yourself. Be careful: in a two-way split test you can only test one idea against one other, and if there is more than one difference you will not know which was responsible for the improvement. You can test three ideas or more against each other, providing they are in the same medium at the same time, as long as they are on different inserts and are separately coded.

Fig. 3c *A powerful appeal for Médicins Sans Frontières.*

Special points

The mechanical process that lifts and inserts the leaflets often needs an edge to grip and paper of a certain size. Do check with the magazine that they can accept your leaflet, making sure they have seen a sample, before you commit yourself to a large print bill. This is a must if there is anything at all unusual about the size or shape of your insert.

You never have a nil response. So, if nothing comes back, the inserts have either not reached the magazine or have not been inserted. It is best to make sure your agency or mailing house is committed to seeing that everything arrives at the magazines before their deadlines. If you have many tests going on in several magazines, it can be a nightmare for a busy fundraiser to check everything is where it should be, when it should be.

If you are inserting in the weekend supplements or a newspaper you will see a distressing quantity of your precious leaflets strewn down the street. Be prepared for this as people are very careless of their environment. It may make you think twice about such inserts; but do wait until you see the actual results before making a decision.

Postcards

Postcards are increasingly used as a fundraising tool because of their strong visual appeal - for example, they are often used as compliment slips.

Nadia just wants to be like the other children.

Member-gets-member schemes

An easy and most obvious way to recruit lots of new members is by asking your existing supporters to sign up all their friends and colleagues. This is probably already happening if you did but know it. The people most likely to join are those just like your present supporters, and people tend to make friends with people just like themselves.

There are all sorts of ways of spurring on this process. You can simply ask your members to sign up their friends but it helps, as usual, to make it easy for them. One way of doing this is to mail them several letters that they can send on to their friends with a suggestion that they join. This is best done in a separate direct mail package with a covering letter, explaining just how important it is to your organisation to recruit new members, and that the most likely new members are those known to your existing supporters.

Make sure that your copy flows naturally through the exercise. It is easy to assume that you can simply ask for something like this to be done without talking about the serious problems you are trying to solve, and how this will help. It will be quite an effort for people, and they need to be convinced it is really important and will lead to an improvement in the situation with which you are dealing.

If you make the letters you enclose self-sealing so that they just need addressing, it will increase the number sent, but can cost a lot more. The cutting and gluing process is not cheap. Shop around for the most cost-effective supplier, but do check the proofs carefully, because the quality can vary enormously. Incidentally, in any print job, if you are using colour, you should always ask to see a colour proof.

This is a fundraising exercise that really benefits from a creative approach. But be careful not to get carried away with ingenious ideas. I have tried sending beautiful colour postcards to supporters for them to send on, but it did not work very well, and I suspect the postcards were so good they went straight up on people's walls - though it may have failed because the cards did not allow enough space for people to send a personal message to their friends. I have tried asking people to copy their friends' names and addresses at Christmas time when they had their filofaxes open to write their cards; and I have also approached new members to send in a short list of their friends who might join. These approaches work, provided you take care that the materials are good and the exercise looks as if it's really important, not just in-house photocopying and a plain letter. But none of them have ever worked as well as when people approach their friends directly.

The best method of all is to have your supporters approach their friends face-to-face. This is the most effective way of raising funds in any case, even if only a few members take part.

If you have an appeal for donations going out to your supporters every month, it may be more effective to insert your member-gets-member scheme in your newsletter. Then it will not clash with an appeal, and has the bonus of saving a considerable amount on postage; but do bear in mind the general rule that it will be much more effective if mailed on its own. As a direct mail appeal to your members will bring in much more profit in the short term, you should not substitute a member-gets-member scheme for an appeal.

Once again, keep testing ideas and checking what other organisations are doing. You should donate to at least six other organisations and file away everything they send you.

Member and donor recruitment: general issues

I have chosen to look at member and donor recruitment together because the techniques are so similar. You may have the luxury of giving your supporters the choice of joining or just donating, but if you choose the latter course you will still need to keep your donors informed and pleased about their relationship with you, if you are to maximise your income. A donors' newsletter is just as important as the members' newsletter. Because the members' newsletter is often long established and run by another department with its own objectives, it is often more cost-effective to recruit donors and reach them through a new newsletter that you design and control yourself. The key difference between members and donors, apart from the annual subscription, is the political difference that members usually have voting rights and donors do not. Members are also inclined to think of themselves as long-term participants in the organisation, and the organisation will often think of them in terms of work that they can do rather than the income they will generate.

Those organisations such as political parties and pressure groups that look to their members to carry out campaigning work (commonly called 'advocacy') will often set up local groups, and it is in those local groups that the real work is done by dedicated individuals who have the time and inclination for such activity. On the part of these activists there is often a degree of resentment, of which you should be keenly aware, when they are asked for additional funds. They frequently see themselves as giving their time rather than their money. This attitude is often also found among staff, who are fearful of upsetting members by the use of fundraising techniques which they see as a bad thing per se, or a necessary evil at best. Some relief can be obtained from this if you are able to separate out the activists from the national members (some of whom will, of course, be or become activists), and if you can allow people to opt out of your appeals to members. Flag the activists on your database and consider carefully when, and how, to approach them for funds.

If your targeting of prospects is accurate you will no doubt mail a few of your existing members, asking them to join. This is sometimes taken as a personal affront ('Didn't you know I was a member?'), but even with the best de-duplicating system currently available it is unavoidable to some degree. Another occurrence in prospecting is that you may find that certain lists or publications are more likely to provide members and others more likely to provide donors. If you only require one or the other, test the media carefully and adapt your literature to suit your requirements. Think too about adapting your organisation to their needs.

Reminders to lapsed members

All your recruitment will be in vain if you fail to retain your members. An efficient subscription reminder system is essential. One or two reminders sent out occasionally will not do. Many of your members will simply not notice them. In survey after survey many lapsed members have said, 'I thought I was a member,' or, 'You have not sent me a reminder.' This is partly because they belong to many organisations and cannot remember which they have a standing order with and which they sent a cheque to even last week. It is also because the best organisations send out five reminders, and, as people become accustomed to that, anything less is not taken seriously. Of course, it may also be that your administration is at fault. Check to make sure the reminders are really being sent to the right people at the right time.

Join several organisations like your own, let your membership lapse and see what happens. Note how long after you stop receiving their newsletter and when you stop receiving their appeals. Lapsed members are a very important source of donations - but only those who have a consistent record of giving in the past. Find out which is which on your database! Keep all the reminder letters you receive and compare their programme with your own. There is always something to learn.

A good reminders procedure is to send:

1   an 'early bird' reminder a month before the renewal is due. This can increase your revenue by bringing forward some subscriptions by a month (much to the confusion of your administration), but more importantly, it will stop their renewal drifting by a month.

2   a second reminder ('Renew now!') at the time of lapsing.

3   a final reminder one month later.

The last two reminders are sent to those segments of the donor-base that are worth renewing. Each stage should be costed against the income from members rejoining, over their expected new lifetime with the organisation. Those people who give very generously are worth sending many more reminders to than those who never give at all.

You should also test additional reminders to see if they are cost-effective (Greenpeace sends five). This must take into account the lifetime value of those renewing and not just the immediate income. (Lifetime value of a supporter is their average donation per year multiplied by their average lifetime with you.)

Lapsed donors

Many organisations have adopted the same procedure with donors as with members. Renewing their donations is a little different, but the difference is only in the copy. Reminding them that a year ago they gave a donation, and inviting them to do the same thing again, can be much appreciated. The number of reminders needs careful testing, and it may be much better to move on quite quickly to appeals for specific work rather than issuing generic reminders about a donation.

Telemarketing to lapsed supporters

Telemarketing is a great way to bring back countless members. I have listened in to many calls in which the lapsed member is charmed to receive an avuncular call, from the organisation they supported, enquiring why they have left and asking them to kindly rejoin. It is also quite possible to bring people back at a much higher rate of subscription than they lapsed at, to be paid usually by direct debit or standing order.

Prospects should be asked first for, say, £10 per month, to give the more affluent members the opportunity of giving at that level; then £5 per month, and lastly for the fee they lapsed at. At the moment £5 per month is a common average, which improves on the usual donation or annual fee of £15 to £20. For your key donors (or donating members) it may be well worth phoning them soon after they have lapsed, to enquire why. They will appreciate the effort you have taken. Lapsing may be due to changed financial circumstances, in which case they are then likely to rejoin when their circumstances improve; or it may be that they have just retired, in which case you may well learn about a legacy. You may also be able to sort out a problem or misunderstanding that they have with your organisation.

It is not unusual to have some 80% of people pledging to rejoin, but sometimes only half of those will eventually come through. It is worth flagging on your database those members brought back by telemarketing, as they will be susceptible to telephone appeals in the future. There are now several companies that specialise in telemarketing for charitable organisations. It is well worth using these, unless you have real expertise, because this is such a powerful approach that it will upset your supporters if not done with sensitivity. You will, however, always experience a number of complaints, as with any fundraising technique. Any call, albeit mild and apologetic, will make a few people complain. This is most likely to happen at the beginning of a campaign when the callers are getting used to their scripts and are a little wooden.

Resting actors are a good choice as callers, as they are used to working from a script and have pleasant voices. Do work carefully on the script with your agency, and test it before rolling it out on all your lapsed members. Telemarketing for philanthropic organisations is still far from realising its full potential. Most organisations think of it only as part of their renewal programme because that affects lapsed members, on the basis that if these people are offended it doesn't really matter. This is a self-defeating philosophy because it locks out a wide range of telemarketing activity. Almost anything you do by letter can be done by phone - more quickly and with a better response rate.

Naturally, this costs more and you need to test its cost-effectiveness. Organisations that use telemarketing a lot often use it to precede an appeal, letting people know how important the appeal is. Alternatively, you can send a letter saying that a call is on its way. This may spur the recipient to action and avoid the expense of the call. As always test which approach your supporters appreciate.

The future of telemarketing

As thousands of people renew their subscriptions to dozens of organisations after telemarketing, we are becoming a telephone-responsive society. This is also becoming manifest in the number of credit card purchases made over the phone, from buying theatre tickets to sending flowers by Interflora and, of course, banking by phone. In later chapters we will look at future stages of this development, including interactive TV and the Internet.

§

Recruiting new supporters can be a humbling experience. Most people will say no. Often 99 % of people will automatically say no or even 99.9 % but that 1% or even 0.1% can be enough to build a mighty organisation solving immense human or environmental problems. If you know how much an individual's lifetime support is worth you can often face such external rejection with equanimity. Knowing their worth and the cost of recruitment, you will also be able to recognise just how vital it is to retain them, and to fulfil the faith you have engendered in your organisation.

4 Inside the Pyramid:
Developing your Supporters and building your relationships

Steadily increasing the income from your supporters and building your relationship with them go hand in glove. As your supporters learn more about your work, have their enquiries answered promptly and accurately, and are thanked quickly and politely, they will become your friends and even your advocates. Neglect this and they will become the opposite.

The prime vehicle for informing your supporters about your work is the newsletter. Let them know how well their donations have been spent and educate them about your cause so they have a real understanding and can pass on your concerns and message. An attractive and well written newsletter will more than pay for itself.

In building and developing the profile of your organisations think about the effect announcements have on your supporters. Appeals should match the urgent concerns you voice in the press, your newsletter should inform your supporters before you launch a major campaign and your staff should be courteous and helpful to all supporters who call up or write in. Make sure that the person answering your 'white mail' and those answering the phone are trained in customer relations and thoroughly familiar with all your projects.

Raising additional funds

The best known method of obtaining additional funds from your members or donors is simply to write to them. As a substantial proportion will have been recruited this way, and an even larger proportion will have joined or donated to another organisation this way, you have a very warm prospect list sensitised to direct mail and therefore likely to respond to this method.

Appeals to members or donors are very similar to prospecting letters. Naturally, you are dealing with a sympathetic and knowledgeable audience, although, if your organisation is rapidly expanding, it is unwise to expect too much sophisticated knowledge from the new supporters (who, incidentally, will also be the most likely to give). You should, therefore, be careful to explain all those internal references and inscrutable acronyms.

This means that you should appeal not just for the organisation in general, but for new, real needs that they would not expect their membership fee or initial donation to cover. This is possibly the most important factor in appeals. They must come across as genuine pleas for additional urgently needed funds, not just the usual bi-monthly appeal for more money.

Successful organisations typically appeal between four and six times in the year, often sending a newsletter between the appeals. The number of these appeals can be increased until the financial return threatens to drop below the cost. In some organisations it is quite possible to appeal twelve times in the year relying on the commitment of supporters who are, of course, usually paid monthly. A typical fundraising programme, however, contains a combination of direct mail appeals with a monthly giving programme and 'soft' fundraising in the newsletter to provide a greater variety of interest for the recipients.

Soft fundraising includes raffles, legacy appeals, merchandising catalogues and member-gets-member schemes.

Taking each element of the appeal package in turn:

The covering envelope

As with all fundraising techniques, some thought needs to go into even this, the simplest of devices in the appeal package.

- Imaginative envelope design can be very effective. An appropriate picture and phrase helps recipients realise what the contents are about and should entice them to open the envelope, but be careful not to mislead them into thinking the appeal is something else entirely. They will not be well disposed towards you if they feel they have been deceived into opening the letter. Different sizes, colours and textures of envelopes are useful in making a distinction between different approaches, and avoid your appeals seeming like a routine affair.

- A return address is important (it need not go on the front of the envelope). Do make sure your membership department is ready to adjust the changes in names and addresses from returned envelopes, which are usually marked 'gone away', 'deceased', etc.

- A window envelope is useful, as you can then place the name and address on the return coupon (positioned to show through the window) and save donors the chore of writing it out for you - which they will inevitably do in a way that differs slightly from your records. The resulting confusion can last for years. Sometimes the donor will just return a cheque without filling in their name, and if you have no name and address your records will not be able to allocate the gift correctly. This will also cost you dearly if you begin donor clubs based on amounts previously given, and you wish to issue end of year letters thanking people for their help. (In the US that letter forms the basis for the charitable tax returns which are deductible against American income tax. Americans giving to a UK charity will also appreciate this consideration from you).

- Naturally, you should use the Post Office's Mailsort system to keep your costs down, unless you are mailing to a special group who you feel should receive something different. By the way, short runs are not liable for the Mailsort discount. A real postage stamp or one of the Post Office's special issue stamps will be appropriate and make the recipient feel more personally involved. A first-day cover can be used to great effect especially if it is relevant to the organisation. Contact the Post Office to discuss the possibility of a special stamp - though they do have a long waiting list, and very few organisations are likely to be accepted. You can also have your logo on the Post Office cancellation stamp - at a cost.

Fig. 4a *Moving text, strong images, theme graphics and a clear 'ask'. This pack has it all!*

The letter

Ideally you should select the most highly respected person in your organisation to sign the letter - but not to write it; this should always be done by a copywriter or experienced fundraiser. Rarely does your CEO have the talent for this, though they may believe they do. If so, try a split test with a copywriter's letter. It will not work unless it is written specifically to bring in donations, and the sincerity and enthusiasm for the work to be done with that money must be clear. These are definitely not thank-you letters or progress reports, which should be kept separate from appeals.

The basic format of the letter is a statement of

- the current need
- what your organisation can do about it
- how the donation will be used
- a very clear request for money.

As far as possible use examples of real individuals and the problems they have that you are trying to solve. One individual with a strong story is much more effective than a dozen, hundred or thousand people. Several such 'cases' can be brought into an appeal letter.

Supporting material

Lots of other material can be added, but they should all build up the case for the donation and be specially designed, not just added because they happen to be around at the time.

A lift letter from an appropriate celebrity (or expert) can help a great deal, as can a leaflet showing the problem in pictures. Imaginative and money spinning additions have included a piece of opaque plastic to demonstrate the effect of cataracts; postcards to MPs protesting at the problem and saying, ' I have today given a donation to help'; and harrowing pictures sent in a separate envelope clearly marked 'Harrowing pictures: do not open if you may be upset'. Personally, I have always been drawn to maps, and find them a very useful and effective addition to an appeal – provided they do not replace the personal stories.

As usual, always test such material by sending out a separately coded control pack, without the enclosure, and seeing which is more productive. Then you will really learn about your donors' preferences and increase your effectiveness and fundraising skills. Try testing something in each appeal.

The FREEPOST envelope

Make it easy for your donors and give them a FREEPOST envelope in which to return their cheque. They will also use it to return letters of complaint, and sometimes stuff the whole appeal back into the envelope before returning it to you, in the mistaken belief that this is an environmentally sensitive gesture. Surprisingly, however, those envelopes will also turn up months and even years later with generous donations. The

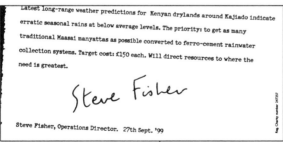

Latest long-range weather predictions for Kenyan drylands around Kajiado indicate erratic seasonal rains at below average levels. The priority: to get as many traditional Maasai manyattas as possible converted to ferro-cement rainwater collection systems. Target cost: £150 each. Will direct resources to where the need is greatest.

Steve Fisher

Steve Fisher, Operations Director. 27th Sept. '99

From the outside, a Maasai house is pure Africa.

Fig. 4b *Here a strong and moving lift element from the Operations Director strengthens an already well thought-out appeal.*

Medical Foundation for the Care of Victims of Torture recently received a donation for £40,000 to an appeal sent out a whole year beforehand.

Try to make the return envelope part of the whole pack by designing it anew each time. Occasionally I have seen appeal papers which are cleverly converted into envelopes for re-use in returning a donation. This is fine as a one-off but is unlikely to be effective each time, as the appeals will begin to lack variety.

The return coupon

Arguably, this is the most important part of the appeal, and deserves quite as careful copywriting and design as any other part of it.

- Give the donor a voice by saying something the donor can identify with. Commonly this is on the lines of, 'Yes, I enclose a donation to support your work for ...' , but I am sure that you can easily improve on that.

- Emphasise the amount you are requesting. This is usually done with a short line of tick boxes to help the donor feel that they are doing the right thing, rather than being mean by giving too little or foolish by giving too much. Donors do fret over such things.

- Help your donors by setting out all the possible ways to pay, including credit card donations and any credit card hotline that you can set up.

- Most importantly, enter the member's name and address on the coupon, using laser, Cheshire labels, or whatever process looks good and is accurate and cost-effective.

- Remember to code each coupon so that you will know from which appeal it has been returned, and which segment of your donor-base it has come from. If you are sophisticated enough to segment your appeals into different categories, try mailing each segment with an appeal for donations the size of which is based on the donors', or groups of donors', past giving record.

Time of year

Whether the time of year makes a difference or not is highly debatable. For example, most fundraisers will avoid August, as a large percentage of your target audience will be away enjoying their holidays - yet many fundraisers will claim to have had their best appeal in August. Personally, I would stay away from July and August but I have had great success in January and February. Will people arriving home from their holiday feel rested and in a generous mood, or will they be fed up with the prospect of returning to work, and broke?

Many organisations appeal before Christmas and this makes sense, as it is traditionally a time of goodwill and giving to charity. Your supporters are more likely to give to you than someone else, but they won't if you don't ask them. Again, many fundraisers, like me, claim to do well in January, because there is no competition and people are relaxed, perhaps feeling guilty after the Christmas indulgences, and, on opening a fresh wage packet, inclined to be generous. On the other hand, other fundraisers think that this is too soon after the Christmas appeals and people need January to get over the usual Christmas extravagances.

Fundraising appeals and issue campaigning

A powerful, well planned fundraising campaign will powerfully advance your organisation's issue campaigning. Sometimes the money invested in generating new members and donors is far greater than that available for pure campaigning purposes. So it is natural for the organisation to look for a strong campaigning message to be used and this should 'fit' with your fundraising concepts.

The fundraising media are high-profile, e.g.:

- national press advertising, which, by its nature, is designed to have impact

- inserts in magazines which are read by thousands of people who, even if they do not join, will be positively influenced

- direct mail, which will also bring your message home to thousands of people.

All the techniques used in these media are intended to generate a response, and so will have been designed and written to be easily accessible and persuasive. The fact that their power is measurable (via the response coupon) means that you know the message is being put over correctly.

Pure campaigning rarely has such a self-correcting mechanism, and so it is hard to tell how effective it is and to revise whatever technique was used if it is not performing as well as expected. Naturally, some campaigning has goals which can clearly be seen to be met, e.g. by the passing of an Act of Parliament – but without a response device in your letters it may not be until the actual vote that your organisation has an inkling of how effective it has been. Having said that, the justification of your expenditure budget is the financial return it will bring. So that is the prime purpose, and decisions on copy, choice of media, etc., must be taken primarily on fundraising grounds within the overall guidelines of the organisation.

Achieving synergy

It is important that fundraising and campaigning go hand in hand through the year to gain the maximum synergy. If your next campaign is on acid rain it is foolish for your next appeal to be on the ozone layer - unless the campaign is a deliberate attempt to include an unpopular subject in the year's work, and the ozone layer happens to be everyone's deep concern at the time the appeal is going out.

Bringing advocacy (campaigning action) and fundraising closer together also helps to build bridges with other departments, staff and committees. If you are seen to campaign, actively and effectively, it will help to create the recognition that fundraising has a powerful role to play at the heart of the organisation.

Taking advantage of the media

Your work will fare much better if, in general, you deal with topics that are featured in the media, especially television, rather than those your organisation particularly wants to highlight. In responding to fundraising literature, members and donors often behave in a very similar fashion to the general public, which reacts to television as if it was the real world and is grateful for the opportunity to help alleviate any dreadful situation that is presented. One TV programme, however, is rarely enough to ensure this. The news itself is much more powerful, but this can be influenced by programmes like the compelling documentaries that themselves become news, and so spill over into the rest of the media.

How effective is advocacy?

Asking the recipient of a fundraising appeal to undertake an act of advocacy often enhances the response, but it needs split testing to see if your organisation's advocacy methods have this result. You ignore split testing at your peril, and the first time you try mixing advocacy and appeals you might get the formula wrong - so:

- test just 10% of your list (not 50%, as is common)
- if you can, test several variations, both of technique and of tone, at the same time. You could, for example, test five different approaches using 10% of your list for each one. This is best done after you know the basic concept is sound.

Linking advocacy with response to an appeal

You must link the act of advocacy with response to an appeal. If you are asking someone to write a letter, they should be asked to use words such as 'I have today joined/made a donation to Save the XXXXs '. Use approaches like, 'Please make a donation and then send our card to your MP. Tick the box on the return form and fill in your MP's name so that we know how many have been posted and to whom can work well, both for your income and your campaigns. If you do not do this you will probably find your supporters send off the cards because it is the easiest option presented to them and fail to make a donation.

What can go wrong

This whole process can, however, misfire badly. If it is not absolutely clear that what you really want, more than anything else, is money, then people will not bother to send it. They will see a campaigning letter, and may campaign or not, but they will rarely respond to a call for money that appears to be just tagged on. It is vitally necessary to make it clear just how important additional funds are to your work.

Thank-you letters

This is a most important part of the appeal because it is the first step to the next donation and, as usual, it should be appropriate and prompt. Speed is very impressive and donors often feel the professionalism you show them reflects the professionalism (or lack of it) in your organisation's charitable work. If you can tell your supporters how well the appeal is going and how much you have accomplished so far, you may receive further donations.

The thank-you letter shows that you care about the individuals' gift, so make sure it is not merely a poor photocopy that devalues the gift. A real letter, signed by the person who signed the appeal letter and referring to the basis of the appeal, is important and will help to build a lasting relationship. It does help if you can quote the exact amount received. Be sure that your software has this capability. If you are signing letters always look at the name and address as well as the amount. You will find countless mistakes in the form of address and often in the full address but also in the £ sign and the spacing of the amount in the letter.

Do not be tempted to let your supporters opt into receiving a thank you letter. You want them to receive this letter even though it is a great effort for your team to send it out. Many organisations use volunteers to do this but the finding, training and losing of volunteers is such an effort it is hard, but vital, to remember how important they are in building your future prosperity cost effectively.

Monthly giving

Monthly giving is a crucial step in ensuring the long-term financial stability of your NGO. It works on the simple proposition that, because most people are paid monthly, it is easier for them to give, say, £10 per month than £50 out of one month's salary. Of course this means that twelve months later you have received £120 instead of £50. More importantly, because monthly giving is either by standing order or by direct debit, you will receive £120 the next year, and the next, and the next, until the order is cancelled. Naturally, there is an attrition rate as people face financial problems, but that is surprisingly low compared to annual or irregular giving.

If your organisation is a charity and the monthly gift is by means of a covenant, then this will last for a minimum of four years and your organisation can reclaim the tax. This is a slightly complicated procedure that seems to baffle many finance departments, who pile up unclaimed tax year after year. Each donor does have to be asked to fill out a short form each year. The Charities Aid Foundation (CAF) will undertake this work for you for a fee, but this is much better than not claiming the tax at all, which happens surprisingly often.

Technically, covenants can be 'variable' by being linked to another event, e.g., the royalties from a book or interest rates. It is not a good idea to encourage these complicated schemes unless large sums are involved and there is a real reason for such linkage which meets the needs of your donor rather than being a fanciful whim. At least one major NGO owes its financial survival to the power of monthly giving, which persisted at a serious level long after the cynic would have thought all links with the organisation would be cut.

Gift Aid

All donations from individuals or companies, no matter how small, are now available for Gift Aid (this scraps the old £250 limit from 6 April 2000), and everyone can join the scheme by a simple phone call, or by sending an email message. This must be followed up within thirty days by a written declaration stating that the donor wishes the charity to be able to reclaim any tax they have paid on the donation. Higher bracket taxpayers can, as before, reclaim the 15% difference between their rate and the next lowest rate for themselves. The declaration can be backdated to 6 April 2000.

It can also be for all donations from 6 April into the indefinite future. A Gift Aid declaration can be revoked on future donation, and it has a thirty day 'cooling off' period, within which it can also be revoked.

An important *new* initiative
from Amnesty International

Fig. 4c *"Partners in Freedom" are the armchair activists who could play a key role in financing your organisation. Research their needs well - and don't neglect to fulfill them!*

Gift Aid declaration forms can be introduced in many inventive ways. For example, they could be on the back of tickets to an event, provided that they referred to a donation not to a fixed ticket price, and the donor could therefore have enjoyed the event for free.

Current conditions are available from the Inland Revenue Claims Branch, St. John's House, Merton Road, Bootle L69 9BB. Remember that for companies, Gift Aid forms cannot be used if the company has paid via its charitable trust or via the CAF (Charities Aid Foundation).

Incidentally, tax relief given under a deed of covenant will now move to be covered by the Gift Aid scheme; but it remains to be seen if this process scuppers the chances of tying in donors to a four year promise, and increases the volatility of donations, which would not be helpful. Covenants should still be regarded as good vehicles to retain commitment over the long term.

If you do not run six appeals in the year, then slotting in a monthly giving programme is easy. If you have reason to believe that your supporters will not accept another appeal, you are faced with the possibility of either replacing an appeal (in which case monthly giving will probably bring in less in the first year, but will more than justify itself thereafter), or taking the higher givers out of your appeal programme and sending them the monthly giving shot.

A hotly debated question is whether monthly givers should be sent appeals as well. Some organisations make a selling point of not sending appeals, but I have noticed that monthly givers soon miss their thank-you letters, and the feeling of involvement that comes from responding to an appeal, and begin donating again. They also forget just which organisation they have a monthly arrangement with, and which organisation they pay their fees to by direct debit - and they often forget completely whether or not they have renewed their subscription. So, I have always avoided promising not to appeal to monthly givers. I really don't think that it maximises your income, and neither does it slow your chances of recruiting such people, because they are giving to help the cause you set out for them, not just to avoid receiving more appeals.

Forms of monthly giving

The basic pattern of monthly giving is a 'donor club' whose members give a certain amount per month and receive special thanks in the form of privileges. These can be as small as a smart lapel badge, or as much as you can afford to give back without nullifying the gift. If the organisation is a zoo, for example, privileges can extend to spending time with certain animals outside of normal visiting hours, feeding and grooming them accompanied by their keepers, meeting the head keeper and discussing future developments, etc.

Different monthly rates

At this point, monthly giving and 'big gift' giving programmes are very similar. You will need to make a clear distinction so that your supporters are not confused. Usually the difference resides in the numbers giving and the level of donation. Monthly giving lies at the mass end of that spectrum. You should aim to bring as many people as possible into the monthly giving programme, but you can also run schemes with different rates and different rewards for much larger monthly gifts. Most of the basic schemes are at the £5 or £10 a month level, though much has also been done recently in asking people to give around £50 a month. This is, obviously, a much greater commitment and you will need to have a very significant reason for asking for that amount, and a very special programme for those givers to enjoy. At that level they will probably need to feel a very important part of the organisation, as indeed they will be. You will also need to ensure that your service to those people is faultless and of a high quality that lasts for all the years you would like to keep on receiving those funds.

Ideally, the higher givers will be treated as a separate part of the donor-base and all communications to them will recognise that they are members of that special group. You may need to set up a separate mailing system and write a special newsletter for them as well. All this will be well worthwhile but, naturally, you should test the appeal on a small segment of the base first to get the proposition right. In particular, you will want to know how much to ask for and what to offer in return. As this is difficult to do for real, a focus group could be used. The Greenpeace 'Frontline' programme is of this nature, appealing to the armchair activist with videos and special reports that put them in the front line.

The Medical Foundation runs a 'Friends of the Foundation' scheme for those who give £30 per month or more. Once a year they are invited to dinner with the Foundation's Director and a celebrity speaker drawn from their long list of Patrons (which was devised to attract useful celebrity support). Friends are also invited to attend an attractive package of events throughout the year. Potential major donors are excluded from this programme, being visited separately and treated as individuals.

Big gifts

The process of treating the higher givers as individuals bridges the gap between monthly giving clubs and big gifts proper. The importance of upgrading your donors into the clubs, or attracting potential major donors into them, cannot be overstressed. These high level clubs are the recruiting ground for your major gift programme: major donors can yield not only substantial annual income, but also funds for major capital appeals.

Approaching major donors

Once potential major donors are identified from among the prominent members of high value clubs, or by such techniques as matching your supporters' names against lists of wealthy individuals, or systematically following up the networks of contacts that your influential supporters (including staff, volunteers and trustees) all have, you must make sure that they identify closely with your organisation's goals before you approach them for a large donation. If you are embarking on a big gift programme of any size then you should consider a full-time researcher who will be invaluable in selecting your prospects.

Prospects can be invited to open days, prestigious events, dinners and any other occasion at which you have the opportunity to explain to them your vision of the future of your organisation, and to enhance their understanding of your work. To maximise your chances of success, you need to know your prospect's current appreciation of your work, and to be able to convince them of the necessity of the next steps you propose. When you feel that you both share the same goals for the work of the organisation, then you are in a position to set up the 'ask' for the maximum amount that the individual will be happy to give. All this requires knowing your prospects in depth, and in particular knowing how to meet their needs for knowledge and recognition.

The 'ask' is best made face-to-face by a friend or colleague of the prospect, who is in the same peer group or profession and who has already given themselves (in fact they really must have given themselves to be effective). It can be done in the prospect's office, or wherever they feel comfortable. It is important to have a set sum in mind, or at least a range of giving options, but do not forget that gifts in kind, and secondments of staff or use of office space can be invaluable too.

In some charities such work is undertaken by Board members, who have been offered a place on the Board for this specific purpose and who have the task of big-gift fundraising written into their job descriptions. Do ensure that the people you engage to make the 'ask' really can ask for money from the right level of prospects. It is wise to run a short training programme for them, in which they brush up their knowledge of the organisation, its successes and its future needs, and their knowledge of the prospects. In the course of the programme they should have the chance to practise asking for money. This will be unnecessary for some, who will be adept at calling in favours and who enjoy the game, but it will be vital for those who are less sure or practised at fundraising.

Legacies

Charities have been at the forefront in persuading the British public to make out a Will and to leave part of their legacy to a good cause, but still less than half of us take that simple step.

As Britain has become increasingly a property owning nation, legacies have become big business. The sale of houses often releases much larger sums than their occupants ever disposed of in their lifetimes, and without a Will the proceeds may not be used in the way they might wish.

Legacies are a potentially huge source of income, and no charity, however small, should be without a proactive legacy programme. CAF reports legacies amount to 33% of voluntary income to the top charities in 1993. Interestingly, Smee & Ford (who provide very knowledgeable consultancy in this field) show only 13.7% of people made a charitable Will in 1994. So we have a long way to go and a great deal of opportunity in a market which is wide open.

Key to success

The key to successful legacy work is to let your supporters understand that a percentage of the residue of an estate is your preference, rather than a set amount of money (which may be greatly reduced in value by inflation), and means that the legacies you receive will be some ten times greater in value than if you were left a simple lump sum.

Fig. 4d *Take care to choose the style of legacy advertisement that suits your supporters.*

Although we tend to talk of supporters in this context, some research has shown that perhaps half the legacies received by charities come from people who had not previously made a donation or become supporters or members.

Taking this into account, most large legacy programmes have featured advertising to the general public, often in the national press, usually offering free legacy advice in the form of a booklet. Naturally, charities hope that those who receive the booklet will leave them a proportion of the residue of the estate.

It is frequently said that these campaigns have been very successful, but they are certainly not run with the intensity that they were in the late Eighties, and I suspect that it is rather difficult to prove a connection between income and expenditure. Legacy income is, however, not usually as tardy as one might suppose. The average time between the making of a Will (or addition of a codicil) and the charity's receipt of the legacy is reliably quoted as being only three and a half years. The current trends may have altered this statistic a little, but it is still a surprisingly short time.

In planning your campaigns for legacies, bear the following points in mind:

• The seasons for making Wills are in the spring, before the family flies abroad for the summer holidays, and just before winter, when people fear the approaching cold.

• Most people seek legal advice on legacies, and you should always encourage your supporters to do this.

• The principal person people turn to when they are thinking of making a Will is their solicitor, bank manager or other financial adviser. For that reason many charities advertise in the Solicitors' Journal and the Law Society Gazette. Many solicitors have told me they use these publications, but there is also a plethora of others designed especially for charities advertising for legacies. I suspect that, with so much money coming into charities via legacies, and so little direct feedback from such advertising, many charities simply advertise anywhere they can.

Fig. 4e *Legacy leaflets are a good way of delivering detailed information at the right time.*

You need, as always, to test the market. The secret is to have an incentivised return coupon: 'Yes, I would like to receive a copy of your free Will guide'; 'Yes, I have left a legacy to you in my Will. Please enter my name in your record of Lifetime Key Supporters, plant a tree in Charity Wood and send me that engraved fountain pen'. These things sound trivial, listed like that, but they are a real indication of a major decision and act of charity, which you should take pains to show you appreciate. You cannot thank someone after you have received the legacy. Of course, working out what percentage return from these coupons makes the expenditure worthwhile is not easy, but a very low return may indicate there is money to be saved on these costs though even a quite small number of responses may in a few years lead to huge profit. Legacy information like this needs to be carefully recorded, old records checked, and a healthy long-term institutional memory and inquisitiveness established.

Legacy leaflets and advertising

To reach your supporters, a legacy leaflet is standard fare. This often goes to all members as an insert in the newsletter and then to all new members in your new member's pack.

Before you write this it is well worthwhile pulling together groups of your supporters and talking them through the whole process of leaving legacies especially what words and sentences are acceptable to them so that you use a language and approach they will appreciate in your legacy material.

- Consult your charity's legal adviser about the current state of taxation and legacies.
- Incentivise the return coupon.
- Set out sample wording for a Will to help people to see how straightforward this can be, but make sure you also make it clear that a standard wording will not suit everyone.
- Advise people to consult their solicitor before writing their Will. It is very easy to make a simple mistake in Will-writing and so fail to achieve what you set out to do. You may have solicitors who are supporters of your charity and could offer an advisory service to members.
- Including a list of the times in life to consider making a Will or adjusting a previous Will can set dates for people to get down to the task. At marriage, for example, previous Wills are no longer valid. Other dates include:
  - buying a home
  - the birth of your children
  - divorce
  - retirement
  - the birth of grandchildren
  - the death of family or friends
  - receipt of a windfall or inheritance
  - taking up a dangerous job or hobby
  - planning your estate and tax position.

But it is the drip-feed approach that works in the long run. To achieve this you need to advertise in a small but readable way in each newsletter then occasionally in any other publication you produce. That way your supporters become accustomed to the fact that legacies can be left to you, and their memories are also jogged on occasion, so that when the time comes to make out their Will they cannot forget that you are interested.

Some people worry about the effect a legacy programme may have on their older supporters, but the thought of death is not necessarily a problem for old people. They have had a lifetime to get used to the subject, and you need not be shy about writing about legacies and Wills. If you do encourage someone to make out a Will you will probably have done them and their family a favour.

Visiting officers

The most progressive organisations now employ visiting officers, who contact the older members or supporters and offer to undertake any light services that they can provide, like shopping, or just calling in for a chat. This help is frequently deeply appreciated by older people, who are increasingly living on their own without an extended family to help them, and who may have contributed considerable sums to the charity when they were working. Naturally, this is no time for a hard sell, and any decision to leave money in a Will must be taken spontaneously, but it can be a very rewarding process for all those who take part. Local group members often make lasting and valuable friendships with national supporters, and vice versa.

Another team activity is visiting solicitors and bank managers to mention that your charity can receive legacies and to leave leaflets and posters. A small volunteer team (best composed of retired solicitors and bank managers!) gradually covering the country in this way has proved invaluable to several organisations, including Oxfam.

One service you should definitely subscribe to is that run by Smee and Ford, 2nd Floor, St George's House, 195/203 Waterloo Road, London SE1 8XJ, Tel: 0207 928 4050. URL **http://ourworld.compuserve.com/homepages/smee/**

They will let you know the details of any legacy left to your charity and any open legacy, where it is left up to the trustees to decide which charity shall benefit. This is a potential goldmine, though in practice charities have had very mixed success.

Raffles

Like their gentleman-burglar namesake, raffles (though run within the law - in this case the Lotteries and Amusements Act of 1976) are fun and make a huge profit.

They can take place perhaps twice a year when books of, say, twenty 50p raffle tickets are mailed to each member and, say, ten books to each local group and other amounts to significant support groups. For an organisation of 100,000 members these tickets typically cost around £16,000 and bring in some £100,000 each time. It is possible to become very sophisticated in allocating additional books of tickets to those keen on selling them, and so run additional raffles throughout the year, but you must make sure that the complexity of this does not outweigh the benefits. Some people object to receiving raffle tickets on the grounds of waste, or on religious or moral grounds. It should be possible to flag these people on your database and to refrain from sending them further tickets.

The rules on raffles

- If you anticipate ticket sales of over £10,000, or the prizes are worth more than £2,000, you should register with the Gaming Board as well as your local authority, who can give advice about your legal position.
- If your tickets' value is under £10,000, and the prizes are worth no more than £2,000, you should register only with the Local Authority.
- Small lotteries, where prizes are less than £50 or have been donated during an event or entertainment, do not count as trading and do not need to be registered. Neither do private lotteries with tickets selling only to members of a club or society or people working together in the same place.
- You need to retain all raffle stubs for a period of four years after the raffle, unless you are given special exemption. This is to ensure a traceable audit trail.
- The name and address of your registered promoter must appear on the tickets.

The tickets

Send a book of raffle tickets to each member. This is usually done with the newsletter, to save postage. Tickets can be sold individually for 25p, 50p or more and a book often holds £5 or £10 worth of tickets. Many members will just buy the whole book, so it does not pay to have books with less than £5 worth of tickets in them. It is well worth testing the selling capacity of your local groups and other associated bodies by sending them several books of tickets.

All tickets should be the same, though of course the serial numbers will differ, and none should have a greater chance of winning than any other.

List the range of numbers that go to each segment of your supporter base to check response, though if you sell many tickets, this can be very time consuming.

It is a good idea to have an attractive cover on a book of tickets and link it to one of your campaigns. You should also give enthusiastic sellers the chance to order more books by putting a form on the back of the cover, but if you do so, be sure to fulfil the order promptly.

The prizes

The key to successful raffles is their first prize. Often this is a holiday for two. For most people that is a problem. Who do I go with? Can I get time off work? Will my husband/wife really want to go there? Can I afford the air fare, or the hotel at the other end? Winners of holidays have an awkward habit of phoning up and demanding the cash equivalent as they are far too old, ill, or agoraphobic to take up the offer.

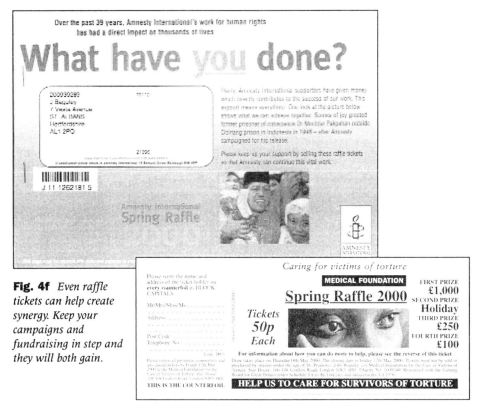

Fig. 4f *Even raffle tickets can help create synergy. Keep your campaigns and fundraising in step and they will both gain.*

An attractive cover on your raffle tickets will help them sell.

You will find a cash first prize of, say, £1,000 works much better. It raises no problems in the buyer's mind, as it can be used to fulfil various needs. Of course, the amount given in prizes must relate to the number of people likely to purchase tickets, and for some smaller organisations a £1,000 first prize would exceed the likely income.

The rest of the prizes should be as good as possible, though they are very much secondary items. These can be donated by friendly local firms or your suppliers, but it will take a personable and persistent individual a lot of time on the phone to obtain these goods. Your own trading goods can be used - but do not overvalue them. They are most likely going to people outside the organisation, so own-branded items will not have the appeal they do for your ardent supporters.

Ten prizes are quite adequate, but some organisations like to have a hundred or more. The main problem with this is that they take hours to draw - particularly when the celebrity insists on rummaging around to find tickets from the bottom of your huge tombola.

The draw

- Do look for a meaningful date to hold the draw of winning tickets, and seek out a celebrity or interesting person to do the draw. If you have a lot of prizes, check that the celebrity has time to draw them all.
- The tickets should be thoroughly mixed before the draw.
- Make sure the celebrity cannot see the tickets, and draws them out one by one. Half a dozen drawn together are likely to have just one name on them.
- Photograph the draw and publicise it in your newsletter and local paper, along with a list of the winners. Many people will be convinced that they are going to win, and quite surprised if they do not. Seeing the draw and list of names will help show the draw was fair.

Let the winners know immediately and post the prizes off straight away. You will have phone calls on the day of the draw from people sure they have won, and you should let them know who the real prize winners are. Publicising the list of winners takes up newsletter space and time, but it is essential to raise the profile of the raffle, and such publicity also helps to show that it was operated fairly.

Recording names and addresses

It may seem a good idea to collect from your ticket stubs the names and addresses of all the people who bought raffle tickets, or have a computer bureau data-capture them (i.e. put all the names and addresses on a computer), and send them a letter asking them to join or donate. You would, however, be mailing people who like to buy raffle tickets, rather than people who like your organisation enough to join - though a test is well worth carrying out. Be most careful that you use a very sophisticated de-duplication system, because you will be mailing many of your existing members, and they will write their names and addresses in a different way on each of the tickets they buy. Be prepared for some surprises. People buy tickets for babies, putting their name and address on the stub. One supporter bought a ticket for his dog. I asked the dog to join. He joined. He was asked for a further donation. He was a very generous dog. He even filled in a member-gets-member list of his friends: Rover, Princess, etc...

§

Building relationships

This process of upgrading supporters by moving them gradually up the steps of the fundraising pyramid can be deeply satisfying as your organisation's income grows but relationship fundraising teaches us that there is much more to long-term profitability than that. The more you can research and understand the needs of your supporters and then meet those needs on an individual basis the stronger the bond will be between you. The stronger the bond, the more satisfying and long-term that relationship will be.

For example, the Medical Foundation for the Care of Victims of Torture has run a programme of five Open Days per year for some time. These allow supporters to meet the Director, visit the premises and chat with staff: but the experience is tightly controlled, and the supporters are led to absorb crucial details about the work of the organisation which encourages them to face the hard facts of the work done by their clinical staff. After the supporters have gone staff compare notes and develop their knowledge of those individuals.

During the rest of the year a series of events, including small gatherings in private houses attended by celebrities, brings key supporters much closer to the organisation. Often potential major donors or those with influence are invited to lunch or dinner with the Director. This whole process of development has been remarkably successful, paving the way for a capital appeal which is rivalling much larger organisations in its income and speed of acquisition.

5 Trading

Trading is not in itself a charitable object, but charities can charge people for services and goods, engaging in what is termed 'occasional fundraising activities', without infringing their charitable status or incurring a tax penalty from the Inland Revenue (trade is usually taxed at Corporation Tax rates).

Trading must only be done occasionally, not regularly, and it must not be in competition with other traders. The public must be buying the goods because they wish to help the charity, and, of course, the profits must be used for the charity's charitable purposes. This is made clear in Inland Revenue leaflet C5.

If trading becomes (or looks like becoming) substantial or regular, then it is best to set up a limited company which covenants all of its profits to your charity. Instead of covenanting (which must be for four years or more), the company could use the Gift Aid scheme to remit funds tax effectively to your charity (it remains to be seen if it can take advantage of the recent relaxation of Gift Aid regulations). If you need to retain profits for future expansion, you will probably be liable to corporation tax like any other company. The Inland Revenue leaflet IR75 deals with the rapid reclaiming of that tax by the charity. Because the company is limited, any losses it makes will not have to be met by the charity. Indeed, the charity could be in default of its objectives if it attempted to rectify the situation.

Inland Revenue permission is also needed for any loans made to the trading company at its outset or later. Repayment of these loans needs careful consideration, as all profits may have been covenanted back to the charity already!

It is prudent, as always, to seek legal advice in the setting up and running of a trading operation of this kind. An accountant's advice would also be helpful in making sure that the two legal entities are entirely separate. The accounts must also be separate, and if there are shared staff and premises, it must be clear which part of the staff's time and what proportion of space and overheads the trading operation will incur. The distinction between the two organisations must be quite clear at all times, and the charity cannot use the trading company to undertake activities on its behalf that it would not normally be allowed to do.

Interestingly, trade can be carried out by the charity if it directly helps the charity's charitable purposes, e.g. disabled people running shops or manufacturing units as part of their training and rehabilitation.

The contract culture

Unfortunately, governments are looking to charities and other voluntary bodies to take up their shortfall in social service provision. They are also harnessing, if not harassing, charities and other NGOs to fit their policies and accountability, by increasingly contracting out services to them, and decreasing straightforward grant funding.

If these contracts are to provide services in the course of fulfilling charitable objectives, they are not trading and can even be charged at a rate high enough to cover overheads and set aside reasonable provision for the future. Independent schools and private hospitals are both examples of charities that do not shrink from charging a good rate. Of course, at some stage, the amount charged will begin to interfere with the concept of benefiting the public. But remember that you do need to cover all your overheads, not just the running costs, or your organisation will be out of pocket. This includes the costs of monitoring and evaluating the services you provide, as well as the management time used in liaison and negotiation.

Do make sure that you have good legal advice that covers all aspects of your contracted services, grants and trading. Incidentally, an area that is coming under increasing scrutiny from the VAT inspectors and the Inland Revenue is that of the incentives given by charities in exchange for covenants or Gift Aid.

The nominal value should not be more than 2.5% of the gift and there is a ceiling of £250, but magazines and other incentives can be deemed to have much higher value than their production costs. Be careful of the cover price on your magazine or newsletter and the value of other incentives. If in doubt check, before you launch a costly scheme that might incur tax and VAT on the whole of the gifts raised.

The key to successfully managing the contract culture is to ensure that your income strategy covers the long term and allows for major funders to drop out and others to replace them. Do not become over-dependent on one source of income, and keep trawling the market for new areas of funding.

Catalogues

Your membership forms a niche market of a certain kind of person. One thing is sure: they like your organisation and probably wish to be associated with it. The Henley Centre for Forecasting, among others, has highlighted the phenomenon that people are increasingly defining themselves in terms of the organisations they support and their profession, rather than the place they come from. They are, for example, beginning to think of themselves as members of the World Wide Fund for Nature, rather than inhabitants of Tottenham.

This enhances the possibility of selling them goods which bear your logo, even T-shirts which make abundantly clear the wearer's allegiance.

Naturally, you will need to discover what kinds of goods interest your supporters. In this respect organisations like the RSPB have an easy task. It is not difficult to think of the products their members will purchase. If you look at a few catalogues it will become obvious that there are several items that most organisations can market, such as T-shirts, tea towels, re-use labels and Christmas cards.

Fig. 5a *Why let your supporters buy from anywhere else ? They will pay more for a T-shirt from you because they gain the "benefit" of supporting and being associated with their favourite charity, as well as the T-shirt itself.*

Trading will add synergy to your relationship with your supporters by; cementing loyalty, spreading your message, giving an easy way for everyone to assist financially, and helping your local groups earn funds and reach the public.

Starting out

If you are starting out to create a new catalogue, begin with the items mentioned above.

- Choose the best designer you can find, and use only good quality materials. (Art colleges can be helpful, but you must direct students carefully and be firm with sub-standard work.) If you produce shoddy goods it will reflect badly on your work and you will not be able to build up repeat purchases, which are the foundation of your future sales. Do not run a competition which offers the winner the prize of having their T-shirt design sold in your catalogue. The designs are invariably awful and no one would be seen dead in them.

- Budget, taking into account that a certain proportion of your stock will not sell. Assume some stock will need to be written down at the end of the year (say 10%), and then allow for 'shrinkage' (say 5%).

- Do not drop old favourites that are selling well, but change the designs slightly to keep them up to date.

- Only buy for one catalogue at a time, to keep stocks down. If you can order small quantities repeatedly and still have them arrive in time (without costing more because of the small manufacturing run), this will also help to keep the stock cost down. This is important as money held in stock cannot be used for anything else and is a waste. Aim for 'just in time' delivery, but stock must arrive in time for people to post them on successfully before Christmas – people won't forget or forgive if you have messed up their present-giving.

- Start small with a few items until you know the kinds of goods your supporters will buy. Do not be afraid to charge a premium for branded items - you have an exclusive item! The usual mark-up is around 2.5 times the purchase price.

Setting out the catalogue

There are many commercial books about catalogue layout, and their wisdom applies to charities as much as commercial firms.

- The cover sets the tone of the catalogue. You can use it to increase sales of your best items and attract people inside with a picture of something you know they will like. Put your best-selling items on the cover, not those you are trying to shift.

- Use the first pages to talk to your customers, setting out your policy and philosophy of trading. Let them know you care about your customers. A celebrity endorsement helps so long as it actually encourages people to buy rather than just saying that your charity is a worthy cause. It is quite acceptable to draft this letter for the celebrity and to allow them to add a personal note or change something if they wish. Some will rewrite your draft improving it greatly, others will just sign the draft.

- Use colour, because your customers will worry whether the product matches other items they have, etc. Do not just use a picture and leave it at that, but mention key points and important details. A simple, clear layout can still show a lot of items per page, but do make sure they are all clearly visible. Your customers will want to see exactly what they are buying, because they cannot call in at a shop, see and handle the goods first.

- People are buying the benefit of having your product, not the product itself. Describe products in those terms, and your sales will increase.

- Make sure you have priced, numbered and described the items accurately.

- Keep a fair turnover of goods by marking down and selling off slow-moving items, but do not let them clog up your catalogue. Keep it looking fresh and interesting. (Use local groups to sell off goods cheaply rather than letting them take up valuable selling space in your catalogue).

- Try out what everybody else does. They may be doing it because it works!

  - Send out your catalogue a long time before Christmas and mention it in your next newsletter.

  - Try two issues with the same contents but different covers. One for summer, one for Christmas.

  - Do not try a spring catalogue until you have established your Christmas market (85% of sales are said to be pre-Christmas).

  - Use celebrity endorsements. They sell products and add glamour to your organisation.

  - Provide a clear and simple order form, and a FREEPOST address to save people finding an envelope and stamp. Insert the catalogue in your newsletter to save postage and avoid clashing with your appeals - but test to see if a separate mailing may not be more profitable.

  - Trading catalogue operations are often run by the Office Manager on a part-time basis to start with. As they grow this becomes impossible and when the organisation's supporters number around 50,000 it becomes worthwhile employing someone full-time.

Giving good service

Complaints will usually come from activists who believe the products should be cheap and the catalogue printed on poor quality paper. The compliments will come from repeat orders by your national members who appreciate receiving exactly what they saw, on time. This is especially true before Christmas.

- It is absolutely essential to have adequate stocks ready to send out on time. Let people know the last date for ordering. If items they have bought as gifts do not arrive in time for them to send on to friends they will not give you a second chance.

- Apologise and explain promptly if you have any problems in supplying goods.

- Make it really easy for people to buy from you and to return the goods if they are not happy.

- Refund money quickly if you have to.

Market research

Survey your buyers and your non-buyers - learn everything you can about them.

• Why didn't they buy anything? (Perhaps your catalogue distribution was not as efficient as you thought it was. Perhaps your goods are too old fashioned, or too trendy, for your members. Are they to your taste or theirs?)

• Are they buying for themselves or to give to others?

• What would your members like to see in the catalogue?

• What have they bought from your competitors' catalogues recently?

• Are your buyers men or women? Is there an obvious reason for that? How should that change the product mix?

Act on the information you receive, and do not ask a question unless you know that you can use the answer.

Increasing turnover

• Send a second catalogue and order form to anyone who buys anything. Give them an opportunity to pass the catalogue on to a friend, and give that friend an opportunity to join or donate to your organisation.

• Allow the purchaser to use as many means of paying as possible - e.g. credit cards, cheques and postal orders. Establish a credit card hotline and make sure it is properly maintained.

• Your order form should also give the opportunity to round up the purchase price with a donation.

Going outside the membership

• Test your catalogue, or a version of it, in the magazines that your members read.

• Try a loose-leaf insert with a FREEPOST coupon to return, requesting a copy of your catalogue.

• Code all these inserts so that you can check which magazines worked best, and code each catalogue you send out likewise, so that you know exactly in which market it has been cost-effective.

Sometimes you can be highly successful by ignoring the conventional wisdom. Lynx was very successful in taking full-page colour ads selling their T-shirts. The WWF was very successful in creating a catalogue that appealed to a very wide range of people outside their list of supporters, enabling them to build up a separate list of purchasers hundreds of thousands strong. They also used a smaller version of their catalogue to send to each purchaser and, on a reciprocal basis, to send to the purchasers of other organisations' catalogues. That way a huge database of catalogue-friendly people can be built up. Of course, you will need to have a well-established catalogue with a large enough range of excellent products that appeal to a wide audience in order to achieve this.

There are commercial mail order companies which cater for charities by providing a goods, dispatch and fulfilment service. These can save you a great deal of time and effort if their kind of goods match your supporters' tastes. Make sure the products offered fit with the expectations your supporters have of your organisation, both for quality and for their likely needs.

Licensing

Licensing deals for charities have their origins in the licensing of well-known trademarks such as cartoon characters, cinema and TV heroes.

Suitable products would be designed by a design company and sold on to a manufacturer who would manufacture the goods and in turn sell the goods on to their usual outlets, or would perhaps find new outlets for such goods. A star like Mickey Mouse would then appear on a bewilderingly large variety of products, from straightforward toys to curtains and bedspreads, as well as coat hooks and torches. A licensing agent would take the copyright owner through the whole process, putting the best deal forward, looking after their clients' interests and maximising their return.

Several charities have gone down this route, with varying degrees of success. World-wide sales of many quite different products can be achieved in ways that an individual charity would never be able to think of, let alone manage making the contacts and developing the organisation necessary. It only really works, however, for key trademarks that are well known, highly respected, and capable of translation into goods people wish to buy. It is, for example, a lot easier for a well known environmental organisation to market soft toy animals than for a charity looking after the homeless to find a suitable product or product range. A great deal of time and energy can be consumed in trying to design appropriate products that do not sell on. If an agent's fees are clocking up at the same time a charity can rapidly find itself making a heavy loss.

Licensing products

Some catalogues feature unique or popular products and have a well-known household name, to which a suitable segment of the market will respond. Amnesty has licensing deals with manufacturers of stationery, calendars, greetings cards and other such items. These feature the positive side of Amnesty's work in pictures about freedom, the candle logo, doves and other appropriate symbols. The calendar pictures are the sort one could wish to see on one's wall, though each has some text about the human rights violations that take place in any countries featured. At this level it is a matter of negotiating directly with a manufacturer. Often this will be someone you already know, who creates a similar product to those in your catalogue. It is often very difficult to make the first deal. Manufacturers find it hard to imagine a product from a not-for-profit charity, but once one commercial product is in the shops it suddenly appears feasible. The fears that dealing with a charity is a nightmare, or that the public will never buy something associated with torture or vagrants, or whatever, quickly fade - especially if sales are high.

You will find that one of the most difficult questions is the extent to which the charity should benefit. Some organisations get over this by saying that they want a certain percentage and a guarantee of £5,000 per year for each product on which their logo is featured. Others demand 10% of the sales price regardless of the market or costs. Others will look at sales each year and negotiate new rates. It is, however, very hard to negotiate up if you have started too low or are unsure about the producer's profits.

The pitfalls

One thing is certain. You must never allow your logo to be used on products without receiving a financial return. Do not accept the argument it will gain you publicity. If it is a serious commercial company they should and will pay.

- Many apparently altruistic companies will try to tell you they are doing you a great favour by featuring your logo on their products. Do not fall for this, and be quite prepared for the deal to fail if no money is forthcoming.

- Make sure you do not accept anything less than a reasonable percentage of the sales price (or of profits if you are going to receive strict accounting, informing you in clear language how much the profit is).

- Sometimes you can simply place your address or phone number on a product. Usually, this will merely result in nuisance calls and is not worth serious consideration. People do not usually join or donate to organisations through products. Of course, if you need people to call for a specific reason this can be a way to reach the public.

Working with commercial retailers

If you are dealing with an external chain of commercially-run shops, a wider deal is quite possible.

- Window space backed up by leaflets (with coupons!) and a counter can for donations can be quite effective. Tread very warily with lesser deals. Leaflets on display are fine.

- Posters in the shops with your name on are probably not much use to you unless you are a local charity and need that sort of publicity.

The type of work you do and the publicity you need will condition your response to these sorts of offers. It may be very effective for your local groups to be able to work with a chain of shops because they have a high street presence, a meeting room, or a management with particular expertise your groups may lack.

It is also well worthwhile to think about the long term. If you are too demanding on day one you may not get a look in on day two, or year two or three. It's all a question of judgement, but negotiating is a two-way process in which both organisations benefit, even if one needs to demonstrate publicly that one is the benefactor (and the other the recipient) of favours.

Local group trading

A local group has an entirely different market from a national headquarters. The group is usually selling goods at events, to passers-by who will linger by a stall and purchase a few items whilst they chat to the stall holder. Another key source of income for local groups is their membership, and their trading officer and/or fundraiser should start by making sure that all group members are aware of the range of goods on offer, and have bought all they wish to.

What to sell

The goods that sell best are relatively low-value items, small and conventional. They are the sort of thing that someone will buy anyway, and can purchase without fear of making a mistake whilst chatting to the stall holder (in fact it often gives them an excuse to chat to the stall holder and learn about the charity):

- greetings cards
- simple, informative publications about the organisation
- goods with the organisation's logo on, such as
  - re-use labels
  - biros
  - stickers
  - badges, etc.

The small outlay needed is often readily available to a local group and the income is useful for its running expenses. An organisation providing such goods will help its local groups a great deal.

At a slightly more ambitious level

- a range of attractive T-shirts
- stationery items
- mugs
- Christmas cards

can greatly improve a local group's income. The key word here is 'attractive'. You will only persuade your groups to buy if the goods are really well designed and people will be pleased to wear them or have them in their homes. A great many organisations have lost large amounts of money through sale-or-return to local groups – do not do this!

Trading goods are not hard campaigning devices. 'I support X hospital' is fine, and people will be happy for others to see that they support X. 'Sack the Home Secretary' is an aggressive statement that few will wear on their chests or want on their coffee mugs. Of course, you must judge your particular public carefully. What sort of designs appeal to them?

Perhaps they like attractive pictures of mountains or rare breeds of animals, but they may also like hard or cheeky slogans. Where and when to sell goods should, of course, be sold every time the group meets the public and there is room to display the goods. Often the mere fact that the group has goods for sale will enable it to mount a satisfactory presence at many local events. Especially valuable are those that the whole locality seems to turn out for, such as pre-Christmas sales and Easter Fayres. There may be many similar stalls, but there will also be customers who are in the mood to browse, chat and buy as they circulate.

If the group is confident enough it can usually make more money by renting a local hall and then hiring out any space it does not need to other organisations for a special event. In this case, of course, there is ample opportunity for them to take the prime position for their own goods. It is well worth while testing several different 'markets' before settling on the best place to sell your goods.

How to sell

1   Buy goods in sufficient quantities to earn a good discount, but not more than you can comfortably shift in the next six months.

2   If they do not sell, reduce the price to your purchase price and try again.

3   If they still do not sell, reduce the price to next to nothing to shift them.

As with catalogues, do not clog up your stall/selling space with unsaleable items. Keep the merchandise moving and avoid having the same old stuff on display every time, but do keep adequate stocks of good selling lines. Maximise your successes, cut your losses and brighten up your image with new items. Shops often have interesting goods on display that will not sell particularly well, but which draw buyers into the shop because they are unusual or very attractive in some way. Your stall can benefit from these 'strange attractors', too.

Shops

Why shops?

Most NGOs depend, as we have seen, on their membership/donor-base for a very large part of their income. A few have significant sums from the government or trusts or from commercial companies, but these are not usually sources of sustainable long-term income. Shops

• offer a reliable way of diversifying your income which is probably subject to a different business cycle than your membership

• can be expanded across the country depending only on the amount you are willing to invest and the availability of prime site, high street premises. (Do not bother with anything less - you will not be seen by those giving or those buying.)

In recessionary times it is particularly easy to open charity shops because the institutional landlords who control most of our high streets are less choosy about who they rent to. Traditionally, they are opposed to charity shops 'lowering the tone' of their shopping parades and, by implication, the rentable value of their commercial properties.

The charity shop market looks saturated. Your high street may have a plethora of different charity shops, and they will tell you there is no point in opening another one; but you should be aware that customers tend to 'do the rounds' of charity shops and come quite long distances to check out a group of several charity shops.

Is a shop a good campaigning base?

If you have the choice of opening a shop for either your organisation's charitable or non-charitable wing you must consider whether it is important for you to use the shop as a campaigning base for your non-charitable activities, and whether your local group members will be likely to play an active role in the shop. If so, that role might need to be restricted. The experience of most charities is that their shop's customers are not interested in the cause, and campaigning leaflets rapidly gather dust. This is not to say that the shop should be devoid of relation to the cause but it must be implicit not explicit.

The high street presence of your shops will make people aware of you, and your fascia and displays should, of course, reflect your name and work. This will, naturally, encourage donations of goods and remind your helpers why you are there.

Attracting the public

Though the British are deemed to be a nation of shopkeepers, sound commercial sense is often abandoned when charity shops are opened. If you follow the example of the smart, well-presented shops of the market leaders you will not do badly.

* In charity shops, appearances are everything. Like attracts like, and good quality attractive clothing etc. attracts more of the same.
* Good quality clothing in attractive surroundings attracts customers who will pay the best prices.
* Helpful, friendly volunteers attract more of the same. (Unfortunately, the reverse is also true, with disastrous consequences for many charity shops.)
* An up-market location in a prime site is far better than a mid-range location - and poor locations should be completely avoided.

Quality control–clothing

Clothing is the mainstay of charity shops. The kind of customer who is used to buying expensive clothing is quite happy to tell the world about the designer label they bought for only a few pounds in a charity shop; but the poor will buy new, cheap, low quality clothing and avoid at all costs appearing to have bought second-hand.

It is difficult to run a good-looking charity shop with a clutter of bric-a-brac and books, which hardly pay their keep. If you start selling junk you will have tons of it delivered the next day, and the day after that. Everyone has junk they would like to give to a good cause.

* Be absolutely ruthless in sorting through the things given to you.
* If you are keeping more than 20% you are not being ruthless enough and the quality of your goods will nosedive. Throw the rest away.
* Clothing can, however, be recycled through the Oxfam Wastesaver scheme by other charities.

Choosing premises

The location

Stage one, as usual, is defining your needs. If you have a choice of towns, start in the best location in the largest town and work your way down slowly.

- Undertake a pedestrian count outside your favoured locations to see which is doing the most business. Simply count the number of people passing on the same day of the week at the same time, and compare shop with shop.

- Check to make sure that there is vehicle access, i.e. that people can draw up and unload easily and quickly, close to the shop.

- Is there a high-class residential area around the shop to provide goods and customers?

- What are the rents and rates, and will they be reviewed in the near future? (If you are a charity you will be entitled to a 50% rate reduction but some councils will give you a 100% reduction. If you are not a charity but have philanthropic purposes you can still apply and may receive considerable relief.)

The shop

Once you have found a suitable area, you still need appropriate premises.

- Look for a shop with adequate frontage so that people can find you and you can display your goods. Give yourself plenty of space to display goods.

- Remember, one third of the floor space will be needed to store, sort and price goods, as well as giving room for helpers to relax and have a break.

- Use a good surveyor and solicitor to make sure you know all about the condition of the premises and the conditions of the lease or sale (e.g. just who is responsible for the roof if there are several floors to the premises, etc.).

Before you open shop

Do not be in a rush to open. Give yourself more than enough time to do the following:

1 Fit the shop out properly.

2 Build up and train a team of volunteers to run the shop (including your shop leader who is by far the most important element in the shop and will ensure its success or otherwise).

3 Attract, process and display goods.

Fitting out the shop

Having an architect design the shop and give detailed instructions to the builders will save a lot of heartache later. Make sure you really approve of the design, and that it is based on the best models. Do not attempt to oversee the fitting out of the premises yourself if you have no experience.

It may prove very costly dealing with builders and shop fitters. Make sure that you have taken health and safety issues into full consideration, including fire exits and that all legal requirements are covered.

Making the most of your space

Starting outside the shop

- The fascia board should be clearly painted so that customers and donors know exactly who you are.
- A hanging sign helps in a busy street (and if it's not busy you should not be there).
- The window and door should be clear, with no handwritten notices. (Neither should there ever be any in any other part of the shop.)
- The two notices that should be clearly displayed are the opening times (with the open/closed sign) and the fact that you need good quality, clean clothing delivered during these times only.

Any window display should be clean, neat, attractive and regularly changed. The door should be open during shop hours with an overhead heater to keep the shop warm in winter. You will need a doormat to preserve the carpet.

Inside the shop

- The carpet should be cheap and strong in a neutral colour, with no pattern.
- Lighting should be good - a false ceiling may be needed if the roof is too high.
- Make a clear space to tell people about your charity, and keep the leaflets stocked and tidy.
- Maximum use should be made of the space without it being crowded: customers should be able to move freely around the shop even when it is quite busy.
  - Flexible fittings are a must, so that you can rearrange the shop at regular intervals and test different ideas.
  - The counter should be near the door (with an electronic till which can divide up the different kinds of items you sell so that you can test which are earning their keep in terms of profit per square feet taken up).
  - Changing rooms are essential but should be as open as possible, because they are the area in which goods disappear. Price tickets are often stuffed behind the mirrors in changing rooms, so have the mirrors fitted outside. Only allow one garment at a time, and try to have extra volunteers to supervise at busy times.
- There should be a phone by the till, and in the back room (so that you can phone the police in case of need; they will often come if you are going to ask an awkward customer to leave).

The sorting room

The sorting room requires special attention, as that is where the money is made. To avoid having sorters bend over for long periods, adequate worktop space is necessary, with industrial bins to hold black sacks for the discarded clothing and rails for those accepted, and shelves for books etc., so that the pricers can come along later and price up the goods.

- A safe area for valuables is essential, as is somewhere for volunteers to keep their bags, etc.
- Tea and coffee making facilities should be safe and easy to use.
- Toilets and washrooms must conform to regulations.

Sorting, labelling and pricing goods

- Discard everything that is torn, dirty or old-fashioned, and be absolutely ruthless in this.
- To assist pricing, it helps to have a guide listing the suggested pricing for different kinds of clothing against the average retail prices.
- Make sure your pricers are genuinely interested in clothing, and let them look at several other charity shops to get the feel of current prices.
- The great fear of people giving quality items is that you will sell them too cheaply. People giving expensive goods like to be asked what they paid for them as it shows you are taking pricing seriously.
- Label and price everything. Nothing must go into the shop unpriced, or customers will bargain with the person on the till and force the price down. (They will also take the labels off anything else that is priced, and try to bargain for that as well.)Often they will pick on the mildest person in the shop late on Thursday night and beat them into giving designer clothes away for pennies: 'It's for my poor dog to sleep on!' I heard it said about a perfect silk dress.
- Make it a rule that if something has no price it is withdrawn from sale immediately (even if the ticket is discovered a few seconds later).
- All clothing should be date-coded and withdrawn from sale after about two weeks.

Displaying goods

- All clothing should be on plastic hangers, which you can easily obtain for free from commercial clothing shops as they receive new clothes on plastic hangers. Never use metal coat-hangers as they look dreadful and tangle themselves up like wild animals.
- Buy smart rails to display your clothing and do not allow dump bins to emerge in the shops.
- Shoes and underwear should not be sold. They are impossible to display well, and do not sell.
- Do not display anything you would not like to receive six of the next day. If you put out only antiques, you will receive only antiques. Bric-a-brac should be restricted to small items of good quality.
- Restrict the area available to books unless they are really selling well. Popular paperback fiction sells well but academic books rarely sell at all.
- Compare the sales per square foot of books, clothing and bric-a-brac and adjust your displays accordingly.

Recruiting volunteer staff

While fitting out is in progress, put in the window a notice with your phone number on it requesting volunteers, and begin to build up a weekly rota of staff. You must have at least two people in the shop at all times. The first person you are looking for is the shop leader. They will make or break the shop. Usually, they are women who live locally, do not wish to work full-time and whose children have left home or are independent. They will enthuse the volunteers and bring in sensible, caring people to run the shop. That team will take time to settle in and there may be several changes of staff before the rota is really set, though after the first year there will hopefully be very few changes.

You will need to build up different teams to sort, repair and price goods. Each is a special skill and it takes time and practice to acquire the necessary experience, which is then invaluable.

Volunteers can come from a variety of sources. If you have a national membership or donor-base they can be telephoned or written to. You should advertise in the local press and put up cards in sweetshop windows. Each method will probably recruit only a few people, but that is all you need before the shop opens and begins to do its own recruiting.

Opening up shop

When everything is ready hold a grand opening day and advertise it widely.

- If you have any celebrities associated with your charity ask them to come, so that you feature in as many local papers as possible.

- Issue a press release before opening day, and afterwards let the press know how well it went.

- Try to arrange for interviews with the shop leader and any volunteers with appropriate and interesting stories to tell.

- Make sure that you have your own photographer to cover the event and send pictures to the press as their photographer will have many calls on a Saturday (which is the usual opening day).

Tips for good public relations

- Create good relationships with other local traders, the police and, especially, the refuse collectors.

- Make sure the back of the shop is clean and tidy. If you have unsavoury or bulky goods dumped on your premises take them quickly to the local dump to avoid more arriving.

Third World goods and new products

Oxfam is the market leader for selling 'third word' craft goods through shops, but beware! Oxfam's profits on these goods come from their catalogue sales to a steady market of subscribers. The goods in the shops are attractive and can sell well, but they do not bring the profits that the second-hand items attain. The cost is an internal pricing transfer and need not be the real market price.

Oxfam's policy is to support co-operatives until they find a commercial market for their goods, then to move on. Naturally, they cannot easily abandon co-operatives whose goods are not selling well. This is an ethical dilemma that those thinking of entering that market should consider carefully. The expense of overseas travel and working with co-operatives to ensure prompt delivery and quality control is very high. To import such goods, you will need very experienced buyers and delivery organisers. Many organisations have been caught with goods stuck in customs, months late or only bearing a passing resemblance to the sample first proffered.

Such trading goods do, however, provide an attractive appearance for the shops - particularly the window display and, in the right location, sell well. It is possible to come to an understanding with manufacturers, to receive their ends-of-lines as the season changes. This can be very profitable but it cannot be relied upon for steady sales through the year. With just-in-time delivery, zero stocks, computerised warehousing and industrial retailing, the goods left unsold have been cut down to a fraction of those in former years. Of course, there is still that happy change of fashion in the high street which passes unnoticed outside the city centres.

§

Last but not least...

Shopkeeping is great fun, and many amusing incidents occur during the day. It is a good idea to have an incident book for helpers to record useful information and anecdotes. This not only serves as a friendly link between people who may never actually meet but also as a very practical one. For example, it can alert helpers to the latest scam by unscrupulous customers, or give the shop leader many good ideas for improvements.

6 Outside the Pyramid

There is, of course, a wide variety of fundraising techniques that fall outside the traditional fundraising pyramid. Instead of depending on known supporters you may look to the general public, or try to secure funds from targeted individuals, trusts and foundations or companies, or from government sources. Of course, many of the people contributing through these techniques may also be members (or donors); conversely, a donor-base is a fine place to start to seek these people. Your supporters can be mailed to invite them to events; you could also look for individuals who are trustees of charitable trusts you might wish to approach, and for august but friendly major company chairpersons, CEOs or MDs.

Events

Probably the best known and most visible of these techniques is the special event. There are at least as many types of these as there are charities - and that is a lot! You will find that successful events usually fall into one of two different categories.

One is the sponsored event, in which hundreds of people undertake a walk, swim, parachute jump or some such collective activity, and collect money from their friends, colleagues and relatives. The other is the kind of event that has an entrance fee, such as concerts and other performances, or where people gather to buy goods, such as village fetes and auctions.

Sponsored events

Sponsored events are good fundraisers for organisations with large membership or local group structures. If supported from the centre with materials, T-shirts and national publicity, even local groups sponsored events can become very serious money makers.

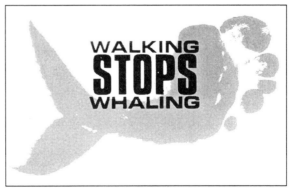

Fig. 6a *Stickers and other appropriate items help to promote events and enhance their attraction.*

Sponsored walks have long been the traditional sponsored activity, but charities have done very well out of sponsored swims, cycle rides, and a large variety of other activities. It helps if you can link up with an appropriate company or add a special flavour to the event. Some years ago Friends of the Earth organised a mass sponsored walk through London's parks, called Ark Day, in which participants, dressed as animals, walked to a huge ark built at the highest point of the city. Thousands of people took part in the spectacular event and enjoyed the day out. There is most likely a feature of your work that would help to raise a sponsored event out of the ordinary. I have seen local groups undertake long tractor pulls for the Young Farmers and bed-pushes for local hospitals.

The funds for sponsored events come from individuals asking their friends and colleagues face-to-face for money for a charity in which they believe. This is a very effective proposition. It is helped if the person asking has a well-designed form to fill in, showing just how the money raised will be used, and if they are enthusiastic and persistent. An incentive to raise a lot of money helps the person asking to say, 'Please give generously because I'm trying to raise the most money so that I can ...' and for the person giving to think, 'I'm being extremely generous this time because I want to help him/her to ...'

Keys to success

Incentives such as a T-shirt for each £50 raised, a jacket for £100 and an appropriate gift for £500, can make far more money than merely selling T-shirts to participants. If you change the T-shirt design each year, people will collect them.

Your key to running a successful sponsored event is to maximise the number of people taking part and to ensure the first gift pledged on the sponsorship form is a large one, because everyone following will agree to give the same amount. You ensure this by simply printing in a sample sponsor and gift: John Brown, Anytown, £35... This looks best if done in half-tone.

Individual expeditions

Charities are often approached by individuals who wish to undertake a particularly difficult or hazardous task or trek, like climbing the Matterhorn or crossing the Sahara on a bicycle. These offers should be treated with extreme caution. They are well-meant, but they show a fundamental lack of knowledge about how sponsored events work. It is very unlikely that people in your organisation, or their friends and colleagues, will give money because someone they probably do not know is undertaking a difficult task. This is not to say that those expeditions do not have their contribution to make. This is really from the publicity that they can garner from the media (often mainly the local media) for the cause.

It may help all your other fundraising if someone is seen to be making such a huge effort to help. The sponsorship, in this case, often comes from companies giving equipment that can be featured in any photographs or filming of the trek, which the company can use for marketing purposes. Occasionally, the participants can raise quite significant sums themselves from affluent contacts, or sometimes from companies, if what they are doing is certain to feature on a television programme. It is important that all this is made clear by your organisation from the start, otherwise the participants may feel badly let down by you, for failing to take full advantage of their hard work by not raising much money.

WALK FOR LIFE

95/96

REF: 322AB

AMNESTY INTERNATIONAL BRITISH SECTION

Please Sponsor (Name) .... (Group name where app.)

of (address) ....

.... Postcode ....

on their .... mile **Walk for Life** on (date) ....

SPONSORS ARE REQUESTED TO PAY THEIR CONTRIBUTIONS TO THE WALK FOR LIFE PARTICIPANT WITHIN ONE MONTH OF COMPLETION OF THEIR WALK FOR LIFE. Please photocopy this form before filling in if you need more space for sponsors, or ring 0171-814-6200 for more forms

Sponsors Name (Block Capitals Please)	Address (including POSTCODE) + Telephone No.	Amount per mile	Total
Tony Morrison	15 Solomon St, Reba, CA4 1AA - 071-123-4567	5.00	10.00
		Page sub total	

Declaration

I have completed my .... mile AI "Walk for Life" and I promise to pay Amnesty International all monies pledged within 1 month of my Walk for Life.

Signed .... **Participant**

Complete box below for total payment only

Total Sponsor money enclosed

Important

Please make all cheques/postal orders payable to Amnesty International. Please do not send cash. Send your sponsor money **WITH THIS FORM** to Walk for Life, AIBS, 99-119 Rosebery Avenue, London EC1R 4RE

Tick if you would like a receipt ☐

Fig. 6b *Note the specimen amount already filled in - how much will the next person give?*

Planning a sponsored event

- Make sure the route goes from A to A, not A to B, or the participants will have a long journey back at the end of their efforts.
- Everyone who agrees to take part should have
  - a route map
  - clear instructions
  - a sponsorship form that can be photocopied.

The form must have a space for telephone numbers because after the event those who take part will need to ring round all their sponsors and chase up the pledges quickly before they go cold.

- If you have a local organiser they will need to know who has taken part in their area so that they can chase up the money likely to come in. It is the organiser's enthusiasm that will keep the event going from year to year and will enable it to become more and more successful. Make sure they have access to this information.
- Design T-shirts to wear on the walk and take photographs of participants to sell to them so they can take them home immediately afterwards.
- Make the event fun and unified in design. If people have endured certain hardships together they become closer, and these events can engender a spirit of camaraderie which helps them to continue year after year. So don't lose participants' names and addresses.
- It is usual to sign (stamp) people in at the beginning and out at the end, so showing that the course has been completed. (A certificate like this helps the pledges to be collected.)
- You will need enough marshals to cover the late starters and finishers, and along the route to help people over roads or with any difficulty they may have in following the route.
- Some drink and refreshment is very helpful during a very long walk.
- Always
  - notify the local police and seek their advice. They will often advise you not to proceed but if you insist they will be very helpful
  - check your insurance
  - take every precaution over safety to eliminate risks as far as possible.

Any open air event can be insured against rain (pluvial insurance). However, this is very expensive, often one fifth of the amount insured. The time you are insuring for also needs careful thinking through. Do you simply insure against rain at the time the event takes place, or for, say, a two-hour period in the morning when people are making up their minds whether to attend, or on a Friday morning for a Saturday event? Personally I prefer to take the risk.

Concerts and open air events

The second type of event is epitomised by the rock concert. Here artists forgo their fee (giving their time or art for free), and the proceeds from the event go to the charity. So, often your only advantage over a commercial venture is that you have saved the fee.

Planning for a concert

The big surprise for most people is just how risky these events are. Most large charities have a horror story or two (some people never learn) about concerts that have lost money and credibility, and induced concert rage, as costs spiral out of control and income fails to materialise. Especially serious are the artists' expenses. After the initial contact with a celebrity you will probably be dealing with their management and you can be sure that they don't care about your charity at all. In fact they will see you as a good chance to fly their star, the band and tons of equipment back from South America for free, as well as an opportunity to have two weeks in the best hotel in town for a large number of people they owe favours to.

Set a limit to expenses, and read the contract details carefully. Most of them are designed to stop the artist being put into a squalid hotel, taking taxis at their own expense, and changing in sordid dressing-rooms - but does the carpet really have to be turquoise, and do they need that amount of root ginger and vodka before appearing on stage? Everything is negotiable - up to a point.

The entertainer's fee is only a small part of your expenses, so you are still left with major costs. You should consider

- hire of the hall
- advertising
- publicity
- programme printing (ticket printing for major rock shows etc. has to incorporate security measures. Do use a speciality printer who is used to this).
- sundry expenses (which can easily amount to more than the total take if not watched rigorously).

When drawing up your budget, allow 10% of the expected income for publicity and have another 10% contingency sum so that you can cover the unexpected. You may need this at the last minute to boost ticket sales. These will be much easier to judge after the first time you run this kind of event.

Points to watch

- When approaching stars, ask the best first. (Who wants to join the worst on stage?)
- Making sure the artist and venue match is extremely important.
- Check carefully that the artist has not just failed to fill a larger venue. If they have just toured, will their fans go yet again to see them? Read the music press to keep in touch if you are planning such an activity.
- If you have more than one artist appearing make sure they complement each other. Do not assume that if you have five completely different artists you will have five times the audience. People will not sit through a performance by someone they cannot stand in order to hear someone they like.

Fig. 6c *Many firms have a budget for charity advertising - and don't forget to ask all your commercial suppliers.*

- You must only reveal the names of artists to the press when they have definitely agreed. This can take some time as their management will try to hold out for as long as possible in case paid work comes up.
- Fix a deadline to decide when all confirmations from performers must be in, and stick to it.
- You should spend enough on advertising to fill the venue, but budget to break even at half full and to be profitable at two-thirds full. It is surprising how often an event is two-thirds full and how often the real break-even point is a full venue leading to a serious loss.
- Straightforward promotional ideas are best. Free tickets or T-shirts to radio shows and newspapers for listeners and viewers who ring in first or who answer a simple quiz correctly (what is your name?) are a very good investment, which gives your show integrity in the eyes of the audience (being linked to their favourite show) as well as publicity.
- Photo opportunity stunts are fun, but the chances are you will have to take your own photos and push them to the press (not forgetting to take your own broadcast-quality video for an electronic news release). Events always take up twice the staff time you have available, but are an excellent opportunity to make the most of your volunteer support. Draft in volunteers early, and give them specific tasks under a volunteer co-ordinator who can organise them into an effective workforce over the time needed. For major venues use professional organisers and promoters.

After it is all over do not forget to thank the stars and everyone who has helped you in any way at all, as well as all the volunteers and staff. You will need them again next year, and they will love to help again if they have received recognition for their effort.

Keys to success

Your key to maximising revenue is to remember that the artist will only attract their usual audience, who will only pay the usual fee for that venue. Check what that was and price your tickets the same. Nobody will go or pay extra just to support your charity.

The key to making events work is to run them year after year. You will find that there is a steep experience curve, and the second and third time you hold the same event (or one very similar) it will be much easier, cheaper and more profitable. Your helpers become professional, the audience returns (it was such fun the last time) and you know exactly what to do.

Art auctions

There are innumerable events that can be held to raise funds, but art auctions are a particular favourite of mine. At their best they bring out a huge spirit of generosity on the part of the artists, auction houses and bidders, and they are great fun. Quite extraordinary sums can be paid when several people decide they must have a certain painting. Your expectations should, however, be realistic. The art market varies greatly from year to year and prices follow suit. Not every painting by a famous artist is worth a lot of money (prints are often worth very little indeed). In fact, most works will go for quite modest amounts. Let the auctioneer know that bidding will

Fig. 6d *Don't stint on the quality of your art auction material. Let it reflect the quality of your art.*

be a little slower than usual and talk through with him how to handle events if you have reserve prices that are repeatedly not being reached. Celebrities' paintings do not sell in art auctions unless the celebrity has a second career as a well-known artist. Celebrity memorabilia is a different event entirely and very specialist.

It is a good idea to move from fine art (oil painting on canvas) one year, to water colours the next, perhaps to cartoons the third year and then to sculpture, before coming back to fine art. Always ask for 'significant' works of art. Do not confuse the issue by mixing an art auction with an art exhibition. Auctions make money quickly. Exhibitions take up huge amounts of time, and cost money to prepare and ship from town to town or country to country. You will need to plan your art auction a year in advance, taking time to cultivate all those whose help you will need and to have the opportunity to overcome the setbacks and problems that will, no doubt, occur. The three elements that need to be brought together are the auction house, art gallery(s) and artists. It is essential to find a sympathetic auction house and art gallery.

Never use an amateur auctioneer: the auction must be conducted professionally. An amateur auctioneer will cost you a very large amount of your potential income. Auction houses often have auctioneers who would like to undertake charity work, and you can sometimes have the finest auctioneers in the land working for you as volunteers. If you have one major work of art for a local auction, consider entering it instead into a city auction where it may obtain a better price, and where your local buyer may well send it the week after. Think about auctioning online through **ebay.com** etc. Online auctions can also be used to sell unsold works of art.

If your organisation is a major national charity or equivalent, start with the auction house, (possibly one of the top three: Sotheby's, Christies or Bonhams), looking for a possible date twelve months or so in advance. As you get nearer the date, seek their advice regarding the quality and nature of the works you have collected and the most appropriate way of selling them. Let the auction house guide you on price, order of sale, number of suitable lots, etc.

The artworks

It is much better to aim for thirty or forty pieces of good quality art than a hundred mediocre works. Of those thirty or forty, there will probably be only half a dozen which are outstanding and it is those which the serious buyers will come for. They will not come to sit through the sale of a large number of paintings they are not really interested in. You do not have to put everything given to you into the auction.

Make sure you have somewhere safe to store the works of art and that you are adequately insured. Always use a suitable van to transport the works and check the size and weight before collecting, or you could be in for a surprise.

The gifts of artworks will come through because of a combination of the profile of your organisation, the strength of your cause and the importance and connections of the person making the 'ask' for you. As is usual in fundraising, the personal 'ask' from a close colleague is the strongest possible way to attract a donation. Learn the connections in the art world that the great and the good associated with your organisation may have. It is well worthwhile to spend time on this first. Often the best way is to put together a committee of these people. Working together to secure the best quality art will enhance the result and be less work for you, as you will have one committee to organise, rather than dealing with each individual separately. As with all such committees the chairperson is the key and they must be well respected and effective, and stay active throughout the project. If you can persuade a major artist to ask persistently for you, you are home and dry.

The galleries

It is at this stage that art galleries will prove invaluable. Their owners have many connections and an extensive understanding of the art world. Your committee people should know gallery owners and it is usual to attract at least one gallery to work with you, helping to make the auction a success. Without a committee, you, or others in your organisation, must have such a connection or you will need to seek help from artists known to you. Another route is to talk to the gallery that handles the work of the artist who donates the finest work. In any case, you will need to work your way through all the galleries who handle your artists and interest them in publicising your auction to their customer list (galleries mail their customers about each of their shows).

The artists

But before thinking about the buyers, you will need to reach the artists. Always start at the top, going for the best artists in their field. Once you have one or more major artists, it is much easier to ask others to join them. Take advice about the best method of approach, which is often to have another artist make the request personally. If a major artist does donate, find out if they would be willing to approach fellow artists - that is how large charity rock concerts are put together (again by face-to-faceor at least telephone presentation). By the way, a good existing work of art will sell much better than something specially created for your organisation. That is fine for merchandising products, but rarely for works of art. Artists may delight in depicting the suffering you are trying to alleviate but buyers may be less enthusiastic about having this hung on their sitting room wall.

Store the works of art with great care before and after the auction. If they are very valuable, use professional storerooms. You may have some left over that can be sold through other outlets or saved for the next time. Always make sure they are insured and move them cautiously. Check the size of the artwork before collecting it. If they are paintings, they will usually be unframed and you will need to frame them for the sale. This can be prohibitively expensive but framers will often do this for free in return for appropriate publicity. It is worth spending a lot of time cutting down on costs by befriending framers. A volunteer with a good voice will be needed to ring round countless companies obtaining all you need, from frames to food, free, to keep costs down to a minimum. (Free drink at auctions is essential, food is inessential, and possibly a distraction.)

Once the venue is arranged and the works of art collected, or suitable arrangements made, you will need to create a catalogue for the sale. This is often the most expensive part of the operation. Good quality colour reproduction is essential if buyers are to be attracted to your event. Make sure the works are fully described, their title, size and medium are important. Always use a professional photographer who has photographed works of art before, (do check their portfolio). It is a professional task, especially if they are large and covered by glass. Focusing on a large canvas so that the final picture is clear from corner to corner requires a specialist. You can recover some of your costs by selling advertising space in the catalogue to your suppliers and others. Set the date of cataloguing carefully, because you will need adequate time to have it printed and to reach the buyers before the sale. That means the setting of a date by which all works of art are ready. Leaflets and advertising are the next highest expenses.

The buyers

Buyers are found through three principal sources. Firstly, through the galleries which already sell works of art by your artists. Secondly, through the great and good in your organisation, including your top donors. Thirdly, through appropriate advertising: try art journals, obtain lists of buyers from other organisations, and talk to journalists about an article on charity art auction bargains. Invite the gallery owner and anyone influential to the private view. (Although your members should know the auction is taking place they should be discouraged from turning up unless they are prepared to bid.)

The auction house will have a lot of advice about the private view and catering on the night. Use the private view as a 'thank-you' and cultivation opportunity for top donors and others - do not forget gallery owners, framers and businesses that have advertised in the catalogue. You should try to ensure the best artists attend and that there is good quality wine as well as soft drinks. As much of the drink, food, flowers, etc., as possible should come free from businesses, for both the private view and the auction itself. (When you have exhausted already friendly companies, you can work your way through Yellow Pages.)

This is a prestige event, so it can also be used for fundraising purposes such as a high price raffle - 'put your business card or signed £20 notes in the hat.' Have photographs taken for your own internal publicity and to highlight the auction in your external publicity afterwards. Do make sure that there are enough volunteers present to cater for all the guests and make sure no one is feeling lost. Ensure they keep a record of the people they spoke to and their interests in your charity. This will be invaluable information for your major donor development officer. To invite people to all such events you should use quality invitation cards, for example with chamfered gold edges and round corners. Select your most prestigious and appropriate person to make the invitation.

The auction proper will take on a momentum of its own and you will need to free yourself from other duties, in order to concentrate on managing the dozens of unanticipated things that occur. Naturally, you may not handle them yourself, but you will need to feel on top of the proceedings by knowing you have allocated all the important tasks to people you can trust and monitoring that they are actually taking place on schedule. On the night, give yourself the freedom to deal with problems by not taking on any major task but let yourself float and liaise with key people.

Take advice from the auction house about the date and timing of the event. It is fine for it to be a weekday and early enough in the evening for business people to attend on their way home. Give the audience time to enjoy their free drinks and look through the catalogue before starting. If you have a lot of lesser works to sell, you could hold a silent auction at the same time whereby people write their bid on a piece of paper below the painting and other bidders add their names and bid more if they wish. This can be quite entertaining but do not let it distract from the main event, perhaps by using a separate room.

Try to avoid reserve prices and percentages going to the artists - you want it all! Some artists, however, like to keep their prices up and in difficult times are loath to give away anything when they could earn from it. The auction house will handle the taking of cheques, etc., at the end of the event and the dispatch of the works of art, but agree on all this beforehand! You will need to dispose of those left over. This can sometimes be done by arrangement with people who bid under the reserve, or those who missed their chance to bid by hesitating. Do not incur storage charges by hanging onto works that are not valuable. Return them to the artists with thanks. If, for some reason, very valuable works are left, auction them off in a regular auction later, but let the artists know this may happen.

My own preference is to avoid reserve prices like the plague. They hamper the natural flow of an auction, which requires some works to go cheaply so others will be scrambled for. Reserves take the fun out of auctions. Having to sell or return works afterwards makes you look incompetent. Everyone asks 'Did you sell out?'. Works sold later require storage, consume huge amounts of time and bring in annoyingly trivial sums.

As always, thank everyone personally and make sure you have included all those who helped, regardless of the size of their contribution.

On the day:

- Let a key person or celebrity speak before the auction to remind everyone to be generous; and, at the end, to thank them (and be prepared to jump up in the middle and enthuse them if things are not going well).
- After the event thank everyone promptly, as usual. The event has not finished until everyone has been thanked, including all the volunteers.

Key to success

The key to successful art auctions is to put as much effort into attracting real buyers as into attracting major painters. Artists will wish to see their work sold properly, for good prices. Remember, they have a market in their work to maintain.

Local group fundraising

Your local groups may provide your organisation with a large tranche of its income, but, surprisingly, many organisations have set up local groups' networks with no culture of fundraising. Often local groups are started by individuals concerned to take part in the campaigning work of an organisation. They are serviced by a groups officer located in the campaigns department and much of their income raising potential may be lost.

Starting local groups from scratch

The first place to look for local support is in your database and files. A search by postcode will reveal the parts of the country where your support is strongest. Usually this will be in the larger cities. If you already know of likely prospects then writing, phoning and visiting key volunteers may give you the nucleus of your groups.

Otherwise a local reception with celebrity speaker and an appeal for individuals to form the initial committee should start the ball rolling. The Freeze Campaign did this on a very efficient basis some years ago. They held a series of meetings across the country, each for some 20–50 people, after work during the week with a local celebrity speaker. A buffet was provided and short speeches, followed by a pitch for help and enough staff there to meet and ask everyone present if they would like set up a group. By the way, you should find it is easier to ask people to become the Chairperson, Treasurer or Secretary (which are the key posts you need to fill) than to give them an unspecified role. If you have no local supporters to invite to these meetings then use the yellow pages to invite people by profession matching those found in greatest numbers on your existing database or those that you wish to form the backbone of your organisation. If you can entice a well-known and respected individual to take a key role before the meeting then it will be much easier to bring into the group good volunteers.

If receptions are not possible, you can write to all your supporters in the locality and ask if they would like to join or set up a local group. Use your newsletter to highlight this programme and to mention all the groups as they form to encourage others. Of course, you should also highlight their fundraising activities so that they can share ideas and encourage each other to raise more. This recognition is tremendously important for local groups as are visits from staff members.

Before embarking on a programme of building local groups do set out their roles and responsibilities quite clearly and agree these at the highest level in the organisation. Will local groups have any voting rights? Will they elect Council members? Will they attend your Annual General Meeting? A simple constitution is important and a sample can be obtained from the NCVO, which is easy to customise and helps to remind you of the areas to be covered. Each of the committee members e.g. Secretary, Treasurer and Chairperson needs a clear job description. The banking arrangements also need to be clearly laid out.

Can the group open an account in your organisation's name? There is no rule of thumb for this. Some organisations are adamant that they will not allow groups to do this. The groups then have to make their own arrangements how they fund their activities. If cheques come to them with the organisation's name on they must pay them into that account or send them to the head office. If they engage in large scale fundraising then funding the up-front costs (and dealing with losses) is not easy. With a bank account in the organisation's name (e.g. Exeter Help Foundation Branch), appropriate cheques may be paid in. However, there is more than one organisation with over £1m locked in local group accounts that their head office cannot use. To avoid this you should set up the accounts with your own bank and no other using a system of back to back banking whereby each month, or year, your bank sweeps through all the branch accounts taking out all funds bar an agreed float. Do ensure that local groups cannot draw funds from your central account or a rogue treasurer could bankrupt your charity. It can happen!

Think how you should be supporting your groups. Do you have posters for them? T-shirts? Trading goods to sell? It is always a good idea to have a simple book of suggested local fundraising events. This should give clear guidance and encouragement, mentioning too all the legal and health and safety implications of the events. When will you visit the groups?; what access do they have to head office?; and how much are they expected to undertake (what is their fundraising target?): these are the fundamental questions you will undoubtedly be asked.

Starting a tradition of fundraising

If you have local groups who do not already fundraise you can turn the situation around but to remedy a situation like this is not easy. It requires a change of culture, which takes time. I have, however, noticed that traditions often take only two years to become established, so if your groups can be persuaded to undertake fundraising activities for two years running, the third year will largely take care of itself. Having said that, the work of starting the tradition remains. One idea is the fundraising week, outlined below; another is to establish a fundraising contact in each group so that you can work directly with a keen individual. The fundraising newsletter, also mentioned below, can be a strong agent of cultural change. Do ensure, however, that the rest of your organisation is supporting this development and is kept informed of your plans and progress.

Fundraising weeks

Fundraising weeks allow you to concentrate on your groups for a short period and, by publicising those groups who are keen to fundraise, begin to influence the others. Fundraising weeks are a well-known phenomenon and many of your local group members will also be members of other organisations which have such weeks. The idea also allows you to use national publicity to assist the groups in their fundraising and, of course, many groups will then receive enquiries which may serve to activate (or re-activate) them.

You could start with an idea like a sponsored walk, flag day or book sale and ask each local group to carry it out at the same time. That way you can provide helpful materials such as flag day instructions, tins, forms, sashes, T-shirts, etc. with reasonable cost-efficiency.

- Let your groups know well in advance what is going to happen. As groups often meet monthly your advance warning should probably go out six months beforehand, with more detailed ideas four months ahead, and any materials for them to use at least three months in advance, (so that the group secretary can distribute them at the next meeting, and catch those who did not attend at the following one).

- It helps to give groups a clear idea of what they can do, and how to organise fundraising events. A group guide is useful, particularly if groups have to pay a fee to head office each year and are largely left to their own devices as to how they will raise this money. Your guide should contain very clear step by step instructions on all the basic local group fundraising techniques, including flag days, door-to-door collections, coffee mornings, jumble sales, car boot sales, running stalls, etc. Join a few organisations and become active in their local groups. It is ideal training for practical fundraising and well worth the time spent. Look at their group fundraising manuals and write a better one for your organisation. Give your local groups an advice hotline to someone in the fundraising department.

- It is very useful to establish a fundraising person in each group to work with, rather than the group secretary, who is often very hard pushed to deal with everything else the organisation asks. Offer the fundraiser a few inducements, such as a training day, priority for much reduced goods from the merchandise catalogue, and a chance to meet with other local group fundraisers each year.

- A newsletter really helps as well, especially if it disseminates good ideas from group to group. Groups learn much faster from each other than they will from someone from head office. Knowing that one group has undertaken a certain kind of event successfully can be a powerful incentive for another group to try it, and perhaps to show that it can do better.

Regional fundraising

There are many local sources of fundraising available to philanthropic organisations. These cover much of the usual range of funding sources such as companies, trusts, individuals, etc. Many charities that work on a local basis as well as nationally derive a large proportion of their income from regional fundraising. Many trusts can only give locally; many companies prefer to give close to home and many individuals are more comfortable giving to someone they know.

A regional programme will often incorporate a dynamic local group structure, but will usually extend beyond that to a series of systematic approaches to all likely funding bodies in the regions.

Regional organisers are essential if the scale of activity is to be sufficient to bring in serious income beyond the activities of local groups. Some organisations train and develop their local groups to approach trusts and companies as well as holding events, competitions and running stalls. Others use their regional organisers, who are usually paid, to undertake these sophisticated tasks on behalf of the organisation or the local groups. If the charity is running local operations such as a hospice then the level of fundraising required will usually demand a very professional team of local fundraisers and support committees rather than the conventional local group. Regional organisers will find these volunteers, plan their strategy and train them to carry it out.

In all this, as in so much of fundraising, motivating the volunteers is absolutely essential to develop a dynamic grass roots operation. This is a hugely responsible task often carried out with little head office support (though the best organisations provide excellent back-up) whilst on it rests the national reputation of the charity.

Flag days

Flag days are a traditional form of fundraising that everyone is familiar with, as they play a part in the lives of most of our high streets. In some, hardly a week goes by without a charity collection. Success here comes from the number of people you have out on the streets. Although it is largely a numbers game, the nature of your cause and public profile is important - as is the material you provide, and training for collectors. Read the Charities Acts 1992 and 1993 to ensure you understand the legal position.

- You will probably need local authority permission to collect. Apply to the Clerk to the Council, and make sure you have permission for all locations in which you wish to collect. Before the event all such permission should have been sought by you, or the direct organiser, and the best collectors allocated to the busiest places.

- Collectors need to be organised around officials who give out the cans, allocate collecting places, and, at the end, collect the money and thank everyone.

- Collectors should be 18 or over and must carry an ID card.

- The official organising collectors should give out sealed and numbered tins, making sure that they all come back with the seal unbroken and that they are counted with two witnesses present.

- Collectors can call out and make a noise, so long as they do this without causing a nuisance. Rattling the can and calling the charity name is the customary practice. If the collector is quiet and retiring, people will just pass by. High streets, stations and anywhere there are large numbers of people are the best places.

- Collectors must not stand closer than 30 feet apart, and definitely not together.

- It helps to have

  - sashes for people to wear, clearly showing the name of your charity

  - collecting tins and leaflets to give out to those interested

  - stickers for contributors to wear so that they will not be asked again, and to show their support.

- Keep a record of the amounts that each individual collects and tell them how much it is when you thank them. Collectors will ask who has raised the most, so keep this in mind. They need to ask permission to collect on private property, shop frontage and railway or underground stations.

- Check the Charities Act 1992 on the regulation of 'public charitable collections', including street collections and make sure you are doing everything correctly. You can obtain copies of the Act from HMSO, St Crispins, Duke Street, Norwich, NR3 1PD, Tel: 01603 622211, or from HMSO Bookshops. Note that this act has been brought into force in stages in consultation with the ICFM and other voluntary sector representatives.

Door-to-door collections

Door-to-door collections are another standby of local groups. Many organisations and societies began with the weekly collection of small amounts of money door-to-door. Door-to-door collections depend for success, like street collections, on the power of numbers: on how many people are prepared to drop envelopes through the letter-boxes of houses in streets near them and pick them up, bulging with cash, a few days later. Also, like street collections, they are regulated by the new Charities Act, which should be carefully perused.

Unlike street collections, however, door-to-door collections have a private feel to them. It is often how well-known the collector is that makes the difference, so collecting locally in your own street can be both profitable and sociable. Collectors can call round together, and much of the fear of going door-to-door is taken away by encouraging volunteers to work in their own neighbourhoods with a friend.

The officials organising the collectors need full instructions on how to run the operation and how to account for the money raised. Door-to-door collections do require materials to be centrally produced. It is well worthwhile looking at several other organisations' envelopes to see which are the most effective and to test out different ideas. How large should the envelope be? What colour? Should you recruit members as well? Do you indicate an amount? All these questions can be answered by testing.

Telemarketing greatly increases the income from door-to-door collections. A phone call enables you to talk with your national supporters, who are probably not local group members, about taking part in the collection. It is surprising how many take part, and the results they achieve. If they do not wish to help in that way they may well be happy to sell raffle tickets or take a small cardboard collecting box which they return when it is full. These secondary actions help to overcome the fact that phone calls by an agency are not cheap. Most of the people called will be pleased to help you and to take part in future years, sometimes increasing your local group support.

Training local groups

Training for local groups can be surprisingly effective if you bring together several groups at a time. There is a wealth of experience in local groups, and they will learn far more rapidly from each other than from you or from an outside expert - though it does help to have that outside professional view if their questions can be answered in a frank and knowledgeable way, accepting the limitations of local groups, but showing how these are best overcome.

Face-to-face fundraising

Not really a local group activity but a very popular extension of the above usually undertaken by consultants who train staff or volunteers to ask people in the street to join or donate to your charity making out a covenant or standing order with Gift Aid on the spot. No cash or cheques are collected. It is a surprisingly effective technique but you will need to be a well known charity or one with a simple and appealing message. Greenpeace has used this idea successfully in many countries and trains its local supporters to carry it out world wide. A full briefing is essential to ensure that your charity's message is clear and that those asking are polite and agreeable at all times. The tone, style and content of the approach is paramount. The approach is one of soft sell and there must be no undue pressure placed on people to give. Care must be taken with older or vulnerable people and people under the age of eighteen should not be approached or signed up. ID badges should be worn at all times and care must be taken with older or vulnerable people. Collectors must be over eighteen.

Let your collectors have clear identification, simple literature and an engaging and direct manner. They must be enthusiastic and love your charity. Their sincerity will be one of the key reasons people are convinced.

It appears that no permission is needed to carry out this activity in public places though the law is uncertain, and it is certainly necessary to comply with the requirements of Part II of the Charities Act 1992 (and the Data Protection Acts 1984, 1998). The same lack of clarity extends to House to House fundraising where staff or volunteers go from house to house asking to leave a leaflet and to call back later to discuss the work of the charity and then seek a covenant or standing order if the person is interested. This appears to be free of the need to obtain a licence but local authorities or the police may at times take a different view. It is always a courtesy to let local police know of any fundraising activity that will take place on their patch.

Government and European Community funds

Both the UK Government and the European Community act like very sophisticated trusts. They have very clear guidelines showing exactly what they would like to support. They also have thorough application forms and staff to assist in the process.

Both the Government and the EU are typical bureaucracies in that their departments occasionally discover they have sums of money left at the end of their financial year which must be spent quickly, or the department's budget will be cut for the following year. So applying towards the end of the calendar year to the EU, or early in the year to the Government, is not a bad idea at all.

It is well worthwhile spending time talking through your application with the relevant official, who can be very helpful. In the case of the EU, you will need to know what is meant by many of the terms in the application forms. They have, for example, a love for acronyms that almost mean something. This avoids the problems of translation into many languages as they have now created an entirely new word readily understandable to all. These do not necessarily mean what they appear to, and your request will not be considered unless the form has been correctly filled out. You are well advised to seek expert advice from a consultant specialising in EU applications and to talk to people who have been successful in their own applications.

Grants from the UK Government

The sources of Government funds are covered in detail by Susan Forrester & Ruth Pilch's book *Government Departments & Agencies*, published by the Directory of Social Change. The Government gives some £2 billion of support to the voluntary and community sector in the UK and this can be a major source of income for voluntary organisations.

The annual funding cycle, which many grants are on, runs from applications in September (Autumn) to a January date for notifications of awards to applicants with the expectation that the programme of activity will commence in February or March.

In your application you will be most likely of success if you play to the department's policy and priorities. Read their literature and talk with officials - listen carefully and ask questions. The information you seek may not be volunteered and civil servants are constrained in what they can say. Their language is often precise and tactful. Do also keep an eye on government statements so you know their current priorities. You should demonstrate that your project is value for money. This can be the deciding factor between applications.

Devolution and other changes, such as regionalisation and the Comprehensive Spending Review, have ripped through department after department and changed their remits and practices. For example, Defence, International Development and the Foreign Office have UK-wide responsibilities, but most others have undergone changes. Many departments have mailing lists of NGOs, and do let them know when major policy changes mean that funds are available to carry out new activities. Clearly, you should check whether this is so in your area of interest.

Unlike the EU, funding from both the central Government and local authorities in the UK has begun to shift towards contractual arrangements to pay for services provided by voluntary organisations to those authorities. The outcomes of these services are monitored and evaluated quite thoroughly, as are, increasingly, the more traditional grants. The tenor is for all payments to further Departmental policy and accountability, rather than on any emphasis the voluntary organisation may care to place on that part of their work.

To maximise your income, think carefully (if not laterally) through both the range of Government Departments that may possibly fund your organisation, and the range of grants and contracts that may be available within any one Ministry or Department. For example, the Ministry of Defence is a strong funder of the Pre-School Playgroups Association and The Scottish Office has funded Alzheimer's Scotland under their Mental Illness Specific Grant, and Childline Scotland under their Section 10 grants.

For further information try the government's websites:

www.open.gov.uk
www.coi.gov.uk (the Central Office of Information)
www.scotland.gov.uk
www.cymru.gov.uk
www.nio.gov.uk

European Community funds

In fact, only a small part of the huge sums available from the EU are really for charities, but the trouble taken to obtain a grant can be more than compensated for by the scale of funds that are then available. Commissioners in the EU are surprisingly willing to meet applicants personally (particularly from pan-European organisations) and to discuss their applications. The better they know you (or rather, your organisation) the better your chances of success.

The Commission has offices in the UK and these are a useful starting point for information, though you will send your application to Brussels to be considered. The EU has large sums of money to disperse, but across only a very limited number of issues. Raising these funds is time consuming and complex but there are several sources of help along the way and there can be huge rewards for the persistent.

The Commission of the European Communities

The NCVO publishes a useful book called *Grants from Europe* by Ann Davidson, which will give you good background information and which offers much more detail than the following brief account. The Directory of Social Change also has a *Guide to European Union Funding – For the Voluntary Sector* by Peter Sluiter & Laurence Wattier, and CAF has a guide called *The Way Through the Labyrinth*.

The Commission of the European Communities maintains offices in each member country. In London the address is 8 Storey's Gate, London, SW1P 3AT. Tel: 0207 973 1992, Fax: 0207 973 1900. This office has a useful library. There are also offices in Cardiff, Edinburgh and Belfast. The Commission itself is at Rue de la Loi 200, 1049 Brussels, Belgium, Tel: + 32 2 299 1111. Officials speak English and are usually very helpful.

The Commission consists of seventeen Commissioners, officially appointed by the Council of Ministers. Their Secretary General co-ordinates the twenty-three Directors General who run the different departments of the Commission. These are known by their numbers, e.g., DG IX, DG XV.

Each DG that you may apply to will have its own application form. These are long, complex and not easily understood. They may have been translated from another language by someone whose first language is not English. Words are used with certain meanings which are not always obvious, but the process of talking to officials, taking advice from other fundraisers who have made successful applications and, where appropriate, talking with officials in the UK or with the NCVO (which has staff working on the European Social Fund – by far the largest pot of money!) will ensure you do not lose out because of misunderstandings over jargon.

When requesting your application form do not also ask about policy matters. Whilst junior officials can send out application forms, only certain officials can make policy statements so your enquiry may be delayed whilst the statement is prepared and authorised. It is advisable to wait about three weeks before phoning to check on progress - don't forget the time difference or the long lunch breaks! Ask your MEP to help if you have any problems. They have good access and are usually dealt with efficiently by the bureaucracy. Applications are often considered early in the year, the financial year runs January to December. It is best to apply as early as you can. The system works by each commission sending out a 'call for proposals' which is published in the Official Journal of the EU and on its website at **http://europa.eu.int/eur-lex/en/oj/index.html**

Though it is said to be much easier to contact the officials as the dates of the calls have often varied each year. Much more information is to be found via the EU's site at **http://europa.eu.int/comm/dgs_en.htm**

Extensive links to the Director Generals can be found on that site, many leading to relevant information that will be helpful for you. Also try **http://europa.eu.int/geninfo/whatsnew.htm** ...which, as its name suggests, has general news about the EU, sometimes including calls for proposals.

Recently the Commission has introduced common guidelines for applications in their *Vademecum on Grant Management* which is a reference for applicants and officials alike.

Projects that you put forward must always be measurable, realistic, and evaluated against their objectives, making an effective difference beyond groups manifestly taking part. Often you will need to have a pan-European dimension to your project, which means having partners in at least two other countries in the EU (one partner taking the lead role). This tries to ensure that knowledge and experience are shared and developed across Europe.

Of course, budgets are not always fully allocated, and funds may become available at odd times during the year, so even if you are officially too late with your application it is worth enquiring about the state of the fund. Grants are, usually, only made once in a year and may take months to come through. The programmes the grants are supporting change every three years on average, so the grants will not be made for very long-term projects (make sure your future funding is secured elsewhere), and you need to be up-to-date with existing requirements. The EU often requests matching funding, which may come from your own government. Sometimes there is a useful fixed percentage for overheads but do not forget to fund as much as is legitimately possible out of the programme budget. You may also be required to provide 10% - 20% of the total grant - the EU rarely pays 100% of any project. You may also only have 80% of the project funds given to you up front. You then need to successfully complete the project, send in your report, and apply for the remaining 20%. This is where things begin to slide if you are being funded for the same or similar work year by year, and an awkward funding gap begins to open up, giving organisations severe cash flow problems.

Surprisingly, a lot of successful applications are from relatively small organisations that have decided to put in the effort needed, whereas many larger organisations do not feel they have the time necessary. Indeed, the success rate for organisations that stay the course is quite high. Naturally, your application needs to be correctly made out, meeting closely the requirements of the DG you are applying to, for it to stand any chance. Of course, larger organisations do have the advantage that they can afford to employ staff specifically to work with the Commission.

In the long term, as usual, it pays to build a relationship. Getting to know your MEP (though it is inadvisable to ask them to lobby on behalf of an application), sitting on advisory committees and networking all help on many levels. The NCVO have a helpful book on the subject called Networking in Europe.

Remember that the EU basically deals with pan-European problems and organisations. Your organisation, networks and applications are all strengthened in the eyes of the EU by being cross-border. For example, if your patrons are recognised across Europe this will help applications by adding appropriate integrity. The EU also appreciates demonstrable government support for your organisation. Another approach is to undertake work directly for the Commission. Check the *Official Journal* for all contracts put out to tender; though these do tend to be large scale projects. It also helps very much if your organisation is well-known to officials. Decision-making, the handling of applications, and the giving of grants have been in some cases infuriatingly slow, leading to huge expense for NGOs as they continue to pay staff salaries in the interim between grants.

The Directors General

These were under review during 1999 when the commissioners resigned en masse and details may still be in the process of change. It is most likely that the responsibilities below will have changed.

The Directors' General areas of responsibility are:

DG I	External Relations, Mediterranean Policy, Relations with Latin America, North-South Relations (includes work combating drug abuse in developing countries)
DG II	Economic and Financial Affairs
DG III	Internal Market and Industrial Affairs
DG IV	Competition
DG V	Employment, Industrial Relations and Social Affairs (includes the European Social Fund, Health & Safety at Work, AIDS, Cancer, Drug Abuse)
DG VI	Agriculture (includes rural development; also free food for distribution to needy people)
DG VII	Transport
DG VIII	Development in Developing Countries
DG IX	Personnel and Administration
DG X	Audio-visual Media, Information, Communication and Culture (includes Citizen's Europe)
DG XI	Environment, Nuclear Safety and Civil Protection
DG XII	Science, Research and Development (includes biotechnology)
DG XIII	Telecommunications, Information Technology and Innovation
DG XIV	Fisheries

DG XV   Internal Market - Financial Institutions and Company Law
DG XVI   Regional Policies & Cohesion
DG XVII   Energy
DG XVIII Credit and Investments – now merged with DGII
DG XIX   Budgets
DG XX   Financial Control
DG XXI   Customs Union and Indirect Taxation
DG XXII   Education, Training and Youth
DG XXIII Enterprise Policy, Commerce, Tourism and Social Economy (includes co-
          operatives and some work with non-governmental organisations)
DG XXIV Consumer policy & consumer health protection.

The key funding areas among the Directors General are:

Unemployment

The European Social Fund (ESF) and the European Regional Development Fund
(ERDF) deal with this area of concern. You should seek advice from the NCVO
(which has an EU section) and the Department of Employment about the former
(ESF Section, 236 Gray's Inn Road, London WC1X 8HL Tel: 0207-211 4732); and
from the Department of Trade and Industry, (1 Victoria Street, London SW1H 0ET
Tel: 0207 215 5000) about the latter, or look at
http://europa.eu.int/comm/dg16/activity/erdf/erdf_en.htm

The ESF deals largely with vocational training matters and job opportunities. Here
some 50% of the funds go to Government work with the unemployed. It is usual for
funds to be given conditional on matching funds from public money.

The ERDF funds go to reduce differences in development between different
countries. Community initiatives like RETEX to help areas dependent on the clothing
and textile industry, RESIDER for declining steel areas and PESCA for restructuring
of the fisheries sector. There are also regional operational programmes started by the
national government, and several other categories of lesser importance, details at
http://europa.eu.int/comm/dg05/esf/esf_home.htm

The ESF and the ERDF along with the European Agricultural Guidance and
Guarantee Fund (EAGGF) (**http://europa.eu.int/comm/sg/aides/en/p1ch1.htm**),
and the Financial Instrument for Fisheries Guidance (FIFG)
(**http://europa.eu.int/commsg/aides/en/p1ch3.htm**) constitute the structural
funds. EAGGF helps to adapt agricultural structures and diversify the EU's rural
areas. FIFG assists the restructuring of fishing industries. The pattern of funding for
2000 – 2006 is now set with a total budget for that period of £149 billion.

Poverty, families and elderly people

Advice on the current programme can be sought from Directorate-General V,
Employment and Social Affairs. The Department of Social Security link is Room 921,
Adelphi, 1-11 John Adam Street, London WC2N 6HT Tel: 0207-962 8411.

Women

Advice can be sought from DG X Women's Information Service, Information,
Communication and Culture, Rue de la Loi 200, 1049 Brussels, Tel: + 322 299 1111.

Also for budget line B2-1420 - Employment – NOW (New Opportunities for Women), try DGV.B.4 Community Initiatives, 27 Rue Belliard, B-1040 Brussels, Tel: +32 2 295 8138. Or, in the UK, The Department for Education and Employment, Caxton House, 6-12 Tothill Street, London, SW1H 9NF, Tel: 0207 273 3000.

There are grants for

- Training, guidance counselling and employment networks for women.
- The development of flexible training packages and programmes.
- Job creation and support for the start up of SMEs and cooperatives by women.
- Measures to disseminate information and raise public awareness of the need for equal opportunities, including the creation of databases and the establishment of networks.

See also budget B3-4012 - Measures to Achieve Equality between Men and Women. There is a UK advisory committee on this matter at the Department for Education and Employment, 4F Caxton House, Tothill Street, London SW1H 9NF and a Sex, Race & Equality division of the same department.

People from ethnic minority groups

In the past, ethnic minorities have not been funded specifically. There are funds that can be tapped, however, under other headings. DG V, for example, had a small budget that can be used to help migrants. Migrant children can be a special category and the ESF has been used for the education of migrant workers. Grants have been made to improve the supply of housing for migrant workers and their families.

For the Promotion and Safeguard of Regional and Minority Languages and Cultures, budget line B3-1006, try: DG XXIV.A.4 Regional or Minority Languages, 7 Rue Belliard, B-1040 Brussels, Tel: +32 2 2995655

People with disabilities

There are grants in many budget lines including the HORIZEN programme for integration of disabled people into employment. There are quite a number of budget lines under which disability would be appropriate; and a careful trawl through the possibilities, bearing in mind how your priorities, and those of the relevant funder, could be integrated, will no doubt throw up several possibilities.

Human rights

Again there are quite a few possible budget lines dealing with specific policy fields like social exclusion, anti-discrimination, etc. For example, if your organisation works with refugees you might like to consider budget line B3-4113 - Action to Integrate Refugees: for pilot projects which look at factors conducive to the integration of refugees, such as education and vocational training (including language courses), housing, access to services, social protection, culture and leisure, etc.

Or B5-803 European Refugee Fund: reception of refugees and displaced persons and voluntary repatriation of persons who have found temporary protection in EU member states, including achieving an equitable balance of responsibility between member states.

If you are working overseas then the B7-70 budget lines will be appropriate. These are for specific regions or aspects of human rights and are currently contained in eleven budget lines, but these do change with the changing external situation e.g. rehabilitation in the Balkans.

Human rights are spread through several Directorates including DGIA (External relations – Europe and the New Independent States); DG VIII (Development – External Relations and development co-operation with Africa, the Caribbean and the Pacific) and DGIB (External Relations – Southern Mediterranean, Middle East, Latin America, South East Asia and North-South Co-operation). Try the website at **http://europa.eu.int/comm/dg1a/human_rights/intro/index.htm**

The Community provides funding for inter-EU co-operation, exchanges and mobility grants. For guidance on funding try Management Services and Public Relations Department, Central Bureau for Educational Visits and Exchanges, Seymour Mews House, Seymour Mews, London W1H 9PE. Tel: 0207-486 5101 or the British Council, Central Information Point, 10 Spring Gardens, London SW1A 2BN. Tel: 0207-839 4382.

Funding is also provided for such cultural activities as exchanges, the restoration of historic monuments and conserving and promoting architectural heritage. Also possible is funding for training and mobility scholarships in art restoration.

For information on funds for sport try DG X.C.6, Sport, 102 rue de la Loi, B-1040 Brussels. Tel: + 32 2 299 9525. Or try the website at **http://europa.eu.int/comm/dg10/sport/index.html**

Outside the EU

The EU's External Measures grants feature in budget lines B7-1 to B7-8 and come under three Directorate Generals; that is DGs IA and IB, dealing with external relations, and DG VIII, dealing with development. It is often important to liaise with the EU delegate in the country concerned. You could try these websites:

DG I   **http://europa.eu.int/comm/dg01/projects.htm**

DGIA   **http://europa.eu.int/comm/dg1a/index.htm**

DG IB   **http://europa.eu.int/comm/dg1B/index.htm**

DG VIII   **http://europa.eu.int/comm/dg08/index.htm**

ECHO (emergency aid) **http://europa.eu.int/comm/echo/en/index.htm**

SCR   **http://europa.eu.int/comm/scr/index_en.htm**

EU delegations   **http://europa.eu.int/comm/dg1a/site/contacts/delegations.htm**

There is also a UK representative on the NGO Liaison Committee EU-NGO Network, c/o CAFOD, 2 Romero Close, Stockwell Road, London SW9 9TY, Tel: 0207-733 7900.

Two useful documents are

* *General Conditions for the Co-financing of Projects Undertaken in Developing Countries by Non-governmentalOrganisations*

* *General Conditions for the Co-financing of Projects to Raise Public Awareness of Development Issues, Carried Out by Non-Governmental Organisations in the European Community.*

DG VIII also publishes

* *Digest of Community resources available for financing the activities of NGOs and other Government and/or decentralised bodies representing civil society in the fields of development co-operation and humanitarian aid* .

This can be found at **http://europa/eu/comm/dgo8/publicat/ngo/digest_en.pdf**

The environment

Grants for the environment are spread across several budget lines. These are; B4-304, B4-306, B4-3200, B4-3201, B4-3300.

The EU umbrella network of environment NGOs is at: European Environment Bureau, 34 Boulevard de Waterloo, B-1060 Brussels. Tel: +32 2 289 1090, or check the website at **http://www.eeb.org**

For the environment, civil protection and nuclear safety try DG XI, and for energy try DG XVII. In the UK contact Environmental Protection, Central Division, Department of the Environment. At the European level try Secretary General, European Environmental Bureau, Rue de la Victoire, 1060 Brussels, Tel: + 32 2 539 0037.

There are also a small number of funds with the King Baudouin Foundation at 21 Brederostraat, 1000 Brussels, Tel: + 32 2 511 1840. These are primarily for Belgium but some seminars and research projects have been funded. Recent concerns are social issues, the environment and land use planning. There are other sources of funds related to scientific research, awareness, education and training, the coastal environment, animal welfare, rural development, biotechnology, energy saving and work on alternative energy sources.

Health

The relevant departments are DG XII for medical and health research and DG V for public and occupational health. DG XXIV also pays a part in consumer health and safety. The budget lines are; B3-4300 to B3-4306, B3-10 and B3-13.

Useful addresses:

Public Health and Safety at Work (**http://europa.eu.int.comm/dg05/phealth/sitemap.htm**) EUROFORUM Building, Rue Robert Stumper, L 2920 Luxembourg Tel: +352 4301 32719

European Public Health Alliance (**http://www.epha.org**), 33 Rue de Pascale, B-1040 Brussels Tel: +32 2 230 3056 or at

Consumer interests

The two budget lines are; B5-100 Promotion of consumer interests, and B5-103 Consumer health and safety. These are part of a broader programme *General framework for community activities in favour of consumers* which runs from 1999 to 2005. This is one of the few areas not likely to have changed by the time you read about it.

It is under DG XXIV (**http://europa.eu.int/comm/dg24/index.html**): the consumers organisation in Brussels is; Consumers Organisation BEUC, 36 Avenue de Tervuren, B-1040 Brussels, Tel: +32 2 743 1590 (email consumers@beuc.org).

The headings I have used above are by no means comprehensive. This is just to give you a flavour of the EU system, and there are many ways of cutting the EU cake. You can search by budget line, by Directorate or, as above, by interest category. If you find no mention of your organisation's area of interest above do not despair. It is quite possible there is a strong budget line just waiting for your application.

There is also a useful publication called *EU Research Funding* available from the Commission's London Information Office.

Company giving

Companies can help you in many ways and each way requires a different approach. If your charity is non-controversial and obviously a good cause, you stand a chance of receiving company funds. Companies are not, however, major sources of income for most charities and give far below the level of American companies. In the US it is part of the corporate ethic to put money back into the community from which your profits derive, or at least in which your workers live. Community Chest programmes, which do just that, have long been a feature of the American way of life, but have not had great success in the UK.

Companies are, however, a lot more organised and less secretive than they were a few years ago. Organisations like Business in the Community, the Per Cent Club (embarrassingly unable to call itself the One Per Cent Club), the Action Resource Centre and the Association for Business Sponsorship of the Arts, have all played their part. The Directory of Social Change publications have also helped strip away the mysteries about who has given to whom.

Business in the Community aims to ensure that businesses are socially responsible and also practically involved with their local communities. Education and Training, Urban Regeneration, Employee Volunteering, Women's Economic Development, Local Economic Programmes and many others are all excellent examples of the programmes that Business in the Community fosters. Enterprise Agencies are also a feature of its work, providing varied assistance to small businesses to develop. Other partnership programmes include the Action Resource Centre that provides secondments and gifts in kind for community purposes. A good secondment of skilled personnel can be of incalculable benefit to a charity, though the cultural differences take some getting used to on both sides. REACH, the Retired Executive Action Clearing House, can be of similar benefit, though after a lifetime of commuting, their executives often prefer to work outside London. Business in the Community will provide information on all its programmes. It can be found at 227A City Road, London, EC1V 1JV. There are also regional offices.

The Per Cent Club members do publish a great deal of information on their charitable giving, and over 100 major UK companies are members. They are listed in Guide to Company Giving by The Directory of Social Change.

Company trusts

Many major companies have set up charitable foundations and these are approached in the same way as trusts. Some have highly developed aims and objectives while others appear to give almost at random. There is a pattern to the development of these trusts. At first, the trust exists as little more than a bank account for the companies' charitable giving - often decided by the Chairperson or CEO. Then the trust acquires a committee and a more settled donations policy. Later on, it may acquire its own capital and begin to move away from a donations policy that, in any way, reflects company objectives; e.g. the Ford Foundation. These trusts may be named after the company or the original owner, or may just have an insignificant name to put would-be applicants off the scent. One major company is famous for always giving anonymously.

Many companies, and individuals, sometimes use the Charities Aid Foundation (CAF) in preference to setting up their own trust. They give their donations, or covenant a sum, to CAF and then tell CAF how to distribute this money. Alternatively, they use the CAF voucher system to direct money to appropriate charitable causes. The charity receives a CAF Voucher which it cashes in like a cheque with CAF. A small fee is charged for this service, which incidentally goes to the National Council of Voluntary Organisations (NCVO) which created CAF.

The marketing budget

Cause-related marketing is the phrase often used to induce companies to take up a relationship with a charity or 'Good Cause'. It is based on research which has shown that companies that have an ethical component to their work attract and retain customers better than those without, if they use that relationship in their marketing. At worst this is simplistic. If you ask people would they rather buy an ethical product they will say 'Yes', but if you ask them would they buy an ethical product from an unknown company you might find that brand loyalty and awareness is a living concept. All that is just to say that you must tailor your approaches carefully. Is your proposal really going to help the company market its products or develop its brand values? As ever, research carefully and fit your approach to the prospect.

Companies' advertising budgets are, however, usually where the money comes from when you ask a company to take an advertisement in your concert programme. The trick here is to imagine how you can help the marketing managers reach their goals. Does the company sell to children or to pensioners or to anyone else you might help them reach? Do you have a schools' programme where, with some lateral thinking, the school, your organisation and the company can all benefit? Do you have a large donor-base that matches the characteristics of a company's target audience? What are your members buying anyway, and would they like to see part of the price they pay coming back to their favourite charity? For once, look for solutions to company problems rather than solutions for your problems.

If you have a large membership of professional people, a company may be interested in offering those people a range of financial services through advertising in your newsletter, or by paying to mail your members (ensure you are registered for trading in the Data Protection Register and your members have agreed to this use of their personal details). If you have the sort of organisation where people enjoy the outdoors, many companies will want to reach your members to sell them boots, rucksacks, sleeping bags, etc.

If the company is looking to market its product with a new socially responsible image, then they may wish to sponsor activities that will help with this marketing concept. For example, Reebok sponsored a World Tour by internationally known rock stars for Amnesty International, which went to several countries around the world. It was a massive sell-out gaining huge publicity, but the cost was even larger (dwarfing the income, so Reebok had to dig deep into its pockets). This level of generous sponsorship is unfortunately very rare.

Some airlines now help good causes by collecting funds via an envelope in the in-flight magazine. This sort of activity may come from the marketing department or the social responsibility fund, or the charity may be required to pay for the material so that the company only gives its time. Do not be surprised if a company has no budget for that kind of venture and can only provide services which it has already budgeted for. If you do not have a more productive use for your money, do not say no just on principle.

Beware, however, if companies just want to put your logo on T-shirts or other goods, without any money coming directly to you. Buyers will expect you to benefit (which is why they bought the goods), and if your logo is worthwhile using it is worthwhile paying for. The publicity you achieve will be negligible but the income could really help. Once you have given away your logo you will find it hard to sell it to another company. Do also think twice about having just your phone number on products. Is this your target audience? Do you really want all these people phoning you to express support or ask for information?

Sponsorship

You will usually find that most of your money from a company's marketing budget will be given in the form of sponsorship. This is assumed to be another distinct area, and if you are in the arts, music, or sports fields, then you stand more chance than most, (though sponsorship of major sporting events is really just advertising by another name). Sponsorship is rarely wholly and exclusively a business expense: much of it is considered to be pure philanthropy, and the charity may have to produce two invoices to separate out the elements. You will find the *Hollis Sponsorship Yearbook* invaluable in locating sponsors, and for keeping up to date with developments. The address for this is Contact House, Lower Hampton Road, Sunbury-on-Thames, Middlesex, TW16 5HG.

Company sponsorship is often planned a year or two in advance, so write early to the person responsible for sponsorship. As far as possible, try to give your potential sponsor a clear idea of the advantage they will gain from sponsoring you. Will this be in reaching clients, gaining prestige, impressing business contacts or rewarding favours? Will it enhance their corporate image, give name awareness, promote a certain product, benefit staff? How will their name and yours be linked? Exactly what publicity will they obtain and in what form, e.g., posters, signs on stage, TV coverage? Will their name be part of the event name, so that it will always be used in conjunction with that event?

Remember, in a recession, sponsorship is often heavily curtailed because its direct benefit to the company is hard to measure, and spending which offers perks to company employees or directors is easily cut. If you are being imaginative in your discussions with companies, for example, suggesting they put up huge prizes, such as £1 million if six dice come up all sixes, or a golfer hits a hole in one, or even suggesting that they sponsor a world rock tour, then it is worthwhile suggesting that they can insure against these events happening, or indeed something like a non-show by a major rock star at a benefit concert. This means that effectively the company pays a premium and removes the risk and liability.

Why companies sponsor events

The advertising associated with events, e.g. major exhibitions, is often worth very large sums and will often be exclusive. A reception can be a very cost-effective way of bringing together say, a couple of hundred people, and key clients can be looked after individually. The company will also look to see if your event fits their brand values. If the company wishes to see itself as traditionally British, it is unlikely to sponsor radical overseas organisations. Building the brand is key, but so is customer retention, and premium staff loyalty and recruitment. If a company is seen as socially responsible it attracts many benefits that feed into the bottom line in the long term.

Arts sponsorship is one area where huge sums can be obtained, and is a specialist field in itself. I would recommend *The Arts Funding Guide*, edited by Anne-Marie Doulton, published by the Directory of Social Change.

Charities that engage in serious sponsorship always ensure that they have a written contract, which makes sure each side knows what is expected. A mutual misunderstanding may have been Oscar Wilde's recipe for a perfect marriage, but it won't work for a sponsorship deal. Both organisations' objectives have to match; they have to understand the effort and resources they will put into the project, and a controversial association cannot be hidden if a contract has to be signed.

In general, charities obtain much less than they imagine possible from businesses. Profits are for investment and shareholders, not for charities. And unfortunately, many innovative schemes can waste a huge amount of company time, for very little reward.

The social responsibility fund

Another company budget is that for social responsibility. To tap this budget you need to be able to command a high profile and to be the kind of organisation that the company's customers love to support. Do not feel you are doing the company too many favours. Interestingly, a survey of European youth has shown that for those under 25, it is the major companies' brand names that have integrity and charisma not charities, though the charity connection does sometimes add a competitive edge to a popular brand name. Again, imaginative schemes with a high profile get the best results. Think out how the company can obtain something special for key customers, suppliers or other significant people with whom they do business. Celebrities are an obvious link.

Cultivate your celebrities carefully, so that they understand how important it is for you if they can act as your ambassadors at company related events. Think beyond a celebrity performing for you for free. All that often happens is that you save their fee for the night and have the headache of putting on an event you know very little about running. Many charities would be better off paying the celebrity, which would allow them to hold the event at the best time of year and actually pack the most appropriate venue, rather than have it two thirds or half full.

Think about secondment of staff to your charity. Could you use a first rate accountant for a year? What would they get out of working for you? Sometimes this arrangement can be mutually beneficial, as companies restructure or individuals need to broaden their horizons and experiences. Often the association persists long after the official period is over. In many cases, however, companies simply wish to be associated with a good cause and to be thought altruistic rather than just profit-oriented. In these cases, your charity will need to have a high profile and be safely non-controversial. It should deal with subjects that the public at large have a great deal of sympathy with, such as medical charities, pets, and children, all in the UK.

The Chairman's fund

Of course, you can go straight for a company donation from the Chairperson or CEO, though it is still best to do your homework and look at the previous pattern of giving. Then you will be presenting the most attractive part of your organisation's work, as far as he or she is concerned. For most smaller companies this is the only route. As always, do not assume the person you talk to has any knowledge of your charity, and be very specific in stating what the problem is and how the money will be spent to alleviate it. Ask for specific amounts. If successful, ask again the following year, after having reported back on how the money was used and what it achieved.

Companies want to create goodwill in their locality and a great deal of company giving is done locally. Your local group may have more success than you would from the centre. They also like to be responsive to their workforce. Many company schemes are dependent on ideas that must originate from their workforce.

VAT

Take advice about both your VAT situation, and how income tax is levied on donations that are charitable, or part charitable. Both the VAT Inspectors and the Inland Revenue have offices dealing exclusively with charitable giving, and the position is often more complex than the untrained eye would ever suspect.

Employee giving

Check to see if the target company has an employee scheme whereby the firm will match employees' donations pound for pound. Payroll giving works well for some charities, but not for all. Charities seem to have settled on three approaches. The first is simply by reminding their supporters that they should enquire at work about payroll giving schemes and try to include their charity in any such scheme. The second is more dynamic, and involves setting up a volunteer team to visit companies and introduce the charity to the workforce. The third is to hire one of the agencies currently promoting payroll giving to companies. This works best for charities that already have a large amount of support and close involvement with companies. All schemes have had mixed receptions. The first is hard to judge. Income from payroll giving may be increasing, but is this due to the fundraising effort, or to an increase in supporters, (or support itself), or to a natural rise as payroll giving spreads around the country? The latter ideas have worked well for some charities and not for others.

Payroll giving schemes are set up by companies under the guidelines laid down by the Inland Revenue and published by HMSO. Money raised for charity in this way is given to a Charity Agency that distributes the funds to the appropriate charity, taking a small percentage for administration of the scheme. Some Charity Agencies are long-standing, and some have been put together by groups of charities pooling their resources. It is rare now for a charity to set up its own agency. The CAF's 'Give As You Earn' scheme is the most commonly used by companies and most major companies are happy with their charity agency arrangements. Charity Agencies do not have a say in how the money is distributed, and therefore do not need to be approached themselves.

Affinity cards

In the heady days of the Eighties, a number of charities made huge sums by teaming up with banks to bring their members a special credit card, from which the charity received £5 for each card taken out and 0.25% or so of the turnover on the card. Charities with a million members were overjoyed when anything from 5% to 10% of their membership took out cards, netting them a windfall of £500,000 followed by an extraordinary amount several times larger than that, as the 0.25% on the huge sums going through people's accounts just before Christmas began to kick in. The cards were well-designed and well-marketed and supporters felt good about spending. Many took out the card just to give the charity £5, (why not?) and then found an additional source of credit very useful. Now, banks are more likely to require that the initial £5 is used to pay for the mailing to your members.

An affinity card does help to build the synergy of your fundraising, placing your organisation alongside those trusted charities that are seen as full of integrity and clout.

Negotiating with banks

Today we have got used to using a plethora of credit cards on a regular basis, often with a high level of debt. But the banks are a lot more cautious, and it can take a long time to persuade your favourite bank that your supporters are the right sort of people for them to bother with. You may be well advised to try a link with one of the American banks currently entering the market, for example, MBNA.

If you have over 100,000 members, mostly in income groups A, B, and C1, you stand a chance of agreeing an affinity card deal with a major bank. Be prepared to negotiate hard over the terms. If any of the great and the good on your board, or known to you in other ways, have connections at a senior level in a major bank, it is worthwhile seeking an introduction. You are more than likely, however, to find yourself negotiating with a marketing manager who has a small budget to develop credit card sales and who has never given to a charity in his or her life, but retains a vivid mental image of the worst charity shops.

- If you have carried out professional demographic surveys of your support base and had the results analysed by an independent agency, that will certainly help - if you haven't, it's time you did.

Fig. 6e *After the first year, profits from affinity cards really stack up.*

- If a bank agrees, before you accept their terms check with other charities for a comparison. Terms vary a lot, including the number of times a 'free' card must be used in a year, and how soon after receiving the monthly statement your supporters need to pay before being charged interest.

- It will be a great help for you to keep up a series of regular meetings with your bank contacts, if only to remind yourself of all the ways in which you should be putting the offer in front of your supporters.

If you do this fastidiously, you will be surprised how much money you make year by year.

Designing the card

You will need to design the card. If you have an artistic streak, this is the enjoyable bit. After bringing the concept through your committees, winning a good deal from the bank, and spending days meticulously reading the small print on the contracts, you can indulge your creative flair on the design. But remember, the design should make it easy for anyone to take out and use in public. They will not do this if it is ugly or in bad taste. Wildlife and sunsets work very well, victims and sufferers do not, logos are just about OK - you should be able to do something more imaginative.

You will have to have your logo copyrighted if you are seeking a Visa card as they require legal protection in using your mark.

Marketing the card

- Inform your members by separate direct mail. As with appeals, the response will be much better than it would as an insert in your journal, and the additional mailing costs will easily be repaid by the increased take-up.

- Let all your new members know in their new members' pack that you have an affinity card. (New members are at their most appreciative of the organisation, and more willing to help at that point than they are likely to be again.)

- It is essential that you keep reminding all your members, at frequent intervals, that they can have an affinity card. Whenever you ask for money, mention that it can be paid for by your affinity card, which will mean the gift goes even further.

Key to success

As with legacies, the real secret of success is to remind people constantly of the opportunity. Eventually, they will feel the time is right for them - but that time will never arrive if you rely on their memories of the original invitation. Having your supporters wondering if you still do a card is not conducive to its being taken up. Your supporters undoubtedly belong to several other organisations, and the chances are, that they are being reminded by one or more of these about their own affinity card.

Warning

Be aware that banks nowadays are a lot more meticulous than they were in the past about who they give cards to, and how high the credit limit is. Your members may not receive anything like the credit limit they had previously, and may not receive a card at all. (Incidentally, the bank is obliged to tell them if this is due to a bad credit rating). You will receive a number of calls on this subject, but they should be referred to the bank, who will give you a contact to sort such problems out. Do not get involved in approaching the bank on a member's behalf. You will need to obtain permission to deal in credit, as you will technically be offering the card to your members. This is covered by permission from the Office of Fair Trading, and is not the legal minefield it appears to be. Your bank or the Office of Fair Trading will supply you with an information leaflet.

The National Lottery

Many charities have claimed that the National Lottery has taken funds that used to go to them and that, with only a small proportion of the stake going to charitable causes, there is a net loss of income to the charitable sector. Others have questioned the grant making policies of the Lottery Board. Be that as it may, the Lottery represents a significant source of potential income and one that should not be overlooked.

The National Lottery Commission website is at **www.natlotcomm.gov.uk.** From this site you can discover everything you ever wanted to know about the lottery - apart from how to win.

There are five categories within which your application must fall. Each has its own distributing body, criteria, eligible applicants and eligible projects. The five categories are: The Arts, Charities, Heritage, Sports and the New Opportunities Fund. Each of these has its own pack, leaflets or application form, and it is advisable to make contact with them before applying, as it is unlikely your application will be considered unless it is accompanied by the correct form. Priorities and practice can change from year to year, and so some of the details given below may well change in the near future.

The Arts

The distributing body is the Arts Council of England, (Lottery Department, 14 Great Peter Street, London SW1P 3NQ,. Tel: 0207 312 0123) - **www.artscouncil.org.uk.** You may also need an application pack and a Detailed Guidance to Applicants booklet. The fund covers all art forms and capital projects. The minimum grant given is £5,000 though joint proposals are possible for larger scale shared facilities. Decisions take up to six months.

Charities

The distributing body is the National Lottery Charities Board. The only ways to apply are to phone for an Application Pack, (Tel: 0845 791 9191) or to visit their website at **www.nlcb.org.uk.**

There are five grant making committees made up from the twenty-two overall Board members. The committees cover England, Wales, Scotland, Northern Ireland and the UK. Grants for the international programme are made by the UK.

An organisation need not be a registered charity to apply but it must be a benevolent or philanthropic organisation, and it must:

- have a constitution or set of rules, defining its aims, objectives and operational procedures (except Parochial Church Councils)
- have a signed copy of its constitution or submit the management committee meeting minutes at which it was adopted
- have a bank or building society account which is in its own name, and which requires at least two signatures on each cheque
- be able to provide a copy of its most recent accounts approved by the management committee and signed and dated (by chair or treasurer), or projected accounts, if it is a new organisation.

Branches of larger organisations can apply, either in their own right if eligible, or if supported by the parent organisation. Professional fundraisers or consultants who are not members of staff cannot submit applications. You cannot apply on behalf of another organisation.

The criteria for grants change each year. The stated aim is to give grants to help meet the needs of those at greatest disadvantage in society and to improve the quality of life in the community. Match funding is not required. Grants in 2000 averaged about £90,000. Grants over £500,000 are rarely given and the minimum is £500. If the total cost of your project is over £200,000 you must provide a business plan.

There is no closing date except for the International Programme. At the time of writing this line opened for applications on 20 September and closed on 17 December. Completed applications must be returned by 28 January, and grants are announced the following summer.

The Charities Board's mission statement is:

"We give grants to help meet the needs of those at greatest disadvantage in society and improve the quality of life in the community". The Board funds development projects which address the causes of poverty and inequality and make a significant improvement to the quality of life of some of the most vulnerable people in the world. It is aimed at UK-based voluntary organisations working abroad.

Heritage

The distributing body is the National Heritage Memorial Fund, (Heritage Lottery Fund, 10 St James Street, London, SW1A 1EF. Tel 0207 747 2087/6/5/4/3/2). Apply first for their Guidelines and Application Pack at **www.hlf.org.uk.**

Eligible projects are those which help secure, conserve, improve and enhance public access to, and appreciation of, tangible heritage assets and add tangible benefits to tangible assets. The minimum grant is £10,000. Applications will be considered by the trustees within five months.

Sports

The distributing body is the Sports Council for England. To apply, ring the Lottery line at the Sports Council for an application pack. You will receive consultation forms which should be sent to all relevant organisations a few weeks before submitting your application. Eligible bodies are only those dealing with sports recognised by the Sports Council. Some sports must be affiliated to their sports national body. Eligible projects are essentially capital projects. Equipment purchase is not eligible unless part of a capital project, a major item to be used for six years and permanently on site, or a pool of equipment for a single sport or for more than the local area.

The New Opportunities Fund (www.nof.org.uk)

This fund gives grants to projects dealing with education, health and the environment.

Camelot

The commercial lottery company has also set up its own charity called the Camelot Foundation which runs two grant making programmes. One is for small grants of up to £5,000, and the other is for large scale collaborative projects between organisations often of several hundred thousand pounds.

Camelot's website is at **www.national-lottery.co.uk.** They are located at One Derry Street, London, W8 5HY Tel: 0207 937 5594. Camelot is a well run organisation with clear criteria and has a rigorous assessment and evaluation programme.

§

In setting up your range of fundraising activities you may find that, initially, you have a large proportion of them either inside or outside the pyramid. Do ensure that you achieve the right balance for your organisation, so you are not exposed to vagaries in any one area of funding. Opening up a new income stream is often time consuming and frequently costly, but in the long term your organisation will only have sustainable growth if it has as many appropriate techniques on the go as it can manage.

7 Charitable Trusts

How to Succeed at Trust Fundraising

By Chris Small, Trust & Corporate Officer, Medical Foundation for the Care of Victims of Torture.

Charitable Trusts are key players in the voluntary sector, and deserve to be regarded as an important element in the fundraising mix. This may be particularly true for smaller organisations lacking the resources to fund and administer mass-market donor recruitment drives. Trust Fundraising costs are low, and the return on investment can be as high as 20 or 40 to 1, particularly when major funding bodies such as the European Union and The National Lottery Charities Board are part of the portfolio.

What is absolutely crucial in securing benefits of this kind for your organisation is that the principles of Relationship Fundraising are adhered to with passion. Without total commitment to research and service, your programme will flounder.

Know who your friends are

The first step towards raising significant sums from trusts is research, which takes a number of forms. If your organisation has a history of making applications, successful or otherwise, the most obvious place to start is your own filing cabinet. Hopefully all previous correspondence with trusts will have been kept in good order in separate files, one per trust. Careful perusal of this correspondence, along with any notes that may have been taken during meetings, conversations or from previous research will be invaluable as you begin to understand the animals you are dealing with. Asking other members of your organisation for information can also yield important clues.

Particular attention should be paid to requests that the Trust may have made of your organisation in the past, for example, that a gap of two years should be left between applications or that it is not necessary to send a general Annual Review with reports. Honouring such requests will set you apart from less careful operators who make extra work for the Trust Administrator - and your chances of success will increase. It goes without saying that you must be conscious of any contributions the Trust has made in the past, and acknowledge this when contact is renewed.

Where no previous relationships with Trusts have been developed, other avenues of research must be pursued. The first task will be to ascertain which of the many thousands of Charitable Trusts in the UK and overseas are your potential funders, a job which is made easier by a wide range of publications, hard and electronic. Good directories and periodicals are a good investment, providing the Trust Fundraiser with information regarding background, general and philanthropic history, grant-making potential, geographical scope and aims, along with guidance as to preferred methods of approach. Charity Commission files and database can also be consulted for information regarding UK registered grant-makers.

Training workshops, special interest groups, seminars and speaker meetings are also useful ports of call for the Trust Fundraiser and should be seen as part of the ongoing process of developing understanding and keeping abreast.

Making the right connections

Once this background research has been completed the fundraising can begin. A list can be compiled of Trusts who may feel a sense of common cause with your organisation. It is worth erring on the side of optimism at this stage as trusts may have broader interests than their directory entry, or other sources of information, may suggest. On the other hand it is important not to waste time with those funders whose priorities are clearly of a different nature.

At this stage, close consultation with project staff and managers within your organisation is very worthwhile. There may be scope for applying for an embryonic project that has not reached the stage of being incorporated into the organisational budget, but which everybody would like to see run. Even with existing projects, it is important to have project staff on-board from the outset. Their collaboration will make all the difference when it comes to writing up the application and, of course, in the matter of evaluation and reporting at the end of the grant period.

Although all good proposals set out clearly the need for your project, along with aims, methodology, expected outcomes and costs, the format of the application must conform to the rules of the individual Trust, and reflect the interests of the Trustees. Careful study of the Guidelines for Applicants and the application form are indispensable where these are employed. In freeform applications the priorities of the Trust should be to your case for support as the key of D Major is to Beethoven's Violin Concerto. In all cases, the funder should reach the bottom line of your proposal with a clear sense of how the objectives of the Trust are going to be met.

All part of the service

The duties of a Trusts Officer vary from organisation to organisation; however in most cases the fundraiser will also be responsible for producing end, and in some cases interim, reports. This will usually be undertaken in conjunction with service providers and should, once again, meet the expectations of the particular funder. Whether a formal contract with Terms and Conditions of Grant is issued or not, it is important that project staff are made aware of their responsibilities in terms of record keeping and general conformity from the word go.

Administration

With individual Trust Officers taking responsibility for portfolios of several hundred Trusts, good administration is absolutely essential. At the level of the Trust Officer's desk, a logical method of central record keeping is a must to ensure that the various cycles of trust-charity relationships can be monitored. At the organisational level, it is important that all members of the charity are aware of the Trust Fundraiser's role, and that all Trust-related business is channelled through the postholder. Disasters occur in larger organisations when internal miscommunication results in Trusts receiving inappropriate correspondence from unauthorised sources, or when correspondence from a trust is misdirected and never reached the Trust Fundraiser's desk. Where a team of Trust Fundraisers is in place (in a single office, or more particularly where a branch system is operated), clear communication between officers is vital if overlap and expensive mistakes are to be avoided.

§

The History of Trusts

There is a lot of mystique to trusts. They are often ancient bodies set up under the will of a philanthropic antecedent for purposes which were noble in their day, but can now strike us as rather quaint. For example, hundreds of years ago they, he or she have wished to assist the gentlewomen of their parish, who have fallen on hard times, or become 'distressed' as it is called. The Will which established the charitable trust may leave the annual proceeds of two fields to this purpose. The fields may now, however, be in the heart of London and earning a huge fortune in rent from amusement arcades. How to find and fund the appropriate gentlewomen could prove a challenge to the current trustees, and a conundrum to grant-seekers trying to make their projects fit this objective. Many trusts are limited by area, and others by much more rigorous criteria. At the outset, it should be said that many trusts only fund organisations personally known to the trustees and do not accept applications.

Trusts are big business. There are some 9,000 grant making charitable trusts in the UK, and they dispense some £1.5 billion. The two largest are the Wellcome Foundation and the National Lottery Charities Board, which between them make grants totalling 35% of that given by all trusts.

Trusts are united only in their great diversity, and the fact of being usually registered with the Charity Commissioners and possessing a charity number. The objectives of a charitable trust were set in the time of Queen Elizabeth I, with an act in 1601, as the relief of poverty, the advancement of education, the advancement of religion and some other purposes beneficial to the community. This was the preamble to the 1601 act, which was later consolidated into those four objectives by a Lord MacNaghten in 1891, and which has now, by and large, stuck as the UK's charitable objectives. They can make grants to other charities or for charitable purposes. Many will only fund other charities.

Though many trusts accumulate capital, the trustees should not do this at the expense of the trust's objectives. They are bound by certain duties and carry a heavy responsibility for the funds under their care. To lessen the restrictions on a charity many now set themselves up for general charitable purpose, rather than restrict their objectives. In the past the investment of those funds has been a cause for concern, both because the companies they are invested in may be damaging to the trust's objectives, and on the other hand because the alternative 'ethical' funds may not be perceived to perform quite so well. It is now generally accepted that though the trustees have a duty to maximise the income of any investments they hold, their over-riding duty is to the trust objectives. Indeed, many trusts make their investments in a range of ethical funds. Trustees are bound to hold the assets of the charity in prudent safekeeping for the benefit of others. Trustees should act rationally, and not be prejudiced in their actions, nor can they derive a benefit from their position. They are ultimately responsible for the charity's actions.

Many trusts originate with companies. Here either the founder or the CEO may have decided that it is appropriate for a profitable concern or good for the company's image. This will often determine the nature of the company's philanthropic activity. Their trust might give to the local football club or day care centre where the company's factories are situated, or they may give to a set cause such as cancer because the founder's wife died from it. Some trusts are deeply caught up in the company's activities, and others are really very independent bodies whose pattern of giving may even involve organisations deeply critical of some of the company's activities.

Only recently have changes in the law given the Charity Commissioners leeway to begin to consider the varying of such wills. In some notable cases this has unlocked huge amounts of money, though there is a real and reasonable reluctance to greatly change what is, in effect, the wish of the deceased, or to guess what their interpretation of the current situation might be if they were still with us.

Your charity may well have begun with a grant from such a grant-making trust. Trusts often like to fund innovative projects for a year or so, until they find their feet and generate resources elsewhere. As a rule of thumb, trusts prefer not to become permanent funders though many will entertain an application from a charity which they helped start for a new or crucial stage of its development.

If your organisation is a new charity, this gives it both a great opportunity and a problem, as you have a relatively short time to get off the ground financially. The backing of a major grant-making body can help, as it shows you are considered worthy of their funds, but you will also need to develop your public profile rapidly to attract alternative funding and support from the public. In the search for publicity you might even find that a grant from a well known trust is news in itself but, of course, the real story you are trying to put over, is your work and how it will alleviate a serious problem.

Your Bible for this is the *Directory of Grant Making Trusts* compiled by the Charities Aid Foundation. The Directory is large and forbidding, but essential reading if you are to research all those trusts who could possibly help you. Fortunately, it is now on CD. It is by no means an exhaustive list of all possible trusts, but will keep you busy for quite a time.

If you require an easier source book, or more in-depth knowledge of the larger trusts, a directory of the top 200 trusts is published by the Directory of Social Change. They also publish a companion volume of the top 200 grant-making companies. These directories are updated every year and new entries appear, so it is well worth being on their publications mailing list. There are also many other local and specialist trust guides.

Target your trusts carefully, and try to learn as much as possible about them beforehand. The Charity Commissioners hold all the accounts submitted by charitable trusts. You can look at them on the Commission's premises. This service has improved in recent years, and the rate of filing of trust accounts has also picked up from a very low rate. One revelation is the size of the average grant. Even for large trusts it can be quite small. The variety of grants given is also a surprise, indicating just how wide objectives can be stretched. Do think about American foundations, which are often ten times larger than their UK counterparts, but remember than US Foundations are not the same as UK charitable trusts and you may need to ask a US funder to pay their donation to CAF America to meet their IRS needs. Alternatively, you could set up your own US '501c3' which is their close equivalent of our charitable trusts or give a complicated legal assurance that your charity is identical to a 501c3 in various important respects (which not all charities are).

Trusts traditionally love new, exciting, innovative projects that can be replicated across the country bringing effective and efficient solutions to obvious needs. This approach gives fundraisers severe headaches, as few projects conform to this optimistic scenario. What organisations really need is core funding over a long period of time, which is usually anathema to trusts who like to switch their funding to new organisations at regular intervals. Effective innovation is a rare animal and trusts, having conjured up its spectre, sometimes take fright at the risk involved. Innovation, by its nature, is new, unproven and not necessarily a safe bet. Rolling out innovation, tried and tested elsewhere, is not difficult to fund at the worst of times.

And always remember, trusts can take a considerable time to make up their minds. They may meet every three or four months, but are just as likely only to meet annually.

Using your contacts

Once you have ascertained which trusts, according to their objectives, can give to you, and which of them are most likely to, the next stage is to match up the great and the good on your organisation's governing body (or other important supporters such as patrons) with the trustees of the charitable trusts you wish to approach. Let your chairperson write and call round all the people who may be connected in any way with someone who is a trustee of a grant-making body, and seek their help either towards a donation or towards a new contact on the right trust. Do this with great sensitivity, because some trusts will react badly to any attempt at 'lobbying', though others naturally give to projects that friends of the trustees have brought to their attention.

Writing the application

- Some trusts have application procedures. If these are mentioned in a directory, obtain a copy and follow them.
- Stunts and 'creative' applications do not usually work with trusts. The best tone to adopt in your application letter is one of efficient enthusiasm.
- State your case clearly on the first side of your letter of application.

Make it clear exactly which problem you are trying to solve, how you are going to do that, why you think you will succeed, and how much you are asking for, to be put to exactly what purpose. Show clearly your methodology for meeting the need and how you will evaluate your work.

Do enclose a realistic budget for the project that is simple to understand and is in keeping with the size of your organisation. State any capital equipment you need to purchase (vehicles, computers, premises) separately from running costs (salaries, travel costs, etc.). Allow for inflation. Set aside a reasonable amount for your overhead costs (management, heating, lighting). This used to be about 10%, though some funders allow 15%, but the drive is now towards 5%, which is often unrealistically low. Try to build in a 5% or 10% contingency sum - you will need it. Do not, however, make your application appear like a desperate bid to cover your overheads even if this is the case.

It helps the trustees to know what you have already done to raise funds. They will prefer it if you have tried other sources first. If you are already part-funded that will be seen as very positive, as will be funding from a well-known charity, which will help the credibility of the project.

Think about partnership with other organisations and how the findings from your project may be disseminated to help other organisations or individuals.

- If you have annual reports and accounts they should usually be enclosed. If not, the audited accounts will do. If you are starting up, a statement of your financial position would be helpful.

- Do avoid professional jargon, and do not assume the trustees are familiar with your work. Clear evidence of need is important. Make sure you give all the relevant facts to build up a complete picture. How many people will you help? When and where will it take place, and how long will it last? Why do you need this amount of money? For exactly what, and why, should money be needed rather than something else? How do you plan to replace the grant when it runs out?

- It is rarely possible to explain all about your work in a covering letter, so it is well worthwhile adding any additional literature or leaflets that you have which will support your case. Make sure these really are relevant and add to what you are saying in your letter.

Do not leave the trust with the impression they will just be asked to fund again next year, or see the project close. Explain how you will continue to fund the project from your own resources (it may be that you expect your revenue funding to be sufficient by then - remember to say why you believe this). If you really need money for just three years, say so, but explain what will happen to the project then.

You will obviously need to establish your credibility. Do this by listing the professionals associated with you, and the great and the good, who may be your patrons: if need be, add a letter from a senior person in the field you are working in, which shows your standing in that field. List your own trustees, if you are a charity, and your senior management team plus the qualifications that make them suitable for this position.

'Building your public image' is not a phrase often found in fundraisers' job descriptions. Yet, it is often a key element in obtaining funds, especially from trusts who like to have heard good things about organisations they are considering. Written documents, press-cuttings, etc. all help to build credibility.

The tone of voice you should use is one of professional competence but private enthusiasm. Let your excitement at the work to be done and your drive and commitment show, but also your professionalism. This must, however, be expressed as far as possible in plain English.

If you are seeking unusually large sums (e.g. for a capital appeal) do ask for a meeting with the trust correspondent, and possibly the trustees. Some trusts will not meet applicants but there is no harm in asking. Only the larger trusts have full or part-time staff, and most therefore may not have the resources for this. Do, however, also ask trusts for advice. Many are repositories of huge amounts of relevant information. For example, their knowledge of other funding sources in your field could be invaluable.

Trusts usually have a limited number of objectives, and it will usually be the case that you are asking for funding for a particular concrete project rather than core funds. This case can be made separately, outside the covering letter, and should be in as much useful detail as possible to clearly explain it.

Do not send the same letter to hundreds of trusts. Most trusts, especially the largest, have a mountain of applications each week, many of which are completely outside their objectives. This only annoys the trust and could damage a later, correctly-made application by giving a poor first impression.

By all means call the trust beforehand to discuss your application, and afterwards to see if it has been shortlisted. But remember that the majority of trusts have no paid staff, so it is only worth calling the very largest that give out their telephone numbers. Most trusts meet infrequently - perhaps every three or six months or sometimes once a year.

Once the trust has received applications and their secretary has sifted them, the trustees, having a large measure of independence, will make up their own minds about whom to support. In doing so they will draw on their own personal knowledge and experience, which is often considerable, take advice from the secretary or 'correspondent', and add any research they feel is necessary. Anyone who can spend time with a trustee, and whom the trustee finds reliable, can help. Though this is often thought of as the key way to obtain money from trusts, the simple written application will usually be your main tool.

Reading your rejection

Read your letters of rejection with an eagle eye. The wording will usually tell you if you are likely to succeed in a future application or if you have a chance to re-apply say, in the following year.

- 'We are not in a position to fund you at this time' is a very positive rejection. Do try again.
- 'Our funds are fully allocated for the foreseeable future' is more difficult. How far can they see into the future? Perhaps as far as two or three years. Does this mean, as it seems to, that they would fund you if they could? At any rate it seems worthwhile to try again later.

- You will often read in trust entries in the various guides 'All funds are currently committed, no applications will be considered'. Understandably, one usually avoids such trusts but a phrase of this nature appears so often, it may just be hiding a shy trust or lazy trustees who wish to avoid reading excellent applications in their area. If you are certain that your needy project is clearly within the trust objectives, and you do not have more obviously productive sources of funds to approach, it may be worthwhile sending a brief 'one-side-of-A4' enquiry to test the waters.

Extending your relationship

You should develop your most likely trusts, and those that have actually given to you, as you would any other major donor. Do not forget to thank them and invite them to see how you have spent their money. You will also be surprised how effective it can be to send them a regular report on the work they have funded.

If you have an interesting events programme do invite trustees to these events and create a positive atmosphere, where they can get to know more about you and your organisation and pass on information about the trust's latest concerns which may, of course, match your own.

The larger trusts will require strict reporting on the projects they support, and there is nothing more annoying for them than to have to chase up such work. So, be prepared, and ensure the staff carrying out the project are aware of this and have built in the time and set up the necessary mechanisms to collect the information - e.g. baseline assessments - against which to check outcomes for the purposes of evaluation.

The Association of Charitable Trusts has begun a very welcome process of encouraging the best practice amongst charitable trusts many of which have tended in the pas, to be opaque and closed organisations. In general, trusts are becoming more open, responsive and likely to enter into dialogue with applicants and professional bodies. Trust accounts are a key document to understanding, and therefore to regulating, their behaviour. This was greatly enhanced by the Standard of Recommended Practice (SORP) from the Charity Commissioners for charity accounting.

§

Trust fundraising is as competitive as any other branch of fundraising and you must be prepared for disappointment. Apply to a series of carefully researched trusts at the same time, but do not make blanket applications. If they all fund your project to excess the cheques can easily be returned, but it is more likely you will need funds from several trusts to make up the total amount you seek. There is also safety in numbers. If a group of trusts fund your work, then the loss of any one trust will not end the project as it might if you had just one funder.

8 Capital Appeals

The ultimate major donor big gift programme is a capital appeal. By their nature capital appeals are quite rare. They are held, on occasions, for pieces of 'capital equipment': that is, equipment that will last for several years. In practice usually this means for a new building.

Because capital appeals are so rarely undertaken, even fundraisers with several years experience may not have lived through one; and because the sums involved are often huge it is common practice to bring in a consultant, or specialist agency, to advise on an appropriate strategy.

First steps

Their first step will usually be to undertake a feasibility study to determine if the appeal can really succeed. This will help to prevent wasting time and effort; and, moreover, will save you from upsetting your key supporters. If your appeal had been premature, you may well have raised a certain amount from your most affluent supporters and then been unable to complete the appeal. This leaves you with egg on your face, and the awful dilemma of what to do with their donations.

The time spent will not be wasted even if it is shown that an appeal is likely to succeed, because it will build the foundation on which the appeal will rest. The feasibility study usually starts with compiling your 'Case for Support', and goes on to interview key supporters, to test both their thoughts about the Case for Support and their willingness to give to the appeal. Do they personally think it is a good idea; would they be willing to make a serious donation; and could they open doors or put in a good word with a charitable trust. They should be warmed-up and sympathetic before you begin, and you should approach them before they have cooled off. The urgent concern you have shown them will not seem so important if you wait six or nine months before coming back to them to ask for their donation.

It is well worthwhile seeking out a reputable firm of consultants who have undertaken several such appeals for organisations similar to yours. The Institute of Charity Fundraising Managers (ICFM) has a list of charity consultants which they will supply on request.

They will help you put together your Case for Support, and conduct the feasibility study. The case sets out the reasons why someone should give to your capital appeal. It is then tested internally, on your senior staff, trustees, and any other important stakeholders, before the external part of the feasibility study. It is often found that key individuals have quite different views about the project, and sometimes key individuals are quite opposed to it. These differences must be sorted out before the study gets under way, let alone the appeal.

Interestingly, the case for support is often the first document a fundraiser will compile on starting with a new organisation. This would be the case for supporting the entire organisation or project, instead of the capital appeal. It is an intensely practical document. At its core lies the question 'Why exactly should a donor give?' If you do not clearly understand the answer to this question, you cannot fundraise effectively. In the USA they say you must be able to make out the case in the time of an elevator ride – and their lifts move fast!

The Case for Support

Your Case for Support should, in its final stage (and it will probably be developed and amended for many months), contain the following building blocks towards donations for your new building:

1   A well worded expression of the problem a new building will solve. This will have been tested on your staff and major donors, and have found favour with them.

2   Supporting testimony from nationally or internationally known figures who will be respected by your target audience. These may include prestigious patrons.

3   Lists of your appeal committees and their members. These may be advisory and support committees, who are there to add weight to your appeal with their names, and your fundraising committees such as a 'Major Donors Panel', and subsidiary panels of interest groups.

4   A schedule of expenditure showing the stages at which you will need certain amounts, for example, to pay the architects. This should run up to completion of the building and its total will be your total ask. In almost every case the initial estimate of building costs or the expected purchase price will shoot up as the appeal progresses. Initial estimates will be confirmed or upgraded by the surveyor, and, if the appeal stalls, inflation may begin to seriously erode the funds you have already raised. This problem has caused grief to many organisations as building inflation can take off suddenly and your appeal target can rise beyond credible reach. One of your most difficult tasks as a fundraiser will be to ensure that you do not promise more than you can possibly deliver, in the face of rising expectations and demands from staff and senior management.

5   A gift list of the amount of gifts, and the number of donations at each amount (the top gift is usually 10% of the total and 80% of the money should come from 20% or more of the donors) (see Fig 8a). This chart will be used in soliciting major gifts and is incredibly useful in making the 'ask'. If the appeal costs rise it will need to be amended. The total should, of course, match the sum set above – less any money from the sale of buildings, or other non-fundraised income.

6   An attractive artist's sketch of the proposed building can really bring the appeal to life by helping the donor to understand how their money will be spent, and to give them an idea of the monument for which they will be responsible. In discussing the building with your architects let them know the type of donor you have: if they are trendy young professionals they may be drawn to a different type

of building than if they are elderly conservative women. The work to be carried out in the building, and the image you wish to project, will be key criteria for the style chosen (and the firm of architects you choose); but the style the donors are likely to give to (or rather, will definitely not give to) must also be taken into account.

7   As detailed a set of plans as possible. They will be easier to produce as the appeal progresses and the architects produce more comprehensive documents. Plans should show the activity on each floor, plus anything else you feel will enhance the case. Gardens, creches and rooms that can be named all help to attract donors.

8   A map of the location.

9   A disclaimer showing how you will handle donations if you raise more than you need (use for ongoing work), or if you raise too little money and cannot build (use for ongoing work), will avoid you having to return donations. This is a legal point and really needs to be made at each stage when you are asking for donations. You are sure to need more revenue income when you move, so this is a legitimate statement. Similarly, if the appeal fails (and quite a few do), then you will certainly need funds for intermediate measures whilst you rethink and amend your strategy.

10 A statement of your fundraising policy - 'we do not accept funds from cigarette manufacturers or suppliers etc.' - prevents unpleasant surprises and embarrassment. A kindly sponsor reading about your appeal may send a large cheque from their company, which causes problems for the people you are trying to help, or an individual may seek to lessen their guilt by donating to your organisation; but either case might be quite unacceptable to your policy setting body.

An attractive professional design for the case for support is important, to put over the image that the building work or project will be carried out to a high standard effectively and efficiently. In the early stages of an appeal, I have used a simple photocopied case for support to show to good friends of the organisation, that I know would not welcome a glossy brochure; but in moving to potential supporters, who are not such close friends, I have found that good design and a clear layout is appreciated.

The feasibility study

The first use of the case for support is to learn just how each of the key people in your organisation feel about the potential appeal. You will need to set up a series of meetings, giving at least an hour to each person. Approaches should be made to the Director or CEO, who will probably have commissioned the study, the senior management team, significant staff members, and the Council or voluntary management body which sets your policies. As you go through this process the initial case will be altered and developed, becoming stronger and stronger. You will need to agree changes with your Director before discussing it to the next set of people.

Once you have internal agreement, you are in a position to talk to those supporters who have made large donations in the past, or are highly influential; for example, the patrons. The top charitable trusts should also be approached, and their advice sought, but only if they are likely to support a request for funds for bricks and mortar. Some charitable trusts will not do this. These supporters will often have a feel for the development of the charity over time. They may welcome this as a stage they think the charity should be at, and may be very willing to play their part in this move. It is essential to have an indication of the possible level of their support. Putting these responses together with your knowledge of the organisation's usual pattern and level of funding, will form the bases of the feasibility study.

There is, however, one key factor that is often overlooked in this study. A capital appeal is usually a very large undertaking, and may often seek to raise an extra amount in the region of the organisation's yearly turnover. This will be a long and difficult task, and it is essential that the key individuals in the staff and voluntary management body are committed to the project, and will remain so in the long term. Capital appeals need enthusiasm to drive them forward, and to survive the occasions when everything seems to be going horribly wrong. In setting income and expenditure budgets for the following year's fundraising programme, there is a clear mathematical progression laid out, which gives a logical assurance to the projected figures. In a capital appeal, which by its nature does not happen every year, the figures are estimated, and so it is not unusual if some parts of it fail to deliver, and others over-perform. For example, several key trusts may decline to make a grant, but the money may be made up by committed individuals, or vice-versa. Naturally, this process can seriously age the person responsible if they do not have strong support.

Once it is known that the appeal is likely to succeed, then the fundraising strategy needs to be drawn up. This will include the likely sources of funds, the programme of asking for them, the schedule of that programme and the resources needed to carry out the appeal.

Capital Appeal strategy

Much like any other strategy document, this will set the pattern of fundraising over the time needed to carry out the appeal. The resources needed will vary according to the size of the appeal, the current fundraising capacity, the length of time needed to raise the funds and the existing support for the organisation.

The Medical Foundation's Under-One-Roof appeal to raise £4.7m, at a time when the organisation's turnover was £3m, required two people full-time in the first full year (after a year of preparation with a consultant), three people in the second year and a strong big gift committee, with key people undertaking personal requests for funds throughout both years, plus innumerable volunteers. This was still dangerously under-resourced for the amount of work that had to be carried out.

The jobs that need to be done are:

1 Creating the Case for Support, and undertaking the feasibility study.

2 Putting together the committees, both active and passive.

3 Researching the donors, including trusts, companies and government, etc. This will continue throughout the appeal.

4 Locating a strong chairperson, and servicing the active committees.

5 Making the requests to trusts, companies, government, etc.

6 Setting up, and sometimes assisting with, the face-to-face 'asks'.

7 Drawing up the marketing plan for the public phase.

8 Arranging the press launch and subsequent liaison.

9 Running the public events.

10 Setting up local group activity.

11 Appealing to, and servicing requests from, existing supporters.

12 Setting up events to mark each stage of the appeal, internal and external: for example, the public launch, which may be a dinner to raise funds followed by a press photo-opportunity.

   As you can see from the length and breadth of the list, this requires a lot of people time from both staff and volunteers. Some of it is quite specialist work; research, major trust applications, setting up committees and running events cannot be left to amateurs without experience.

Calculating the costs of the appeal

After ascertaining the human resources the cost of activities needs to be determined. This will involve thinking about:

1 Salaries and volunteer expenses.

2 The cost of the Case for Support.

3 Consultants' fees (you may ask them to take you through the whole appeal). Include a contingency, in case you need to bring a consultant in when you are going through a difficult period.

4 Research costs, such as the cost of running parts of your database against that of a research agency with a rich list, or the cost of keeping up-to-date lists like Who's Who, People of Today, Charitable Trusts lists, Companies lists and various other rich lists.

5 The cost of setting up events, both nationally and locally.

6 The cost of a PR company (unless, say, your chairperson will lend you his/her company's PR firm), plus the costs of a marketing plan for the public phase, and of any profile-raising you may need.

7 The cost of dinners, lunches, travel and flowers (or other thank-you gifts).

8 If you will be looking to the US for funds, you may need to set up a 501c3 company there, and put together a US voluntary board. The cost of travel to see individuals, companies and foundations needs to be included. If you go on to run events, etc. there, that will need to be included at the outset of the appeal.

   It is important that the fundraising costs are thought through at the beginning, at least as far as that is possible, because they are a legitimate part of the appeal costs, and it is difficult to explain that the appeal target has increased because you have just added in new fundraising costs.

The timetable

Again, this will be influenced by the feasibility study. The Medical Foundation planned about a year of research and preparation including an exhaustive search for a chairperson, and committee preparation; then one year of internal work, going personally to as many existing top donors and likely major givers as possible (including an appeal to their supporters); followed quickly by a launch of the public phase at a dinner and photo-shoot, with celebrities at the building site. In the latter they had been fortunate to secure early on a donation from a Swiss foundation to buy the land they needed. Thoughtfully, the foundation required the land to be sold, and the funds returned, if the appeal failed.

In practice the timetable became a rather soft template, with important individual 'asks' being undertaken before the chairperson was active, the supporters being approached before the public launch, and the income prior to the public launch taking longer than expected to arrive (and coming from slightly different sources).

Getting the campaign underway

The organisation's existing strengths and weaknesses will determine much of the work to be done, but a typical sequence may be as outlined below. Once the strategy is agreed and the resources are allocated, the next step is to undertake two tasks simultaneously. One is to develop your research into individuals, trusts and companies, and the other to organise and print the case for support.

It is a good idea to run your list of supporters against that of a research agency to identify, say, your top 100 potential donors in depth. This will give you all the known facts about them that might be useful (and does not conflict with the Data Protection Act), and will no doubt throw up some millionaires you did not realise were among your supporters.

You will need to then put them in order of approach, and feed into that list any others who are close to you. Some of these you should approach early on, and some you will need to take time to determine who is best to approach them. Usually, the best person to make the 'ask' is a family member, friend or colleague, or someone in the same peer group - business CEO to business CEO, architect to architect, etc. - or someone with a higher status in the same sector (not, for example, a Lord asking a businessperson). However, the person you have in mind to make the 'ask' may be incapable of doing so. If that person cannot be trained or encouraged, then the 'ask' is best made by another competent and experienced person accompanying them. Sometimes this is the Director or a patron, or more often the chair or another member of the appeal committee.

Putting the case for support together should now be a straightforward activity, though support groups and committee members need careful handling. In the early stages only the support groups and letters from key individuals will be needed, so that you can use the case for support to recruit your active committee or committees. A combination of writing, phoning and visiting will secure letters of support and committee members. You may choose to call these groups, boards or panels, as some people are put off by the thought of committee work. Essentially, you are giving them a place of status, in return for using their name to help promote the appeal.

It is useful for at least one committee to be composed of people who are very high in the profession that deals with the problems your organisation is solving. Their support will add weight and credibility to your appeal.

The key committee, which in the case of small appeals may be the only committee, is the major donor panel. The absolute key person is the chair of the appeal. A very good chair will have done this before: he or she will be enthusiastic at all times, make one of the largest donations, and come up with a list of people they will approach. Several of these will give handsomely, and come onto the major donor panel. I have, however, heard as many stories of ineffective chairs as of good ones.

They must command enough respect to set the tone of the appeal, but more importantly, they need to be able to bring in a large percentage of the appeal target. This means they will usually be the CEO of a major firm, that has suppliers that they can lean on to make a major donation (at the top end of your giving pyramid), or have equal clout to this. Their donation will frequently be the largest one you receive. Finding the right person will most likely take you several months. Do not be pressured into choosing someone not quite right, but equally remember that the costs of building are probably mounting up as the months fly by.

On a small scale, a big gift committee can run a capital campaign with little else than encouragement from existing staff, and close co-operation from the director. This situation is rare, and committees usually need servicing, enthusing and pushing to obtain the most from them.

Big gift committees

One simple system is to group your key donors in a committee. The chairman must give financially, and so must each committee member, or they will not be effective in asking others to give. They should meet say, three times only in the following six to nine months to:

- List at least six people they are going to ask for substantial funds, and decide how much they expect to receive. (This avoids the same people being approached twice).

- List persons whom they have approached, any additional prospects they can propose, and any people not yet approached.

- Tidy up those final requests and thank all the committee members for their generous support in raising such a huge amount.

Key to success

The key to the whole thing is a persuasive chairperson, who has the clout and integrity to both ask the right people onto the committee, and ensure they undertake their tasks. In particular, the follow-up work the chairperson does a couple of weeks before the second meeting is crucial. Here he may need to call on the services of the staff to help with a presentation, or he may have to accompany a wavering committee member to ask for a donation at the end of a meeting with a particular donor. Another vital key to the whole process is to secure that first major gift (often

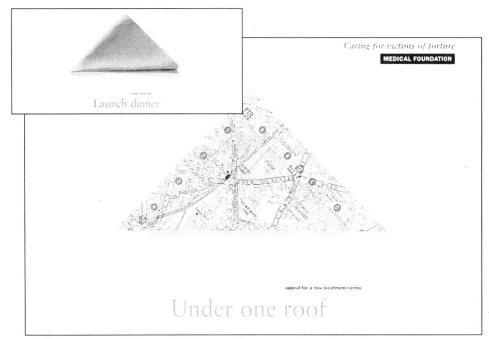

Fig. 8a *A common design style helps to build your capital appeal brand.*

from the chairperson), which will then stand out as a target for others and a signal that the appeal is likely both to succeed and to attract the right level of giving.

Other committees to consider include the following: an appeal advisory group, consisting of people who have been through this before, or have expertise to add, can help you greatly, especially in avoiding pitfalls, and a marketing panel can help design your appeal literature including the logo, Case for Support, public launch documentation, etc., and advise you on raising your profile to assist the appeal. The latter may also be able to come up with free publicity, materials and PR, sometimes even putting their own PR company at your disposal.

- It helps if committee members have a breakdown of the number of gifts needed at several different amount levels (which will match that in your Case for Support), so that a potential donors' giving ability can be matched to one of those amounts. Resist the temptation to let your committee members go for all the smaller sums.

- Sometimes, if you cannot reach a good estimate of how much someone will be prepared to give, you can have three sums in mind and say something along the lines of, 'We are looking for two people who can give £X, four who can give half that amount, and six who will give a quarter of it. Would you care to join any of those groups?'

- Knowing how much to ask for, and actually asking for it, is crucial. If you are seeking to raise £1m you will probably need one donation of £250,000, two of £100,000, four of £50,000, and so on.

Number of Gifts	Amount of Gift (£)	Income (£)	Total (£)
1	500,000	500,000	500,000
4	250,000	1,000,000	1,500,000
9	100,000	900,000	2,400,000
1	450,000	700,000	3,100,000
1	725,000	425,000	3,525,000
22	10,000	220,000	3,745,000
30	5,000	150,000	3,895,000
40	2,500	100,000	3,995,000
54	1,000	54,000	4.049,000
70	500	35,000	4,084,000
80	250	20,000	4,104,000
TOTAL			**4,104,000**

Fig. 8b *Schedule of Gifts.*

Obviously, the key amounts are £250,000 and £100,000 and these should be raised first, or the appeal may flounder. If you can raise one gift of £500,000 this will make life a very great deal easier. Start with obtaining the top gift and work your way down.

Whatever your target, you are unlikely to raise it all from big gifts. It is much more likely that one third will come from big gifts, one third from medium and one third from quite small gifts.

- Researching into known supporters and their contacts is the key to finding the top gifts.
- You will often find that affluent supporters have access to all sorts of opportunities that could help your organisation at a later date. Gifts in kind from companies are an obvious idea. It is much easier for companies to give products, or other supplies, than cash, but this is not a substitute for appeal income. Contacts with trustees of charitable trusts that could help are very useful, as is access to celebrities and decision makers. Working through your supporters on the basis of who knows whom is much more effective than making a direct approach from the outside.

I have undertaken this same process in India with a group of local industrialists, who were keen to raise funds in their country for local projects. In this case, this was to help the poor improve their very small businesses (micro-enterprises), which had previously only been supported by European and Australian organisations. The hardest part was finding the chairperson, but it did not take long to come up with an extensive prospect list. Names from this list were allocated to those who knew them to make the approach - naturally, this was usually the person who had put forward those names.

Before the chair

There is no reason why you cannot begin to fundraise before the chair is in place. There will be both charitable trusts and individuals whom you know so well that an outsider (even a well respected and powerful one) will be no better than your Director or Chair of the Board in making the 'ask'.

Traditionally the appeal will be split into two halves. The first is the private phase when you approach those you already know, and do not whisper a word of the appeal to the press. This is because if a major donor hears about the appeal they may be moved to give a donation, but that donation will usually be far less than if they gave after a face-to-face meeting, with the right person asking them. They will then be 'inoculated' against making the big gift. Later comes the public phase, when you ask all and sundry to give, and invite the press to publish and praise you (you will need a launch stunt or photo-opportunity, but remember the press look for controversy - so provide it). It is customary only to launch in public when you have raised half or two-thirds of the total needed. This is to avoid having egg on your face if the appeal fails - you really should not fail with half in, but that will depend on the effectiveness of your public appeal strategy.

Internally you will ask: key supporters, trusts that have already given, companies who support you; and, as appropriate, the lottery, the European Union, the Government, etc.

Externally you move on to the mass of your supporters, local groups, new trusts, other organisations, the public through the press, posh dinners, events (large and public mixed with small and private) and as many small committees (lawyers, teachers, mountaineers, etc.) as possible. As always, keep researching and approaching individuals face-to-face throughout the appeal. Individuals, trusts and the lottery are likely to give the largest amounts. Your research will uncover potential donors, such as those in the Times Rich List, major trusts and top companies. When you put together your various committees you should ask each member if they know any of these people personally, if they have a business relationship with them, or if they know of anyone they can approach who knows them.

Capital appeals take far longer to complete than people realise. Your Director and trustees will undoubtedly become impatient and worried at some stage. Your key task is to keep everyone concerned motivated, enthusiastic and believing it will succeed. If this falters then the 'asks' may not succeed and someone might pull the rug from under the whole appeal.

Appeals demand a huge amount of work, and you will need adequate staff and voluntary support. Your consultancy will advise on how many staff and volunteer supporters you need for the size of appeal, and the work to be done – do not under-estimate this. At the time of writing I am half-way through the Medical Foundation's capital appeal for £4.7m for a new rehabilitation centre, and have handed over control of my former fundraising department entirely to a new fundraising manager (promoted from within), thus leaving myself, and two other staff members, entirely free to concentrate on the public phase of the appeal.

The 'ask'

Much more important than the chairperson is the 'ask'. Being able to do this successfully underpins the whole operation. The 'ask' should be preceded by research into the prospect's links with the organisation, their motivation, and their ability to give. Each of these areas can involve extensive preparation from internal and external records, not forgetting the Internet. It should also be preceded by years of development, meeting the prospect in the field, and developing their understanding and devotion to the organisation.

From that basis the right person can be selected to make the 'ask' which will then be of the right amount, for the right reason, in the right place and at the right time.

Asking

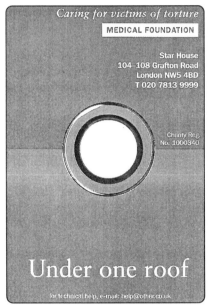

Fig. 8c *This CD-ROM card (shown actual size) introduced major donors to the capital appeal. It contains a self-running mini-presentation and links to the Medical Foundation's web site.*

I have found it easiest to meet in the prospect's own office, where they are comfortable and relaxed. A short period of settling in, with talk of the journey or the weather, allows people to feel comfortable with each other. Then a few words briefly touching on their past involvement, to acknowledge their position in relation to the organisation, followed by a simple reiteration of the problem. That is to say exactly why this building or piece of equipment is so vital, and why their donation is needed - 'We will not succeed if we do not have your help'. Then move on to the level of help needed. Here it is often useful to have the 'pyramid of giving' from the Case for Support, and to point them at the top levels of giving. Ask for an amount but then don't say anything. If you fill the silence to ease the embarrassment, you will lower the amount or let the donor off the hook. It may take a few seconds for the donor to calculate how much they are prepared to give. If you wait, and have done your homework correctly, you will usually be rewarded.

§

A very useful case study of a highly successful capital appeal is Marion Allford's book *Charity Appeals,* which will tell you much of what you need to know. This cites the very successful 'Wishing Well' appeal she ran for the Great Ormond Street Hospital.

Developing and Managing a Fundraising Department

9

If you were starting a new organisation from scratch:

- You would first need to estimate where your likely sources of income lay. Often the initial gifts come from trusts, from the Government or a wealthy individual. In either case, you would need to work out how long this money would last, and estimate the chances of a repeat donation. (Those who have given already are nearly always the most likely sources of additional finance.) If there is a lot still to be gained from the original source, your first appointment might be someone able to further develop this aspect of income, leaving you free to investigate new sources.

- The next step is likely to be the development of the donor-base, and you will need someone to run it who, in the early stages, will also be undertaking the donor development and your appeals for extra funds. If you are fortunate and this works well, the position will need to be split to create one position more concerned with database management, and another concerned with marketing.

- After that, it is really a question of following the best-performing sectors; but be wary of building up 'events' ahead of the donor-base, as the latter is a far more stable area of income.

Merchandising is often one of the first posts to be created in a fundraising department but, unless the membership/donor-base is at least 20,000, and better still, over 50,000 strong, this may not be financially attractive compared with other posts, which move your supporters higher up the fundraising pyramid. 'Following the best performing sectors' should, of course, be reflected in your long-term (three/four/five-year?) strategy, which should be agreed with the organisation via the planning process, and properly resourced through the budgetary process. This objective, and the subsequent development of a department to support it, is really at the centre of any successful fundraising strategy.

Ensuring full support from your organisation

It is essential that the whole organisation is behind your work.

- The first step is to nurture your plans carefully through the planning process. The resource implications must be spelled out as early as possible, so that further income generation is acknowledged to be based on development of the department. It is immensely difficult to request successfully additional staff members on the basis of workload if this has not been planned and agreed beforehand (preferably a few years beforehand), as you will be arguing for fundraising staff against programme staff, and that is not easy.

- Remember to back up requests on the part of processing departments, like Finance and Membership, who will have to cope with the additional income your work produces; otherwise the process will break down, and your financial and numerical reports will be out of date, and provide information too late for you to act on. The servicing of your members/donors will also fail and, as well as being less responsive to your appeals, they will leave earlier than they would normally. Members, as distinct from donors, are surprisingly resilient, but it is very unwise to trade on this by letting your service to them deteriorate. They will assume that the efficiency you display towards them reflects the efficiency with which you conduct your programme work.

Organisational structure

The chances are that your fundraising department has grown up on an ad hoc basis like that of most NGOs. Very few are designed from scratch and very few are re-engineered as thoroughly as the pains of most NGO 'restructuring' might suggest.

At the heart of any sizeable fundraising operation is the donor-base. Yet in many organisations this is located in the membership department, whose mission can be to defend the members from the nefarious fundraisers. Often the membership has voting rights, and is the political master of the organisation, not simply a donor-base to be nurtured solely for its disposable income. So placing it outside the fundraising department, frustrating though this is, has a logic which may defeat all attempts to relocate it.

This is not to say that you should not put forward cogent arguments for improving the situation, and demand at least a very high level of service both from the Membership department and from the members' newsletter. This is often another key fundraising tool, which can be mislocated in any one of several departments (Campaigns, Communications, Membership, the Directorate), and which will cling on, limpet-like, against all encouragement to move it to a new home.

Despite this negative beginning, the fundraising department can gradually become acknowledged within an NGO as a full department in its own right, rather than an adjunct of finance or the ugly duckling of the wonderful events programme. To emerge from these gloomy places into the light of day, a sense of mission is needed, and with it the clear idea that the fundraising department is responsible for the entire income generation of the organisation, not just for one small corner.

Possible structures and staffing

There are many ways of arranging a fundraising department and many ways of splitting up the tasks into jobs. The difficulty of setting out a model is compounded by organisations' differing proclivities to use agents or do the work in-house.

- One model is to centralise around the pyramid, using agencies for specialist tasks such as advertising, direct mail, loose-leaf inserts and the dispatch of mass mailings, but perhaps retaining the database and cheque processing in-house.

- Here, trawling for new members and donors is undertaken by one member of staff, who is responsible for advertising, loose-leaf inserts, direct mail (prospecting) and member-gets-member schemes.

- They should perhaps be responsible for membership renewals as well, (as this is a form of prospecting with a very hot list). This is usually more than one person can do, and so agencies are used to make it all physically possible. This can vary from one overall agency to several (which gives greater expertise, but takes more effort to manage). These can be an advertising agency, a direct mail agency or a space-buying agency, all backed up by various printers and a mailing house or houses.

- To this work is often added that of the direct mail appeals, which usually use the same agency as the one used for prospecting. These are, however, quite different disciplines and can be separated without undue loss of synergy. If they are divided, then a second staff position may be needed, to undertake the work of gaining additional funds from members and donors. This will include appeals, monthly giving, 'big gift' appeals, capital appeals, legacies and raffles.

- Again, this is more than one person can handle, and agencies can be used. When a major campaign is launched, such as a new monthly giving scheme or capital appeal, new staff may be needed for the duration of the appeal.

- The opposite model, too, is quite appropriate, i.e. taking in-house as much work as possible. Once professional staff know enough to instruct agencies successfully, (and they will usually have to instruct advertising agencies very carefully to obtain direct response, not prestige, advertising), they are quite capable of hiring the necessary designers and printers, and can cut out the agency commission, and in so doing retain a high level of professionalism and job satisfaction. Cheque processing and database management, on the other hand, are routine tasks that have little 'fit' with most NGOs' culture, and can quite easily be undertaken externally.

- In practice, you will find, NGOs seem to oscillate every few years between external databases and internal systems. 'Never again!' is said about each method - until the next time!

- Another possible option is a full service agency that handles all fundraising communications to your donor-base. If this option attracts you, do check the agency's references carefully and ensure that all parts of the agency are as professional as you need, not just, say, their direct mail department. Personally I feel that knowing your supporters and how best to fundraise from them is an NGO's core competence, not to be left, at its heart, to any agency.

- Above all, whichever route is chosen, the reporting mechanisms must be first-rate so that feedback on fundraising activity is fast and thorough, allowing adjustments to be made constantly to the various programmes. Advertising, for example, needs daily feedback on response rates to allow press options to be fully exercised.

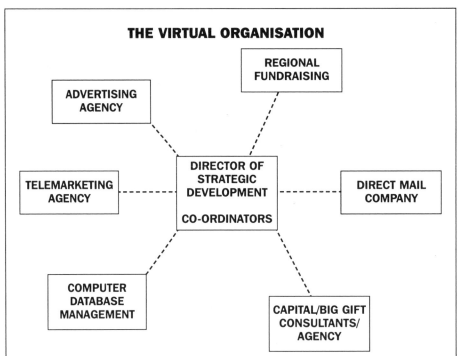

The virtual organisation is ideal both for those organisations who do not consider fundraising to be a core competence and in times of rapid change those who do not wish to employ many staff who may lose their positions if growth falters or goes into reverse.

It does demand, however, a very high level of trust and co-operation between the Director of Strategic Development and the key agencies and consultancies involved. These may need to be locked-in to provide exactly the right services at the right time and cost.

There is a strong body of thought that the core competence of many charities and other NGOs is their ability to retain and develop a strong supporter base and that everything else they do can be contracted out or bought in. So be very careful that the links in your virtual organisation provide adequate safeguards and that it is not set up just because the Council wishes to wash its hands of fundraising responsibility.

The decisions to go virtual is a strategic one to meet changing market conditions and most organisations will choose a hybrid using select agencies to complement in-house expertise.

Fig. 9a *The virtual organisation needs few full time staff.*

Departmental officers

A typical department of an organisation of 100,000 members and with £10m turnover could have:

- A Fundraising Director to whom the rest of the department reports; this is a management role involving little or no direct fundraising work. The Fundraising

Director should be part of the senior management team and should report to the Director.

- A Trading Officer who handles the catalogue and other merchandising methods.
- An Events Officer who organises national events and liaises with any local groups structure.
- A Membership Development Officer who handles
  - direct mail work (both prospecting for new members and organising internal appeals, including legacies and big gifts), loose-leaf inserts, advertising, and member-gets-member schemes
  - the Membership Department, processing the income and membership records
  - the Membership Newsletter. (This gives the organisation the means of developing that warm relationship with members that is essential if you are to maximise your income, though it may not be possible in an established NGO).
- A Company Officer who works with commercial companies and often Trusts and Foundations as well.

DEPARTMENTAL STRUCTURE

Head of Department

Trust Officer

Membership Officer

THE EARLY YEARS

A typical structure for the early years. There may be a local groups officer if the organisation has developed that structure.

The database and recruitment materials are often designed and produced in-house.

Fundraising Director

    Trust/Charity Officer
    Legacies

Trading Officer
    Catalogue sales
    Licensing/shops

Regional/Local Groups Officer
    Groups
    Local shops

Events Officer

Membership Development Officer

    Donor-base management
    Advertising
    Direct mail/leaflets

LATER YEARS

This structure can have several external agencies, eg. an advertising agency, a direct mail agency and the database may be held externally.

Officers and the Director may have assistants or specialists working for them.

Fig. 9b *How a typical NGO fundraising department can be structured.*

- A Regional Fundraising Officer. This is often the first post that charities establish. A team of local fundraisers across the country reports to the Regional Fundraising Officer in establishing local fundraising drives, setting up local groups and seeking local publicity. It is a good idea to have one fundraising 'Week' in the year, supported by national advertising and concentrating on one or more activities like a door-to-door collection, flag-days or sponsored walks. This centralises the regional fundraisers' functions, but depends very much on the establishment of a network of local supporters.

The officers listed above may need assistants, depending on their workload, and should have an ample supply of volunteers to call upon. This is particularly true of outside events. Volunteers who have helped with these functions in the past are invaluable.

In this kind of set-up you will also need the services of

- an advertising agency
- a direct response company
- possibly, a separate mailing company
- an external computer bureau
- the occasional services of consultants as you expand into new areas.

The charity wing

Many campaigning organisations are legally split between a charitable wing, that can receive Gift Aid donations, covenants and all other forms of charitable giving, and a membership-based campaigning wing to which people can belong as members, as well as giving donations. This is the case for organisations like Friends of the Earth, Greenpeace and Amnesty International.

If your organisation has this arrangement, then, as well as the above posts, you may need a charity fundraiser who will solicit gifts from which tax can be reclaimed. You must be very clear, however, exactly where you want the bulk of your income to go. If most of your work is undertaken by the non-charitable wing, then it cannot receive any money from the charity for non-charitable work, and you may be better off foregoing the reclaiming of tax paid, and making sure that most of your income goes to the non-charitable body. The other way round is, however, quite acceptable, and the charity can legally receive any money the non-charitable body cares to give it. (You will naturally want to make sure that donors' wishes are respected.)

One twist to all this is that membership cannot, usually, be covenanted, because a covenant is a promise to pay 'for no material consideration', and the usual newsletters and other membership services will amount to material consideration. Covenantors often think they are members, and there is actually no reason why you cannot send your covenantors a newsletter, so long as that has not been promised as an inducement to become a covenantor. You should also be careful not to confuse the covenantors, who may wish to vote as members, or the members, who may think they are members of the charitable trust.

It is quite normal for the charitable trust to grow in size until it is financially the largest partner - legacies are often the cause of this. All things being equal, any professional fundraising campaign will do rather better for a charity than a similar non-charity. People are used to Gift Aid and other forms of charitable giving. Legacies are, in any case, such a huge source of income for most organisations that they often deserve a staff post all to themselves (though this post is often combined with the trust officer's position).

A key area for staffing is special events. This is often the area where the fundraising department starts. It is also traditionally an area with a chequered past. Many of the reasons for that are to do with events that have cost the organisation a lot of money at some time or other. The charismatic events organiser who comes to grief over a large-scale production is a familiar figure. Events can, however, be a very valuable source of income and sometimes, more importantly, a great profile-raiser for the work of the organisation.

Events, if they are to be of any size, need a team to run them. This means staff and volunteers. Even if your organisation does not normally use volunteers (why not?), events cry out for lots of dedicated assistance from lots of people. Paying for it all will knock a large hole in your profits. The number of staff will be determined by the number and scale of events, but there is usually a need for PA assistance, as the work consists both of high-level contacts and negotiations, and the more mundane work of endless letters, phone calls, and extensive following up of promises and half-promises before the event, and thorough thanking of everyone after it. It also requires reasonable computer skills, to organise the mailings lists and the records, so that they can be used by other members of the team.

The trading manager role

Often the trading manager's job grows out of the office manager's position, (as does the volunteer manager's job). Running a successful catalogue with 100,000 members, or even 50,000, is a full-time job, though the burden of work does vary through the year. This may be evened out partly by a Spring catalogue, but these are not always successful. The trading manager will, of course, also develop the licensing deals and any merchandising operation to, or with, shops.

Corporate and trust approaches

Your organisation may be one which appeals strongly to the corporate sector. If the potential interest and income warrant it, a full-time corporate officer or even a whole team may be needed. Trusts, on the other hand, rarely require more than one person despite the huge number in existence. Again, this is really a matter for experience. If either sector responds on such a scale that you have difficulty keeping up with it, then the likely funds will outweigh any increased expenditure in this area. It is very important not to let a flood of enquiries go unanswered, as this will give the impression that your work is as unprofessional as your fundraising, and you will lose donations.

The Head of Department

Naturally, you will need a head of department (HoD) to guide, motivate, monitor, praise and discipline the fundraising staff, and to set targets based on the budget and ensure they are met. As the work expands the HoD will need to be aware of staff workloads and request assistance or new posts well before there is a crisis. The HoD needs to play a key role in the organisation's long-term strategy, development and planning.

The HoD should also be aware that fundraisers are 'role' based whereas most NGOs are 'rule' based, i.e. fundraisers see rules as a means to accomplish the task in hand, and if the rules obstruct this they will bend or seek to overthrow them, whereas the rest of the organisation will probably see rules as guidelines for good conduct in accomplishing tasks properly, and will be less than sympathetic to apparent breaches. In commercial companies the same dichotomy is apparent between marketing and research on the one hand, and the rest of the organisation, particularly accounts and production, on the other.

Job design and staff appointments

It is important for fundraising jobs to have clear boundaries where responsibilities end, so that applicants know exactly what is expected of them. It is also important to set realistic targets, so that staff are not demotivated by apparent failure: an income of £15,000 will be thought a disaster if the budget was £20,000, but a wonderful success if it was £10,000.

Job descriptions are essential in drawing the boundaries around fundraising positions, which otherwise can get very confused. This should be done largely by income source rather than a loose area of work, e.g. 'events' and 'membership recruitment advertising' rather than 'promotions' and 'press work' - in which case who promotes the events in the press? Some organisations have dispensed with job descriptions altogether, as rapidly changing market conditions have demanded flexibility, but that cannot be done effectively without other linked transformations.

As it becomes apparent that a new position is needed, it is essential to

* think through the implications for everyone in the department, as other changes may consequently be required
* look at whether the position is really a permanent one, or whether the workload is only a reflection of a temporary increase in income, and whether the work could not better be done outside the organisation or by a key volunteer.

Recruitment

Advertising

You will need to follow your equal opportunities policy in advertising for fundraising staff, but within this you might like to consider The Guardian on Mondays (media and marketing) or Wednesdays (public appointments), the ICFM Newsletter, and Professional Fundraising magazine. There are also an increasing number of agencies specialising in fundraising and other 'charity' staff.

Keep your eye on the salaries paid for various fundraising positions. With the huge retreat of state money from welfare provision in the past few years, fundraisers have been in great demand and there is a very limited supply of people with serious fundraising experience, so salaries have increased faster than for most other NGO positions. Some NGO salaries are, however, locked in a time warp so their advertised levels of remuneration will appear derisory.

Make clear in the advertisement:

- exactly what the job entails
- the qualities and experience you are looking for
- the salary and other benefits you are willing to give.

The interview

The interview is far more important than subsequent training, yet most organisations devote much more energy to training. Ensure you have a written job description for the post and person specification to fit that job description. Then agree a set of questions to reveal the qualities, or lack of them, that you have listed in the job description. Keep a score of the answers. It is all too easy to forget what the first candidate said when you are interviewing the fourth. Keep all documentation and notes after the interviews, in case you are faced with a legal action at a later date. Remember, anything you write down may appear in court.

- Take time to let the interviewee relax and answer all questions fully.
- Make sure you have thought through your questions well, and that they will allow you to discover if the interviewee has the experience and qualities you are looking for.
- Make sure that the interviewee talks for at least 80% of the time.
- Talk through their CV with them in detail to see if they have really had the experience it seems to show, or if it is just selective to make it fit the job description and advertisement.
- Think carefully about a written test and 'in-tray' exercise. This can be very revealing.
- Let the staff they will be working with meet the candidates, and preferably have at least one member of the department on the interview panel.
- If, at the end of interviewing the shortlisted candidates, you are not sure which to appoint, do take the time for second interviews. It is surprising how this clarifies issues, and how much additional information you can learn.

Interviewees are also interested in how you put the job over to them. It is easy to lose good candidates by making the job seem unattractive. Do not assume, because they have read the advertisement and the job description, that they know all about your organisation or the work they will be doing. How they perceive you as someone to work with is very important. Of course, it will not do to oversell the position. People often remember very clearly what was said to them at the interview. Offers made at the interview, even if only orally, constitute offers under the contract that you are negotiating.

The Institute of Personnel Managers (IPM) issues a very useful recruitment code. Their address is IPM House, Camp Road, Wimbledon, London SW19 4UW.

Induction

Induction to the department is crucial in enabling new members of staff to perform at their best as soon as possible. The objectives of the induction process should be clear, and it should be a priority for the HoD to make sure it goes smoothly.

New members of staff will also need to know a broad range of people in the organisation with whom they will be interacting, and how to make the necessary contacts for any research into programme work they will require. Apart from the purely human needs of meeting everyone, and getting to know where all the basic resources are, the next most important piece of induction centres on the translation of programme activity into effective fundraising language, whether written, verbal or visual, and on the approvals needed before publication.

Staff development and training

You will find it much more rewarding to think in terms of employee development rather than just training, which tends to mean courses to gain certain skills or improve techniques. These are necessary and important, but assisting staff to develop in a wider context, (perhaps by acquiring new experience, or by moving on in the organisation), or remotivating them after several years of the same type of work, will give your workforce much greater strength and dynamism.

If your organisation is progressive enough, try rotating staff members through different parts of it. It really helps to have worked in departments like finance, communications or campaigns. Staff will not only gain a new understanding, they will also collect friends and allies. Letting fundraising staff know exactly how the finances of the organisation are progressing will be much appreciated, so long as they can also see where the income they generate, and the expenditure they incur, fits into the overall picture.

Training courses

There are now many well recognised fundraising training courses. The best known are run by the Institute of Charity Fundraising Managers (ICFM) and the Directory of Social Change. These courses provide both basic training for those entering the profession and more advanced training in specialist subjects. The ICFM also runs an annual convention, which is highly recommended. Other courses are advertised from time to time in the fundraising press.

Promotion

In many NGOs there is no career structure as such. People do move from voluntary work to staff posts and then to senior positions, but promotion tends to be possible only by moving to another organisation. Many people are understandably reluctant to do this.

Within a fundraising department this can be ameliorated by training volunteers and staff, so that they are ready to apply for vacancies as they fall open. To some extent positions can be shaped for the people moving into them, but this is dangerous if carried too far. What happens if they leave soon afterwards? Can you find another person with the skills that fit this special job? Will you have to restructure the department again?

It is often difficult for staff with special skills like merchandising, trust fundraising, or running events, to move to the stage of running a department. More often, the jump is made by those with marketing skills who work with direct mail, advertising, and other direct response media. The transition can, however, be made by building up your CV to include the skills required, (including management), by training and experience. Sometimes a spell in a parallel position in marketing will help, or a move to a smaller organisation where the 'fundraiser' does everything.

Redundancy

Redundancies are rarely handled well. They usually come in the wake of long financial problems, when the organisation has finally accepted that it should scale down its work, and delay has made things so grim that redundancies have to be made with undue speed.

For a fundraising department, there is often the early psychological problem of knowing that the income budgets have not been met, and that for this reason the charity's work will suffer. This is exacerbated when individuals' positions are on the line.

Naturally, as income drops, fundraisers should see their resources increase to cope with the problem. This, unfortunately, does not happen very often, and NGOs are likely to take the foolish step of laying off people equally across departments, or putting everyone on part-time, when they should be increasing staff time devoted to fundraising. This only aggravates the situation, and means that fewer funds will be raised, so speeding up any redundancies.

Inter-departmental conflict

Fundraisers are often anxious to complete tasks within strict budget and time requirements. This process is often accompanied by a high level of tension and relative uncertainty about the outcome. It is not surprising that fundraisers can clash with departments working to a different timescale and priorities. For example, another department may prefer to have programme information checked by a particular person, rather than have an advertisement go out on time, or to meet auditing requirements rather than take time to let Fundraising know immediate details of the returns on the day's advertisement.

An organisational culture which respects fundraising is essential, in order to create the positive climate that will welcome new initiatives and the resulting changes. An over-dynamic fundraising department which upsets peoples' lives by creating continuous organisational change is rarely appreciated, as most people prefer a quiet, orderly life with a large degree of security. Rapid growth, new employees starting and new programmes beginning mean that staff positions change, and the position of older staff in the organisation changes too. Having been accustomed to being a vital part of a small organisation, in direct contact with the director, staff may feel devalued if they find themselves having to report to a new person in a distant part of the empire.

Preventing clashes and wars saves an enormous amount of time and energy. Once an interdepartmental war has started it can rumble on for years through the evolution of an organisation, weakening it and holding back its development, as well as making the working lives of staff intolerable.

- The key to war prevention and peacekeeping is to anticipate the areas of clash, and to agree procedures for staff to follow which meet their needs within the agreed priorities of the organisation. In the customary NGO free-for-all you will find this may not be welcome medicine, but it is far better than the disease!

- Thorough planning, which goes hand-in-hand with good communication, helps a lot. If all other departments know that fundraising is going to double the membership in a year, they can expect their correspondence to double as well. The postroom, Finance and Membership will be able to plan how to cope with the influx, and, if the means by which those people will be brought on board is well known, provision can be made for the necessary information to reach Fundraising, and the approval givers can be prepared for the material that comes their way.

- Above all, avoid surprises, so that people can plan to take fundraising needs into account at all levels. It is necessary both to alert senior management, so that they can tell their departments what to expect as part of their work, and to make early contacts among staff at lower levels, so that everyone to be affected is personally informed and brought on board. This also acts as an insurance policy, in case management is inefficient. Above all, don't forget your friends in the postroom!

An organisational culture which respects fundraising is essential, to create the positive climate that will welcome new initiatives and the resulting changes. These transitions need very careful handling, with a strong emphasis on understanding just how important the changes are in achieving the organisation's objectives. If this is not clearly comprehended by all staff, change will be vigorously opposed.

How to get fundraising ideas through committees

One of the most frustrating aspects of a fundraiser's life is seeing brilliant fundraising ideas turned down by committees for seemingly irrelevant or illogical reasons. Many fundraising ideas can be agreed by the HoD, but these are usually ideas whose cost can be accommodated under existing budget heads, and which do not run counter to any current policy. Other ideas may need the Director's approval because they involve interpretation of policy, or have a significant public impact. (Naturally the Director must personally approve anything that will bear his/her signature.)

Ideas outside current policy, or in grey areas, or that require additional funds, will most probably need approval by a subcommittee of the council or board which governs the organisation. This is usually the finance subcommittee on which the head of fundraising should sit. Or they may need approval by the board itself on the recommendation of the subcommittee, or by recommendation from the Fundraising Department to the Director to the Finance Subcommittee to the Executive Committee to the Council - this is not unusual! Any ideas involving something new, like telemarketing, have little chance of success in those circumstances, as it usually only takes one strong individual on a committee to object and the idea will be rejected, or so circumscribed that it is not worth carrying out.

Sometimes, of course, committees just like to say 'No'. They have passed everything for ages, and feel the need to establish their authority by saying 'No' to something. If you can sense when this is the case just give in quietly, ask for the ostensible reasons, and bring the project back later with the problems dealt with.

In fact, this is often the way forward with complex projects where the committee does not fully understand what is being proposed - they may not even have read the paper, especially if it is long - and needs at least one more chance to discuss the idea. Committees that are pushed often say 'No'.

- Committees respond much better to pulling - having all the positive aspects of the project set out before them. Do not highlight problems but make sure they have been dealt with clearly in your written report. Let committee members raise them if they will, and answer them by understanding the point they are raising but demonstrate that it will be taken care of, or show that, though relevant, it will have minor impact compared with the intended result.

- If you contradict a committee member, do so without signalling your intention by saying 'You may not agree to this', or any such remark that gives them time to frame a negative response. Just make the contradiction directly and clearly. Often this will not meet with a reply at all. (This technique should be used sparingly. It is better to be the friend of a committee.)

- If you can answer the first person to speak against the idea, do so. Signs of a fight, before committee members have voiced an opinion, will give them pause to consider both sides.

- Count how the 'vote' will go as soon as you can, and offer a compromise if it helps: 'I think we are mostly agreed on this, but I'll carry it out in September instead, to avoid any problems,' is the sort of remark that lets the chairperson wind up in your favour.

- Cultivate your chairperson, who is usually the key to unlocking committee decisions in your favour. Whatever you do, do not show up the chairperson in public.

- Chat to all the committee members informally in the breaks, but do not use these for obvious lobbying. You are forging relations for the future, not the present, though you can strike a deal if that looks like a good way forward. Work on the committee members before the meeting by keeping them informed of positive progress. Overt lobbying can be very helpful but can also misfire, and you will need to judge this very carefully. Lobbying by local groups really helps if they have elected the council members.

- Large council meetings are often the easiest, because only a few people will speak, and usually only once; you can contradict them emphatically (but not rudely), knowing that their vote does not matter much, but that you will influence the quiet members, who will not vote against something to which all objections have been clearly answered.

- Above all, your confidence in the matter is crucial, and means more than the statistics. Self-confidence impresses committees. They feel that they can rely on someone who is self-confident, even if they think the person is probably wrong.

Managing suppliers

Your ability to raise funds effectively will often depend on the quality of your interaction with your agencies, be they direct marketing, telemarketing, advertising or simply printing. As with staff, careful recruitment is essential. You will need to have a clear idea, on paper, of the brief you are giving the agency (or supplier), the budget they will have to spend and the return you are looking for, in financial and non-financial terms, as well as the equivalent of a person spec. Do you wish for a highly creative team, or a very reliable operation, or one that is knowledgeable and has a good track record in say, setting up successful programmes of loose-leaf inserts into magazines? Add a timetable to the brief so that the agency knows when you want each activity to happen.

It is worth taking the time to interview a series of agencies (at least three) and asking them to pitch for the business. Do tell any existing agency that you are doing this. It will save embarrassment when they read about it in Campaign magazine before you let them know. Do ask your existing agency if they would like to pitch as well – they could surprise you.

Regular meetings to look at the progress and the relationship are essential. I would suggest these happen at least quarterly for any major contract. Depending on your system for monitoring results, you or your agency should supply them in an agreed format at regular intervals. The format should be sufficient to judge progress according to the criteria for success that you have set. If you have set up a management agreement with, say, a direct mail agency then they will usually be analysing and presenting the figures.

You should have a written contract with each agency. The conditions of the 1992 Charity Act need to be followed if you are employing an agency to actually raise funds for you. In this case do ensure that those donating to you through this organisation are aware of the percentage of income that the agency receives.

If you hire a consultant to carry out specific activities or to give you advice you will need to draw up a written contract and to specify exactly what you need, a schedule of activity and the rate of remuneration that applies.

§

Working in a successful fundraising department can be a very rewarding experience, as successes in fundraising can be clearly recognised. Another satisfying and interesting aspect of fundraising, which lies behind the creativity inherent in the work, is the whole psychology of giving. The next chapter looks at some of the issues involved.

10 Mr and Mrs Chequebook at Home

The Psychology of giving

So why *do* people give away money, and why do they keep on doing it? If you cannot answer that question you cannot begin to fundraise, because you will have no real idea of what to say to people that will really convince them to join, or donate to, your organisation. You may even say many things quite innocently, which will put people off your organisation for life.

Finding out the facts

The simple answer is to ask them. Get together a few groups of, say, six to nine people who have given to your organisation, and put a range of questions to them. This is usually a very revealing exercise - but beware. People love to tell you just what they think you want to hear, and it is much more effective if you use a professional agency to undertake these 'focus group' exercises.

Once you have a clear picture of just why people are attracted to your organisation, you will need to weigh up the evidence carefully. If they are attracted for the reasons that you set out in your fundraising literature, are they just parroting back what you have said? It is a useful corrective to ask another set of people why they did not join or give to you. It could be for the same reason, and that you are putting people off as well as attracting them.

So you need to test your research against your own professional judgement, but do not just dismiss what people say, if it conflicts with your own views about what is effective. Test out what you learn. If you do not test, you really do not know.

Keeping the relationship alive

If donors have been giving to you for a long time and donating regularly, they expect to see that you have done something positive with their money. They need not just a thank-you letter, but a way of knowing that their donation has achieved their objective in giving. So reporting back after an appeal, or after the problem you are working on has appeared in the media, makes a big difference to the donor. If they have confidence that their money is well spent, they will give again and again.

Using your newsletter

The usual means of keeping people informed is your newsletter, sent out about four times or so each year. Do you really need to send it out more often? Is three months too long to leave your members in suspense, or, worse still, leave them open to approach by another charity? Either way, four issues a year is common and, though the readers will always say that they would give up the newsletter to save you money, they would also rapidly drift to another charity if they ceased to hear from you.

The newsletter also allows the organisation to mature and develop in the eyes of the donor. For example, let them know:

- how the needs of the people you serve are changing, so that they will come with you when radical change happens, as it does every few years in the voluntary sector. If it hasn't happened to your organisation yet, it is unusually unresponsive or about to explode. Prepare your donors for these changes.

- when you take on new staff, and what important work those staff will do.

- everything that you find interesting about working for your organisation.

- how much the latest appeals have made, and how you are now dealing with the problems you set out in the appeals. This feedback develops donors' confidence in the organisation, and brings them up the fundraising pyramid, enhancing the warm feeling they have for you - which will develop their generosity.

If things go disastrously wrong, let donors know as soon as possible, and they will give again to help you. If they learn about it from the media, they may feel let down and leave. Always tell the truth in these circumstances, and let donors have a clear idea of what went wrong and how you intend to go about putting it right. Do not be afraid of offering donors their money back, if you cannot spend it in the way you said you would. In fact, you are obliged to do that. In practice, organisations have found that the gesture is really appreciated, and few people ask for their money back. Often more donations come in. Honesty is a highly valued commodity today.

Varying your communications

As new means of communication develop, be prepared to use them in your fundraising to keep the relationship alive. Nothing kills relationships like repetition.

- Vary the size and style of your newsletter.

- Use video to communicate.

- Do you have an email list of top donors? If so, use it to update them on your programme and to reach them when items relating to your organisation break on the news.

- Use the ubiquitous fax machine (but use it sparingly).

Varying the scope, size and style of your communications helps to maintain readership interest, but the content needs to move with the other changes. Keep it lively, but in a style in keeping with your organisation's spirit. You may have a very conservative readership that is frightened of change. But if that is the case, why is it so? Is your membership profile ageing along with demographic trends, or are you failing to bring new blood into your organisation? Can you shift the trend or should you start new groups of supporters with a different ethos, to secure your income on into the future?

Motivating your donors

Do not take your donors for granted. Keep asking them what they want out of the relationship - you might be surprised! Surveys, questionnaires, focus groups and telephone calls all serve to let your donors pour out their hearts to you. If you have never undertaken a questionnaire, then you will be surprised just how many people will take great pride in telling you all about their personal feelings for the organisation. This can be immensely rewarding, if you have the courage to respond positively to all that you learn.

You may learn that amongst the key motivators are simple rewards that will not take up much of your time and effort, compared to their value to the donor. These are likely to vary a great deal from organisation to organisation, because the psychology of the donors will be different, but common motivators are visits to your hospital, offices, centre, sanctuary, first nights, etc. Seeing the work taking place is a special privilege for those who have helped to make it happen. Having special access outside the normal visiting hours when no one else is around can be very rewarding for your donor.

Open days

An open day, for example, can really develop the relationship - but you must take care that it does not work against you. Make sure staff are happy to be showing people around, rather than resentful at spending another Saturday at the office. See that the day's agenda is well planned, from travel there and back to refreshments at appropriate times, as well as explaining the work and letting the donors enjoy the experience. Knowing the organisation, they may have lots of detailed questions, and experienced members of staff should be on hand to deal with the enquiries in appropriate depth. Let them rattle old skeletons that may be lurking in the closets, so that they have good answers when their friends ask them similar questions.

The Medical Foundation holds five open days per year, which are advertised in its newsletter. About twenty or thirty donors come each time. They are given light refreshment, then split into two groups. One group is shown round the building for half an hour, then meets a clinician for a moving half hour discussion about their work, and finally spends an hour with the Director, whose experience helping torture survivors is long and deep. The other group meets the Director first, then has its tour, and lastly meets the clinician. At the end both groups have more refreshment and there is a soft 'ask' for money which covers all the costs involved. Most importantly, the tour is not just peeking into empty offices. The visitors are presented with case histories of torture survivors, showing the suffering they have endured, and how the organisation works to help. These case histories are remembered and have a profound effect. Indeed the whole half day is surprisingly often the prelude to a deepening or very serious involvement by the supporters. We have tracked many major donations and acts of help back to these open days. Along with the special events the organisation runs, they give the impression of a small, easily accessible, very special and professional organisation. That is exactly what our supporters tell us. We can also offer a visit to any potential major donor or celebrity without qualms, because we know that they will be well received within this regular programme.

Recognition

Certificates and registers of supporters, tree planting in donors' names, and mentions in the annual report are all valuable ways of rewarding donors and building the relationship; but make sure these are ways that your donors will appreciate. That is not easy to do because asking the question directly will often be met by the modest answer, 'Oh no, I would not like that at all,' whereas in private, the donor may well be quietly proud that their name is engraved on the new hospital wall-plaque, or whatever. Incidentally, I have been very surprised at the number of people who have come forward in a capital appeal I am running, and asked about naming rooms.

Asking donors how they feel other people might respond will often give you a stronger clue to their own likes and desires. Some people could be embarrassed by the kind of recognition mentioned - but they will give, usually anonymously, or tell you their wishes quite clearly.

Personal contact

Often, personal contact is the strongest motivator of all. If you have a director, celebrity or key player in your organisation whom the donors will know quite well, either in relation to your work or from their role in public life, then you have a powerful motivator who can create a lasting impression on your supporters at meetings, and, more effectively, face-to-face. It is likely that this person is very busy, but do try to free up their time to make a strong impact on your major givers, or prospective major givers, at dinners or face-to-face meetings.

There are theories in favour of having such meetings in either the supporters office, or conversely in your own Director's office. I prefer to visit major donors in their own office or home, because it is easier to arrange, and the donor is relaxed and inclined to be generous to their guests. At your office you are in charge and have the psychological upper hand, but your donor may feel under pressure, which is bad for the kind of long-term relationship that brings rewards to both parties. Under pressure to give, the donor may make a relatively small donation for the sake of form, rather than commitment. So, if you take the time and trouble to formulate a view on your donors' needs, and test that view in practice, you will gradually learn how to develop the relationship beyond the immediate one-donation-at-a-time scenario to the mutually profitable fields of long-term commitment.

Phoning home

Double-glazing salespeople have given the phone a bad name as a means of communication; but a call from an old friend you thought had forgotten you is a pleasure to receive. When the old friend is your favourite charity, it is also quite touching and personal. That is not a moment which should be left to chance. Well-planned and thought-out calls are a pleasure to receive. Calls with a cast-iron script are a cause for concern. By all means use the phone to ask for donations of all sorts, but do it sensitively to appropriate people, and take great care to ensure that those who have any objection to calls are not phoned again. Make sure all questions asked are eventually answered, though the caller will rarely be able to answer them all and must say if they do not know the answer.

If you have interesting news or information that your members might like to hear, then phone them as you would your friends but, as with your friends, phone those with whom you have reached that stage of the relationship. Phoning someone who has made a small donation to tell them news about a project they will not know of can be counterproductive, but phoning members to ask them to write to their MP about an issue which has just come up can be very productive. Calling major donors to let them know good news about a project they have heavily invested in will be very welcome. Who calls is important. Anyone who is keen, well-spoken and informed can phone, asking for a letter to be written, but the person who sought the donation from the major donor is the best person to call with the news, unless another caller is obviously of higher standing in the organisation. Keeping in close touch with your donors can build a lasting relationship beyond the usual telemarketing to lapsed members.

The word telemarketing itself inhibits our understanding of the possibilities. To use the phone only to bring back members or reactivate donors is to miss a great part of its value. Naturally, faxes, email and all other forms of communication are also useful devices for keeping in touch, provided they are used sensitively and imaginatively to build the relationship.

From the cradle to the hereafter

New supporters

Your fundraising will be targeted at your core market by age, education, profession, geographic area, etc. But working exclusively in that market is limiting and you risk the problems many organisations have faced, such as the support base becoming progressively older and older, or that the organisation is seen as representative of only one small part of the population, or only of interest to one segment or gender.

If you devote a relatively small percentage of your budget to testing new ground and investing in new age groups, you will be both opening up the opportunity of discovering that your target market may be much larger than at first envisaged, and also taking advantage of the fact that testing alters the perspective of the market. Seeking new members should also serve to educate all those who are approached and make them more aware of your work. Because such prospecting is in new fields, this may be the first opportunity these people have to learn about your organisation, and therefore, they may in time become supporters.

Conventional wisdom says that people have thought seriously about joining an organisation at least three times before they eventually take the plunge. So it may take, say, a series of advertisements backed by direct mail to eventually open up a new market.

Many organisations have found that their student membership will leave after their student days, but return after marriage and children. Of course, there is no telling if they would have joined anyway, if the student programme did not exist, but it is a common sense deduction to link them together until more rigorous analysis has been done. Sometimes students are an easy catch, but an unprofitable one, and if recruitment is aimed principally at students, who often pay a reduced fee, the membership of the organisation may expand impressively but the income falter. Of course, students make good activists. They have the time to help, but rarely the disposable income, though that will come as they move into the professional classes.

Schools fundraising

A few years ago many national NGOs had small teams of educational staff who toured schools, giving talks about the work and concerns of those NGOs. Some of these had great educational value, others were thinly veiled or naked fundraising approaches. Eventually evaluations of their educational performance found most of them wanting in their ability to reach even a small proportion of the nation's pupils or students. To do this thoroughly at classroom level would require huge teams of educationalists. It is much more likely now to find organisations seeking to influence the national curriculum or teacher training so that their concerns form part of the overall educational process. Naturally, fundraising has been left out of this process, though there is good reason to suppose that the impact of environmental studies will keep the green movement afloat for many years to come.

There is still a great deal of money to be made from classroom-based fundraising, but it is labour-intensive, and schools should demand a high educational content linked to any appeal for funds. It helps if your organisation has a strong component of teachers within its membership, because they can often be mobilised to support your work, and appreciate that you will need to include an element of fundraising.

At a local level, it can be useful to the school for you to run an assembly, and to be allowed to ask for funds on the back of that work, but increasingly, schools will be looking for a long-term relationship, which of course will be most effective for you as well. Take the time to talk to teachers and educationalists about adapting your materials and talks for different age groups, and arrange a programme with the school so that you can eventually cover the whole intake. Set out the *educational* goals you expect to achieve as clearly the fundraising goals, so that the schools can see your objectives. Do check that you are really meeting all your overheads, because it is easy for staff to believe strongly in the educational work and fail to realise the fundraising objectives. When you first set up this programme the returns you expect, and how you will judge staff performance, should be absolutely clear.

Because you are dealing with a great number of individuals, think through various sponsored activities related to your organisation, or stay with the simple sponsored walks and sponsored swims, etc. Look at any small objects that children could collect, related to your organisation, that you could then use or sell, e.g. stamps or silver foil (where there is a market). This technique has been perfected by Blue Peter and is a good standby, but do ensure you can cope with the volume of goods you might receive. At a national level you may find it possible to link with a national company that wishes to reach the schools market, and is willing to invest a reasonable sum in sponsoring a range of fundraising activities to increase its brand recognition by teachers or pupils.

Don't forget that education and fundraising can also be fun for kids. An element of humour and imagination will go a long way in your schools' fundraising.

Grandparents

US and Canadian universities have pioneered the development of fundraising from the parents and even grandparents of their alumni. It is quite obvious, when you think of it, that proud parents or grandparents who may not have been to University themselves may be eager to help by donating to their children's or grandchildren's university. This also helps to fill the gap before the student is earning much money. Incidentally, time and distance make the heart grow fonder, and universities which keep in touch with their alumni find it pays off in a few years time with even the most rebellious students.

Adapting to your market

A full fundraising programme will cover all age groups and all segments of society, adapting to the conditions and psychology of each market as far as it is profitable in the long run. This often requires considerable adaptability on the part of the charity. You may be used to linking celebrities with your advertising in tabloid newspapers, but they will not be effective in the broadsheets. This change of tone and emphasis is often very difficult for a charity's policy makers to accept. It is easy to become used to a certain language, and to fear that another way of writing or putting over the message will not carry the same content, or will trivialise or misrepresent the organisation. You must take care here to make sure that the essential message is clear and be prepared to show how each segment of the population will react to, and understand, what you are saying. It is very instructive to talk to charities already operating in that segment, to learn how their fundraising is received.

§

A key part of adapting to your market is understanding its culture, particularly its moral values. The next chapter tackles some of the questions of morality that may arise during your fundraising.

11 Moral Issues

The use of 'shock tactics' in fundraising has caused a lot of debate, and in some organisations concern about it has got to such a point that making the simplest case for supporting your organisation may have to be watered down so much, in case someone is offended, that no one will ever feel it is particularly important to help your cause.

The distinction between 'shock' and 'offence'

The Advertising Standards Authority (ASA) makes a very useful distinction between shock and offence. Basically, it is wrong to offend someone; but the nature of many charities' work is such that it is not surprising if it shocks.

Shock is a natural reaction to the horrors we are trying to alleviate. Offence is more difficult to define, but its essence is the gratuitous hurt that people feel when they are the targets of an attack. Unfortunately, this can happen inadvertently if copy is not thought through from the reader's perspective. Naturally, biased and bigoted people will claim to be offended by many things, but anyone intending to put forward a strong case for supporting a needy cause must take that in their stride.

Fig. 11a *You can shock but not give offence.*

Setting out factually what has happened to people, however shocking, cannot legitimately be held to be giving offence.

Barnardo's

In January 2000 the ASA rejected 28 complaints attacking a series of advertisements that Barnardo's had run in the national press featuring a baby injecting heroin. The ASA said that Barnardo's had tried to convey a 'serious and important message' in using this 'stark image'. When the advertisement had first appeared the Committee of Advertising Practice (which writes the code administered by the ASA) had asked publications not to use it. Barnardo's said "We are a charity trying to raise awareness of our work aimed at creating better futures for children and young people threatened by disadvantage abuse and neglect. This message is clearly reflected in our advertising". The ASA said "Because the advertisers used the image to raise awareness of the seriousness of drug abuse, and the action that could be taken to prevent it, the advertisement was unlikely to cause serious or widespread offence or undue distress".

Individual cases

In seeking to give potential donors the chance to empathise with suffering individuals, it is necessary to let them know just what has happened to those individuals. Group suffering rarely has the same effect, and mass tragedies can only be comprehended through the stories of single people, but you do need to consider the wishes of those people whose plight you depict. Nearly always, they are more than willing for their story to be told, but you should ensure that those who do not wish for publicity are not exposed.

- Changing names and some other details to protect identity is quite legitimate.

- As far as possible, you should identify the people in photographs, which should not be used without thought for the subjects or the reasons why they were taken.

'Composite' cases

The use of 'composite' cases raises more questions. Here charities give a typical example of the kind of person they are setting out to help, rather than giving a true case history. These pictures often combine several case histories into one story. This can give a more correct image of who is being helped by the donor's money, but you should be very careful to make it clear what you are doing, so that people are not misled into thinking you are presenting an actual case.

- A composite should never be a substitute for proper research.

- Be very wary of the copywriting of composites, as this can tend to shift from a typical case towards an extreme, which may not truly reflect your work.

- If in doubt, use real cases, and vary them through your campaign, so that the differences in cases comes across.

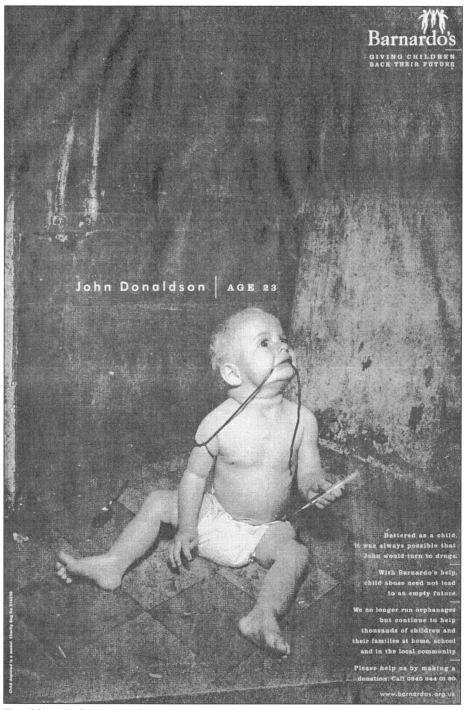

Fig. 11b *The furore around this advertisement has given Barnardos valuable additional publicity*

Respecting privacy

There are two kinds of privacy that you should be aware of:

- the privacy of the people you are helping
- the privacy of the subjects of your campaigns - members and donors.

The privacy of those you are helping

The importance of considering the privacy of those you are helping is common to both fundraising and issue campaigning. It has been highlighted by cases of disabled people, who have felt that they were being made into objects of charity, and not recognised for their talents or for the problems they faced in their everyday lives.

Remember that every campaign carries at least two messages:

- the clear call for funds
- what you are saying in general about the set of people or conditions you are trying to help.

Featuring disabled people in asking for funds can also cast them as helpless individuals. Showing starving children can also carry a message of hopelessness about the country they are in, and depicting rain forest destruction can lead to simplistic assumptions about the perpetrators. There are no clear guidelines for these cases, but you do need to consider all the messages you are sending, and how they square with your organisation's overall aims and objectives. No one wishes to end up doing more harm than good, and you will often have to make some hard decisions, but that is preferable to inadvertently campaigning against yourself or giving up an excellent fundraising campaign because of uninformed worry. Asking the people you feature for their opinion can be an eye-opener and every fundraiser should do it.

The privacy of the donor

When there is a disaster in a small town, everyone rallies round to help. People knock on each other's doors, ring each other up, and write to people further away who could help. This is perfectly normal and praiseworthy human action.

When the disaster is in another country or another town, or even not quite so visible, we are often suddenly afraid that people may be offended if we ask them for assistance, and we worry about putting undue pressure on them to help. This is the fear of poor excuses - and it can paralyse organisations.

Many people feel that they should help, but do not really wish to, and to avoid making a plain statement of this fact, they hide behind a variety of simple subterfuges. First among these is to attack the medium, rather than the message: 'It wasn't that I didn't want to help, but I don't think you should send junk mail, phone people up, spend all that money on advertising or put leaflets in magazines - it's such a waste.' If accepted at face value, all this would leave a fundraiser rather baffled in the search for a universally acceptable means of fundraising.

People react differently to different media. Some people love it when their favourite charity calls them up personally. Other people don't like it at all. Some people like to sit and read through long letters explaining what a charity does, and why it needs money. Others regard this as junk mail, and a threat to trees. There is no universally acceptable means of fundraising, and there will be some objections to everything you do. Be prepared for this, and think through how you will respond to the most likely criticisms. If people tell you they do not want to receive telephone calls, take note of it and do not call them again. If you cannot record and deal with thi,s you are not ready for telemarketing. You must also de-duplicate your list against the Telephone Preference Service (TPS) list.

Other media are harder to deal with. When undertaking reciprocal mailings, you should, however, de-duplicate your list both against the other organisation's list and against the Mailing Preference Service (MPS) scheme, and ensure that the lists you buy are similarly treated.

The Mailing Preference Service and the Telephone Preference Service are to be found at: 5th Floor, Haymarket House, 1 Oxendon Street, London, SW1Y 4EE Tel: 020 7766 4410 and Fax: 020 7976 1886. Their website is at **www.dma.org.uk** and their e-mail address is mps@dma.org.uk

If your targeting is accurate, people may receive several mail shots from you, and will see your advertisements and read your loose-leaf inserts. They take this personally, with a touching faith that every communication you send out is targeted deliberately and personally at each individual who reads it. Often you will write to your own members, asking them to join. Even if you de-duplicate (using specialist software to eliminate duplicate names and addresses) bought-in lists against your membership list, you are still likely to do this, as people write their names and addresses differently on different forms. Adding a phrase like, 'if you are already a member, please pass this appeal on to a friend' can assist you in not offending your members and increasing your support.

The Data Protection Act

The Data Protection Act, appropriately passed in 1984 and augmented in 1998, sets out to protect personal privacy under threat from the rapid development of computer systems capable of holding and processing vast amounts of information on individuals. The 1998 Act is far more stringent that the 1984 Act.

For the full details look at www.dataprotection.gov.uk

The new act is so all-encompassing that every fundraiser should be aware of its contents and should take a systematic approach to its observation. All organisations should have policies in place, to ensure that staff conform to the data protection principles. A working knowledge of the eight principles is essential.

These are:

1 'Personal data shall be processed fairly and lawfully and, in particular, shall not be processed unless –

- at least one of the conditions in Schedule 2 is met
- in the case of sensitive personal data, at least one of the conditions in Schedule 3 is also met.'

This principle introduces the idea of 'sensitive personal data', which is personal data consisting of information about

a) the race or ethnic origin of the data subject

b) their political opinions

c) their religious beliefs or beliefs of a similar nature

d) whether they are members of a trade union

e) their physical or mental health or condition

f) their sexual life

g) the commission or alleged commission by them of any offence, or

h) any proceedings for any offence committed or alleged to have been committed by them, the disposal of such proceedings or the sentence of any court in such proceedings.

Unless you have a thorough knowledge and certainty about your right to process and hold such data my advice is not to hold any such sensitive personal data. The conditions for holding or processing such data are much tighter than for other personal data including, in some cases, 'explicit' consent.

2 'Personal data shall be obtained for one or more specified and lawful purposes, and shall not be processed in any manner incompatible with that purpose or those purposes.'

3 'Personal data shall be adequate, relevant and not excessive in relation to the purpose or purposes for which they are processed.'

4 'Personal data shall be accurate and, where necessary, kept up to date.'

5 'Personal data processed for any purpose shall not be kept for longer than is necessary for that purpose.'

6 'Personal data shall be processed in accordance with the rights of data subjects under this Act.'

7 'Appropriate technological and organisational measures shall be taken against unauthorised or unlawful processing of personal data and against accidental loss or destruction of, or damage to, personal data.'

The New Act not only requires the registration of 'personal data' which is 'automatically processed' (by computer), it also covers other records including card-index files. The Act also allows 'data subjects' access to that information, and to have it corrected or deleted. On receiving a written request, the data user is obliged to give an individual a copy of that information. The data user can charge a limited fee per entry for supplying that information. A request should usually be met within 40 days. If not, individuals can complain to the Registrar (an independent officer reporting directly to Parliament), or to the courts. Most fundraisers will be 'data users', who control the contents and use of personal data on their donors or potential donors.

This can be personal data on individuals as well as information about companies, charities, etc., and includes any information about living, identifiable individuals, even just their name and address. Charities must be registered with the Registrar under the various categories for which the data is intended to be used. It is important to register in every category which you are likely to need, as failure to register is an offence. Some of these categories are decidedly quirky - for example, the Registrar regards reciprocal mailings as 'trading' not 'direct mail'.

The Registrar has drawn up a series of Guidelines which can be obtained from the Information Services Department, Office of the Data Protection Registrar, Wycliffe House, Water Lane, Wilmslow, Cheshire SK9 5AF, Tel: 01625 535 777, Fax: 01625 524510, where registration forms can also be obtained. When you apply to register you will need to state:

- the personal data held
- the purpose for which it is used
- the sources from which the information may be obtained
- the people to whom the information may be disclosed, i.e. shown or passed on to
- any overseas countries or territories to which the data may be transferred.

Think carefully about every other use of personal data in your organisation and make sure you are registered for it.

You must be clearly aware of, and follow, the broad principles of good practice contained in the 1984 Act. These are that personal data must be:

- obtained and processed fairly and lawfully.
- held only for the lawful purposes described in the data user's entry.
- used only for those purposes and disclosed only to those people described in the register entry.
- adequate, relevant and not excessive for the purpose for which it is held.
- accurate, and where necessary, kept up-to-date.
- held no longer than is necessary for the registered purpose.
- accessible to the individual concerned who, where appropriate, has the right to have the information about themselves corrected or erased.
- surrounded by proper security.

If, for example, you collect signatures on a petition, the data cannot be used to send those people a request to join your organisation, however briefly, unless you are registered for that purpose and the code is followed.

You should be sure that you:

- have obtained the information fairly, (e.g. have stated clearly in the main copy on that form that you will hold it electronically, or asked those signing to tick a request box for membership information).
- can record the data accurately.
- are able to adequately protect that data, and will not keep it for an unreasonably long time.
- can prevent casual passers-by reading such data off the screens of authorised users.
- can ensure only authorised users in your organisation access such data.
- delete files when they are no longer relevant (and know just when this is).

To thoroughly understand the requirements, you need to have a good knowledge of the Guidelines which are quite comprehensive. It is apparent, however, that some elements have not been thought through and others are not keeping up with the changing pace of technology.

It is in the public's and the NGO's interest for mailings to be as exactly targeted as possible, yet some of the guidelines seek to restrict the information held so that organisations are obliged to mail many more people than is necessary. Building up large amounts of information on donors enables their needs to be closely catered for, yet the direction and tenor of the guidelines is against this. If you engage in reciprocal mailings you are advised to state this, and seek permission from all donors or members at the point at which they join the organisation. To do this would clearly make it impossibly expensive for many organisations to recruit through newspaper advertising, and would affect all other recruitment methods. A more sensible approach would have been to acknowledge that receiving information from like minded organisations is part and parcel of being a member or donor in the 3rd Millennium. This would also avoid countless other individuals receiving letters that are inappropriate, and enable charities to grow cost-effectively.

One phrase over which fundraisers and the registrar may well disagree is: 'As guidance in this respect the Commissioner would advise that data controllers consider the extent to which the use of personal data by them is or is not reasonably foreseeable by data subjects. To the extent to which their use of personal data is not reasonably foreseeable, data controllers should ensure that they provide such further information as may be necessary'. Of course, someone making a donation to a charity would expect to be welcomed on board with a telephone call, to receive further requests for donations, newsletters, raffle tickets and requests to join other organisations. Unless you have cut yourself off from the world all this is quite reasonably foreseeable. However, I would expect a degree of apoplexy from some older data subjects who have steadfastly ignored any changes since the wheel was invented.

Today, many homes are equipped with computers linked to the Internet with email facilities and databases on CD-ROMs. Thousands of people may be in breach of the Act as they build up lists of names and addresses and process them for a variety of business related purposes.

There are, however, some exceptions to the 1984 Act and registration may not be necessary where personal data are:

- held in connection with personal, family or household affairs or for recreational use.
- used only for preparing the text of documents.
- used for calculating wages and pensions, keeping accounts or keeping records of purchases and sales for accounting purposes only.
- used for distributing articles or information to data subjects.
- held by a sports or recreational club which is not a limited company.

In relation to the final two points, data subjects must be asked if they object to the use of their details. You have been warned! Check Guideline 6 carefully if you intend to rely on an exception.

Ultimately, the Guidelines are only the Registrar's view of the Act and not a substitute for it. Your own view may be equally correct until a precedent is established through a court case, of which there have been a number already.

Europe-wide legislation has now been incorporated into the 1989 Act but not yet tested in the courts. As we have a legal system based on precedent, the exact meaning of the law will not become clear until it has been tested in practice in the courts. Do endeavour not be the subject of those tests.

Handling complaints

Complaints arrive well ahead of money, often by phone. It is important that people in the organisation know this, or your appeals will have a bad reputation early on. This is hard to shake, even if they become very successful financially. Keep your switchboard, press office and mail-opening room informed, so that they can deal professionally with taking calls, handling complaints and passing them on to be dealt with by the right person - usually you!

Always be ready to apologise and explain. Your members will understand, if you are prompt and courteous. Naturally, if you have made an error, do apologise and give a full explanation of how it came about. Someone who complains and is dealt with satisfactorily will often become a more convinced supporter than before.

Occasionally, you will have letters from people who are obviously bigoted, or incorrect in what they say, or who feel they have a genuine case for complaint when you have done nothing wrong. In these cases you can do no more than state your case clearly and simply. You may feel that you can never convince that person you are right, but you should always reply courteously. If, however, phone callers are abusive you can just put the phone down. Letters that are rude or offensive go straight in the bin, though sometimes they can be very funny. Do not make an issue of these or try to reply, unless you want to receive another.

More difficult to handle are letters from the seriously disturbed, that start out just slightly odd, but by the second or third letter are manifestly deranged. Again, this correspondence must be brought firmly to a close by clearly stating your case, and saying that you do not want any further correspondence on the subject. You may choose to reply one last time, stating that you will not reply to any further letters, but it is best to stop as soon as possible. Such correspondence can be very time consuming and distract you from your real goals. Often, such correspondents will write to several people in the organisation, keeping long pointless exchanges going indefinitely. It is best if one person takes over all answers and brings them to an end.

Acceptance of funds

The acceptance of funds with an easy conscience is all about preparation. Most fundraising organisations have evolved a set of guidelines for their fundraising operation. This will prevent its work being hindered and make it clear just what, and who, the organisation can accept from, before the asking is done. Doing this before you ask for funds saves an enormous amount of time and trouble later. Imagine your chagrin when your Executive Committee decides that a cheque for £50,000 from a major company must be returned, because a subsidiary of theirs in Ireland doesn't allow unions in their factory.

The rationale behind most guidelines is to permit the maximum income acquisition possible, without undermining the mission of the organisation. Some organisations say they will accept any funds without strings attached to them, and if the funds come from those they work against, so much the better. However, you may like to consider that PR companies advise such businesses that setting up a large charitable fund is an effective way to influence the public and to let themselves be seen in a good light.

Guidelines are, however, notoriously difficult to construct in such a way that fundraising is not inadvertently crippled. A policy on accepting funds from companies may simply say, 'We will accept no funds from any company which harms the environment'. This statement will then need extensive qualification to deal with the interlinking of companies through the structure of multi-nationals, the raw material supply and product delivery companies. The obvious questions are, 'What exactly constitutes harm?' and, 'What about a company that is making great progress, should it be encouraged?' Faced with that sort of guideline, it is tempting to give up on companies altogether. Similar problems come from over-simplistic guidelines on the arms trade, tobacco companies and those who have links with impoverished countries or repressive governments.

Some organisations, like the Campaign Against the Arms Trade, can provide a detailed and lengthy blacklist. Any such list, covering a fair range of ethical issues in even a fairly straightforward way, will include most companies. It may appear easier to say who you could accept money from, if it were not for the fact that there are no perfect companies in this imperfect world. Some, however, are struggling to improve, and it can help to recognise this in the manner of many ethical investment trusts. Unfortunately, those that might appear on such a list today could disappear tomorrow, thus undermining the cast-iron list approach.

Another, more flexible concept, is to say you will accept no funds from a source that would lower your organisation's standing in the eyes of the public, and then let each case be judged on its merits by the recipient body of your organisation; which can raise any questions it may have to a higher level of your organisation for advice.

This is largely a question of empowerment and trust in the common sense of each separate part of your operation, (which for most organisations will simply be the head office). Until case histories have accrued, however, it may be sensible to mitigate such freedom with an approvals procedure for requests for donations over a certain level, and from any particular industry with which you are at odds.

Some organisations impose a percentage limit to prevent large donors from appearing to control the organisation. No more than ten percent of gross income is common, this is impractical for small organisations with a very low gross income - where will the first donation come from? This form of control also runs into problems when a capital appeal for, say, a new building, is contemplated. Here the early donations, which will be large, will often dwarf the normal gross income and the building may not succeed without those large donations. So, a method needs to exist whereby rules on acceptance of funds can be mitigated to suit the organisation's real needs and objectives.

Other organisations say simply, 'All funds are welcome but not earmarked for any specific project'. This is often found in large membership organisations where there are few funds from Trusts. If you wish to increase your Trust fundraising, this rule would be crippling, as Trusts like to sponsor discrete projects. It also raises another problem, in that membership organisations making frequent appeals for funds will cite different reasons for each appeal, and will need to make very clear to donors that their money is going into the general pot if that is indeed the case. Many organisations welcome donations for specific projects, and deliberately carve up their work into such projects. This makes fundraising easier and brings the donors much closer to the work of the organisation, making repeat gifts more likely.

Acceptance of funds policy

So, what is to be done? Each organisation needs to take time to consider the questions cited above in the light of the overall framework of maximising income, without damaging the work it is doing. As a fundraiser, it is in your interest to draft an 'Acceptance of Funds' document, and ensure it passes through the relevant committees before you begin fundraising. Ask other organisations in your field for copies of their Code of Practice to help you, and to bring out all the issues for discussion, so that the debate does not occur year after year, as executive members think of new ethical issues to consider.

§

The Medical Foundation for the Care of Victims of Torture's Fundraising Guidelines:

The guidelines for solicitation and acceptance of funds by the Medical Foundation are designed to enable its fundraising to be efficient and effective without compromising its objectives or bringing the organisation into disrepute with its supporters or the general public.

Decisions regarding the solicitation and acceptance of funds is delegated by the Trustees to the Director. The day-to-day administration of these guidelines is carried out by the Director of Fundraising.

1. The Medical Foundation will neither accept nor solicit funds from companies engaged in manufacturing instruments of torture or supplying such instruments.

2. The Medical Foundation will neither accept nor solicit funds from arms manufacturers where those arms have, or could be used for, repressive purposes, or from companies supplying such equipment.

3. The Medical Foundation will not accept funds or solicit funds from companies where that association would lower or diminish its public and/or private support.

4. The Medical Foundation will not accept funds where the acceptance of such funds would cost the Foundation more than the intended donation; or where the receipt

of such funds has conditions attached to it that are unduly onerous, costly or incompatible with its objectives; or where the Foundation has first to spend its own money to secure the donation and the assets of the charity would be under undue or inappropriate risk.

The Corporate Sponsorship Policy of the Westport/Weston YMCA, Westport, CT, USA

The Westport/Weston YMCA will seek and accept corporate sponsorship from organisations whose goals and activities are consistent with the mission. The mission states:

The Westport/Weston YMCA enriches the community by developing youth and strengthening families, while promoting healthy lifestyles for adults, emphasising honesty, caring, respect and responsibility in its programs and services.

The Westport /Weston YMCA may

- Use sponsors' names in event literature
- Announce sponsorship during events
- Inform members of sponsorship in member mailings
- Display sponsors names within the YMCA and at YMCA events
- Permit product display and distribution of sales materials at the YMCA and during YMCA events

The Westport / Weston YMCA will not

- Give out its membership list to sponsors
- Promote or endorse specific products
- Guarantee sponsors' 'good name'.

The Westport / Weston YMCA will strive for consistency between sponsorships so that there is equity in what we provide and what sponsors provide.

With thanks to Cathy Onyemelukwe, Director of Development, Westport/Weston YMCA for posting this on the 'Subscribers to fundraising' Internet discussion group.

12 The Internet

The Internet is by now hardly a new tool for fundraisers, but it is certainly an under-utilised one. In equipping a fundraising department with IT equipment, databases and email, it is essential to allow each person access to the Internet so that they can take advantage of its opportunities. Unless it is easily accessed, and information can be downloaded simply the benefits will be lost. If staff have access on their own computers they will pick up Internet skills easily, and begin to incorporate them into their work.

Starting directly with a key fundraising site look at **http://www.fundraising.co.uk.** This is an exceptional service to fundraisers maintained and developed by Howard Lake. It has extensive coverage of all that is new in UK fundraising and a host of features and services. If you have not already visited the site I would recommend that you spend plenty of time browsing through it until you are quite familiar with all it has to offer, and then come back to the site on a regular basis because it is frequently updated. It also has a host of jumping-off points (links) to other organisations and fundraising discussion groups. However, because this site is so comprehensive, a lot of what follows is based on the US experience, to add a further dimension to your Internet investigation.

Email discussion groups

These are what the name implies. Every day every member of a particular group receives an email containing all contributions to the ongoing discussion, which may be, and often are, from all over the world. If you are a novice with discussion groups, below you will find a slightly adapted version of Michael Gilbert's guidelines for the Online Fundraising Mailing List, which are a very good example of the kind of netiquette you should follow. Please read them before you join an email discussion group:

1. Keep commercial speech to a tasteful level that is consistent with the traditional culture of online mailing lists. In other words, commercial messages are welcome if they are an answer to a question, or if the authors have already established themselves as a trusted participant in the list, that is, that they are on the list for more than just a chance to market it.

   If you are in doubt as to the appropriateness of a message, please send it first to the list master.

2. Do not send list management messages (such as messages to unsubscribe) to the list. If someone does send such a message, do not reply! Send such messages to the management address given at the end of each list posting, using the appropriate commands in the body.

3. Be nice.

4. Contribute. Offer your solutions and experience as well as your problems. If you collect answers from people, summarise them and post them back to the list. Your knowledge is a community asset. So, in fact, is your ignorance. Questions are good.

5. Quote or copy only the minimum amount of a preceding message that is necessary to establish context. In other words, don't quote an entire previous message just because this happens automatically with your email software.

It is well worth sampling the groups whose links you can find on www.fundraising.co.uk. (Note that the **http://** is often dropped in giving net addresses, but you still need to use it to access the site). Also note: the words net, Internet or web are used interchangeably below.

If, for example, you are interested in charity law (and you'd better be!) try the discussion group CHARITYLAW-UK by sending an email to listserv@charitychannel.com putting SUBSCRIBE CHARITYLAW-UK in the body of the message and ignore the 'subject' space. Alternatively try the website at **http://CharityChannel.com/Forums**

Starting your own fundraising site

The obvious place to start is everyone else's site. Take time to trawl through a lot of sites. There are huge differences between the quality of the sites, and the methods of making donations and building relationships on-line. You should donate to several sites and see what happens next. The follow-up, or lack of it, will be most revealing and remind you that, notwithstanding the hurly-burly of a modern fundraiser's life, out there sits many a donor just waiting, and waiting, and waiting for your response.

Once you have a good idea of what the competition is up to, join in an online discussion group about site building and development. For example, email **autoshare@gilbert.org** putting 'sub fundraising' in the text body to subscribe to a US based discussion group. It is time it became more European. To unsubscribe email the same address putting 'unsub fundraising' in the body. Remember the US will come online during our afternoons. Do be a passive 'listener' for a while, and do not join in until you understand the netiquette of any group you are joining. There is also a linked website at **http://CharityChannel.com/forums**

Building your website

If you are still interested in building a website, then you should think about registering your domain name as soon as possible, because many .org.uk names have already been taken. Incidentally .org indicates you are a not-for-profit organisation, and .uk indicates you are based in the UK. Once the domain name is added to http://www, or an equivalent, it becomes your URL or Uniform Resource Locator -

i.e. your address on the Internet. Should this be your whole charity name, or a version that people may find easier to locate? For example; the Medical Foundation for the Care of Victims of Torture's address is **www.torturecare.org.uk.** Though no one knows the charity by this name, it is easier to remember and causes far less confusion than some of the alternatives. Don't forget to register your address with as many search engines as possible, and then keep renewing that registration so that you do not slide down the search engine list.

When you have your domain name (from say, **www.register.com** at about $50 per year) you should let your organisation's IT officer become the webmaster and create your site physically according to your needs. It is not impossible to create the site yourself, and you do not really need to know how to write in HTML (hypertext mark-up language), though of course it helps. Try downloading Dreamweaver from Macromedia for a free 30 day trial to see if you are up to it. This is available from www.macromedia.com and has its own tutorials. You could also try Microsoft's rival www.microsoft.com/frontpage/ or one of the free programs. Be warned, however: the process of designing and developing an effective website is specialised and time-consuming: you could toil in your own, or your employer's, time for days and weeks and end up with a less-than-acceptable product.

Setting up a site from scratch can also be done cheaply through **www.seeuthere.com** which has a host of useful services to offer.

Before you tack fundraising pages and a secure credit card donations system onto your existing site, make sure that it is well maintained. That means not only that it should have extensive coverage of your organisation's work and whole area of interest, but that it should be regularly updated. For example, your press releases should be there with extensive links to background information. All the news that is fit to post should be there, checked and updated daily. Look at **www.refugees.org**.

You are beginning a whole new relationship with your supporters, and it is best to get it right from the start. The first people to your page will be your keenest supporters and you do not want to disappoint them.

Attracting people to your site

Ask your IT specialist to place appropriate 'meta tags' onto your site. These are invisible flags that search engines look for as they browse the web in search of the answer to enquiries. If, for example, you are a wildlife charity, one of your tags may be 'wildlife' but you may also have 'birds' or 'environment' plus quite a few others. This means anyone putting these words into a search engine will have your site address (URL) pop up on their screen. This is why, whatever you type into any of the major search engines, amazon.com pops up. Think through these tags carefully and review them on a regular basis; they are very important for the traffic-flow through your site. Another helpful technique in increasing flow is to set up reciprocal links with lots of other sites, however vaguely connected to your business they might be.

Lastly, ensure your supporters and potential supporters know about your site. Put your Internet address prominently on everything you print. Write about your site in all your literature and encourage visitors.

Asking for donations

Direct marketing techniques apply in much the same way to online requests for funds, but we tend to forget all the rules when we set up our 'ask' on our website. Do place say, three revolving pages, with different codes on the return device, so that you can test which idea works best. If you then change the one with the poorest response for a better idea every few months, you will gradually build a more and more effective site.

Secure donations systems are now easy to set up via almost any web hosting service at around $20-40 per month.

Do let people pay by any possible means, or post or fax you their donation. Not everyone is happy with putting their credit card information onto the net. And don't forget to ask for their email address: internet users are already media-savvy, to some degree, and an email response is usually a good indication that you may be able to develop a full online relationship with them.

Look at forms on

http://secure20.client-mail.com/actulink/forms/join/shtml

http://www.christianchildrensfund.org/sponsor_today.stm

http://secure5.nmpinc.com/icrclink/forms/help_icrc.htm

There are, of course, countless UK examples.

Auto responders are a very good idea, as they speed your thanks directly to the donor in record time. You can follow this by another email after, say, a month, to thank them again and to send details of the project their money was spent on, including a link back to your website with pictures, a recorded message, etc. - not forgetting another 'ask'. Re-contacting online donors by the same method they gave in the first place would fit the usual pattern of giving; though it is too early to say just how effective this will prove to be.

Permission fundraising

Let me begin a digression. There will be many of your supporters who would enjoy an online relationship with you; whereby, they receive your newsletters, information and fundraising appeals by email rather than through the post. You cannot, however, assume that anyone who gives you their email address is willing to have this kind of relationship. Likewise the end benefit to you is not yet certain, because Internet fundraising does not have a long enough track record to reveal the answer.

It is, however, likely that there are people who would prefer this and fundraisers have begun moving down this route. The way to judge who is interested is simply to ask them. At the same stage as asking for their email address, or in your first email communication with them, let them know exactly what you intend, and see if they are interested. Do make sure, as always, that your organisation is up to speed on this, or you will merely frustrate your donors as their newsletter fails to arrive and your email system goes down yet again.

This process is also designed to meet the new more stringent data protection requirements. Until there are a number of court cases (UK law is based on precedent for the final interpretation of the law), we will not know quite how this act will be understood. It indicates that charities can respond to people who make donations in the manner which those people would naturally expect.

Today people would expect, if the charity were half-way efficient, to go on a database and be asked for additional gifts, as well as being sent regular information on the charity. They would also expect to be contacted by a range of means, from letters to email to the telephone, and to hear from like-minded organisations; but the small number of people who take a virulent dislike to ever hearing again from someone they have helped seems to have formed the mind-set of our legislature and the Data-Protection Agency.

This means we may need to take extreme pains to inform people what we will do to contact them in future. Permission fundraising is based on this. Certainly through the Internet it is advisable to ask supporters if they would like to receive news and appeals, and to hear from other organisations giving them the chance to opt into the scheme if they wish. If you think that they may like one part of your scheme but dislike another, then you could let them opt out of any part they do not welcome.

In the wider direct marketing picture it may become necessary or advisable to adopt this approach in its entirety. This would mean that all the people whose names and addresses etc. that you have data captured would have learned just how you intend to approach them, and you would not need to ask them to opt into or out of your programme. It would mean, however, that you would have quite large prospecting coupons, and that some of your potential supporters might be put off by your scheme. So far, fundraisers have been rightly cautious of this approach but if they truly believe in their fundraising programmes then why the reluctance to expose them? Perhaps because supporters come to accept the programmes only when they learn more about the organisation and become closer to it. Unfortunately, this process is likely to be stifled by over-zealous interpretation of the Data Protection Acts.

Becoming 'sticky'

Commercial Internet sites that work best are those that have a strong degree of 'stickiness'. This means that a customer stays in the site for a long time, and returns to browse or make repeat purchases. To achieve stickiness, you will need to create interesting content tailored to your supporters' interests and needs. These can be much wider than your organisation's most immediate concerns. Do you have a daily, or hourly, hot news site which gives the latest information in your area of concern. If you are an international organisation, are you linked to **http://babelfish.altavista.com**? Have you spent hours trawling through the net to see what other gems would be of interest to your supporters? The idea is to build less of a site and more of a 'portal' to their life-styles. If they begin to bookmark your site, and use it as their first port of call to the net, you will be a long way down the road to stickiness.

- There is an interesting study on 'e-commerce trust' about brand building online at **http://www.sapient.com/cheskin/**

- Is your trading catalogue on the net? By the way, GTA Technologies offers free shopping cart software on
  http://www.shoppingcarts.cc/netorderform/welcome.asp
- If you have Front Page (authoring software) also look at
  http://www.richmediatech.com/
- Also recommended to me for marketing tips has been
  http://www.marketingtips.com/t.cgi/28198/

Points to consider

Do you use the net auctions to shift donated goods and gifts in kind? Do you take part in net activities that leave a trace to your site? When you join in discussion groups, and so take part in the Internet communities, do you use your site address everywhere you can (without offending netiquette)?

Are your supporters creating dot-com companies? If you do not know the answer to this question, it is time to ask them. This is not only in order to be in pole position for access to their forthcoming fortunes, but to create those links to popular sites, and to achieve real-world networking to other dot-com entrepreneurs. The Harvard Business Review now refers to the online new economy as the economy and the old off-line economy as the old economy. This sea-change in business is being taken very seriously as a permanent step and not a bubble and we, as brilliant fundraisers, should be thinking along the same lines. Even if some parts of the bubble bursts the economy will never revert to what it was and the steep learning curve will continue to throw up winners at the cutting edge and losers who do not adapt. As Andy Grove, CEO Intel, said 'only the paranoid survive'.

Your next job?

To see how effective links are, look at Fundraising UK's links under recruitment. This gives access to a range of sites and opportunities such as: PeopleBank: The Employment Network, where you can register your C.V., the ICFM member recruitment update, Professional Fundraising magazine, Progress Magazine from Charity People (one of many charity recruitment agencies), Third Force News (Scottish Council for Voluntary Organisations for jobs in Scotland), Third Sector magazine, Working for Charity (a charity that runs introductory courses in the voluntary sector) and many more. If you fancy a well paid fundraising job in the USA then there are links to Career Search Online, the Chronicle of Philanthropy, Community Career Center, Idealist Job Search, National Opportunities NOCS, Nonprofit Jobs and the Nonprofit Career Network.

Charity portals

An additional activity to building your own site is to link to one of the charity portals which set up shop for a series of charities on-line. These are US based and I would avoid signing an exclusive agreement with any one of them at present:

- **www.4charity.com**
- **www.greatergood.com**

- **www.charitableway.com**
- **www.igive.com**

You can also start researching similar sites via Puttnam Barbers's 'Resources for fundraising online' at **www.nonprofit.org/npofaq/misc/990804olfr.html.**

Also whilst you are there look at www.nonprofits.org/, and check out research by Alison Schwein at: **www.inhervisions.com/nonprofits/cm-intro.htm**

You might like to consider setting up a 'click and donate' site if you can find a backer, like the following:

- **www.thehungersite.com**
- **www.peaceforall.com**
- **www.ecologyfund.com**
- **www.endcancernow.com**

If you visit these sites and click on a button the sponsors donate funds to the organisation. Note they are .com not .org sites, and hope to build market share through this crazy but wonderful exercise.

Sites of the future

Virtual reality may one day offer donors the possibility of entering the restricted world of disabled people or see hardship through the eyes of a child. Affinity for the suffering of individuals could be literal. The phrase, 'If you were in their place you would think differently,' could be put to the test. In a world where it is easy to insulate yourself from human problems, virtual reality could be profoundly moving, and re-sensitise people whose conscience has been deadened by pervasive materialism.

The Internet currently offers many useful possibilities for fundraisers. It is an immense information resource that can provide you with information on countries, businesses, events, breaking news, etc. but perhaps the most important area is that of research into individuals and their backgrounds, whether these are celebrities or business people. To do this simply feed in the person's name (use 'exact match' where you have the option, e.g. on Yahoo's 'advanced search') to one of the search engines and see what comes up:

AltaVista	**http://www.digital.altavista.com**
Excite	**http://www.excite.com**
Infoseek	**http://www.infoseek.com**
Hotbot	**http://www.hotbot.com**
Yahoo	**http://www.yahoo.com**

This information is extremely useful in big gift fundraising, or for quickly checking the background of someone you are about to meet and have not had time to research thoroughly. It is well worthwhile spending at least an hour per week familiarising yourself with the possibilities.

The association of Professional Researchers for Advancement (US) has a mission statement and donor bill of rights at
http://weber.u.washington.edu/~diamb/apra/APRA.html
There are links to several prospect research sites on
www.geocities.com/baja/cliffs/8433/index.htm
Auctions are now established on the net. If you wish to auction items look at:

www.pages.ebay.com/charity/

www.etapestry.com

www.charitableway.com

www.ten97.com

The Internet also provides a powerful tool to link to other fundraisers around the world. If you are already connected to an email system you will appreciate the ease of communication that it affords.

Within international organisations, email provides a very rapid and straightforward way to communicate across time zones and physical distance. Given a person's email address, you can send messages to them wherever their computer is located. As email can also be sent and received via laptop computers, this can often be wherever their laptop happens to be in the world. If, for example, you are visiting alumni prospects in Seoul and need information on a person or company in bulk, then this can be taken from a colleague's computer files in Edinburgh and enclosed with the reply to your email message directly to your laptop, where you can read on screen or print out or update the information.

Given the nine hour time difference, your message can be sent from, say, your hotel room in the evening at 21.00 hrs, when it will be 13.00 hrs in your office in Edinburgh. That gives a whole afternoon for information to be compiled, which you can pick up first thing in the morning before you start work the next day.

If you are working for an organisation where there are several fundraisers in the country or world-wide, they can be linked by email in a discussion or information forum which people can add to at an appropriate time for them.

Email appeals

Much vaunted as the next way to raise huge sums on the Internet, email appeals appear to have faltered as a mass medium for recruitment. Emailing thousands of people, who have not given you their email address, with the same appeal is frowned upon. Called 'spamming' it is more likely to invoke an angry response with your email system being brought down by the surge of irate replies than to generate huge sums. Yet thoughtful email appeals on current disasters to likely prospects should stand the same chance as direct mail appeals. Much more likely to succeed are, of course, appeals to existing supporters.

To make this work you must not forget all your direct marketing and go back to a simple 'ask' without explanation but integrate your programme work into the appeal and always have a real reason for asking at that time and a note of urgency coupled with a suggested amount and how the money will be spent.

More interesting ideas involve treasure hunts through the net, virtual world tour concerts where the donor can hear their favourite groups play just for them, quizzes and auctions. You should also consider using CD-ROM business cards. These ingenious cards are CDs the size of business cards, and not only can they display words, music and video clips, they can also provide a link directly to your website. The quality is excellent and they provide an easy way to put across your message and let potential donors see your work. The Medical Foundation has used them successfully in its capital appeal with downloadable or emailable donations forms.

To add slight note of caution for anyone who thinks they will attract a million new donors and charm a fortune from their pockets. There is some research on: **http://www.craveronline.com** which shows that though 50 million Americans over 18 have Internet access, and currently give their time or money to good causes, most have never visited the website of a charity, and only 3.5 million say they have given online.

Foundations, trusts and companies on the web

There are quite a few specialist fundraising sites that offer lists of trusts and foundations. Indeed, most large trusts now have their own site and online applications for funds are becoming common. Online rejections may, however, not be far behind!

Trusts vary greatly in their use of the net. The basic site will have a short history of the trust, along with their grant-making objectives and procedures. Many, however, go a long way beyond this in being able to respond online to email queries, and in attempting to create online communities and satisfy research needs in their areas. Much grant-making produces research and reports which are placed on the net to ensure wide, cheap and rapid dissemination for which the net is an ideal medium.

Maintaining this kind of informative and interactive site is, however, costly and time consuming. Many charitable trusts cannot afford this expense and, of course, many are quite shy and retiring, not wishing their largesse to be readily accessible to a wide audience. These trusts often prefer to give secretly, away from the public gaze, sometimes because they are afraid of being over run with requests they cannot meet or even service.

Do look at the links to US foundations on **www.fdncenter.org** which is an interesting site in its own right. The Foundation Centre provides links to hundreds of grantmaker sites and even provides 'folders' for grant making organisations to set up shop on the web. This is a simple and effective service which quickly puts their information in front of a wide audience. Their main list of foundations can be queried by subject and geographical location, so that you can build up appropriate lists of funders.

For a look at US Foundations' sites check:

Ford Foundation	**http://www.fordfound.org**
Soros Foundation	**http://www.soros.org**
The Heinz Endowments	**http://www.heinz.org**
The Bell Atlantic Foundation	**http://www.bellatlanticfoundation.com**

These are a variety of the better sites of the larger US foundations. Remember that US foundations, though larger than UK charitable trusts by a factor of 10, usually give within the US within their own state. The larger foundations will sometimes not entertain requests for small amounts of money, but will only give to serious players whose work is completely within their current objectives. As mentioned elsewhere, UK charitable trusts are not equivalent to the US 501c3 foundations, and it is often easier to set up a 501c3 in the states to receive donations or to use CAF America's service. This means that the donor can reclaim the tax paid under the Internal Revenue Service (IRS) rules. To do this from a donation to a UK charity, the charity would need to sign a legal document showing how they were equivalent to a 501c3 – and many are not.

Similarly, US companies are using the Internet for a huge variety of purposes from selling their goods, to buying their components, as well as selling or buying services and putting out corporate information such as their Annual Report and Accounts and details of their directors.

US companies tend to be much more philanthropic than their UK counterparts, and often have a very focused programme of grant making, as well as a lot of gifts-in-kind, including secondments, which can be of substantial help to organisations. Companies frequently like to demonstrate their giving, support for the community and public spirit on their sites. The larger companies have separate foundations with their own Internet presence. Check:

- The Foundation Centre's corporate grantmakers on
  http://fdncenter.org/grantmaker/corp.html
- And the CAF CCInet on
  http://www.charitynet.org/CCInet/frames/fpages.html
  Also try:
- Hewlett Packard   **http://webcenter.hp.com/grants/index.html**
- Apple Computer   **http://www.apple.com/education/**
- Ben & Jerry's   **http://www.benjerry.com/foundation/index.html**
- Intel   **http://www.intel.com/intel/community/**
- Coca-Cola   **http://www.cocacola.com/co/scholars/index.html**

Virtual foundations

Of course, the future is happily unpredictable and in time your whole organisation may be online like the Virtual Foundation: **http://www.virtualfoundation.org/**

In general

The Internet is now part and parcel of every professional fundraiser's life. Whatever aspect of fundraising you are concerned with, there are opportunities out there to be exploited and information to be utilised.

My advice is to start by spending at least an hour each week going through site after site, joining discussion groups, using search engines, making donations and seeking information. Once you have a thorough grounding in the possibilities, the ground will have undoubtedly moved and you will need to keep up with developments. You can do this through a regular visit to Fundraising UK's site and by joining a least one discussion group.

The Internet is littered with dead sites that no one seems to maintain. If you are going to set up a site and use it to attract new donors or communicate with existing donors, make sure that it is kept up-to-date. For this to happen, control over the information should be in the hands of those with an interest in seeing it is updated regularly. Often this will include at least one member of the fundraising team. It is easy to forget to take information about events off the site after they have happened, or not to mention the result in your news area. Do put up plenty of email addresses for your staff. Let your supporters communicate directly with the right staff; this is becoming much more important as the huge increase in mobile phones accelerates phone usage. As people becoming increasingly used to making phone calls to sort out everyday matters, and access services such as banking, a key problem in charities is how to deal with the mass of incoming calls. Diverting as many of these on to email allows staff to deal with them as and when they have the time, and gives time for the response to be planned.

Do not think of yourself in a narrow category. Try to become the first site of the day for your supporters, and think through their related sets of issues. This is not specifically about your organisation; it is about creating an information resource your supporters will benefit from and, therefore, return to over and over again. Their concerns will be much wider than your organisation's immediate remit and catering for those concerns in an imaginative way can bring stunning results. If you look again at refugees.com you will see this in action, with their world-wide information on human rights giving a strong reason to come back to the site over and over again.

As ever with cutting edge technology there will be a few winners whose imagination puts them ahead of the game - make sure you are one of them.

13 Future Developments

Now we have lost our fear of using credit cards on the Internet (thank you, amazon.com) and are busily buying all manner of goods, including our shopping from Tesco, several possibilities have been opened up. One is that we can all shop in the comfort of our own front rooms, by the convenience of interactive digital TV. All we will need to do is flip to the shopping channels, select our goods, and feed in our credit card number for rapid delivery. That is, if we can tear ourselves away for long enough from the interactive game shows, where we can win a million pounds, or the interactive soaps, where our choice (expressed by digital voting) will determine who marries whom and what happens next.

This will also revolutionise charity giving. If you a see a dreadful situation on TV, you will be able to help straight away by sending a credit card donation, that minute, to an appropriate charity, and probably by the end of the programme see help arrive with your name or company logo plastered all over it. If you are feeling charitable at the end of the month, (shortly after pay day), you will be able to search through a series of charity commercials, and donate to whoever you like, instantly, effortlessly, and with the full knowledge of millions of other viewers, if you so wish.

Most people will have already given their charity a copy of their credit card details, and will merely signal the amount of their latest donation much as we buy books through Amazon's one-click purchase scheme. There will also be charity Internet sites that act as brokers (rather than portals to charity sites) for a range of charities. Then the monthly or annual giving by an individual or family will be a question of filling up the 'shopping cart' with donations, and one-clicking to send the money. More information and ideas about this are in the chapter on Internet fundraising. The organisations that benefit from this will be those that have mastered the art of projecting their concerns on television. Those that fail will be those that do not have the resources or the imagination.

Making television work for charities

Currently, not many organisations can make television work for them, and very few are even experimenting with moving images and concepts. Many others have had their fingers burnt by allowing advertising agencies to overrule their common sense. No one would today allow an agency to place an advertisement in a newspaper without a coupon, (though some agencies still try) but when it comes to television we are no longer on safe ground. We may feel sure that the commercial should have had a telephone number on it all the way through, and a voice saying 'Call the number right now', but we do not like to say so. Somehow it gets tacked, reluctantly, on the end, (not to spoil the creative effort), and our press advertising is supposed to benefit mysteriously from the prestige of our charity being seen on TV.

Just as fundraisers have learnt to control advertising agencies over press work, we will need to learn the tricks of our trade over TV commercials, and insist on the most effective direct response methods being used, with no concessions to raising the profile or winning awards. If the commercial works in raising funds, it will win those awards anyway.

Interacting with television

More importantly, fully interactive television has begun, and charities need to master the necessary techniques at speed. As with the Internet success, this will be about market share and market share depends on building a strong brand image with moving brand values. As we have seen, even this is not good enough on its own, and success demands a large amount of funds to be spent on promotion of the brand, brilliant PR to capture the media, or word of mouth from a really effective use of the media. And the media will not be TV advertising by another name. The ability to mix together web images and TV means we can, for example, have a virtual fashion show with live presenters. Individuals could take the part of the fashion models using avatars to walk down the catwalk. To make money, designer patterns could be downloaded to your home computer (for a donation), clothing purchase delivered by bike anywhere in a few hours, access to the programme could be limited, fashion houses could pay to take part, etc. Here the etceteras are limitless, but they do depend on understanding a very complex interaction - albeit one we will all soon no doubt be living with. Simple appeals for funds could link a large amount of information with a TV appeal, but this information could be selected by the viewer and available on screen as they watch. This could consist of information about the problem, your organisation and how the appeal is going, minute by minute. In the space between programmes, instead of watching advertising, the viewer could revert to your website but my guess is it would need to be radically improved, carrying at least real-time footage of current developments.

Survival of the fittest

When it starts for real, the first few charities to become established will build up a learning curve that will be very hard to catch. Mistakes will be very costly, and the barriers to entry of new participants will be high. Competition between organisations with the same theme will be cut-throat, as huge amounts of money will flow to those which are successful: and that could impoverish those which are not. Good, almost iconographic, concepts will become the hallmark of certain charities. If Friends of the Earth were to use birds as their theme, how would that affect the RSPB?

Direct Response Television (DRTV)

This has proved its worth for a number of charities, though it tends to work best for the big name organisations. Already, there is a lot of practical information for those wishing to advertise on television and ask for a response through the telephone. This has come from tests and trials in the UK and USA for home shopping and for charities. Assuming that you are seeking a direct response from a telephone number placed on the screen during your commercial, to be at all successful you will need an agency to handle the response. There are several good agencies now with relevant experience. British Telecom itself has agency facilities, and if you are going to put on a telethon or a spectacular where the response will be huge, you must discuss it with them beforehand, as thousands of calls can be generated in a very short period.

The secret of DRTV

The secret of successful direct response commercials is your ability to handle the volume of calls generated. For years many more calls were lost than received, as lines jammed, and people could not get through. Well-equipped agencies can capture a much higher percentage of calls than ever before, transforming events. In some regions, DRTV accounts for 20% of TV advertisements, and that figure is growing rapidly. A good agency will record all call details carefully and switch to a recorded service if calls begin to go over their capacity.

Call capture is the name of the game. You may wish just for an automated service, but live operators can check details and begin to build a relationship. Talk through their scripts very carefully and ask people outside the organisation to let you know what they would think of such responses. Call capture must be quick, efficient and very polite. Your agency will need to know if your target is money or list building, what kind of people are likely to call, what questions they might ask, and how many calls that could be generated. This is very difficult to estimate the first time around.

One BBC's Children in Need programme resulted in 200,000 calls via Local 0345 numbers (charged at local rate). These were handled by 1,750 operators in over 50 centres. It successfully raised £17M. Incidentally, the call rates are changing, and you will need to select the appropriate rate for your situation, which may well not be Freephone. You must arrange with British Telecom how these calls will be charged and paid for. The options range from Freephone 0800 to premium lines on which the caller pays the maximum rate for the call.

For most fundraisers, that sort of mass appeal is an unlikely occurrence, (coming perhaps once in a lifetime), and you will have to buy your time on television instead. This is the big stumbling block, as it is very expensive, but DRTV is said to work best outside peak times and to a selected audience. That is why Cable and Satellite networks attract a lot of DRTV. You will still need to keep the budget low, and it is certainly not necessary to have a lavish creative spend. In fact, it is probably counter-productive. You will need to discover which channels your target audience watch, and when. Test out your ideas as cheaply as possible, i.e. on as small a scale as possible. You will also need to let your audience relate to you simply and emotively, so beware of pressure from your agency to adopt an intellectual or complex approach.

A classic campaign

You may well remember the NSPCC 'Ellie' campaign. If you can obtain a copy, view it several times. Then look at a typical commercial break and at other DRTV ads. Only when you have fully understood the difference between commercial advertising and successful DRTV appeals should you begin to think about using this medium. If, in the eyes of the general public, your charity answers a real need, you're in a position to create a successful TV appeal. If, however, you feel you cannot make the public share your perception of the importance of your organisation's work, perhaps a TV appeal will not meet your charity's needs. And if you do not feel that your charity's work is very important, perhaps you should change your job. In any case, you will have to think about the appeal commercial from the point of view of your donors. Why do they give to you? What do they see in their mind's eye when they make out a cheque to you?

Think 'Timing for TV'

Timing is very important. It is a factor you probably have not needed to think about in other fundraising media. You will need as long as it takes to put over your message and bring people to act. Any longer and people will turn off. It is worth experimenting with a 30 second commercial at the start of a break and 10 seconds at the end - for those who did not have their pens handy. Thinking in seconds can also improve the rest of your fundraising work. If you can't say it on the back of a bookmark you need a better copywriter. (But a great copywriter holding the reader for a full page will bring amazing results!)

People are not going to stand up and phone you unless you tell them to very clearly. Use a strong call to action - 'Phone us now... Pick up the phone and call now. Please don't wait to call... We are waiting for your call now...'. Part of that clarity is having the phone number legible. It is recommended that it is at least two inches high and in the centre, middle or centre bottom of the screen, in a colour that will stand out from the screen, and preferably steady, not flashing. An easily remembered number helps a lot.

It is always useful to signal clearly that this advertisement will ask for a response. Do not surprise your audience. Whilst they are getting over the shock, the time for action will have passed. Let them feel they want to respond, not that they are being pushed into calling you. As in all response devices, let the viewer know just how much you are asking for and let them know what you will do with this sum if at all possible. Remember that you are really after repeat business, rather than the maximum amount of money on the night. The number of people who have made a donation is more important than the total amount. If you are going to work with your favourite advertising agency, choose the specialist teams who understand direct mail. Never go for prestige advertising. It will cost you a great deal for very little response.

Responding to demographic trends

Age may play an important part, as younger professionals give to their causes through TV and older viewers stay with press ads and direct mail. This means that charities have to keep a very careful check on their supporters' age profile, to avoid being wiped out as the age of those using TV to give rises inexorably. Conversely, fundraisers may need to segment their appeals with care. Do you advertise for legacies on TV, to get into the Wills of young professionals, or do you advertise in the press to reach the older generation? Can you afford to do both? We could be entering a very uncertain era, where the old adage of 'test, test and test again' becomes the most important touchstone of our efforts.

Much more importantly, demographic changes are arguably the largest current external challenge to fundraisers. Those people now in their sixties, seventies and eighties are said to give out of duty. Traditionally they gave relatively small amounts (a heritage of wartime prudence?) but on a consistent basis, to a select few charities. They also keep on giving, almost obstinately, unless the charity really upsets them. Fundraisers relying on these people - and most charities' typical donor has been an elderly lady - are now faced with a wake-up call of alarming proportions. The next generational cohort of donors are the baby boomers and we are selfish, fickle and demanding. Baby boomers are numerous and have lots of money, which they give in large amounts. They cannot see the point in making a five pound donation which will be used up in processing charges. They are more likely to give £50, but they won't give again unless they are satisfied with their interaction with the charity. Boomers won't put up with inefficiency, or charities that are not addressing their concerns. There is no giving from duty or loyalty. They will move to the next charity as soon as they perceive a new problem that needs solving, and they will move on if the charity doesn't seem to be sorting the problem out pronto.

Well educated and politically aware, boomers are reached through leaflets in magazines, direct mail and all new media. Boomers expect charity literature to be professionally written, and well presented. Poor quality paper and badly printed photographs will not say economy and careful use of funds to them. It will say 'We are hopelessly unprofessional in everything we do and we will waste your donation on poor quality trash'. It costs much more to recruit a boomer, and it may take two years before it becomes profitable, but the profit will be considerable if you can retain their interest. They are living longer, and believe in spending their parents' money, which is now coming down to them in the form of houses they do not need. The effect of the lack of adequate pension care for their long healthy old age is likely to be met as much by continued economic activity as by frugality (not a boomer characteristic). Boomer children, if they have any expectations, are going to be disappointed, as boomers like to spend (on themselves) and party (lifestyle is crucial for them).

Boomers need to be nurtured and brought into the work of the charity, in the same way they buy into commercial goods. The brand name is one they have to be happy seeing on their coffee table. What is the lifestyle of a donor to Amnesty International, to Oxfam, to the British Heart Foundation, to UNICEF, to Save the Children, etc.? Which will boomers support? Re-branding is essential right now for many charities who are blindly ploughing on in the face of falling incomes. Boomers want to know just what their money is buying, and expect to be thanked quickly and offered the opportunity to see over the work. Once they feel a part of the organisation boomers will give large sums. At this stage they like to meet celebrities. The 'me' generation expects to have its rewards.

Think also about the fact that women are working en masse, and have developed new life styles that do not resemble those of charities 'little old lady' donors. We need a completely new approach to capture and hold their interest. In showing supporters around the Medical Foundation (we have five Open Days per year) I am always struck by the questions men ask about numbers of clients, total income of the organisation and the number of staff. Women on the other hand ask about the interaction between clients and clinical staff. Like all generalities, if observations like this are to be used in say, segmented appeals to donors, then they need careful testing.

Beyond the boomers are their dot-com Thatcherite children that don't give anything away, and generation X'ers who have absolutely nothing to give anyway. However, the picture is not entirely bleak, and every cohort has passions and can be reached, but churning out the same old appeals just will not work. There are now strong generational differences at play and we need to respond to them.

These are laid out in Judith Nichol's fascinating book *Global Demographics – Fundraising for a New World* in which she explores the giving patterns of each of these cohorts in detail.

Ethnic minorities

The other demographic quality of the UK is its ethnic mix. In my experience, charities do not have a particularly good track record of promoting staff from ethnic minorities (in particular black and Asian staff) to middle or senior management positions. Neither have they attracted donations from ethnic minorities. These donations will, of course, go more often to needy minority projects. Indeed, as minority populations establish themselves in a new country, profits will be ploughed back into building businesses, and salaries into helping other members of the family survive and develop. We are, however, now at a time when mature minority populations have the ability to make both ordinary gifts and very large donations, but with some notable exceptions this is not taking place.

I have no magic formula to address this, but I suspect that this problem will only be solved when charities promote ethnic minority staff with ease, and their experience begins to permeate the literature, outlook and branding of the charity. I do not think this is so much likely to lead to fundraising campaigns aimed at ethnic minorities, as that it will capture the individual who is ready to give, but would otherwise be put off by the way the charity promotes itself. This is all to do with subtle indicators of a lack of inclusion and understanding, rather than (except in some cases) a completely naff approach.

Bar-coding

As a fundraiser, I am deeply fascinated by supermarkets' checkout tills, with such huge amounts of money passing through such a small space so quickly.

- Why not introduce your organisation's leaflet next to all those tills, with a simple bold appeal and a barcode so that donations can be rung up? £5 to 'Save the Snails' would appear on your grocery bill alongside your cabbage, etc., and at the end of the month the chain of stores would pay a huge sum into your organisation's bank account.

- Of course, barcodes have many uses. Your organisation's membership card could have a barcode on it so that your members, too, could give £5 every time they shopped; and when they took part in your AGM they could be booked in, out, and vote, all by means of their card. They could also use the card to pay reduced fees on a large range of products. It might even reduce your membership drop-out rate considerably.

- Barcodes could also reduce your processing time and cost for appeals. Next to each address on the coupon a barcode could be read, instead of the membership number being entered or the whole name and address being typed into your database.

The Post Office should not be far behind in being able to deliver letters by means of barcodes. This would mean much greater accuracy for deliveries and for your database memory.

Barcode readers are relatively inexpensive and their speed and accuracy are very high. The only current limitation on their use is your imagination. Eventually, they will be used by all charities - but you can steal a march on them and move up the learning curve by investing in the technology now.

Psychographics

An interesting development in targeted direct mail has been submerged in the direct mail recession, but can be of great interest to fundraisers looking to broaden the membership of their organisations.

Different people respond to different approaches

Psychographics assumes that people have a range of different psychological views of the world and different ways of relating to it, and so need approaching in a way that corresponds to their individual psychology. For example, if you are raising funds for sheltered accommodation for elderly people, you might be using mailing lists which include those who are very patriotic, those who are very international, those who are very self-centred, and those who are altruistic. Each of these people will react differently to the emphasis in your message, so it is prudent to put your message in language that the people will take in.

Identifying the differences ...

In order to tell which people on your mailing list fall into which categories, a free offer is often used. This is on the lines of 'If you send for more information you will receive a free gift. Kindly tick the box for the gift you require.' The gifts could be tea-towels with the flag of your country, or a map of the world, a scarf, or a book-token sent on their behalf to a friend. Obviously, this will not be a foolproof system, and you can, no doubt, find better and more appropriate examples of gifts than mine.

... and the advantages of knowing about them

This exercise will, however, enable you to approach your audience with a much better chance of speaking their language. It will also solve several problems for you. For example, should you mention that a large proportion of the people you will be helping are ex-servicemen, or do you feature the multi-racial aspect of your work, or do you emphasise that the donor's name will appear on a plaque on the wall of the building, or that a tree will be planted for every donation given?

This technique takes some time and trouble to think through and get right, but it is especially useful if you are raising a limited amount of large donations. The cost of issuing four different letters could be easily repaid. It also pays to tailor your letter in a similar way to different mailing lists, all of them addressing different psychologies. (And shouldn't you be writing rather different appeal letters to men and women, to old and young supporters?)

Of course, your psychographics cannot just stop at the acquisition stage. It is equally important to follow this through by recognising people's differences in the rest of your communications. With high-value donors this can be very rewarding over their lifetime with you.

Creative ideas

I am probably at my happiest thinking through a simple but promising variation on an old fundraising idea. It continues to amaze me that this is possible but each year new ideas continue to present themselves.

For example, as I write, the Medical Foundation for the Care of Victims of Torture is starting a charity auction of 'characters'. Several best selling authors have agreed that we will auction the name of one of the characters in their next book. So, if I win the bidding, a character in their book will be called 'John Baguley'. Simple but promising and hopefully it will be a good fundraiser. This is one of five auctions the charity is running in a twelve month period. Two of the others deserve a mention for their ingenuity. One was an auction of the manikins that painters use to help draw the proportions of human figures. Well known artists and celebrities were sent plain wooden manikins and asked to paint or decorate them. Many responded with exquisite designs which were sold at Waterstone's huge bookshop in Piccadilly, some fetching surprisingly high prices. The Foundation was Waterstone's charity of the year. The other, currently in preparation, is an auction of architect's models to be held at the RIBA. The President of the RIBA is also Chair of the Foundation's capital appeal, and the Managing Director of the Richard Rogers Partnership. Here the ideas on their own were not quite enough, but the long-term building of bridges and networks has begun to serve the charity well.

i-events and the me-generation

Events have, over the past few years, become the neglected child of our fundraising departments. Once we sang and swayed together during huge Wembley benefit concerts, laughed hysterically at Amnesty's Secret Policeman's Ball, or trudged footsore and weary from Land's End to John O'Groats. Today, so many organisations have had their fingers burnt attempting to create larger and larger events that directors and trustees are rightly loath to take on the risks involved. And perhaps we too have changed. We no longer march in the numbers we did or join causes with the same enthusiasm. The environmental and human rights organisations struggle to keep their numbers up and only the largest charities are making headway in developing their income.

Partly, I suspect, this is the changeover in wealth, described above, from charities' traditional supporters (the dutiful old) to the newly rich baby-boomers (the me-generation) who are more fickle and demanding, and, as they age, less and less likely to leave home for a good cause.

The canny fundraisers I know are now grooming their events for a new role. Far from their days of fame and fortune, celebrated and admired in the national media, their new role is almost invisible to the outsider. Less prime time television than a few discrete photos in Hello and more likely an exclusive gathering in Belgravia than mass participation at Wembley. Perhaps more glamorous now, attired in Farhi and Prada, the neglected child is coming of age as a sophisticated accomplice of her elder sister, the big gift fundraiser. These are the i-events which are tailored to suit small groups of people. Like your personal computer they can be arranged almost to an individual's taste.

Typical of this approach has been the Medical Foundation's evenings of Words and Music for no more than sixty people at a time, in supporters' own homes such as exclusive mews cottages or spacious Hampstead houses. The evenings are free and the entertainment superb. Invitations are sent to carefully selected supporters who are encouraged to bring their friends. The invitee is famous, often one of the charity's patrons like John McCarthy, and the entertainment is provided by a mix of celebrities, authors, actresses, playwrights, etc. reading from works relevant to the organisation. These could be, for example, poems or prison writings on freedom and there may be music from artists in exile or songs by refugees. Most importantly, all themes are strongly in tune with the charity's ethos. Finally the organisation's director, Helen Bamber OBE (fast becoming a celebrity in her own right), will talk directly and movingly about her work and ask for covenants or pledges. At the end of the evening a time for light refreshment allows people to mix and mingle.

Surprisingly, each evening raises well over ten thousand pounds. Perhaps a third of this comes from those who cannot attend (but may want to remain on the invitation list). The evening is exclusive and the gathering small enough for the supporters to talk with the celebrities but it is also deeply emotional, not shying away from the organisation's subject matter. The choice of writing and song, its delivery and the final pitch for funds is carefully orchestrated to elicit the strongest response in terms of awareness and donations.

These evenings are, however, only a part of the much longer term programme that brings in affluent supporters (and new celebrities) and binds them to the organisation. Even with larger ticket events, such as evenings at the Piccadilly Theatre with Michael Palin and Seamus Heaney (sponsored by Waterstone's), the most profitable part of the event will, in time, prove to be the after show drinks where a few supporters have the chance to meet the stars and network.

The keynotes then of this sea-change in strategy are that events, whilst profitable in themselves, are becoming devoted to servicing big-gift fundraising. All those individuals developed through the small but glamorous evenings will, at the right time, and for the right reason, be approached for a major contribution, often amounting to tens or hundreds of thousands of pounds. i-events are also smaller and more exclusive. Baby-boomers do consider what they receive in return for their generosity. They are not purely philanthropic, and charities must provide unique events for them. If they are to compete in this market this means access to celebrities or occasions that the supporter would not normally encounter. However, it should be recognised that these events are not jollies, but rather meaningful and thought-provoking gatherings imbued with the charity's values and serving its mission. At the end of each event the staff and volunteers should be brought together to discuss all the individual supporters they have talked to. In this way you can develop useful insights into your key supporters' thoughts about the charity. Your supporters will believe that you have an institution memory. If they have spoken to one of your staff about a problem, idea or thought they have, they will expect you as an organisation to remember it. This exercise is invaluable for your future fundraising, but do ensure that if you take notes, they do not conflict with the Data Protection Act. i-events are lifestyle events, and should be just as professionally conducted as the organisation conducts its charitable work. Draughty church halls and badly-printed invitations represent carelessness and poor organisational ability, not thrift, to your professional supporters.

On the subject of professional supporters, a sea-change is happening in their charitable involvement. As work becomes increasingly a twenty-four hour occupation people prefer to associate with someone in the their profession rather than someone from their locality. Local groups are being replaced by professional groups. Today's equivalent of The Oxford Committee for Famine Relief would be The Lawyers Action Group for Refugees. This means thinking in terms of profession not locality when you plan events. For example, organising sponsored events for professions (with firms competing against each other), rather than with local groups, will allow you access to those at the top of those professions. Quality not quantity is the new hallmark.

Even concerts are becoming smaller and more exclusive. Can your star perform for a private party? If so, you will make more money in the long run and influence more people with far less risk than if you hire a major venue. In moving to this kind of event it is important that you are using the right celebrity. Do they know and understand your organisation? Are they really advocates for you? Is their image the right one for your organisation? Usually ticket prices for concerts reflect the star's going rate, because people come to see the performer and will not pay extra because it is a charity performance. In exclusive concerts with the right celebrities and venue the sky is the limit. Careful research into your supporters is absolutely vital in pitching these events. If you have not already carried out some demographic research into the wealth of your supporters, I will wager they are far wealthier than you suspect; and in the right circumstances will make larger donations than you dreamt possible.

Supplementing this research with standing networks of well-matched supporters (often from the same profession) can make all the difference when selling tickets. Committees align today's need to network with the fundraiser's need to shift high-price tickets to stunning events. Fashion shows and opera seats, concerts and dinners all need committees to replace the impersonal mail-out with the personal touch. Face-to-face fundraising and judicious use of the phone can work wonders in selling those £500 boxes and £150 seats. Committee fundraising is enjoyable and turns the event into a social gathering with people talking, making connections and becoming ever closer to your charity. So, bring back the committee!

Auctions are another form of event ripe for the individual treatment. Minor celebrity cast-offs will not make the grade. To attract and cultivate your future major donors you need significant gifts from first-rate artists. Naturally, the people who will pay nearest to the market price will be the people who already collect those artists' works. To attract them, consider a more up-market venue, a professional auctioneer and personal invitations. Can you also obtain help from the artists' galleries? Consider too the poor artist afraid his market value will be brought down by charity prices. Should you consider a hybrid auction and sale with 33.3% of the sale price going to the artist?

So, welcoming and integrating the neglected child back into the family means a change in the planning of each event, and a strategy which sets events as a key part of the fundraising mix, not an isolated, risky venture half-justified by a possible rise in public profile. i-events are a powerful trend with plentiful long-term profit.

Changes in the law

In common with many other Western governments, our current government has, within limits, continued to pursue the previous government's policy of state withdrawal from expenditure on the provision of social services, and has looked for a parallel, though not equivalent, strengthening of the work of the voluntary sector.

As part of that strengthening, it has been made progressively easier for charities to claim back the tax that donors have paid on various donations. Now by the donor making a simple declaration, all tax paid on the donation can be reclaimed by the charity.

Other changes are to be expected, and a careful eye needs to be kept on such government moves in each budget. This is professionally undertaken by the ICFM and NCVO on behalf of philanthropic organisations, but it is essential for all fundraisers to know exactly how the law is interpreted on each fundraising activity, and to keep abreast of all new developments. Fundraisers and finance officers need to be particularly vigilant over VAT, which is being collected with almost religious zeal from almost every possible charitable transaction.

The Charities Act 1992

The Charities Act 1992 is particularly far-reaching, and you should be familiar with its implications. It covers three areas of fundraising:

- the employment of fundraising agents and agencies

- the reporting of financial details to the Charity Commission

- the control of public charitable collections (basically door-to-door and flag day collections).

The idea is to protect the public from fraud as far as possible, to make charities more accountable, and to regulate the growing number of collections. It is stressed that, "the Government fully supports responsible fundraising for good charitable causes". Some controls are, however, felt to be essential. A balance is therefore to be struck between enabling and regulating charitable fundraising.

Interestingly, this legislation was held up whilst the Deregulation Task Force's views were being formed. This was the eighth Deregulation Task Force, set up in September 1993, to look specifically at charities and voluntary organisations, (the other seven having been business Task Forces). The current proposals for legislation take into account discussions between the Home Office and the Task Force.

Proposed legislation

We should note, on the positive side, that proposals for legislation increasingly talk about charities and 'organisations with philanthropic purposes,' in the same breath. However, this is not always followed up in the same spirit in subsequent legislation.

For example, such non-charitable but philanthropic organisations will be disadvantaged, as the granting of national exemptions from the requirement for local authority permission to hold street collection passed from the Home Office to the Charity Commissioners, (who will only deal with registered charities). Consequently, such organisations will need to apply for permission to every local authority in whose area they wish to collect. This will greatly add to the burden of work by both NGOs and local authorities, and make it exceedingly difficult to co-ordinate collections across the country effectively - if, indeed, this will still be possible. The costs of such collections will thus be greatly increased.

In drafting new legislation, the Government has, however, also sought the advice of charities, appropriate individuals and organisations through documents such as the consultation document issued by the Home Office Voluntary Service Unit on public charitable collections (Part II of the 1992 Act). This is part of an ongoing consultation process that is being carried out as this significant piece of legislation is shaped and put into practice. The ICFM has followed this closely and represented the interests of professional fundraisers, informing them as developments have taken place.

Predicting the future

Unfortunately this is rarely possible with any degree of certainty, but the rapidly changing external environment in which we work makes it essential for us to keep a watchful eye on trends in fundraising. Ensure that you innovate faster than your external environment changes.

14 Fundraising in Other Countries

In business it is often the second company to move into a new field which maximises its income, rather than the initial trailblazer, but it is rarely the last few to change who benefit. One area that has quietly been gathering steam is fundraising outside the West, particularly in the Asia Pacific countries. The next chapter looks at overseas fundraising, and identifies some interesting possibilities.

The key source of overseas funds for work in the UK is the EU, which is dealt with in Chapter 6. Technically, there are a variety of overseas foundations which could support projects in the UK. *The International Foundation Directory* (Europa Publications) gives a good flavour of what is available, as does the *Directory of Organisations concerned with Peace and Security* (published by the Directory of Social Change). There is also a huge directory of American foundations called *The Foundation Directory*, published by The Foundation Centre, New York, which lists US Foundations. It is simpler to check their website at **http://www.fdncenter.org** but you should not take the trouble unless you have exhausted all the possible UK sources of funds, and feel that your work is foundation-friendly, and you have someone knowledgeable to undertake the spadework for you.

It is also quicker to check in *US Foundation Support in Europe* (By Ruth Lauer & Steve England, published by the Directory of Social Change) or to read *The Directory of International Funding Organisations* (published by CAF). If you do need to look further, the Charities Aid Foundation has a collection of US Foundation literature at its London Offices. If you work for an international organisation with branches or projects overseas, you may be well placed to tap not only the UK market, but also foundations and organisations in other countries, to fund those branches or projects. In many instances, it may be more effective for you to assist them to submit the final application themselves. For example, your Eastern European branch in Hungary may be totally inexperienced in approaching foundations, and yet the local Soros Foundation may wish to fund just the kind of work that they undertake.

For applications involving more than one country, however, it may be preferable for you to approach their offices in London or New York. However, the application will succeed, more usually, if you assist your local branch to develop the skills necessary to place a successful application, carry out the work, evaluate it, and report back on progress in meeting objectives. Many international organisations either have branches in other countries that are dependent on them for financial support, or fund projects in other countries, never suspecting that they may well be able to raise their own funds locally, thus enabling the local branch to achieve a degree of financial and political independence. In most developed 'western' countries there is a healthy fundraising culture, with professional fundraisers and fundraising conferences and workshops at which skills can be learnt and exchanged. Most advanced are the USA, Canada, Australia, South Africa and Europe.

In Europe, the principal fundraising event, in October of each year, is the International Fundraising Workshop at Nordwijkerhout in the Netherlands. Started in 1981, the Workshop has become an annual three-day event. Fundraisers and directors come from over 30 countries and from all continents. It is run by the International Fund Raising Group (a non-profit making trust) which has a permanent secretariat in London - International Fund Raising Workshops (IFRG) Ltd. 295 Kennington Road, London SE11 4QE. Tel: +44 (0)207 587 0287, Fax: +44 (0)207 582 4335.

International workshops

In the past few years, a flourishing and rapidly expanding international programme of workshops has been set up, mainly by the IFRG. Workshops have been held in many countries including India, Mexico, Zimbabwe, Taiwan, Hong Kong and Eastern Europe. Many more are planned, giving comprehensive global coverage. International organisations like the World Wide Fund for Nature (WWF), HelpAge International, Greenpeace, Oxfam and Amnesty International are sending their overseas staff and partners to these workshops, and are often running additional internal workshops to facilitate fundraising in all the countries in which they operate. This has come about because of a gradual realisation that every country has a relatively rich, educated, middle class who are used to giving to religions and political parties (both of which run very sophisticated fundraising programmes in nearly every country).

These people are also linked by the same communications media of sophisticated newspapers, television and radio. They share the same aspirations and an increasingly similar culture which paves the way for them to participate in philanthropy. Those organisations that have understood the potential, (for example,there are over 100 million middle class people in India), are frequently operating in a competition-free environment. Techniques such as direct mail, advertising and telemarketing are hardly used by NGOs outside the West, yet they can bring huge rewards.

The non-profit sector overseas

The non-profit sector is rapidly developing in many countries around the world. Indeed, it is often the fastest-growing and least-mapped sector in those countries. A feel for this can be obtained by reading *The emerging nonprofit sector - an overview* by Lester Salamon and Helmut Anhier (published by Manchester University Press). This is a serious academic work mapping out the sector in France, Germany, Italy, Japan, UK, US and Hungary. Their definition of the non-profit sector is rigorous, but probably wider than most peoples' expectations. It is not a book about fundraising. Similarly CAF publishes a series of profiles on the sector in UK, Bulgaria, India, Russia, South Africa and the EU.

What follows is based on my own experience of working in different countries and gives only a flavour; which in many cases is sadly far from being up to date.

Fundraising in India

Some years ago I worked in India for Mr K. S. Gupta for Lok Kalyan Samiti (LKS), a Delhi based family and medical welfare charity which specialises in eye operations. For a long time he has been running a sophisticated and very profitable fundraising campaign. His newspaper advertisements ask the reader to save one person's eyesight by sending LKS the equivalent of £5 in rupees, in return for which they receive a photograph of the person whose eyesight they have saved. As LKS then has the name and address of the person who gave, we then wrote to them at the time of various festivals, with a message such as, 'This is Holi, the festival of colour. Blind people can see no colours. Please be generous again and sponsor the rebirth of light for 2, 4, or 6 people', 'This is Diwali, the Festival of Light ...', 'This is Independence Day, blind people have no independence...'

This has been repeated several times a year. Not only is this simple system effective, but variations and new ideas are tried out constantly. Newspaper editors were approached for free space, (using an important newspaper contact who first gave free space himself), which resulted in many free advertisements across India. This meant that the advertisements needed to be translated in several languages, and the picture of a person with bandaged eyes had to be changed to suit the various newspapers' readerships (a Sikh for Sikh newspapers, etc.).

Direct mail lists were not available and so other ideas were tested. Telephone directories were tried because most people with a phone would be reasonably well off, and would have been in the same house for about four years. Their address would often reflect their occupation. Residents' associations were approached to use their newsletters, especially in areas where teachers or other caring professionals were known to live. Company contacts were tapped for their client lists. The 'Who's Who' of India was mailed for celebrity support, and every contact with LKS was placed on the mailing list.

The expansion of names and addresses was such that before long the whole system needed computerising. Now LKS has many thousands of donors across the country. Naturally, a newsletter is sent to each donor and new ideas are tested there too. For example, birthdays and remembrance days are popular. The newsletter also lets people know much more about the organisation they support and there is a set invitation to visit LKS and see the work in progress.

LKS has been able to tell European development agencies that it could now manage without their assistance, and it has been an inspiration to other NGOs on the sub continent. Many other organisations are also fundraising effectively in India. Examples include the children's organisation CRY India, Aide et Action and HelpAge International, which has for many years run thousands of sponsored walks in schools, and which has over the past few years branched out into many other activities including an impressive Art Auction. All these and many more agencies are now assisting with the running of annual fundraising workshops in India, which can teach any NGO dozens of new ideas.

Mr Gupta has now written his own book on fundraising *How to raise Rs.10 million Year after Year* (published by OEU Networking Group Trust, M-2 Green Park (Main), New Delhi-110 016, India, available directly from the publishers).

Fundraising in South America

Peru

The economy of Peru has been devastated by a long civil war, and the horrors of massive international debt. Many people feel that they have dropped rapidly down the class structure in the past few years. NGOs are often substantially funded from abroad, though most are also engaged in a degree of fundraising locally. The techniques of fundraising are often similar to those used in Europe. For example, the Peruvian Foundation for the Conservation of Nature was the most advanced and impressive fundraising organisation I visited. Trained in Canada, their fundraiser has raised substantial sums from top business people by organising seminars, dinners and meetings at which they are personally targeted as individuals. She also raises funds through direct mail to lists in the USA, though direct mail in Peru has not worked for her, and events have not been as successful as expected.

Chile

Here, by contrast, the professional classes are feeling well off, and the country has an air of successful economic and social progress. Two of the many organisations that raise funds locally are Compartiendo La Mesa and the Hogar de Cristo. Both their Directors are impressive fundraisers, working with relatively small organisations and developing their own approaches to fundraising. Their work is very similar to the work being done by kindred organisations in Europe. Door to door collections, by large numbers of volunteers, of relatively small amounts of money on a regular basis, give an echo of various schemes in England. Dinners with celebrities are popular, and trading goods and other promotional items help to give a positive image of the organisation. Art auctions, street collections and concerts have also been held in Chile.

Venezuela

The days of very rapid development of the Venezuelan economy are over. Now, with the attempted coup d'état in 1992, and increasing social instability, the professional classes are less sure of their disposable income, but there is still a great deal that can be done as the country is relatively wealthy. I visited Bioma, an environmental organisation specialising in protected 'park' areas, which is expanding its local income at a great rate. Likewise, ANAPACE, (a charity dealing with cerebral palsy), is making large sums from all the classic western donor-base fundraising techniques. Organisations which cater for a problem that does not distinguish between rich and poor (such as diseases like cancer), are well placed to run basic donor pyramid-based fundraising operations. They can be sure that a reasonable number of wealthy people have been affected or know of other people who have been affected.

These people are the ideal target group as they have both knowledge and disposable income. Often the donor-base grows out of a simple victim support organisation offering advice and/or assistance to those affected and their families. From this base a more substantial operation can grow, but this is a major step to take and will require a larger investment for much smaller returns than the early days. The organisation would do well to realise that it is moving into a new era, and that it will have to resource and support that move steadfastly until the expected returns kick in.

Fundraising in the former Soviet Union

Until recently, philanthropy has been a state concern and collections were taken in the workplace (the hub of Soviet life) for various charitable endeavours. 'If part of a co-operative's income (profit) is donated to the Lenin Soviet Children's Fund, the Soviet Peace Fund or the Cultural Foundation of the USSR, or used for other charitable purposes, it shall not be subject to taxation.' This is a quote from the Draft Law, 'On Co-operative Economy in the USSR', which makes an interesting contrast to the basic definitions of charity and philanthropy once current in Soviet society. For example:

- 'CHARITY. Aid hypocritically rendered by representatives of the ruling class in an exploiter society to a part of the poor population in order to deceive the workers and divert them from the class struggle.' Great Soviet Encyclopaedia 1950.
- 'PHILANTHROPY. Bourgeois charity, aid to, and protection for the poor.' Dictionary of the Russian Language 1987.

As the pace of change quickens, new fundraising ventures are evolving. Concerts are held to raise money for drug addicts, street stalls raise funds for the miners, lotteries are held, etc. One organisation recently active is The Soviet Peace Fund. Set up in 1961 and collecting public and private funds which are used to run international peace congresses, it helps the victims of war and aggression and those suffering from natural disasters. In 1987 it raised 273,400,000 roubles from tens of millions of people.

The Soviet Cultural Foundation, founded in 1987, is one of the most important philanthropic organisations. It has organised benefit concerts, performances, sales and auctions for the restoration and protection of cultural monuments and to assist artists. The Lenin Soviet Children's Fund was also set up in 1987 to tackle the enormous problems in the childcare field. One of its first tasks was the payment of 6 million roubles to cover teachers' salaries in orphanages.

Donors are by no means naive, as this letter to Izvestia in 1988, (quoted in Philanthropy in the Soviet Society by Vitali Tretyakov) shows. 'The workers at my factory were told to send one day's pay to the Peace Fund, but no one was very enthusiastic about doing this... The workers said openly the Peace Fund had an oversized bureaucratic staff, and it did not want to finance its members' trips abroad or pay their salaries. Why aren't reports on the Fund's spending regularly published by the press? At our meetings we decided to transfer our money to the Children's Fund, in particular to one specific children's home. Please understand that we don't grudge our money for concrete steps linked with the struggle for peace, and we are ready to help orphans and problem kids. There is no problem as far as the victims of the Chernobyl accident or natural disasters is concerned. But we have had enough of bureaucracy!' A. Chizov.

Does this sound familiar? Incidentally, by 1988 the Fund had twenty-three permanent staff members and their salaries were paid out of money earned by the fund itself and not from donations. As Eastern European societies have opened up, many international organisations have begun fundraising workshops and conferences. So far, these have had limited success. There is little in the way of financial resources to set up serious fundraising from scratch, entrepreneurs are not easy to find, (let alone in voluntary organisations), and staff and volunteers' circumstances change rapidly.

There has also been the problem of 'looking expectantly to the West' rather than facing the less pleasant task of trying to raise money within crumbling dislocated societies. As, however, much of Eastern Europe becomes Central Europe and prosperity comes to some countries there will be increasing chances to raise funds for philanthropic causes. Since writing this a flood of agencies and western funds has flowed into the former Soviet Union. The question now is how to sustain and develop the local NGOs that have emerged as the initial funds dwindle and the expected economic miracle is tardy in arriving.

Fundraising in Africa

Africa has a rich tradition of family philanthropy. Often as someone gains wealth their obligations to the wider family grow at the same rate. There are also the well trodden paths of political and religious fundraising. In many countries NGO fundraising has reached quite sophisticated levels.

Zimbabwe

In Zimbabwe, for example, even in 1989 the Salvation Army were using mailing list techniques, (and legacies were left to hospitals like St Giles', though few NGOs were seriously trying to raise such funds). The Rotary movement was using casinos set up in hotels to raise funds for specific charitable work (gambling was illegal unless for charitable purposes). Street collections were popular, though the sums raised were not large. Charity concerts were often held in the largest venues, sometimes with international artists, and Christmas card sales, jumble sales and other sales of almost anything were also held.

Schools' fundraising was big business with much money going to help fund the schools themselves, for example, through sponsored bicycle rides. The late Sally Mugabe's Children's Fund was very active in schools. Their fundraising included an exciting sponsored dance marathon. Extensive schools' fundraising has also taken place for the Save The Rhinos Project with a goal of £1M, though there was apparently a shortfall from this target. Gifts in kind from industry are quite common. HelpAge Zimbabwe have received scrap cloth, reject enamel, tyres for their refugees programme, cement benches for one of their homes, etc. Industry and commerce give large sums to prestigious projects, such as the Mayor of Bulawayo's Fund, or the Child Survival Programme, because of the influence of their powerful patrons, but the business community has been heavily pressured by Government to contribute to many events and celebrations and has become rather resistant to lesser appeals.

Blocked funds

In some countries, the government does not allow foreign companies to repatriate their profits. Such profits are known as blocked funds. Blocked funds are often a major source of large-scale donations but the results can also be quite small-scale. If you have a branch or project in a country that has blocked the repatriation of currency to the UK, it is always worthwhile asking the DTI for a list of UK companies operating there, and contacting them all, asking for them to release their profits to your charity. If some of them have helped you in the UK, this may open up the way to a serious donation in currency you can use but they cannot.

If large sums and an American company are involved, try talking to the central bank in the country where you are operating, to see if they will release the funds to the UK for a brief period. The company can then offset the donation, (to a UK registered charity), against tax liabilities before returning the rest into the block within a strict time limit and paying a small fee to the central bank (say 2 or 3%). Or try suggesting half the blocked funds are used for charitable purposes in the country where they are blocked and the other half repatriated, (or some such variation of percentages). As globalisation takes a hold, the free flow of money around the world has lessened the amount of blocked funds, but some are still in existence. If you are sending funds overseas, it is often more effective to send something like a tractor which can be readily sold for far more than it cost, (including shipping), to increase the funds you have available for your project.

Do not forget the commercial disciplines of doing this. For example, poor countries are littered with tractors that have no spare parts, so you should send at least two years' worth, or no one will buy your tractor. (The sale should, of course, have been arranged beforehand). In Zimbabwe there were some commercial ventures raising funds for charity. Jairos Jiri had two shops selling handicraft goods, and the then Bulawayo Council for the Welfare of the Disabled, (now the National Council), had a model shop in Bulawayo selling clothes made on the premises by people with various disabilities. Embassies in most poor countries are a very useful source of funds and Zimbabwe is no exception. Though the sums available are not large by European standards they can make a very significant difference, as can the use of vehicles or a word from the ambassador to the right person.

From the above it can be seen that there are three fundraising sectors in the country. One, largely outlined above, is by organisations like Rotary, the Soroptimists and other NGOs. The second is political party fundraising and fundraising using the party network. This has been done very successfully, for example, by ZIMOFA (the Zimbabwe Mozambique Friendship Association) which had links to Zanu PF, the ruling party. The third sector is the Church and Mission fundraising which appears to be fairly undeveloped, being based on churches or missions meeting their own needs with little fundraising at a national level. Churches do occasionally undertake second collections, as they have done for both ZIMOFA and the Rhino Campaign.

Fundraising in Pacific Rim countries

The wealthy economies of the Pacific Rim countries have begun to attract the attention of several foreign NGOs, some of whom have been working for several years to build organisations capable of unlocking the huge wealth that has built up. Sometimes this has been merely fortuitous. Oxfam in Hong Kong, for example, received a large legacy, some years ago, which prompted it to think of becoming more independent by raising funds locally. Now it runs a sophisticated system like any European NGO and raises a considerable sum each year. Oxfam also organises as arduous but successful sponsored walk called 'Trailwalker' over 100 km of countryside. This was organised originally with the Gurkha regiment, and grew year by year.

Hong Kong also has a famous flag day pitch, and the few organisations that are fortunate enough to receive permission to fundraise there can be assured of a good return for their effort. Theoretically, no organisation that is merely a branch of a foreign NGO is able to operate. All such organisations must become local under the Chinese basic law. This does not seem to have made much practical difference to NGOs operating in Hong Kong.

Japan, South Korea, Singapore and Taiwan are obvious targets. They are rich countries, even after the economic turbulence of the late 90s, with excellent communications systems and middle class lifestyles similar to those found almost everywhere in the world.

Taiwan

Taiwan has a variety of effective local fundraising NGOs. They employ many techniques including the use of television, which was pioneered by the Children Burn Society. The Chinese Children's Society is also very effective, raising money through a series of programmes, including sponsorship, direct support for their child protection programmes and the soliciting of contributions to their scholarship fund. I was also rather taken with the Buddhist organisation that fundraises through business offices. First asking permission, then going from floor to floor collecting funds face-to-face. This has proved exceptionally efficient in raising donations year after year.

Korea

Korea is open to all kinds of fundraising. One human rights organisation has rapidly developed its income by writing to all the lawyers in the country, and following that up with a telephone call. This combination has proved its worth over and over again.

Singapore

Beneath the famous twin towers of Singapore there are many fundraising schemes operating. The Singapore Community Chest, for example, has a huge corporate programme for its Community Chest that upholds some 50 charities in Singapore. Regular payroll-giving provides 70% of its income but corporate donations often match employee giving, funds raised through their corporate network of various trade sectors and transaction based events provide the remaining 30%. Individual businessmen sometimes demonstrate their charitable side publicly, for example, Sanwa Bank's newly appointed General Manager asked for donations to be made by corporate well-wishers instead of the usual flowers and gifts.

Japan

Japan has many NGOs receiving funds from a variety of sources. Once registered as an organisation capable of receiving funds, it is possible to solicit gifts from industry, trusts and rich individuals who can be extraordinarily generous. Registration, however, is not easy: applicants are required to lodge several million yen in a bank account and follow a complicated legal procedure. In all these tiger countries there are trusts and foundations to which applications can be made. Often they have been set up by companies now staffed by young MBAs educated in America and Canada, who bring back the American business ethic to their home countries. Buddhist organisations, in particular, are both effective fundraisers and distributors of charity. The fastest growing local NGO in Taiwan is a Buddhist organisation that raises its funds by direct person to person contact, often in offices.

China

In mainland China, as opposed to Hong Kong, it is still perfectly possible to raise funds, but this must be done in conjunction with the government's aims. The stance is one of offering assistance to the government to meet its stated objectives. It is not one of being an independent organisation with its own objectives. The China Youth Development Foundation's 'Project Hope' has raised huge sums (over 1 billion yuan) to help over 1.55 million school dropouts in poverty-stricken areas, repairing old, ramshackle school buildings, setting up over 3,600 new 'hope' primary schools, and equipping poor rural primary schools with books and teaching aid facilities.

One of their most successful techniques is to encourage people to place their funds in a special bank account the interest from which is used by the Society for educational purposes. Donors can also link directly to projects by naming or sponsoring buildings and activities. They have also worked with the People's Bank of China to issue 20 million 'Project Hope' commemoration coins - a first ever for a non-banking institution. These are given as gifts in thanks to donors and have a very high value of collection.

In the Pacific Rim, more so than in other parts of the world, fundraising is best done through your local organisation to avoid cultural gaffes. In beginning to introduce new fundraising ideas to your branch, be prepared for a long wait before you are 'accepted' and another wait before your ideas are fully considered, especially in Japan where decisions are made more collectively than in the West. Bear in mind that middle management is very important in Japanese companies. New ideas will certainly not be implemented until the relevant group in the NGO feels they are the right way to go. Full responsibility for decision-making is rarely given to individuals in Japanese companies but, once made, decisions will be put into effect quickly and efficiently.

As in most Far Eastern cultures, it is important not to put people on the spot. Remember it is far easier to elicit a polite, positive answer than a negative one. A little thought and sensitivity will usually make uncertain meanings clear. Asking questions that cannot be answered with a 'yes' or 'no' helps. One way of conveying 'no' in Japanese is to say something is 'difficult' but that does not necessarily mean the end of the affair. The word 'wakarimashita' is often translated as, 'I understand', but it means that you also agree. Asking for 'co-operation' means more than just trying hard. It means agreeing to do what is asked. Doing what is requested wins great appreciation in Japanese society, and debts are repaid in due course. Patience in discussion is also rewarded, and silences are not the negative experience they may be in the West.

Direct mail is effective in Japan for commercial companies, despite the recession, as well as for NGOs. Greenpeace made good use of this technique when the environment was a popular local issue. Use handwritten (calligraphed) envelopes to rich donors and trade on the loyalty they have to an organisation that they have taken the important step of joining. Trading goods also sell well, especially traditional items such as Christmas cards. T-shirts are also popular, though few designs will travel effectively from Europe.

Two organisations that are designed to help businesses but can also provide useful information to NGOs, are JETRO, the Japanese External Trade Organisation, (a non-profit semi-governmental organisation from which some of the advice above is taken) and the Japan Business Consultancy (19 Somerset Place, Bath, BA1 5SF, Tel: 01225 444190).

Fundraising in the Middle East

In Islamic countries, mosques are places where funds can be solicited by the poor, but fundraising as a professional activity is largely unknown and untested. Funds are usually raised on a personal basis from the very rich. There are, however, various enterprising operations, such as cooperatives of women in Pakistan making shawls to raise funds for women's education in the region. With the polarisation of societies in North Africa, the creation of donor-based NGOs is difficult. For example, simply registering as an organisation can take many years, if it happens at all. Incidentally, in Israel, charitable funds have traditionally been sought from the West, but there are many local foundations, and NGOs are developing sophisticated fundraising techniques.

§

It is my belief that many NGOs should be developing strategies based on globalising their operations, and as a key part of that process, evening out their income flows between the US, Europe and the Asia Pacific countries. In particular many NGOs could benefit in the medium- to long-term from serious investment in developing a donor-base in the tiger economies of the Pacific Rim.

This is the basis for research being undertaken with the Open University and the cooperation of over 50 international NGOs. It appears that a few have quite extensive fundraising operations overseas with both training and starter funds for their branches and partnerships. The pattern of globalisation is, however, a very mixed picture, with little overall strategic thought replacing a quite random pattern.

The best organisations are targeting countries like India, Brazil and China (Hong Kong); setting up branches that are geared to fundraise from the word go and have both training and funds at their disposal. These organisations should rapidly overtake and possibly exclude those who still pay for their branch salaries and office costs from the centre. The latter model appears to attract only programme staff who cannot switch to fundraising, and do not believe it possible in their country. This limits the organisation's effectiveness and prevents its expansion unless it is willing to sink large sums into the country year after year. Playing catch-up is going to cost these organisations dear, if they want to grow in years to come.

The drivers that are propelling commercial firms to globalise are apparently less effective on NGOs, because they cannot find the same cost savings; nor are they aware of being squeezed for market share. The latter will only become apparent when they try to expand their supporters overseas, or appoint international fundraisers to their senior management teams or at the top of their international divisions. Whilst international development is seen as a minor part of the programme work overseas, the situation will not improve. It is still difficult to think not in terms of raising funds here to spend there, but in global terms to raise funds in competition with others wherever the funds may be located, and to build a global organisation, not a home based charity.

The global organisation confers huge benefits not just in income generation terms, but in long-term policy-making, because it absorbs the cultures in which the charity must be effective and guards against rapid changes in the external environment being ignored or unseen until it is too late.

To survive in the long term an organisation needs to innovate faster than the changes in its external environment. In a globalised world these changes may come from anywhere.

15 Careers in Fundraising

Fundraising is one of the fastest-growing professions in the Western world. Fuelled by the withdrawal of government support from social services of all kinds, and the growth of that part of the population that social scientists call 'inner directed', fundraising now provides one of the most interesting and worthwhile careers of the new millennium.

You will need to have an interest in marketing, and in people's motivation for giving, as well as a desire to work in the 'charity' sector. An entrepreneurial attitude is essential, though the necessary practical skills can be acquired through training. Underlying all that, a passion to help people and improve the world will give you the unrelenting drive you will need to survive and flourish in the non-profit sector.

Career paths

If you are thinking of becoming a fundraiser, there are several possible routes to follow. Many years ago fundraising was considered a suitable occupation for aristocratic ladies with a social conscience or ex-army officers without one. The governing bodies of charitable organisations were filled with the great and the good, but today they are often run by those elected by the grass-roots, and the great and good are only allowed to put in an occasional appearance on such bodies as appeal committees (where they can be invaluable). So marrying into the aristocracy, joining the army or doing great service to your country are not now recommended routes to gaining employment as a fundraiser.

Today there are two main paths. The first is to work your way up inside an organisation, starting perhaps as a volunteer in the fundraising department (or sometimes as the volunteer fundraiser), and later obtaining paid employment with the same organisation. This will probably be enhanced by taking a series of courses from organisations like the Directory of Social Change, the Institute of Charity Fundraising Managers (ICFM) or Charity Consultants Ltd. The other way is to work commercially acquiring an appropriate marketing skill such as direct mail, advertising, retailing or just business management (an MBA is still very rare in the sector and commands more respect), then learning how to apply that skill in the voluntary sector (which can be a very daunting experience).

A hybrid version of these two paths is also beginning to develop with people acquiring the necessary skills by taking courses and then applying for fundraising positions with the charity of their choice. Needless to say, it is very difficult to build a successful career if you limit yourself to one organisation, and career development usually involves moving from one voluntary organisation to another. The largest and most prestigious charities carry the most weight when it comes to assessing your record. On the other hand, with the withdrawal of government from all manner of social funding around the world, there is a dramatically increasing demand for fundraisers with a good track record. This is most keenly felt in the capital appeal field (where experience is difficult to come by), with the need for large sums of money to finance new hospital buildings and the like.

The Certificate in Fundraising Management

This is now the key course in fundraising management for professional fundraisers. It is a competence-based programme set by the Institute of Charity Fundraising Managers (ICFM) as a vocational qualification at NVQ level 3/4. This book has been revised to complement the requirements of this certificate. For further details see the ICFM's website at **http://www.icfm.org.uk.**

Voluntary organisations are rarely the caring lifestyle workplace they aspire to be, and can mirror some of the worst faults of the commercial world, with staff displaying every trait from ruthless ambition to pigheaded incompetence. In general, however, their work is to a very high standard of efficiency and effectiveness, which would be the envy of the commercial world if it realised just how well they are performing.

The volunteer's route

There are many levels of entry into fundraising. At the simplest, you can volunteer for work with almost any charity and the chances are you will be welcome to assist, though the fundraising department may not need help immediately, and you may have to begin somewhere else in the organisation, such as the campaigns, press, or office management departments. Though this may seem very attractive from the outside, the principal work of volunteers is mundane and repetitive. There is never any guarantee of moving to paid work, though it does often happen. When it happens, it tends to be because the volunteer either has skills the charity needs, or acquires a proficiency which is indispensable in an area where the charity wishes to expand.

It is important to stress that many volunteers spend years doing virtually full-time jobs without ever having the chance of being paid. Having worked as a volunteer in the organisation to which you are applying for a job, does, however, confer many advantages over someone from the outside or someone who has no experience of NGO work at all. You will rapidly learn a great deal about the inner workings of voluntary organisations and obtain a feel for the life.

NGOs are not lifestyle organisations where the most enlightened social theories are practised, but are often stressed, under-resourced organisations, struggling to cope with the most serious problems of the age. Their commitment to being caring and consultative organisations, frequently degenerates into faction-fighting, in which staff deploy all the campaigning skills they usually reserve for changing the world. But it must be said that charity work can also be extremely rewarding in a personal sense. The organisation, for its part, will learn about the volunteer's capabilities at first hand rather than through the restrictive means of a CV and interview.

Volunteering as a first step can also be done simply at local group level, where anyone interested in fundraising is often welcome and can pick up a great deal of practical experience. Though this is often necessarily restricted in scope, dealing mainly with a variety of small events, trading from stalls and bringing in local membership fees, it does offer many useful insights, both into an organisation you may be interested in working for, and into the psychology of giving, which will hold you in good stead in the future years of your career.

Local groups are often both the grass roots of national organisations and the democratic heart of those organisations. As such, they often elect regional representatives who sit on the voluntary council or board of the charity, and determine its policies. There are, however, many, many forms of local group structure, some purely for fundraising, some purely for carrying out the programme of the organisation. Their relationship with the charity's fundraising departments varies equally; but there are few local groups that are not at some point encouraged to undertake specific fundraising activities supported by the centre, sometimes in a charity week allowing the national organisation to use national publicity to support local fundraising.

With a local group background, all other routes can still be pursued, but the immediate level of entry would be as a local groups' fundraising officer. This would usually require a few years' experience and should be bolstered by undertaking appropriate courses.

The commercial route

At the other extreme, charities are increasingly drawing in people who have worked for both advertising agencies and commercial direct marketing companies, often with charity clients. It is preferable, if not essential, of course, to have worked with those charity clients. Again, if this experience is expanded by fundraising courses or by volunteer work, that helps to build an impressive CV, and this will bring you to the interview. Your CV will need to be good, because in the current market there are often a number of applicants for any charity position. The more popular charities have huge numbers applying for some of their posts. Naturally, a business qualification of almost any sort, from OND Business Studies to MBA, also helps.

The larger charities often have posts for advertising managers, direct mail officers, direct response officers, etc., all of which can be approached through this route. It would be unusual to move directly from a commercial company to become the head of a fundraising department, but this does happen, and commercial experience of managing a team is a very useful attribute. It is more usual for the directors of charities to be drawn from the business world by charity councils eager to instil commercial reality into the management and development of charities' incomes.

For specific fundraising positions there are many obvious commercial parallels. Work in a chain of charity shops will be accessible to those with similar commercial experience; the merchandise catalogue of a charity needs just the same skills as its

How to be recruited as a fundraiser by a recruitment agency

By Alison Whitely, CharityPeople

As fundraising becomes more targeted and competitive, individuals aiming to succeed can improve their chances of finding a suitable post by harnessing the expertise of agencies like Charity People.

Agencies will work with you to identify and maximise your skills through interviews, advice and discussions throughout your initial job search and subsequent job changes. They will recommend improvements to your CV and relevant training. They will also suggest research you could be profitably undertaking.

Perhaps most importantly, a good agency will have taken the time to know its clients, the employing organisations, and will advise you frankly on matters of culture, salary and promotional prospects, offering you insights you may not achieve through a direct approach.

Opportunities within fundraising are becoming broader and more accessible; where ten years ago you were unlikely to enter a fundraising career above administrative level without a background in the Not for Profit sector, now your experience in sales, marketing, business development and management will ensure that you attain an appropriate level within the sector, and that your existing skills are recognised and supplemented with a thorough induction and appropriate training.

Basic steps, then, to finding your first or next job in fundraising are:

Maximise any voluntary experience you have

For those at the beginning of their careers, without a proven track record on which to trade, you would be well advised either to make the most of voluntary experience you have gained to date, or to supplement your training and education with some voluntary contribution to the sector. Your commitment to a career in this sector is important, both in ensuring that you will feel the benefits are sufficient, and in persuading an employer that the organisation has spent precious resources wisely in recruiting you.

Individual qualities which will boost your application and help you to impress in your first and subsequent fundraising roles are dynamism, enthusiasm, persistence and tact.

Take advice from your consultant on application, interview and presentation

At Charity People we serve the interests of both client and candidate by ensuring that there is a good fit. We want to send candidates to our clients who have researched the organisation, whose commitment to and interest in the Not for Profit sector is strong, and whose skills and experience will enable them to make a positive impact.

Know your skills and express them clearly on your CV

Be clear on your CV. Ensure that you explain how you have achieved, as well as listing those achievements. Keep it relevant, and where possible tailor the CV to the job in which you have an interest. Leave out irrelevant and outdated information.

Take an interest in the work of the organisation, not just the role that interests you

It will be apparent at interview if you have an interest in the mission of the organisation. If you don't, you will be wasting the time of the organisation and their feedback will not be good.

Keep in regular touch with your consultant

Keeping us up to date will mean that we are able to offer you immediate opportunities. Being able to talk confidently about our candidates helps us to develop and maintain the good relationships with employers which ensure that we are able to offer you exciting job opportunities. We often learn of vacancies before they are advertised, and many of the vacancies we handle are never advertised.

Network

It is essential in a growing sector that we all keep abreast of new developments and continue to cultivate contacts. Your job opportunities will be improved by your networking activities. Attend shows, conferences and any meeting which will add to your knowledge or contact list.

Get qualified

Take advantage of any relevant training or secondment opportunities which will enhance your prospects in your current role. Study outside of work to develop new skills if you are looking to change jobs. Be aware of legislation relating to the job.

If you are contemplating your first move into fundraising, whatever your background, speak to a Charity People consultant in complete confidence for advice and support.

commercial partner; and the talents needed to raise money by a host of other means have their commercial equivalents. In fact, charity work often requires both much more sensitivity, e.g. in telemarketing, and a much harder commercial edge, because competition is very tough and you are asking people to give money away, not to buy a product they need.

The training route

This is becoming the most frequent way by which people choose to become a professional fundraiser. Most applicants favouring this route already have degrees, often in subjects relevant to the charities' work, or, more importantly, in a commercial discipline; but they augment this by undertaking both a period of volunteering and a foundation course with the ICFM, and subsequently a series of courses on specific topics with either the ICFM or the Directory of Social Change. This whole bevy of certificates and diplomas can only be beaten by experience, and that, preferably, with a major charity.

If you are going down this route, then it pays to be selective, dovetailing the courses you take to the position you are after. If you intend to move up the career ladder, from assistant to member of a fundraising department, to director of fundraising, to becoming a CEO, then no specialism must be maintained for long. A head of department will usually have a specialist knowledge of the direct response industry, because that is where most of the income will probably come from, but that is by no means universally true.

One of the best places to start your training is part-time with the Open University. This allows you the luxury of working in one job whilst acquiring the skills necessary for the next. The list of useful organisations at the end of this book has the addresses of the principal organisations, mentioned above, which offer training courses. Write or phone them for a current list of courses on offer.

The external environment is changing so rapidly for fundraisers, as for everyone else, that it has become commonplace to say that your training will never stop.

Changing jobs

It is more likely that you will find your next job outside your current charity. Promotion is by no means assured, and a charity career is a rocky one, as charities rise and fall in the same way as other businesses. Often the breakthrough to promotion will come from your Rolodex of business cards and contacts, and you should cultivate with great care your contacts in other organisations.

Make sure your triumphs are known outside your current employment, and make good use of the charity press to advertise yourself. The charity press often seems to be growing daily, and *Professional Fundraising*, *The Third Sector* and *Charity* are all widely read. In the US the *Chronicle of Philanthropy* has a large circulation. There are also various discussion groups opening up on the Internet which make interesting reading. They tend to be based on the US not-for-profit sector, but will give an interesting insight into their methods and could even lead to your next position.

Changing charities

It may be a wrench for you to think of leaving your favourite charity to improve your prospects, but once that challenge is taken, it is usually seen that there are many organisations with equally important claims to your devotion. Causes are also much more interlinked than it can appear from the confines of your first charity. Changing charities also gives a breadth of experience that will enhance both your everyday work and your future prospects.

The changing profession

In the past few years fundraising has really taken off as a profession, acquiring a respect that many other professions seem determined to lose. Fundraising departments have grown rapidly in many organisations, developing a set of fundraising managers and directors who were scarce on the ground not so long ago. The latest trend has been international, with an increasing number of fundraising managers training the overseas branches of international charities to fundraise in their own countries. These glamorous international fundraisers hold aspirational positions that require great experience, cultural adaptability, entrepreneurial spirit, a love of airports and laptop computers, and the ability to function in all temperatures without sleep!

The challenge of fundraising in every possible environment has reinvigorated many organisations. At one extreme, as the newly industrialised countries of the Pacific Rim emerge, there are fundraisers tapping into the wealth being created there, especially fundraisers from Western universities following their affluent alumni back home. At the other extreme, there are fundraisers in the very poorest countries, locating the inevitable class of rich and affluent people, and going to work on them.

Charity employment agencies

A very good way to acquire a position in fundraising is to take your CV to a charity agency. They have the time and knowledge to give professional advice on your career planning, and the type of CV you should be building in order to stand the best chance of the position you are seeking. Charity agencies are often called upon to provide fundraisers for charities or to help with the recruitment and selection process. In doing this they frequently suggest appropriate people who are on their books.

The Internet

The Internet hosts a wide variety of fundraising and other charity positions. Look at **http://www.fundraising.co.uk** - this site will lead you to many advertisements for charity work, some of which are mentioned in the chapter on Internet fundraising.

§

§

Fundraising is one of the key professions for building a better world. It has the power to transform societies and the way they operate. It can take the dreams of thousands of individually powerless donors and turn them into a force for positive change. I hope that this book will help and inspire you to make your work for such changes more effective and efficient.

Ten Principles Of Fundraising

1. The Pareto principle

80% of your income can come from 20% of your supporters. Learn who they are, develop the relationship, and approach them for more until the ratio comes true.

2. 'My friend the fundraiser'

People give to people, not to organisations. They give to help end suffering, so in your fundraising bring them as close to the victims as possible but become their friend in the process, and build up the relationship for long-term giving.

3. 'Thank you!'

Always say 'thank you', and say it promptly. It is a common courtesy and shows respect for your donors and gratitude for their generosity. If you do not say 'thank you' you do not deserve another donation. Thanking people helps to cement your friendship. Do not try to get out of it.

4. How much?

Always let people know how much you would like them to give. It makes them feel comfortable and makes you look competent. If there is no indication of the amount you need people worry that they may be thought foolish for giving away a lot, or mean for giving just a little. Whilst they deliberate the immediacy goes out of your request, and you may lose the donation altogether.

5. Testing, testing, testing

Until you test, you do not know. You can have a hundred theories about your fundraising programme and your donors, but until you actually run one idea against another you do not really know which one works. It is easy to do in some cases, such as direct mail, and harder in others, such as advertising - but is essential in all cases. Always try to learn something each time you carry out an idea, and always test ideas on the smallest statistically relevant sample possible.

6. The myth of the Magic Lunch

It is said there are no free lunches. Yet we tend to believe that our supporters give us money and receive nothing in return. Is this true? Just what do they receive? What happens at the magic lunch? If you cannot answer these questions, ask people. If you do not know why they support you, you cannot fundraise effectively and efficiently.

7. The product cycle

All products, including your fundraising devices, go through cycles. In the early days they will be costly as you learn and test in small quantities; then, when the formula is working, the money will roll in - but after a while the market will be saturated, the public will tire of your approach, or you will just appear old-fashioned and irrelevant. Be prepared for this and prepared to respond rapidly to such changes. In some cases you can revamp your appeal. In others your organisation will need a radically new approach. For example, there are signs that common-interest groups are replacing local groups, so organisations dependent on local groups should consider restructuring based on professional classes.

8. Make it easy

Surprisingly, the least effort can put people off giving. They are well intentioned, but if they have to find a stamp the desire to give will have gone long before the stamp turns up. Use FREEPOST envelopes, print the donor's name and address for them, fill out their bank details, ring them up and remind them - it all helps more than you would imagine.

9. 'We're different.'

When I worked for Oxfam, people told me that it was hard to fundraise because people liked to give to local organisations like Friends of the Earth. When I worked for Friends of the Earth people told me all the money goes to people, not the planet, and it was easy for organisations like Amnesty International. At Amnesty it has been said that Oxfam has an easy time fundraising for disasters. When I went to India... Yes, it will work for you. No, it's not easy.

10. The truth

Always tell the truth. Do not be tempted to make your case stronger than it is. If your organisation makes a mistake or things go wrong, do not hide it. The press is waiting for charities to slip up. Nothing makes a better press story than a saint who has sinned.

Useful Books

Both the Directory of Social Change and the Charities Aid Foundation have a wide range of fundraising publications. Their book lists can be obtained respectively from the DSC, 24 Stephenson Way, London NW1 2DP Tel: 0207 209 1015 (where the DSC also have a bookshop) and the CAF, Kings Hill, West Malling, Kent ME19 4TA Tel: 01732 520 000.

The Voluntary Sector Legal Handbook

Adirondack, Sandy & Taylor, Sinclair James
Directory of Social Change (DSC), 1996, ISBN 1 873860 79 X

Charity Appeals

Allford, Marion
Dent/Institute of Charity Fundraising Managers (ICFM), 1993, ISBN 0 460 86191 3

Relationship Fundraising

Burnett, Ken
White Lion Press, 1992, ISBN 0 9518971 0 1

A Guide to the Major Trusts, Vol. II

Casson, David
DSC, 1995/96, ISBN 1 873860 64 1

Directory of Grant-making Trusts

Charities Aid Foundation (CAF), 1996, ISBN 0 904757 994

Grants from Europe

Davidson, Ann,
National Council for Voluntary Organisations (NCVO), 1993, ISBN 0 7199 1382 9

Guide to Company Giving

Ed. Casson, David,
DSC, 1995, ISBN 1 873860 31 5

The Arts Funding Guide

Ed. Doulton, Anne-Marie
DSC, 1994, ISBN 1 873860 31 5

The Central Government's Grants Guide

Doulton, Anne-Marie
DSC, 1995, ISBN 1 873860 73 0

EU Research Funding - a guide for applicants

Commission of the European Communities
London Office, 8 Storey's Gate, London SW1P 3AT.

Hollis Sponsorship and Donations Yearbook

Hollis Directories Ltd., 1996, ISBN 0 900 96755 2

Guide to the National Lottery

Hurd, Howard
1995, ISBN 1 873860 67 6

A Guide to the Major Trusts Vol. I

FitzHerbert, Luke
1995/96, ISBN 1 873860 49 8

Networking in Europe

NCVO, 1995, ISBN 0 7199 1460

The Borderless World

Ohmae, Kenichi
HarperCollins, 1994, SBN 0 00 638364 5

Ogilvy on Advertising

Ogilvy, David
Guild Publishing, 1985

The Tom Peters Seminar: Crazy Times Call for Crazy Organisations

Peters, Tom
Macmillan, 1994, ISBN 0 333 62864 0

The International Foundation Directory

Hodson, H. V. (Ed.)
Europa Publications, ISBN 0 46653 66 6

Peace and International Relations

Forrester, Susan
DSC, 1994, ISBN 1 873860 58 7

The Foundation Directory

Olson, Stan (Ed.)
The Foundation Centre, New York

US Foundation Support in Europe 1994/5

Lauer, Ruth & England, Steve (Eds.)
The Directory of Social Change, ISBN 1 873860 34 X

Fundraising on the Internet

Lake, Howard
Aurelian, 1996, ISBN 1 899247 06 8

Data Protection for Voluntary Agencies

Ticher, Paul
DSC, 1999, ISBN 1 900360 47 0

The Voluntary Agencies Directory

NCVO publications, updated annually.

The Seven Habits of Highly Successful People

Covey, Stephen

Simon & Schuster, 1992, ISBN 0-671-71117-2

Targeting the Powerful: international Prospect Research

Hack, Vanessa

Aslib, 1997, ISBN 0 85142 365 5

Trust Monitor

Newsletter - Ed. Susan Forrester

DSC, ISSN 1369-4405

Useful Addresses

Advertising Standards Authority (ASA)

2-16 Torrington Place, London, WC1E 7HN

Tel: 0207 580 5555

Angal

68 First Avenue, Mortlake, London, SW14 8SR

Tel: 0208 788 5464

Manufactures collecting boxes, etc.

Arts Council of England, Lottery Department

14 Great George Street, London, SW1P 3NQ

Tel: 0207 312 0123

British Council, Central Information Point

10 Spring Gardens, London SW1A 2BN

Tel: 0207 839 4382

Youth exchange grants, cultural relations policy, etc.

Business in the Community

227A City Road, London, EC1V 1JV

Encourages community involvement in job creation and corporate responsibility, and administers the One Per Cent Club.

The Camelot Foundation

One Derry Street, London, W8 5HY

Tel: 0207 937 5594

The Lottery Board's own charity.

Chapel and York Ltd

PO Box 50, Lingfield, RH7 6FT

Tel: 01342 836790

Helps UK organisations seek grants from the US.

CAFOD (Catholic Fund for Overseas Development)

2 Romero Close, Stockwell Road, London, SW9 9TY

Tel: 0207-733 7900.

Central Bureau for Educational Visits and Exchange

Management Services and Public Relations Department, Seymour Mews House, Seymour Mews, London, W1H 9PE

Tel: 0207-486 5101

The national information source for educational visits and exchanges.

Charities Aid Foundation

King's Hill, West Malling, Kent, ME19 4TA

Tel: 01732 520 000

Publishes Directory of Grant Making Trusts, runs charity voucher scheme, administers covenants, gives advice to charities on tax, etc.

Charities Advisory Trust

Radius Works, Back Lane, London, NW3 1HL

Tel: 0207 794 9835

For charity trading advice.

Charity Appointments

3 Spital Yard, London, E1 6AQ

Tel: 0207 247 4502

Helps charities fill key jobs.

Charity Commission

Harmonsworth House, 13-15 Bouverie street, London, EC4Y 8DP

Tel: 0870 333 0123

2nd Floor, 20 King's Parade, Queen's Dock, Liverpool, L3 4DQ

Tel: 0870 333 0123

Woodfield House, Tangier, Taunton, Somerset, TA1 4BL

Tel: 0870 333 0123

Registers and regulates charities.

Charity People

38 Bedford Place, London, WC18 5JR

Tel: 0207 833 0770

email: charity@dircon.co.uk

A charity recruitment agency.

Charity Recruitment

40 Rosebery Avenue, London, EC1R 4RN

Tel: 0207 833 0770

Charity recruitment agency

Chronicle of Philanthropy

Box 1989, Marin, Ohio 43305, USA

Tel: + 1 (800) 728 2819

email: subscriptions@philanthropy.com

Interesting US fundraising journal.

Commission of the European Communities

8 Storey's Gate, London, SW1P 3AT

Tel: 0207 973 1992, Fax: 0207 973 1900

The Commission itself is at Rue de la Loi 200, 1049 Brussels, Belgium,

Tel: + 32 2 299 1111.

Crucial Color,

4 Kingstanding Business Park, Kingstanding Way, Tunbridge Wells, Kent, TN2 3NP

Tel: 01892 512055

Printer who is used to printing fundraising material.

Crossbow Research

79 Portland Avenue, New Malden, Surrey, KT3 6BB

Tel: 0208 942 2012

email: crossbow.research@virgin.net

Supporter research agency.

Data Protection Registrar,

Information Services Department, Wycliffe House, Water Lane, Wilmslow, Cheshire, SK9 5AF

Tel: 01625 535 777, Fax: 01625 524510

Registers users of personal information held electronically.

Department of Employment,

ESF Section, 236 Gray's Inn Road, London, WC1X 8HL

Tel: 0207-211 4732

For information on the European Social Fund.

Department of the Environment,

Environmental Protection, Central Division, Room A132, Romney House, 43 Marsham Street, London SW1P 3AT

Tel: 0207-276 8146.

UK Government department dealing with environmental protection.

Department of Trade and Industry,

Investment and Development Division, 232 Kingsgate House, 66-74 Victoria Street, London, SW1E 6SW

Tel: 0207-636 2556

For advice on the European Regional Development Fund.

Directorate-General V, Employment and Social Affairs,

Room 921, Adelphi, 1-11 John Adam Street, London, WC2N 6HT

Tel: 0207 962 8411.

C4 Avenue de Cortenburg, 1040 Brussels, Belgium

Tel: +32 2 735 1671

EU Directorate responsible for European Social Fund, Health and Safety at Work, etc. London address for information.

Directorate-General X,

Women's Information Service, Communication and Culture, Rue de la Loi 200, 1049 Brussels, Belgium

Tel: + 32 2 299 1111

EU Directorate for Women's Information Service, etc.

Directorate-General X

Audio Visual, Information, Communication and Culture, Rue de la Loi 200, 1049 Brussels, Belgium

Tel: + 322 299 9366

EU Directorate for audio-visual media, etc.

Directory of Social Change

24 Stephenson Way, London NW1 2DP

Tel: 0207 209 4422

Great booklist and fundraising courses.

European Environmental Bureau

Rue de la Victoire, 1060 Brussels, Belgium

Tel: + 32 2 539 0037

Provides information and represents NGO members' interests.

ExecuCare

Collier House, 163-169 Brompton Rd., London, SW3 1PY

Tel: 0207 589 4567

Charity recruitment agency.

Forster Munroe

13-27 Brunswick Place, London N1 6DX

Tel: 0207 251 4890, Fax: 0207 251 4860

'Alms' computer database software supplier for charities.

Fundraising Research & Consultancy

1 Royal Crescent, Cheltenham, Gloucestershire, GL50 3DA

Tel: 01242 522 323

email: frc@frc-ltd.demon.co.uk

Major donor research and capital appeal specialists.

Halfpenny Press

Caxton House, Holbrook, Ipswich, Suffolk IP9 2QS.

Tel: 01473 328400

Specialist printers of raffle tickets, etc.

Hollis Sponsorship and Donation Yearbook

Contact House, Lower Hampton Road, Sunbury-on-Thames, Middlesex, TW16 5HG

Tel: 0181 977 7711 Fax: 0181 977 1133

Human Rights Foundation

13 Rue Van Campenhout, 1040 Brussels, Belgium

Tel: + 32 2 299 3243

For the promotion of human rights. Also small grants for innovatory projects worldwide.

HMSO

St Crispins, Duke Street, Norwich, NR3 1PD

Tel: 01603 622211

HMSO Bookshop, 41 High Holborn, London, WC1V 6HB

You can obtain copies of the new Charities Act from either address.

Inland Revenue Claims Branch

St John's House, Merton Road, Bootle, L69 9BB

Considers claims for tax exemption.

Institute of Charity Fundraising Managers

208 Market Towers, Nine Elms Lane, London, SW8 5NQ

Tel: 0207 627 3436

The professional association for all fundraisers and consultants. Sets standards, runs courses, etc.

Institute of Personnel Managers

IPM House, Camp Road, Wimbledon, London, SW19 4UW

Advice and codes of conduct on personnel matters.

International Fund Raising Group

295 Kennington Road, London, SE11 4QE

Tel: 0207 587 0287

Organises fundraising workshops globally, including the major annual European workshop in the Netherlands.

John Rodd & Associates

Coombe House, Stoke Hill, Chew Stoke, Bristol, BS18 8XF.

Tel: 01761 221702

Helps you get the computer database advice you always wanted.

Japan Business Consultancy

19 Somerset Place, Bath, BA1 5SF,

Tel: 01225 444190

For advice on working with Japanese companies in the UK.

JETRO (Japanese External Trade Organisation)

Publications Department, 2-5 Toranomon 2-Chome, Minatu-Ku, Tokyo 105, Japan.

For information on Japanese companies.

Millennium Commission

2, Little Smith Street, London, SW1P 3DH

Tel: 0207 340 2001

Administers the Millenium Fund.

National Council for Voluntary Organisations,

Regent's Wharf, 8 All Saints Street, London, N1 9RL.

Tel: 0207 713 6161.

Represents and advises NGOs on a wide variety of issues.

National Heritage Memorial Fund,

Heritage Lottery Fund, 10 St James' Street, London, SW1A 1EF.

Tel: 0207 747 2087/6/5/4/3/2

National Lottery Charities Board,

7th Floor, St Vincent House, 30 Orange Street, London, WC2H 7HH

Tel: 0345 919191

Administers the Lottery fund for charities.

Open University Business School (OUBS)

Walton Hall

Milton Keynes MK7 6AA

Tel: 01908 274066

The Open University Business School offers a number of postgraduate modules and programmes of interest to serving or would-be fundraisers. Probably the most interesting is the new Professional Certificate of Management in Public and Non-profit Organisations, which is accredited by the ICFM. Additional modules are likely to be offered in the next few years.

Other Creative,

43 Charterhouse Square, London, EC1M 6EA

Tel: 0207 600 9339

email: other@other.co.uk

A very creative direct marketing agency.

Paul Barker Consultancy,

4 Verney House, 1B Hollywood Road, London SW10 9HS.

Tel: 0207 376 5322

Great direct mail agency.

Personal Telephone Fundraising (PTF),

Tower Point, North Road, Brighton, BN1 1YR

Tel: 01273 698 697

email: info@ptf.net

Popular telemarketing agency.

Professional Fundraising,

United House, North Road, London, N7 9DP

Tel: 0207 700 3479

email: tmd.press@btinternet.com

The UK's professional fundraising magazine

The Razor's Edge,

GFI Solutions Ltd, FREEPOST, The Claremont Centre, 39 Durham St., Glasgow G41 1BR

Tel: 0141 427 7939, Fax: 0141 427 1413.

Supplier of the computer database software 'The Razor's Edge'.

Smee & Ford,

2nd Floor, St George's House, 195/203 Waterloo Road, London SE1 8XJ

Tel: 0207 928 4050.

Runs a will reporting service for charities and much more.

Sports Council National Lottery Unit,

PO Box 649, London WC1H 0QP

Tel: 0207 388 1277 and 0345 649649 (Lottery line).

The Foundation Center,

79 Fifth Avenue, New York, NY 10003 4230

Tel: + 1 212 620 4230

http://www.fdncenter.org

Useful Organisations

The Institute of Charity Fundraising Managers (ICFM)

by David Parker, ICFM

The Institute of Charity Fundraising Managers was established in 1983 to provide a membership body that is committed to the highest standards of fundraising in fundraising management and practice within the voluntary sector.

Since then it has attracted over 3000 individual members and 209 national, regional and local charities as affiliate members. ICFM continues to grow rapidly within the UK and is increasingly recognised internationally.

All members of the Institute agree, as a point of membership, to abide by its Code of Conduct, Codes of Practice and Guidance Notes.

Its mission is to promote the highest standards in fundraising, furthering knowledge, skills and effectiveness in all aspects of fundraising. The Institute fulfills its mission by developing standards of practice which encompass strict adherence to law; appropriate ethical practice in relation to the cause for which support is sought; public accountability; and respect for the rights and wishes of donors and clients.

The Institute sets out to achieve these goals by attracting and maintaining a substantial membership which is effectively trained; has a thorough knowledge of proven fundraising practice; is sure of its professional standing and skills; works towards optimum cost-effectiveness; and is valued, respected and successful.

With an established code of conduct and operating within a policy framework agreed by its members, the Institute endeavors to meet its mission and assist members in this quest.

In 1998 the Institute launched a professional qualification for fundraisers, the Certificate in Fundraising Management (the Certificate). The Certificate is a vocational qualification based on occupational standards or competences. Competence is a wide concept, but in relation to the Certificate it means demonstrating, through evidence, those qualities of personal effectiveness that are required in the workplace. It encompasses planning and organisation of work, innovation, coping with change and the ability to work with co-workers, managers and others.

ICFM oversees the work of 11 regional groups across the UK, providing members with opportunities to meet locally, to share experience, to discuss ideas and to explore and respond to policy formulation, emerging legislation and new fundraising developments and techniques. More regional groups are currently being established to provide increased access for ICFM members. The ICFM-operated National Fundraising Convention is the major national focus for fundraising activity in the United Kingdom, run over three days in Birmingham. The ICFM is recognised by government, the Charity Commission and increasingly throughout the voluntary sector as the lead body in providing self-regulation in fundraising practice, and is represented on the World Fundraising Council.

Any individual or voluntary organisation actively engaged in fundraising is eligible to gain individual, organisational or corporate membership to the ICFM or its Charitable Trust.

More information about the ICFM and its activities is available on the ICFM website at: **http://www.icfm.org.uk**

National Council of Voluntary Organisations (NCVO)

On its Internet site the NCVO describes itself thus:

The National Council for Voluntary Organisations (NCVO) is the umbrella body for the voluntary sector in England, with sister councils in Wales (Wales Council for Voluntary Action, WCVA), Scotland (Scottish Council for Voluntary Organisations, SCVO), and Northern Ireland (Northern Ireland Council for Voluntary Action, NICVA). NCVO has a growing membership of over 1,000 voluntary organisations, ranging from large national bodies to community groups, volunteer bureaux and development agencies working at local level.

NCVO is a highly effective lobbying organisation, and represents the views of its members and the wider voluntary sector to government, the Charity Commission, the EU and other bodies. It is also at the leading edge of research into, and analysis of, the voluntary sector: its work in this area carries considerable weight with decision makers. NCVO's role is to represent the voluntary sector and serve its diverse membership, and to provide a collective voice.

NCVO also provides high quality information and advice to voluntary organisations, through its helpdesk, publications, NCVO News, events, and information networks. To help voluntary organisations make the best use of limited funds, NCVO also offers a range of money-saving deals on key services of use to charities or voluntary groups. There is more detailed information at: **http://www.ncvo-vol.org.uk**

Directory of Social Change (DSC)

DSC describes itself as an independent voice for positive social change. They help voluntary and community organisations become more effective by identifying and acting on the current, emerging and future needs of the sector. They do this by providing practical, challenging and affordable information and training.

DSC publish over 100 books: fundraising directories and guides, handbooks and journals on fundraising, management, communication, finance and law.

Their training and events programme aims to empower charities with the skills and information they need. They run over 200 courses and events throughout the UK for people at all levels of their career. These cover fundraising, organisational development, management, finance, law and skills development. DSC also organises Charityfair, the 3 day annual learning and networking forum for the voluntary sector offering over 200 workshops plus the largest exhibition of advice and services for the UK voluntary sector. It takes place at the Business Design Centre in London each spring.

For more information on DSC and for a free book list and training guide contact the Marketing Department on 020 7209 4422, or by email to info@dsc.org.uk

Index

Practical Exercises for ECDL

Syllabus 4.0

We work with leading authors to develop the strongest educational materials in computing, bringing cutting-edge thinking and best learning practice to a global market.

Under a range of well-known imprints, including Prentice Hall, we craft high quality print and electronic publications, which help readers to understand and apply their content, whether studying or at work.

To find out more about the complete range of our publishing, please visit us on the World Wide Web at: www.pearsoned.co.uk

Jackie Sherman

Practical Exercises for ECDL

Syllabus 4.0

An imprint of **Pearson Education**

London · Boston · Indianapolis · New York · Mexico City · Toronto · Sydney · Tokyo
Singapore · Hong Kong · Cape Town · Madrid · Paris · Amsterdam · Munich · Milan

Pearson Education Limited
Edinburgh Gate
Harlow
Essex CM20 2JE
England

and Associated Companies throughout the world

Visit us on the World Wide Web at:
www.pearsoned.co.uk

First published 2006

The questions and exercises found in this book have been written especially for it. You can find official sample questions on the EDCL website: www.ecdl.com

All product and company names are ™ or ® trademarks of their respective owners. Pearson Education Limited has made every effort to seek permission to use the screenshots used in this book.

European Computer Driving Licence, ECDL and Stars Device, ECDL, International Computer Driving Licence, ICDL International Computer Driving Licence and logo, ICDL, and e-Citizen are trade marks of The European Computer Driving Licence Foundation Limited ("ECDL-F") in Ireland and other countries.

Pearson Education Ltd is an entity independent of ECDL-F and is not associated with ECDL-F in any manner. This courseware publication may be used to assist candidates to prepare for the ECDL examination. Neither ECDL-F nor Pearson Education Ltd warrants that the use of this courseware publication will ensure passing of the ECDL. Use of the ECDL-F Approved Courseware logo on this courseware publication signifies that it has been independently reviewed and approved by ECDL-F as complying with the following standard:

Technical compliance with the learning objectives of ECDL syllabus 4.0.

The material contained in this courseware publication has not been reviewed for technical accuracy and does not guarantee that candidates will pass the ECDL examination. Any and all assessment items and/or performance-based exercises contained in this courseware publication relate solely to this publication and do not constitute or imply certification by ECDL-F in respect of the ECDL examination or any other ECDL-F test.

For details on sitting the ECDL examination and other ECDL-F tests in your country, please contact your country's National ECDL/ICDL designated Licensee or visit ECDL-F's web site at www.ecdl.com.

Candidates using this courseware publication must be registered with the National Licensee, before undertaking the ECDL examination. Without a valid registration, the ECDL examination cannot be undertaken and no ECDL certificate, nor any other form of recognition, can be given to a candidate. Registration should be undertaken with your country's National ECDL/ICDL designated Licensee at any Approved ECDL Test Centre.

ECDL Syllabus 4.0 is the official syllabus of the ECDL certification programme at the date of approval of this courseware publication.

ISBN 10: 0-13-147958-X
ISBN 13: 978-0-13-147958-6

British Library Cataloguing-in-Publication Data
A catalogue record for this book is available from the British Library

Library of Congress Cataloging-in-Publication Data
A catalog record for this book is available from the Library of Congress

10 9 8 7 6 5 4 3 2
10 09 08 07 06

Typeset in 10/13 pt Stone Serif by 30
Printed by Bell & Bain Ltd., Glasgow

The publisher's policy is to use paper manufactured from sustainable forests.

Contents

Introduction

Learning to use a computer, as with any new skill, requires two things: finding out what is involved and then practising until you are confident you can perform the tasks successfully. Passing the ECDL demands even more practice, as most Test Centres now offer online tests where you have to demonstrate in a limited time that you can carry out all the basic tasks expected of competent computer users.

Although there are many books on the market that teach you how to use a computer, very few contain exercises that encourage you to practise what you have learned. However, to pass the ECDL you need to be sure you can use the various applications fully. That is why this book has been written. When read in conjunction with the ECDL Complete Coursebooks and 'How to Pass' Workbooks by Brendan Munnelly and Paul Holden, you can now learn how to create documents, spreadsheets, charts, presentations and databases, use browsers and e-mail systems, and then check that you have understood and gained the necessary skills by working through the relevant exercises at your own pace.

About the author

Jackie Sherman has been involved in teaching and assessing IT courses at further education colleges since 1996. She also trains staff in an education department and writes courses for distance learning colleges. Her online activities include being on the National Tutor Database for LearnDirect and answering IT questions for the YouCanDoIT column for www.laterlife.com. Jackie is ECDL-qualified and is the author of two successful IT books.

Acknowledgements

We are grateful to the following for permission to reproduce copyright material:

Microsoft® Office screenshots reprinted by permission from Microsoft Corporation; Model answers in Chapter 7: Exercise 1 from www.bbc.co.uk/weather/5day.shtml?id= 3263, British Broadcasting Corporation; Exercise 2 from www.laterlife. com/, Laterlife.Com Limited; Exercise 3 from www.waitrose.com/ online_shopping/ index.asp, Waitrose; Exercise 3 from www.Iceland.co. uk/, Iceland; Exercise 4 from www. mkisc.org.uk/, Rob Stubbs and the Milton Keynes Ice Skating Club; Exercise 5 from www.google.com/ search?hl=en&ie=UTF-8&q=skating+rinks&btnG= Google+Search, Google Inc.; Exercise 6 from www.drumaneeaquatics.co.uk, Drumanee Aquatics; Exercise 7 from www.nrm.org.uk/html/home_pb/menu.asp, reproduced courtesy of the National Railway Museum, © Trustees of the Science Museum, 2004; Exercise 10 from www.toysrus.co.uk, Toys R Us Ltd.; Exercise 13 from www.guardian.co.uk/, © The Guardian; Exercise 14 from www.firstchoice.co.uk/holidaydeals/index.cfm?step=holiday_ search_ results&page=3, First Choice Holidays plc.

In some instances we have been unable to trace the owners of copyright material, and we would appreciate any information that would enable us to do so.

Questions and exercises

Each section in Part 1 contains between 20 and 30 questions or exercises designed to test your knowledge of the ECDL syllabus. These increase in complexity as you work through the section. At the beginning of each exercise, the main skills required to complete it are listed and the following symbol ⟨ECDL⟩ refers you to the relevant section of the ECDL syllabus in case you need further guidance.

Model answers to most of the questions and exercises can be found in Part 2.

Good luck!

The seven sections within this first part of the book relate to the following ECDL modules:

Module number

1. Concepts of information technology
2. Using the computer and managing files
3. Word processing
4. Spreadsheets
5. Databases
6. Presentation
7. Information and communication

Concepts of information technology

This module tests your knowledge of the basic facts about computers, whether you know your rights and responsibilities as a computer user and how computers are used in everyday life. You will also be asked some general questions about the Internet and e-mail.

Subjects covered in this section:

Advanced questions

ECDL module

5.	E-mail	**1.5.2**
6.	Copyright	**1.8.1**
7.	Portable computers	**1.1.2**
8.	Hardware	**1.2.4**
9.	RAM	**1.2.2**
10.	Formatting disks	**1.2.6**
11.	Shareware	**1.8.1**
12.	Pointing devices	**1.2.3**
13.	Modems	**1.4.4**
14.	'Zipping'	**1.2.6**
15.	Storing information	**1.2.2**

INTRODUCTORY QUESTIONS

1. Name a common desktop publishing application and explain its purpose.

2. In businesses, computers are often networked. Give three reasons why this has advantages for the organization.

3. What is the reason for using passwords on computers? Why do you see ***** when you type your password?

4. List three ways in which a hospital might use a computer to improve the delivery of health care.

5. Explain the purpose of keeping backup copies of files.

6. Name two sources of computer viruses. What steps can you take to reduce the risk of catching viruses?

7. What is the main purpose of the Data Protection Act? Give one reason why each of the following organizations might keep personal data on computer:

   a) bank
   b) school or college
   c) doctor's surgery.

8. How does system software differ from application software? Give one example of each.

9. What is the difference between the Internet and the World Wide Web?

10. Explain the term GUI. Give two advantages of GUI compared with earlier methods of working with computers.

11. Name three different means of communicating using the telephone network. Which method(s) require the use of a computer?

12. What might you find in the i) A: drive, ii) C: drive and iii) D: drive of a computer?

13. Name the four main stages in the development of software systems. What is the role of a programmer?

14. What term is used to describe the setting up of a business on the Internet? List three advantages and three disadvantages of shopping online.

15. Give two reasons for using floppy diskettes for storing files.

ADVANCED QUESTIONS

1. Which five steps can you take to ensure that you work safely with your computer?

2. What is a CPU? How is its speed measured?

3. Name three activities that can be carried out when using online banking facilities.

4. Describe the difference between laser and inkjet printers.

5. Give three reasons for using e-mail rather than the post when sending messages.

6. Why does copyright matter when searching for pictures on the Internet?

7. What is a common name for a portable computer? Describe three ways in which it differs from a desktop computer.

8. List two input and two output hardware devices in a computer system. Select one output device and describe briefly how it works.

9. What does RAM stand for? In which two ways does it differ from ROM?

10. Explain how to format a floppy diskette. How often should you format the hard disk? Select one option:

    a) once a week
    b) once a year
    c) only on special occasions
    d) you cannot do this – you must return the computer to your supplier.

11. What is shareware? What is the difference between shareware and freeware?

12. Why are pointing devices used with a computer? List four different types of pointing device and describe briefly how one of these works.

13. Why would you use a modem? How do modems work, and what is their current top speed?

14. Explain the term 'zipping'.

15. What measurement units are appropriate for the following (select from gigabytes (GB), megabytes (MB) and bytes):

    a) hard disk
    b) RAM
    c) CD-ROM
    d) floppy diskette.

MODULE **2**

Using the computer and managing files

This module will help you to check that you can give your machine instructions, that you understand the desktop and that you can work with Microsoft Windows. You will also be tested on your knowledge of how to work safely with a computer and how to organize your work into folders.

Subjects covered in this section:

Introductory questions		ECDL module
1.	Shutting down your computer	2.1.1
2.	File types	2.3.3
3.	Using the **Help** menu	2.1.2
4.	Changing the size of a window	2.2.2
5.	Working with printers	2.5.1
6.	Restarting your machine	2.1.1
7.	Exploring your computer	2.1.2
8.	Exploring folders	2.3.2
9.	Using Find	2.3.6
10.	Zipping	2.3.7

Exercises		ECDL module
1–2	Creating files and folders, renaming and deleting folders	**2.1.3, 2.3.2, 2.3.3 and 2.3.5**
3–4	Copying, moving, renaming and deleting files	**2.3.3, 2.3.4 and 2.3.5**
5–6	Working with multiple files, using Find	**2.3.4 and 2.3.6**
7–8	Saving a file into a folder	**2.1.3**
9–10	Using Print Screen and printing a file	**2.1.2 and 2.5.2**

INTRODUCTORY QUESTIONS

1. Describe the process for shutting down your computer. Why is it wrong to simply turn off the power?

2. **a)** Name two common image file types.
   b) Identify which types of files have the following extensions:
   .txt   .htm   .xls   .doc

3. Use the **Help** menu to provide details of where the calculator is located on your computer.

4. Explain how to change the size of a window on the desktop.

5. What is the name of your default printer? If you were also linked to a different printer, how would you change the default?

6. Describe three different methods for restarting your machine if it freezes.

7. From the desktop, find out and note down your computer's operating system, RAM and processor.

8. Open the Recycle Bin or My Documents folder, reorganize the contents to display full details, and note down three different types of file that it contains and the dates the files were deleted or modified.

9. Use the Find facility to locate any file or folder named Notepad. Note down the number of items listed and the main folder location.

10. Describe the steps to take in order to compress or zip several large files.

You need to know how to:

▶ Create a folder

▶ Open a word processing application and start, name and save a new document.

▶ Create subfolders inside a folder

▶ Rename or delete folders

2

Exercise 1 1. Open My Documents (or a floppy disk if preferred) either on the desktop or within Windows Explorer.

2. Create a folder and name it **Numbers**.

3. Inside the **Numbers** folder, create two subfolders and name them **Large** and **Medium**.

4. In Word, start a new document. Type the word **Eleven** and then save the file with the same name. Note the default location where you are saving the file. Close the file.

5. Create and save five more files named **Three**, **Seven**, **Two**, **Four** and **Six**. Make sure all files are closed and then either close or minimize Word.

6. Re-open the **Numbers** folder and rename the two sub-folders. They should now be named **Even** and **Odd**.

 Module 2, sections 1.3, 3.2 and 3.3

Exercise 2 1. Within My Documents or on a floppy disk, create a folder named **Food**.

2. Inside the folder, create three sub-folders and name these **Fruit**, **Veg** and **Salad**.

3. Open Word, create five files and save them with the following names: **Lemon**, **Carrot**, **Potato**, **Apple** and **Blackcurrant**. Either type the file name in the document before saving or save blank files. Close all the files and either close or minimize Word.

4. Return to your folders and rename **Veg** so that it becomes **Vegetables**.

5. Delete the **Salad** sub-folder.

 Module 2, sections 1.3, 3.2 and 3.3

You will need to know how to:

▶ Move files into folders

▶ Copy files into folders

▶ Rename or delete files

Exercise 3
1. Locate the file named **Three** and move it into the **Odd** sub-folder.

2. Locate files named **Seven** and **Eleven** and move them into the same sub-folder.

3. Locate the files named **Two**, **Four** and **Six** and move them into the **Even** sub-folder.

4. Copy the file named **Seven** into the **Numbers** folder.

5. Re-name this file **Number 7**.

6. Re-open the **Odd** folder and delete the original file named **Seven**.

 Module 2, sections 3.3, 3.4 and 3.5

Exercise 4
1. Locate the **Lemon** file and move it into the **Fruit** folder.

2. Locate **Apple** and **Blackcurrant** and add these to the **Fruit** folder.

3. Rename **Blackcurrant** so that it is named **Blackberry**.

4. Now locate the **Carrot** and **Potato** files and move them into the **Vegetables** folder.

5. Place a copy of **Apple** in the **Vegetables** folder and rename the file **Leek**.

 Module 2, sections 3.3, 3.4 and 3.5

You will need to know how to:

▶ Move or copy more than one file at the same time

▶ Find files or folders

2

Exercise 5　1.　Use the Find facility to locate the **Number 7** file created earlier.

2.　Note down the full details of file type, size and date it was last modified.

3.　Now open the **Even** sub-folder.

4.　Select all the files and move them together into the **Numbers** folder.

5.　Delete the **Even** sub-folder.

6.　Finally, open the **Odd** sub-folder and copy all its contents into the **Numbers** folder.

 Module 2, sections 3.4 and 3.6

Exercise 6　1.　Use the Find facility to locate the **Potato** file. Note down its size, file type and the date it was last modified.

2.　Open the **Vegetables** sub-folder and move **Leek** and **Potato** together into the **Food** folder.

3.　Copy **Carrot** into the **Food** folder and rename this file **Carrot tops**.

4.　Delete the **Vegetables** sub-folder together with any files it still contains.

 Module 2, sections 3.4 and 3.6

EXERCISES 7 AND 8

You will need to know how to:

▶ Save a file into a folder

Exercise 7
1. Open Word and start a new, blank document.

2. Save the file with the name Ten into the Numbers folder.

3. Now create a new file named Orange and save it into the Fruit subfolder.

4. On the desktop or within your file management program, check that the file Ten is listed inside the Numbers folder. Re-name the file Ten times table.

5. Now check that Orange is inside the Fruit subfolder. Copy it into the Food folder and re-name the copy Orange blossom.

6. Locate the file Carrot tops and delete it completely.

7. Finally, create a new folder named Managing My Files and move the following four files into it at the same time: Lemon, Apple, Orange and Blackberry.

 Module 2, section 1.3

Exercise 8
1. In My Documents or on a floppy disk, create the following three folders: German, Italian and French.

2. Inside the Italian folder, create two subfolders named Male and Female.

3. In Word, create a file named Gatto. Save it into the Male subfolder.

4. Now create the following five files and save them into the folders shown in brackets: Casa (Female), Libro (Male), Regazzo (Female), Haus (French) and Tavola (Female).

5. On the desktop or within your file management program, open the Female subfolder. Locate the file Regazzo and move it into the Male subfolder.

6. Copy Gatto into the French folder and rename the file Chat.

7. Copy the file Tavola into the German folder and rename the file Tafel.

8. Finally, move the file named Haus into the German folder.

 Module 2, section 1.3

You will need to know how to:

▸ Use the Print Screen facility

▸ Print a file

Exercise 9
1. Open the file named Gatto.
2. Type the following words: The Italian word for cat is gatto.
3. Update your file to save the changes and then close the file.
4. Now open the file named Haus and type the following text: The German word for house is Haus.
5. Save these words and then close the file.
6. On the desktop or within Windows Explorer, open the Male subfolder, and then open the file named Gatto.
7. Print one copy and then close the file.
8. Locate and open the file named Haus and print two copies.
9. Close the file and Word.
10. Open the Male folder and use Print Screen to take and print a picture of the contents.

 Module 2, sections 1.2 and 5.2

Exercise 10
1. Locate and open the file named Orange.
2. Type the following words: The word orange means the same in English and French.
3. Save these changes and close the file.
4. Open the Managing My Files folder and move Orange into the folder named French.
5. Now open Orange and print one copy.
6. Close the file and Word.
7. Open the French folder and use Print Screen to take and print a picture of its contents

 Module 2, sections 1.2 and 5.2

MODULE **3**

Word processing

In this module you will test your word processing skills. In the ECDL exam you will need to show that you can create, save and print documents that are formatted attractively, and that you are able to incorporate images or items brought in from elsewhere and can move or edit these as appropriate. You will also be tested on the various features that are available to help you work efficiently with long documents.

Subjects covered in this section:

Introductory exercises		ECDL module
1–2	Creating, changing, saving and printing a document	3.1.1 and 3.6.2
3	Opening and saving a new version of a file	3.1.1
4–5	Using the automatic spelling and grammar checker	3.6.1
6–7	Selecting and fomatting text; saving different file types	3.1.1, 3.2.2 and 3.3.1
8–9	Aligning text and changing line spacing	3.3.2
10	Indenting a paragraph; using **Edit | Replace**	3.2.5 and 3.3.2
11	Changing margins; using Print Preview to check a document	3.3.3 and 3.6.1
12–13	Changing the page orientation; moving and copying text	3.3.3 and 3.2.4
14	Bullets and numbering; inserting the date automatically	3.3.2
15	Copying formatting	3.3.1

Advanced exercises		**ECDL module**
1–2	Headers and footers; inserting a page break; printing selected pages	**3.3.3 and 3.6.2**
3	Inserting symbols	**3.2.1**
4	Using the **Insert** menu; saving files into a new folder	**3.3.3**
5–6	Working with Clip Art	**3.4.2**
7	Change case; hanging indents	**3.3.1 and 3.3.2**
8	Adding borders and shading	**3.3.2**
9	Creating and editing tables	**3.4.1**
10	Applying an AutoFormat to a table	**3.4.1**
11–12	Working with tabs; applying a font colour	**3.3.1 and 3.3.2**
13	Working with styles and templates	**3.3.1 and 3.3.3**
14–15	Setting up a Mail Merge	**3.5.1**

EXERCISES 1 AND 2

You will need to know how to:

◗ Create a simple document

◗ Make amendments

◗ Save a file

◗ Print a copy

Exercise 1 1. Open your word processing application and, on a blank page, enter the following text in capitals:

SURFACE FEEDERS

2. Press **Enter** twice and type the following text, only pressing **Enter** when you are ready to start the second paragraph:

All the fish found 'just under the surface' have a perfectly straight back, which allows their upturned mouths to get right up to the surface. Foods which float for some time are ideal for these fish.

A common surface feeder is the Glass Catfish. This fish is a native of India and is very active and lively. It can reach a size of about 5 cm and is best kept in shoals.

3. Check the text for errors (i.e. proof-read). To correct mistakes, click on the error with the mouse or use your arrow keys to move the cursor and delete or insert letters or spaces as necessary.

4. Save the file as **Surface Feeders** onto a floppy disk, or into the My Documents folder on the hard disk or, if working on networked computers, into a designated area.

5. Print one copy.

6. Now make the following changes:
    ● After upturned mouths insert the following text:
      (ideal for scooping up floating foods, usually insects)
    ● Replace the name Glass Catfish with Zebra Danio.

7. Add your own name on a new line at the end of the text and print a copy of the amended document.

8. Update the file to save the changes.

9. Close the document.

 Module 3, sections 1.1 and 6.2

Exercise 2

1. Start a new document and enter the following text:

   THE POTENTIAL OF MUSIC

   Teachers generally provide a stimulating environment for children in their classes, with respect to sight and touch, but more can be done. Other experiences may be overlooked. One of the senses which can be educated quite easily is hearing. Sounds are all around us in the secondary school and with careful structuring they can even become organized sounds – music.

   Children make sounds all the time – they talk, shout, cry, scream or sing. A good way to focus on sounds is to tell stories needing 'sound effects', such as those of police cars, ambulances, trains or ghosts.

2. Proof-read and correct any errors.

3. Save as The Potential of Music.

4. Print one copy.

5. Now make the following amendments:
   - Change secondary school to infants.
   - Delete the phrase: but more can be done.
   - Insert the following text after ... focus on sounds is:
     to use rhymes and poems and

6. Add your name at the end of the document and print one copy.

7. Save the changes you have made to update the file.

8. Close the document.

 Module 3, sections 1.1 and 6.2

EXERCISE 3

You will need to know how to:

▶ Open a file saved previously

▶ Save a file as a different version of the original

1. Open the file Surface Feeders.

2. Insert a third paragraph:

   The Siamese Fighting Fish is hardy, but you can only have one male in a tank otherwise fighting will break out. If you want to see it display, put a mirror at the side of the tank. Aquarium-cultivated strains usually have bodies and fins of one colour, apart from the Cambodia Fighter that has a cream body and coloured fins.

3. Change the heading to: FIGHTING FISH

4. Proof-read and correct any mistakes.

5. Save this as a new file with the filename Siamese Fighter.

6. Print one copy.

7. Close the document.

8. Open the file The Potential of Music.

9. Add the following paragraph:

   One activity teachers can try is to sit the group in a circle. Everyone claps three times, then leaves a space equivalent to three more claps, and then everyone claps three times again. How the gap is filled is up to the teacher, but you could alternate between 'oohs' and 'aahs'.

10. Change the heading to: MUSIC GAMES.

11. Proof-read and correct any mistakes.

12. Save this as a new file with the file name Clapping.

13. Print one copy.

14. Close the document.

 Module 3, section 1.1

EXERCISES 4 AND 5

You will need to know how to:

▶ Use the automatic spelling and grammar checker

Exercise 4 1. Start a new document and type the following text as shown, retaining spelling mistakes to the words quarter, blood, arteries and oxygen:

Heart Disease

Heart disease causes a quarrter of all deaths in Britain. It is the biggest killer of middle-aged men in the developed world.

You need a healthy heart to pump bloood around your body, and heart muscle needs food and oxygen for it to keep contracting. These are carried in the coronary arteries. If the arnteries get blocked, then it can cause heart disease. The risk increases if you smoke, become overweight or take no exercise.

A total blockage or thrombosis can cause a heart attack. Here the supply of oxygeen is cut off, there are severe pains in the chest and the affected part of the heart is damaged.

2. Proof-read and use the automatic spelling and grammar checker to correct any mistakes.

3. Save the file with the file name Heart Disease.

4. Print one copy.

5. Now make the following amendments:
   - Change the title to read: The Problems of Heart Disease
   - Delete the final sentence in paragraph two beginning The risk ... .
   - Add the following sentence to the start of paragraph three:
     The artery wall can become rough and this can cause the blood to clot and block the vessel.

6. Update the file to save the changes.

7. Print one copy.

8. Close the document.

 Module 3, section 6.1

Exercise 5 1. Start a new document and enter the title of a favourite book or film followed by the word Uncorrected.

2. Type out two paragraphs outlining the main story.

3. Leave any spelling or grammar mistakes uncorrected – if necessary, add a few extra letters to some words to create mistakes – and save the document with the book or film title as the file name.

4. Print a copy of the uncorrected document.

5. Now correct all the mistakes, using the spelling or grammar checker where possible.

6. Change the word Uncorrected to Corrected in the main title.

7. Save the file as a new version with the file name Book/Film Title 2.

8. Print a copy of the corrected document.

9. Close the document.

 Module 3, section 6.1

You will need to know how to:

▶ Select text

▶ Format text

▶ Save files as different file types

Exercise 6
1. Open the file Heart Disease.

2. Make the title bold and underlined.

3. Select the complete text and increase the font size.

4. Select the final paragraph and format it to italic.

5. Save the changes.

6. Add a new paragraph, formatted to Arial, 14 point, underlined:

   You can take care of your heart by eating more poultry and fish. Cut down on fried foods and red meat and always eat plenty of fruit and vegetables.

7. Save and print a copy of the document.

8. Close the document.

9. Reopen and save as plain text, changing the name to Heart Disease – New type.

10. Close and then reopen the file, making sure you search for plain text files. Print a copy and compare it to the document you printed earlier.

 Module 3, sections 1.1, 2.2 and 3.1

Exercise 7
1. Start a new document and enter the following text:

   ONE POT WONDER
   (Serves 2 – 3)

   4 lamb chops
   700g peeled and diced carrots, potatoes and swedes
   pinch of dried oregano
   15ml tomato puree

   Preheat the oven to gas mark 7. Tip vegetables into a shallow ovenproof dish and arrange the lamb chops over the top. Sprinkle over the herbs, season then roast in the oven for 15 minutes.

Mix the tomato puree with a cupful of hot water and pour over the chops and vegetables. Continue cooking for another 20 minutes.

2. Proof-read and save as One Pot Wonder.

3. Print a copy of the recipe.

4. Select the title and format to bold.

5. Select the list of ingredients and format to italic.

6. Select the instructions, increase the font size and apply a different font, e.g. Times New Roman or Courier.

7. Select the title and add a double underline via the **Format | Font** menu.

8. Save these changes and print a copy of the amended recipe.

9. Save a second version of the file as a plain text file with the name OPWplain.

10. Close the document.

 Module 3, sections 1.1, 2.2 and 3.1

EXERCISES 8 AND 9

You will need to know how to:

▶ Align text

▶ Amend line spacing

Exercise 8 1. The following items are available on a hotel breakfast menu:

fruit juice or cereal
fried egg, sausage, bacon, fried tomatoes, fried bread
grilled kippers
toast and marmalade
tea, hot chocolate or coffee

2. Type out a menu with the title Breakfast at Hotel Belle Vue. The food items should be arranged as five separate courses with at least one line in-between each item, and all text should be centred on the page.

3. Format the title so that it stands out, e.g. increase the font size, make it bold or underlined, etc.

4. Separate the courses with symbols, e.g. """""" or +++++.

5. At the bottom of the menu, enter the following text, left aligned:

Breakfast will be served from 7.30 – 9.00 a.m. Please note that some items on the menu may change according to availability as we like to offer the freshest ingredients in our meals.

6. Add today's date at the top of the menu, right-aligned.

7. Save as Breakfast and print a copy.

8. Double space the final paragraph, left align the date and then print a copy of the amended document.

9. Update the file to save these changes, and then close.

 Module 3, section 3.2

Exercise 9 1. Create the following document, proof-read it, and save as Viruses:

Catching the Fever

Viruses are an unpleasant fact of computing life we could all do without. However, by being aware of the nature of the problem you can guard against the risk of PC infections.

If you've yet to be infected by a computer virus, you're in a dwindling minority. There are now so many viruses in circulation that it's almost impossible to use a PC for any length of time and not encounter one. Cutting through the hype about viruses isn't easy though, particularly when some computer users add to it by forwarding bogus virus alerts to all and sundry.

2. Centre the title and format it as bold.

3. Fully justify the main text.

4. Change the line spacing of the first paragraph to 1.5, and double space the second.

5. Add the date at the bottom of the document, right-aligned.

6. Apply an alternative font to the whole document.

7. Increase the font size of the title text to 14.

8. Save these changes and print a copy. Then close the file.

 Module 3, section 3.2

EXERCISE 10

You will need to know how to:

- Indent paragraphs
- Use the **Edit | Replace** menu

1. Create the following document, proof-read and correct any errors.

   IT'S OK TO GIVE ORDERS

   Good behaviour in kids is required not as a whim of parents but to make practical living easier. Unlike parents of the Victorian era, we do not need pointless obedience, such as brushing one's hair before tea, but we do ask kids to co-operate to make life easier.

   When kids don't co-operate, the parents find their life inconvenienced. Soft parents will soon find they are being given the run-around. However much they want to give in and not inhibit their children's creativity, these parents find they are very angry and tired of the troubles this causes, and attempt to restore order. Feeling steamed up, they may lash out and discipline their kids in a way that they and the child know is somewhat out of control. This is bad for everyone concerned and there are more successful ways to give orders.

2. Save as Orders and print a copy.

3. Indent the first paragraph by 1 cm from the left margin.

4. Using the **Edit | Replace** menu, replace the word kids with the word children wherever it occurs (four times).

5. Left-align the title and underline the word OK.

6. Add the following text as a new paragraph, indented by 1.5 cm from both the left and right margins:

   Be clear in your own mind: It's not a request or open to debate, it's a demand which you have a right to make.

   Make good contact: Stop what you are doing, go up close to the child and get her to look at you.

   Be direct: Say, "I want you to .... now. Do you understand?" Make sure you get a "yes" or "no" answer.

7. Save these changes and print a final copy.

 Module 3, sections 2.5 and 3.2

You will need to know how to:

◆ Check a document in Print Preview

◆ Change margins

1. Create the following document, proof-read it and save as Gardening:

Mr & Mrs S.M. Tyler
Green Acres
17 Bathurst Close
Bath, Avon
BT3 7PY

The Editor
Greenfingers Magazine
44 Old Station Yard
Kingley
Wellington
WT5 7LL

22 May 2002

Dear Sir

Early Hellebores

You may like to know that I followed the advice in last month's edition of your magazine and ordered 26 Hellebores.

When they arrived, they were planted under a fir tree at the bottom of the garden, which you indicated in your article was an ideal spot.

According to your column, the plants would flower profusely from January until late April, and would give my garden much needed colour at this damp and dank time of year.

Unfortunately, I have wasted £35!

Only three of the plants have flowered, and these were a sickly sight. The rest provided a feeble show of leaf and then gave up and dropped all their foliage.

Frost damage was clearly visible on many of the plants and they obviously needed far more light and water.

I am very disappointed at the poor advice I received and have cancelled my subscription to your magazine forthwith.

Yours with regret

S. M. Tyler

2. Increase the left and right page margin by 2 cms

3. Print a copy of the letter.

4. Make sure the document extends just over onto a second page – if necessary, add extra spaces after Yours with regret.

5. Check in Print Preview and then use **Shrink to Fit** to reduce the letter to one page.

6. Reformat Mr Tyler's address, e.g. make it italic and/or apply a different font.

7. Using the ruler, decrease the width of the right margin by approximately 1 cm.

8. Print a copy of the amended letter and save as a new version with the file name Gardening 2.

9. Close the document.

 Module 3, sections 3.3 and 6.1

EXERCISES 12 AND 13

You will need to know how to:

▶ Change to landscape orientation

▶ Move or copy text

Exercise 12 1. Start a new document, select a font size of 14 point and type the following text, centre aligned:

Come to a Party!

2. In a smaller font, type the rest of the invitation and save as Party:

Jane & Rick
Invite .... to their
House Warming
on
Saturday, 22 June
at
12 Rymans Road, Reading

3. Change to landscape orientation and check your document in Print Preview.

4. Close Print Preview and move the line at 12 Rymans Road, Reading so that it appears *above* the date.

5. Increase the font size of House Warming to 16 point and format to italic.

6. Copy House Warming so that the first line of your document reads:

Come to a *House Warming* Party!

7. Print a copy of the invitation and save the changes before closing the file.

 Module 3, sections 2.4 and 3.3

Exercise 13 1. Open the file Breakfast.

2. Move grilled kippers so that it appears after cereal.

3. Copy the phrase Breakfast at Hotel Belle Vue so that it also appears at the end of the menu.

4. Now make the following amendments:
   - On the line below cereal, add the following:
     (choice of tomato, orange or pineapple juice)
   - Change fried egg to read: fried, boiled or scrambled egg

5. Delete cereal and replace with stewed prunes.

6. Add an extra course after prunes:
   Porridge, Muesli or Cornflakes

7. Change to landscape orientation and alter the left and right margins and/or spaces between courses so that the menu fits centrally on the page.

8. Update the file to save the changes and print a copy of the amended menu.

 Module 3, sections 2.4 and 3.3

EXERCISE 14

You will need to know how to:

- Add numbers and bullet points
- Format number or bullet style
- Insert the date automatically

1. Create the following document:

THE VERY BEST OF FRANCE

Normandy: alluring medieval villages, upmarket 19th-century seaside resorts, the island-abbey of Mont St Michael and endless windswept beaches on the Cotentin peninsula.

Brittany: magnificent beaches lining the north coast, dramatically wind-battered west coast, gentler bays in the south and rolling countryside inland.

Burgundy: a wealthy region of forests, meadows, magnificent ancient cities and some of the world's great vineyards.

The Alps: holidays in the mountains, less crowded than the Mediterranean coast, ski lifts to take you up to the peaks for long hikes and après-ski haunts for morning coffee.

2. Add today's date above the heading.

3. Format the place names to bold and underlined.

4. Save the document as France and print a copy.

5. Number the paragraphs.

6. In the first paragraph, reorganize the text so that it forms a bulleted list, deleting the final and. It should be set out as follows:

   1. <u>**Normandy**</u>:

      - alluring medieval villages,
      - upmarket 19th-century seaside resorts,
      - the island-abbey of Mont St Michael
      - endless windswept beaches on the Cotentin peninsula.

7. Repeat this formatting for the other three paragraphs.

8. Re-format the bullet points in the final paragraph so that they have a different appearance, e.g. select squares or ticks instead of black circles.

9. Indent the paragraph beginning The Alps by 1 cm from the left.

10. Increase the left margin of the page to 4 cm.

11. Save the changes and print a copy of the amended document.

 Module 3, section 3.2

You will need to know how to:

▶ Copy formatting from a selected piece of text

1. Type in the following text:

    Flats

    Living in a flat means plumbing and drainage emergencies can cause problems above and beyond those experienced by house owners. After all, leaking water wherever it comes from won't just cause damage to your own property. It can also cause considerable distress to neighbours and can have potentially disastrous results if you are away for a while.

    However, there are also great advantages to flats. For example, if you are on a fifth floor or above, the views can be fantastic, and burglars are less likely to carry your heavy furniture or electric goods down many flights of stairs or in full view of other residents if they are brazen enough to use the lifts. This makes flats a good choice for those who are away for a good part of their working day.

2. Format the main heading by changing the font type, increasing the font size and making it bold and italic.

3. Fully justify the first paragraph.

4. Double-space the second paragraph and indent it by 1 cm from the right margin.

5. Add the following subheadings to the two paragraphs: *Plumbing* and *Views*

6. Copy the main heading formatting and apply it to the subheadings.

7. Centre the main heading on the page.

8. Save as Flats and print a copy.

9. Now add the following paragraph at the end of the document, keeping the list single spaced:

    Here are some of the emergencies that can happen to flat owners:

    1. Burst pipes
    2. Leaking washing machine
    3. Nail through heating pipe
    4. Blocked kitchen sink
    5. Blocked toilet
    6. Leaking radiator valve

10. Update the file and print a copy.

11. Move the last paragraph so that it becomes the second paragraph under *Plumbing*.

12. Change the numbered list to a bulleted list. Make sure the paragraph justifications are retained and print a final copy before saving and closing.

 Module 3, section 3.1

ADVANCED EXERCISES

EXERCISES 1 AND 2

You will need to know how to:

▶ Add headers and footers

▶ Create a page break

▶ Print selected pages

Exercise 1 1. Open Gardening 2.

2. Start a new page after ... all their foliage.

3. Add Hellebores as a header and your own name and page numbers as a footer.

4. Start a new page after Mr Tyler's signature and enter the following text in italics:

    Spring flowers can be the most welcoming as they cheer up dull wintry days. They are often white, pale blue or yellow and contrast well with dark green evergreen leaves. Summer flowers are usually more brightly coloured – oranges, reds and purples – but can fade very quickly.

5. Print a copy of the final (current) page only, and save the file as Gardening 3.

6. Now delete the header and add the word Flowers somewhere in the footer.

7. Save this change and print page 1 of the document only.

8. Close the file.

 Module 3, sections 3.3 and 6.2

Exercise 2 1. Type out the following text:

Watercolour Painting

The size of a painting is very much a matter of personal preference. There are no rules, but if working small, say 6 x 4in., gives you confidence, that's fine. On the other hand, it can be exciting to work large and it can increase your enthusiasm. If you ever feel you are getting stale or need a change, try working in a different size and you might be amazed at the different work you create.

When painting from nature, the natural arrangement you are confronted with is often the best way to give your work credibility. There are so many different aspects to capture including the temperature, weather, stage of growth and seasonal nature. The same garden in winter, autumn or high summer will look unbelievably different.

2. Save as Painting and print a copy.

3. Create a page break after the first paragraph and double space the second paragraph.

4. Add the following paragraph subheadings: *Size* and *Composition*

5. Add the following text as a footer: *Exercise on Painting*. Insert the date and page numbers as a header.

6. Indent the first paragraph 2 cms from the left margin.

7. Reformat the main heading – apply a different font and underline – and make the document text italic.

8. Print page 2 only of your document.

9. Save the changes and close the file.

 Module 3, sections 3.3 and 6.2

EXERCISE 3

You will need to know how to:

❯ Insert special symbols or characters

1. Start a new document and type the following text:

Word processing packages often allow you to use symbols or special characters to liven up your documents. You should be able to find a book, telephone, pair of scissors or smiley face when using Wingdings fonts, or insert symbols for hearts, diamonds, spades and clubs when searching the gallery of Symbols.

2. Save as Symbols.

3. Now add a title – Special Characters – underlined and centred at the top of the page.

4. Start a new paragraph after … your documents. and insert the following text before You should… :

   A good use for these pictorial symbols is for children's games. For example, if you typed a message in a normal font and then applied Wingdings to the text, it would be impossible to read. Offering the alphabet code for each symbol would then allow a child to decipher the message.

5. For each mention of a special character such as a book or telephone, insert the appropriate symbol into the text – you should find eight. (If you cannot find, e.g. the symbol for clubs (♣), find an alternative and change the text as appropriate.)

6. Indent and double space the second paragraph only.

7. Add a footer showing the date and your name.

8. Save the changes, print a copy and then close the file.

 Module 3, section 2.1

EXERCISE 4

You will need to know how to:

▶ Add page numbers via the **Insert** menu

▶ Save a file into a new folder

1. Grimble & Denton, estate agents of 22 Wattis Road, Boscombe, Bournemouth BN5 2AA want to sell a seaside flat. Produce a two-page description of the property (start page 2 with kitchen details), attractively formatted and set out, based on the following information:

   Address of the property: Flat 49, Seaview Road, Southbourne

   Price: £250,000

   Summary: A beautifully appointed ground floor 3-bed property with excellent sea views and balcony, situated close to the picturesque beaches of Southbourne. Included in the price are fitted cupboards, electric hob, carpets and barbecue. There is a garage behind the property which is in a well-kept block built around 1950. Internal inspection highly recommended.

Hall: Carpet, entryphone, radiator.

Sitting room: Large French windows to balcony, seaviews, fireplace, radiator, TV point, telephone point, shelving, Venetian blinds.

Dining Room: Wood floor, radiator, window to rear.

Bedroom 1: Seaviews, fitted cupboards, carpet, radiator.

Bedroom 2: Window to rear, shelves, radiator.

Bedroom 3: Window to side, fitted cupboards, radiator.

Kitchen: Breakfast bar, tiled floor, fitted cupboards, sink unit, electric hob, plumbing for washing machine, door to communal gardens.

Bathroom: Gold taps, shower unit, green suite, glazed window to rear.

2. Add page numbers using the **Insert** menu.

3. When saving the file, first click the **Create New Folder** button in the **Save As** dialog box to create a folder labelled Bournemouth, and save the file into this folder with the file name Property.

4. Close the file and close your word processing application.

5. Reopen Property (you may first have to locate and open the Bournemouth folder) and make the following amendments: Bedroom 2 has no shelves; the kitchen has a wall-mounted electric oven; and there is also a Study with a glass chandelier and wooden floor.

6. Save the amendments and print one copy before closing the file.

 Module 3, section 3.3

EXERCISES 5 AND 6

You will need to know how to:

▶ Insert Clip Art

▶ Amend Clip Art, e.g. resize, crop or border

▶ Delete Clip Art

Exercise 5 1. Open Property, click below the estate agent's address and insert an appropriate picture from the Clip Art Gallery.

2. Resize the picture and align it centrally on the page.

3. Amend the picture, e.g. by adding a background colour and border, cropping one area and increasing the contrast.

4. Print page 1 of the document displaying the picture.

5. Insert a text box in a space at the end of the property details.

6. Return to the gallery and find and insert a different image into the text box. If necessary, resize the picture inside the box.

7. Drag the box so that the picture is positioned on the right of the page, and add colours and borders.

8. Add today's date as a footer.

9. Update the file and print a copy of the last page only.

10. Close the file.

 Module 3, section 4.2

Exercise 6 1. Start a new document. Enter the words: Welcome to Boscombe Zoo on one line and Open every day except Christmas Day a few lines below.

2. Centre the text and make the heading italic, font size 24 point.

3. Save the file as Zoo into the Bournemouth folder.

4. In the space between the two lines of text, insert a picture of an animal from the Clip Art Gallery.

5. Centre and enlarge the picture so that it fills about a quarter of the page – check in Print Preview. Make sure the sentence beginning Open every day ... remains below the picture.

6. Add a thick, coloured border to the picture via the **Format** menu.

7. Add the following bulleted list below the picture, indented by 5 cms from the left margin and formatted attractively, e.g. bold, font size 16 or 18 point:

    ● Circus spectacular show twice a day
    ● See the animals being fed
    ● Cuddle baby lambs and goats
    ● Restaurant and cafe open all day
    ● Take a train ride round the zoo

8. Print a copy of the poster, first adjusting the picture size if necessary to make sure you only print on one page.

9. Now delete the picture and insert an alternative that can be on either an animal or circus theme but must be positioned *below* the bulleted list. Use the cropping tool to cut off any unwanted edges and add a coloured background.

10. Format the bullets to a different style.

11. Print a copy of the amended document.

12. Update and close the file.

 Module 3, section 4.2

You will need to know how to:

▶ Change case

▶ Apply hanging indents

1. Start a new document and type the following text:

STANLEY ROAD HOSPITAL TRUST

The following opportunity has arisen for a clear-thinking, caring individual to join our acclaimed Trust as a full-time ASSISTANT. You will help trained nurses assess need and deliver care to the many older patients at our brand new SALTWOOD ANNEXE.

For the post, we are looking for an exceptional person. You must have first-aid training, good communication skills, be patient and caring and enjoy working flexibily.

To apply, please send us a full c.v. together with the names of two referees.

For further information, write to Marion Hobbs, Saltwood Annexe, Webleton Hospital, Grundy Close, Chesterham. Or phone her on 0166778 2349.

2. Print a copy and save as **Hospital**.

3. Using change case facilities, make the following amendments:

   a) change the heading to title case (i.e. Stanley Road Hospital Trust).

   b) change c.v. to C.V.

   c) change ASSISTANT to lower case

   d) change SALTWOOD ANNEXE to title case (i.e. Saltwood Annexe)

4. Move the second sentence, beginning 'You will help trained nurses ...' so that it becomes the second sentence in the second paragraph. Ensure there are no extra spaces.

5. Centre align the heading.

6. Apply hanging indents to all the paragraphs.

7. Update the file and print a copy before closing.

 Module 3, sections 3.1 and 3.2

EXERCISE 8

You will need to know how to:

◆ Add borders and shading

1. Create the following document, proof-read it and save as Advert.

SEE-RIGHT-THRU DOUBLE GLAZING

Who can you trust to install double glazing?

Few people are experts in double glazing, So if you're looking to improve your home with PVC-U windows, doors or a conservatory – and don't fancy entrusting such a major decision to a possible cowboy – use us.

One call and you will be in touch with a nationwide network of approved, fully trained installers who are monitored regularly by a team of inspectors.

We use only the best materials, and there's a free 20-year guarantee.

Call now on Freephone 0800 444555 for a no-strings quotation.

SEE-RIGHT-THRU

The name to trust

2. Centre the text, then increase the font size for the heading and make it bold.

3. Delete the word us at the end of the second paragraph and replace with SEE-RIGHT-THRU copied from the end of the document.

4. Apply a thick, coloured border to the heading and check that it extends across the width of the page.

5. Apply shading to the heading background.

6. Box the last paragraph so that only the text is bordered.

7. Insert an appropriate picture from the Clip Art Gallery (e.g. windows, houses, etc.) just below the heading and centre it on the page.

8. Replace each mention of THRU with THROUGH using the **Edit | Replace** menu.

9. After the sentence ending ... guarantee, insert the following numbered paragraph left aligned:

    1. We are fast
    2. We are careful
    3. We leave the site tidy
    4. We are the best.

10. Move the paragraph beginning **One call** ... so that it follows the free-phone number.

11. Print a copy and close the file, making sure you save the changes.

 Module 3, section 3.2

3

EXERCISE 9

You will need to know how to:

▶ Create tables

▶ Edit tables

1. Start a new document and type the title: Landscombe College Evening Classes.

2. Insert the following table, ensuring all columns are wide enough to display entries on a single line and row heights are at least 0.6 cm:

Title	Day	Tutor	Time	Room
Bee-keeping	Monday	Jamie Green	7–9 p.m.	B3
Yoga for Beginners	Tuesday	Pat Hurt	6.30–8.00 p.m.	Hali
Calligraphy	Monday	Serena Holden	10–12 a.m.	C14
Car Mechanics	Wednesday	Jack Byrne	6–8 p.m.	Workshop
Watercolour painting	Tuesday	Nancy Smythe	2–4 p.m.	B9

3. Save as **Classes** into a new folder named **College** and print a copy.

4. Add two new classes after 'Yoga':

- Computing for Beginners on Thursday, at 3–5 p.m., in Room C14, tutor Howard Maynard
- Advanced Yoga on Wednesday, at 7–9 p.m., in the Hall, tutor Pat Hurt.

5. Delete the Calligraphy course record, making sure you don't leave empty cells.

6. Centre align all headings except Title and format the text so that it stands out, e.g. use bold and/or increase font size.

7. Apply different borders and shading formats to the table.

8. Save the changes and print a copy.

9. On a line below the table, type the following sentence:

New students may like to know that the following videos acquired by the College are relevant to this term's classes and may be available for hire.

10. Create and format a new 5 × 5 table containing the following data:

Title: Yoga For All
Presenter: The Graceful Goddess
Hire charge: £1.50
Length: 110 mins
Available: On loan

Title: Bees For Life
Presenter: William and Sarah Price
Hire charge: £2.50
Length: 150 mins
Available: Yes

Title: Know Your Car
Presenter: Ray B. Wise
Hire charge: £3.00
Length: 90 mins
Available: Yes

Title: Keeping Bees
Presenter: Walter Mitts
Hire charge: £1.50
Length: 90 mins
Available: On loan

11. Add your name as a header, right-aligned, then update the file and print a copy before closing.

 Module 3, section 4.1

You will need to know how to:

▶ Apply AutoFormats to tables

1. Create a table of six items such as books, records, films, etc., and classify them under at least five headings, e.g. author, title, price, category and publication date. Make sure all data is fully displayed.

2. Save with a suitable file name and print a copy.

3. Delete the second record, making sure you don't leave any empty cells.

4. Add a further item as record number 5.

5. Choose an AutoFormat and apply it to the table.

6. Move the table so that it is centred on the page.

7. Increase the font size for the category headings and make all data entries italic.

8. Add a footer to include the text My Table, the date and the exercise number.

9. Format the exercise details in the footer to bold and underline the date.

10. Update and print a copy before closing the file.

 Module 3, section 4.1

EXERCISES 11 AND 12

You will need to know how to:

▶ Use and set tabs (⮕)

▶ Move the position of tabs

▶ Apply a font colour

Exercise 11 1. Enter the following column headings across the page:

Make   Type   Price   Colour

2. Set out the following information using tabs (⮕). Use decimal tabs for Price and left or centre tabs for the other details. Set the Type column at 4 cm and the Price column at 8 cm.

Miele → oven → £153.99 → black
Electrolux → fridge-freezer → £245 → white
Tricity → cooker hood → £76.99 → silver
Servis → dishwasher → £196.50 → brown
Philips → washing machine → £279.99 → white

2. Save the file as Household items and print a copy.

3. Format the column headings to blue, underlined.

4. Add the following item:

Hoover → upright vacuum cleaner → £89 → red

Move the Price column to the right (and/or Type column to the left) to ensure all details will be fully displayed.

5. Save and print an updated copy. Close the file.

 Module 3, sections 3.1 and 3.2

Exercise 12 1. Enter the following data using tabs. Set centre tabs for Surname, decimal tabs for Per cent and right tabs for the numerical data.

CLASS MARKS 2000

First Name	Surname	Maths	Science	English	Per cent	Total
Janet	Brown-Smythe	40	35	38	75.33	113
Peter	Smith	23	38	46	71.33	107
Richard	Wellington	31	48	40	79.33	119
Harry	Longbottom	15	23	37	50.00	75
John	Baker	38	26	22	57.33	86
Mary	French	50	50	50	100.00	150

2. Save as Marks and print a copy.

3. Format the headings to italic, the names to bold and the numerical data to red.

4. Add the following student details below the entry for Richard Wellington, making sure the columns are adjusted to display the data fully:

Danielle-Celeste Courvoisier, Maths 23, Science 44, English 19, 57.33 per cent and a Total of 86.

5. Update the file and print a copy before closing.

 Module 3, sections 3.1 and 3.2

You will need to know how to:

▶ Apply styles and use templates

1. Type in the following company name and centre it on the page: Home Decorating Ltd.

2. Below this, type the following memo:

   To: Denise Watermill, Marketing Manager
   From: Arnold Morton, Ceramics Department
   Copied to: Head of Purchasing
   Subject: Bali and Hong Kong
   Date: (today's)

   With regard to the recent sales, I am writing to let you know that there was a huge demand for the new lines we purchased from Bali and Hong Kong. Many customers asked when we would be stocking smaller items such as soup bowls, spoons and tea cups, and I feel such items would almost walk off the shelves if we had them in stock.

   I suggest we have a meeting as soon as is practicable to discuss purchasing more items from the Far East, and a possible television advertising campaign to accompany these new goods.

3. Save as Ceramics and print a copy.

4. Now apply the following formatting: Heading 1 style to the company name; Heading 2 style to the subject of the memo; a lower level heading style to the date and people's names and job titles; and a body text style to the main text.

5. Update the file and print a copy.

6. Copy the main text of Ceramics into the clipboard and then select a memo template from those available, in order to create a different version of the memo.

7. Paste in the main text and type in the names, job titles and company name.

8. Format the text as you like and save as Ceramics 2.

9. Print a copy and then save and close both memos.

 Module 3, sections 3.1 and 3.3

You will need to know how to:

▶ Create a data source

▶ Carry out a Mail Merge

Exercise 14 1. In a new document, type the heading Wilmington College, Derbyshire, apply italics and bold format, and centre it on the page. Now use this document as the basis for a mail merge.

2. Set up the following data source containing only the fieldnames shown, save as Staff and enter all the records:

Firstname	Surname	Department	Food
Marion	Peters	Business	crisps
David	Holmes	IT	pizza
Ken	Jackman	Business	salad
Mel	Griffiths	English	quiche
Beverley	Garland	IT	jelly

3. Type the following memo, inserting field names as shown:

To: <<Firstname>> <<Surname>>,<<Department>> Department
From: (your name)
Date: (today's)
Subject: End of Year Party

As spokesperson for the course, I am writing to ask you to come to our final session in the Staff Room on Friday at 2.00 p.m. We would like to hold a party as a fun way to end the course, and would like you to bring some <<Food>> as a small contribution.

Please let me know if you are unable to attend.

4. Check that all records have been merged.

5. Print a copy of the document displaying field names.

6. Merge to a new document and print three memos displaying data taken from the database.

7. Save and close the data source and main document files.

 Module 3, section 5.1

Exercise 15 1. Start a new document and then create the following data source to use for a mail merge. Save as **Names** and enter all the records.

Title	Firstname	Surname	Town	Age	Allowance
Mr	James	Smith	York	62	£2,400
Mr	Paul	Black	Leicester	64	£3,580
Mrs	Jean	Kenton	York	72	£4,000
Mr	Harry	Oldham	Birmingham	62	£2,400
Mr	Peter	Witton	York	69	£3,765
Ms	Sarah	Danby	Leicester	66	£3,245
Mr	Harry	Smith	Manchester	69	£3,765
Miss	Sally	Black	Birmingham	77	£5,490

2. Create and edit the following main document, inserting appropriate field names as shown.

<<Title>> <<Firstname>> <<Surname>>
<<Town>>

Date: (today's)

Dear <<Title>> <<Surname>>

Extra payment

As a resident of <<Town>> who has reached the age of <<Age>> and who has been living in the city for 2 years, we have the power to pay you an extra <<Allowance>>.

This will be sent in the form of a cheque to your home address at the end of the month.

Yours sincerely

Gordon Best

On behalf of the Inland Revenue

3. Print a copy of the main document showing the field names.

4. Now print two copies of the document displaying details taken from two different records.

5. Save the main document as **Payments** and update the data source before closing both files.

 Module 3, section 5.1

Spreadsheets

This module tests your knowledge of spreadsheets and charts. In the ECDL exam you will need to know how to set up a spreadsheet, format numbers and text and use formulae to perform a range of calculations. There are also exercises in this module on sorting data, functions such as Average and Sum, and creating and amending different styles of chart.

Subjects covered in this section:

EXERCISES 1 AND 2

You will need to know how to:

- Enter text and numerical data
- Amend cell entries
- Widen columns
- Perform simple calculations
- Save and print a spreadsheet

Exercise 1

1. Create the following spreadsheet:

	A	B	C	D	E
1	DARTS				
2	Name	Score 1	Score 2	Score 3	Final score
3	Marion	8	11	3	
4	Harry	12	22	6	
5	Steve	3	5	18	
6	David	18	16	5	
7	Joan	9	12	11	

2. Enter a simple formula in cell *E3* to work out **Marion's** final score (*i.e. Score 1 + Score 2 + Score 3*).

3. Calculate final scores for all the other darts players.

4. Save the file as **Darts** and print one copy.

5. On a new row, add the name **Elizabeth-Jane** and scores of **11, 15 and 20**.

6. Widen column *A* to display all names fully.

7. Calculate Elizabeth-Jane's final score in *E8*.

8. Change **Steve's** Score 2 to **9** and check that his final score is updated automatically.

9. Change **Marion's** name to **Marigold**.

10. Print a copy of the revised spreadsheet and then update and close the file.

 Module 4, sections 1.1, 2.1, 2.3, 4.1 and 7.3

Exercise 2   1.   Start a new workbook and create the following spreadsheet:

	A	B	C	D
1	SHOPPING			
2	Item	Cost (£)	Number	Final price (£)
3	Catfood	0.4	10	
4	Milk	0.38	4	
5	Loaf	0.87	2	
6	Marmalade	1.15	1	
7	Pasta	0.56	3	
8	Pineapple	1.3	2	
9	Lemonade	0.89	3	

2.   Enter a formula in *D3* to calculate the final price of Catfood (i.e. *Cost ×
     Number*).

3.   Work out the final price for all other items.

4.   Save the file as **Shopping** and print one copy.

5.   Now amend the entry in cell *C2* to read **Number Bought**, and widen
     columns *C* and *D* to display the full entries.

6.   Make the following changes: **Pasta** costs **49p**; replace **Pineapple** with
     Melon; and increase the number of pints of **Milk** bought to **6**.

7.   Check that the final prices are updated automatically and print a copy of
     the amended spreadsheet.

8.   Save and close the file.

 Module 4, sections 1.1, 2.1, 2.3, 4.1 and 7.3

EXERCISES 3, 4 AND 5

You will need to know how to:

◆ Format text and numerical data

◆ Align cell contents

◆ Calculate totals using the SUM function or AutoSum

◆ Open a previously saved spreadsheet

Exercise 3 1. Reopen Shopping and right-align all column headings except Item.

2. Type Total in cell *A10* and enter a formula in *D10* to work out the overall total for the shopping bill.

3. Format data entries in the Cost and Final price columns to currency.

4. Change the title in *A1* to SHOPPING AT SUPERMART and increase the font size to 14 point.

5. Print a copy of the amended spreadsheet.

6. Now make the following changes: Marmalade costs £1.35 and a loaf is 93p. Check that the total is updated automatically before saving and closing the file.

7. Open Darts and format all the scores to display two decimal places.

8. Right-align all column headings except Name.

9. Format the players' names to bold.

10. Select all the entries on the spreadsheet and apply a different font.

11. Save as Dart2 and print a copy before closing the file.

 Module 4, sections 4.3, 5.1 and 5.2

Exercise 4 1. Create the following spreadsheet, ensuring all data is fully displayed:

Shares					
Months	Bellings	Thatchers	Gordington	Lowden	Witneys
Jan	2.4	12.6	22	0.5	18
Feb	3.7	13.2	14.6	0.96	16.5
Mar	1.6	7.9	18	1.3	17
Apr	0.75	5.6	30.3	4.1	17.8
May	4.9	14.1	31.7	3.7	16.4
Total					
Average					

2. Calculate the total for Bellings' shares.

3. Calculate totals for all other shares and save the file as Shares.

4. Format all numerical entries to currency and two decimal places.

5. Calculate the average price of Bellings' shares (i.e. *Total/Number of months*).

6. Work out all other averages and format the Average row as currency to one decimal place.

7. Format the title to bold and the column headings to italic.

8. Centre the column headings.

9. Save the changes and print a copy.

10. Now make the following amendments: Thatchers' share price in April was £6.40 and Gordington's in January was £24. The name Witneys should be changed to Morgan.

11. Update the file and print a copy of the amended spreadsheet before closing.

 Module 4, sections 4.3, 5.1 and 5.2

Exercise 5 1. You and a friend had the following meal:

Melon (you) £1.25
Soup (friend) £1.00
Steak & kidney pie (both) £4.50 a portion
Chips (you) 80p
Jacket potato (friend) 75p
Salad (both) £1.25 each
Ice-cream (you) £1.10
Apple pie (friend) £2.10
Coffee (both) 85p per cup

2. Set up a spreadsheet with the title Restaurant to show both your meals: type your names in cells *B2* and *C2* and enter all the food items in column A. Make sure cells contain only numerical data (i.e. no 'p' for 'pence'). Leave cells blank if you did not have a particular item.

3. Widen columns to display the full entries, format prices to currency and right-align your names.

4. Add a row labelled TOTAL and enter formulae to calculate both bills.

5. Apply bold format to the name of the person with the more expensive meal.

6. Save as Restaurant and print a copy of the spreadsheet.

7. Close the file.

8. Reopen Restaurant and make the following changes: ice-cream cost 95p; you had two cups of coffee; and your friend had fruit salad at 90p instead of apple pie.

9. Did the same person have the most expensive meal this time? If not, change the name in bold.

10. Update the file and print a copy of the amended spreadsheet before closing.

 Module 4, sections 4.3, 5.1 and 5.2

You will need to know how to:

◆ Copy cell entries and date series

◆ Insert or delete columns and rows

Exercise 6 1. Create the following spreadsheet:

Own Brand Cereal Prices					
SHOP	Gateway	Waitrose	Tesco	Co-op	Safeway
Size of pack (gm)	500	750	450	1000	1500
Price per pack	2.5	2.8	2	4.5	3.75
Cost per 100 gm					

2. Work out the cost of 100 gm **Gateway** cereal using the formula *Price/Size × 100*.

3. Copy this formula along the row to work out the cost of 100 gm of all the other cereals.

4. Format the shop names to italic and right-align.

5. Print a copy of the spreadsheet and save as **Cereal**.

6. Now insert a new column to the right of **Tesco** and add the following details:

   Asda, 1000gm pack costs £3.50.

7. Copy across the formula to calculate the cost of 100 gm of **Asda** cereal.

8. Delete the column containing the entry for **Waitrose**.

9. Insert a new row below the title and type: **Comparison**

10. Format the prices to currency.

11. Increase the title font size and apply bold format.

12. Save and print the amended spreadsheet before closing the file.

 Module 4, sections 2.3 and 2.5

Exercise 7 1. Create the following spreadsheet:

Dates	Postage	Coffee/Tea	Cleaning	Stationery
January	13.5	11	14	15.75
	7.65	2.5	14	17.38
	19.38	3.45	14	20.75
	9.23	4.15	17	9.5
	11.68	2.17	17	12.45

2. Insert a new row 1 and type the heading: PETTY CASH EXPENSES.

3. Copy the date series down the first column.

4. Add a new row Totals and enter a formula to calculate total postage costs. Copy this formula across the row to produce totals for the other items.

5. Adjust column widths and format the column headings to bold, font size 14. Format all numerical data to currency.

6. Save as Office and print a copy.

7. Now insert a new column after Cleaning headed Furniture and enter £385 for March and £37.99 for May. Calculate the total for Furniture.

8. Make the following changes:

    ● cleaning in April is now £14;
    ● coffee costs £3.50 in February;
    ● the Stationery heading should now read Stationery/Disks.

9. Update the file and print the amended spreadsheet before closing.

 Module 4, sections 2.3 and 2.5

Exercise 8

1. Create the following spreadsheet and save as Bookings. Reformat the Price column if it displays dates. Widen columns to ensure all data is fully displayed and print a copy.

Holiday Bookings					
Date of Booking	Surname	Villa	Start date	End date	Price
02-Feb	Billings	Caprice	01-Jun	08-Jun	209
25-Feb	Derbyshire	Miramar	15-Jun	22-Jun	354
03-Mar	Winslow	Capri	25-May	1-Jun	567
15-Mar	Harris	Nuit	15-Jun	22-Jun	248
07-Apr	Davis	Miramar	20-Jul	27-Jul	422
16-Apr	Pentford	Soleil	18-May	25-Jun	680

2. Right-align all headings except Date of Booking and format to bold. Left align data in the Date of Booking column.

3. Format all prices to currency, to display the £ symbol and no decimal places.

4. Apply a different date format to all dates, e.g. 02-Feb becomes 2/2/02.

5. Add a new row heading: Total and work out the total income for the holiday bookings.

6. Insert a new column between End date and Price headed Max. number and use the following table to enter the correct figures:

Villa	Max. number
Caprice	5
Miramar	4
Capri	6
Nuit	3
Soleil	4

7. Head a new column Price per person and enter a formula to work this out for the first booking (*Price/Max. number*). Copy the formula down the column to find the price per person for all bookings.

8. Format the Price per person column to currency and two decimal places.

9. Make the following amendments: Billings should read Browning; the price for Nuit should be £295; delete the Davis booking completely, leaving no empty cells.

10. Copy the title Holiday Bookings to a new row underneath the spread-sheet data and format it to bold.

11. Realign any entries to neaten the spreadsheet appearance.

12. Update and print a copy of the amended spreadsheet before closing the file.

 Module 4, sections 2.3 and 2.5

EXERCISES 9, 10 AND 11

You will need to know how to:

♦ Add borders and shading

♦ Change page orientation

♦ Print to fit one page

Exercise 9 1. Create a spreadsheet to show the following recipe details:

Pizza			
Item	Quantity for 2	Cost per item	Final Price for 2
Strong flour (lb)	1.5	0.70	
Yeast (sachet)	1	0.20	
Fat (oz)	2	0.40	
Olive oil (tbs)	3	0.30	
Tomatoes	2	0.25	
Mozzarella (oz)	6	0.80	
Spicy sausage (oz)	4	0.85	
Onion	1	0.30	
Total			

2. Enter a formula to calculate the final price of **strong flour** and copy this formula down the column.

3. Enter a formula to add together the entries in the final price column to find the overall cost.

4. Right-align all column headings except Item.

5. Format quantities to two decimal places, and all prices to currency.

6. Add a border and shade the background of the column headings. Then shade the Item column entries a different colour.

7. Save as Pizza and print a copy.

8. Insert a new column between Quantity for 2 and Cost headed Quantity for 30. Enter a formula to work out the quantity of flour needed to make pizza for 30 (i.e. *Quantity for 2 × 15*). Copy this formula down the column and format to two decimal places.

9. Change to landscape orientation.

10. Type your name in *L2* (or the cell after the dotted lines indicating the edge of page 1) and check in Print Preview that your name is on page 2.

11. Go to **Page Setup** and select the option to **Fit to 1 page**. Now check in Print Preview that your name is visible alongside the spreadsheet data.

12. Print a copy of the amended spreadsheet.

13. Save and close the file.

 Module 4 sections 5.3 and 7.1

Exercise 10 1. Create the following spreadsheet with the title *TVs* and save the Workbook with the same name.

Make	Price	Size of screen (ins)	Features
Westwood	159.99	20	Stereo
Jacksons	198.75	14	Televideo
Merit	229.99	14	DVD-player
Piccolo	99.99	14	Silver
Bradleys	179	17	Silver
Clerical	79.99	2.3	Pocket-size

2. Format the prices to currency and two decimal places.

3. Right-align all headings except **Make** and format all headings to bold.

4. On a new row, type the row heading Total and enter a formula to work out the total cost of all the TVs.

5. On a row below that, headed **Average**, enter a formula to work out the average price (Total/6).

6. Save and print a copy of the spreadsheet.

7. Now insert a new column headed: **Teletext** between **Screen** and **Features** and enter **Yes** for all TVs except the **Clerical**.

8. Add a further column headed: **No. in stock** and enter the following data:

    Westwood   20
    Jacksons   14
    Merit   2
    Piccolo   12
    Bradleys   5
    Clerical   8

9. Make any further changes necessary to width of columns or alignment and add different borders and shading to improve the attractiveness of the spreadsheet.

10. Check the spreadsheet in print preview and change to landscape orientation.

11. Print a copy of the spreadsheet, making sure it prints on one page.

12. Save and close the file.

 Module 4 sections 5.3 and 7.1

4

Exercise 11 1. Create the following spreadsheet and save as Writing:

Writer's Costs				
MONTH	PENS	PAPER	DISKS	COFFEE
JAN	2.5	3.7	1.8	0.65
FEB	3.67	9.5	3.5	2.4
MAR	1.8	2.7	4.85	2.5
APR	5.5	0	2.7	0.9
MAY	2	3.45	1.1	2.45

2. Right-align all column headings except MONTH.

3. Add a new column headed *TOTAL* and enter a formula to calculate the total costs in January. Copy this formula down the column to find the total for other months.

4. Insert a new column after *PAPER* and before *DISKS* headed *TRAVEL*. Enter the following data:

   Jan: 15.34, Feb: 7.78, Mar: 12.9, Apr 22.5, May 5

5. Check that the *TOTAL* column now includes travel costs.

6. Work out and enter the Overall Total at the bottom of the TOTAL column and add this text as a row heading in column *A*.

7. Work out the average expenditure per month and display this figure under the overall total. Use the formula *OVERALL TOTAL divided by 5* (i.e. the number of months) and enter Average as a row heading.

8. Display the expenditure figures as currency to two decimal places.

9. Display the *TOTAL* column figures in Integer format (i.e. whole numbers).

10. Apply borders and shading to enhance the appearance of the data.

11. Landscape page orientation and print a copy of the spreadsheet, fitting it on one page.

12. Save and close the file.

 Module 4 sections 5.3 and 7.1

You will need to know how to:

- Use absolute cell references

- Apply AutoFormats

Exercise 12 1. Create the following spreadsheet and save as **Meal**.

	A	B	C
1	Food	Price(£)	Discount offered
2	Omelette	4.50	
3	Salad	2.00	
4	Chips	1.50	
5	Fudge cake	2.75	
6	Tea	0.85	
7	Total		
8	Final Price		
9	Discount is:		
10	5%		
11			

2. Enter a formula in *B7* to calculate the total food bill.

3. Enter a formula in *C2* to calculate the discount offered on **Omelette** (i.e. **Price** × **Discount**). Use the cell address *A10* in the formula, *not* the actual figure 5%.

4. Copy the formula down column *C* to work out the discount on other meal items without first making *A10* absolute. What do you think the formula will look like in cell *C3*? (The result will look wrong because the formula will include a reference to cell *A11* that has nothing in it.)

5. Return to cell *C2* and absolute *A10* in the formula, i.e. it will become A10. Now copy the amended formula down the column to replace the original entries. All discounts should now look correct.

6. Calculate the total **Discount offered** in *C7*.

7. Enter a formula in *B8* to work out the final price for the meal (i.e. *Price Total – Discount offered Total*).

8. Reformat the spreadsheet to show currency and apply your preferred AutoFormat. Save and print a copy.

9. Change the discount shown in *A10* to (a) 10% and (b) 17.5%. Check that the final prices change and print the two new versions.

 Module 4 sections 4.2 and 5.2

Exercise 13 1. Open a new workbook and on the first line enter the title **Sale of Tiles for January**. On the row below the title enter the following column headings:

Code number Colour Price of pack Cost of 1 tile Packs sold Final price

Adjust the column widths to display the full entries.

2. All column headings except **Code number** should be right-aligned.

3. Enter the following data (to retain a '0' at the start of each Code number, either format column *A* to text first, or press ' before typing the first '0'):

	A	B	C	D	E	F
1	Sale of Tiles for January					
2	Code number	Colour	Price of pack	Cost of 1 tile	Packs sold	Final price
3	005	Red	6.5		20	
4	041	Blue	8.75		35	
5	018	Green	4.95		30	
6	019	Green	18.45		10	
7	049	Blue	33.5		5	
8	006	Brown	3.25		25	
9	TOTAL					
10	No. tiles per pack	25				

4. Save the file as **Tiles** and print a copy of the spreadsheet.

5. Enter a formula to calculate the **Final price** of packs of **Red** tiles sold that month (i.e. *Price of pack* × *Packs sold*). Copy this formula down the column to find the final price for all other tiles sold.

6. The Tile Company decide that **Blue** tiles coded **049** should be listed in a different category. Delete the complete entry for these tiles.

7. Now make the following amendments: the price of packs of **Green** tiles, code 018 is £7.95 and the colour of tile 041 is **Black**.

8. The **Brown** tiles should have been entered as **Patterned–Brown**. Amend the entry and widen the **Colour** column to display this name in full.

9. Calculate the cost of one red tile (i.e. Price of pack/No. tiles per pack) using the cell address and *not* the figure 25 in the formula. Copy this formula to find the cost of each type of tile sold and format the entries to currency.

10. Calculate the total number of packs sold and the total of the **Final price** column.

11. Save these changes.

12. On a row below the **Red** tile entry, insert a new row and add the following details: **Yellow** tiles, code number 026, each pack costs £12.45 and the number of packs sold is 14. Complete all entries for these tiles making sure all totals are updated.

13. Reformat all remaining prices to currency and apply an AutoFormat to improve the appearance of the spreadsheet.

14. Change the number of tiles per pack shown in *B10* to **50**. Check the new cost of each tile and border the row of the *cheapest* tile to make it stand out.

15. Print a copy of the amended spreadsheet before saving the changes and closing the file.

 Module 4 sections 4.2 and 5.2

Exercise 14 You need to buy new carpets for a sitting room, bedroom and bathroom, so create the following spreadsheet to help you work out the cost.

1. Name and save the spreadsheet as **New Carpets** and enter the following column headings:

Room Length (ft) Width (ft) Area (sq ft) Area (sq metres) Cost (sq metres)

2. Enter the following measurements:

Room	Length (ft)	Width (ft)
Sitting	14	10.5
Bed	9	8.25
Bath	6	7

3. Enter a formula to work out the area of the sitting room carpet in sq ft (i.e. *Length* × *Width*) and then copy this formula down the column to work out the areas for the other carpets.

4. Print a copy of the spreadsheet.

5. One sq ft is equivalent to 0.0929 sq metres. Type this figure into cell *A9*.

6. Enter a formula to convert the area of the sitting room carpet from sq ft to sq metres (i.e. multiply it by 0.0929) using the cell address *A9* in the formula and *not* the actual figure. Copy this formula down the column to work out the areas of the bedroom and bathroom carpets in sq metres.

7. The sitting room carpet costs £22.85 per sq metre, the bedroom carpet costs £19.25 per sq metre and the bathroom carpet costs £8 per sq metre. Enter these prices into the Cost column.

8. Now head a new column Final Price and enter a formula to work this out for the sitting room carpet, i.e. *Cost per sq metre* × *Area per sq metre*. Copy this figure down the column to work out the final price for all three carpets.

9. Add a new row headed Total and total the cost of carpets in the Final Price column.

10. Format the Cost and Final Price columns to currency and all other numerical data to two decimal places. Right-align all column headings except Room and apply your own choice of borders or shading.

11. Update the spreadsheet and print a copy that fits one page before closing the file.

 Module 4 sections 4.2 and 5.2

You will need to know how to:

- Add headers and footers
- Centre headings across the width of a spreadsheet
- Use the AVERAGE function

Exercise 1   1.   Set up the following spreadsheet showing the distribution of money to various charities over six months.

	A	B	C	D	E	F	G	H	I
1	Charity Contributions								
2									
3	Charity	Percent	Jan	Feb	March	April	May	June	Average
4	RNIB	50%	1000	1840	645	2500	2340	1158	
5	Birds	12%	240	442	155	600	562		
6	Lifeboats	5%	100	184	64		234	116	
7	Sue Ryder	25%	500	920	322	1250	1170	579	
8	Oxfam	8%		294	103	400	374	185	
9	Total		2000			5000		2315	

2.   Enter a formula in *B9* to check that the percentages add up to 100.

3.   Enter appropriate formulae to work out the missing January, April and June entries (i.e. *Percent × Total*) and **February**, **March** and **May** totals.

4.   Use the **AVERAGE** function to display average contributions to the various charities.

5.   Add formatting, a border and some shading to improve the attractiveness of the spreadsheet, and realign entries as necessary.

6.   Format contributions to currency with no decimal places.

7.   Centre the heading **Charity Contributions** across the width of the spreadsheet.

8.   Add *DISTRIBUTION OF MONEY* as a header and your name and the date as a footer, and then save and print a copy before closing the file.

 Module 4 sections 4.3, 5.3 and 7.1

Exercise 2

1. Create a spreadsheet to show your expenditure over four months. Your income is £200 per month, but in the second month you earned an extra £45.

   Your outgoings were as follows:

	1st month	2nd month	3rd month	4th month
Heating	£25	£25	£25	£25
Food	£75	£30	£60	£45
Travel	£5	£12.50	£5	£2.50
Entertainment	0	£15.50	£5	0
Clothes	£65	£13.45	£48	£7

2. Format the spreadsheet attractively and add borders and shading. Save as Expenditure.

3. Insert a new row 1 and type the heading:

   Expenditure over four months

   Centre it across the width of the spreadsheet.

4. Add your name and the date as a header and *Exercise 16* as a footer.

5. Add rows as necessary to show your total expenditure each month, your income and what was left over.

6. In a new column headed **Average**, work out the average amount you spent in each category.

7. Save and print the spreadsheet.

8. Insert an extra row for **Newspapers & Magazines** below Travel: you spent 75p each month. Check that the totals take this row into account and that all entries are fully displayed.

9. Delete the entire row showing **Entertainment** expenditure and then insert an extra row above **Heating** labelled **Holidays**. Enter £350 for the third month only and make sure the totals have been updated.

10. Save the changes and print a copy showing the new totals.

 Module 4 sections 4.3, 5.3 and 7.1

Exercise 3 1. Create a spreadsheet to show the average temperature in different locations, using the following data:

Temperature °C						
	Jan	Feb	Mar	Apr	May	Jun
Brize Norton	4.3	3.7	6.3	7.9	11.4	14.4
Oxford	3.7	4.2	5.8	8.4	11.7	14.9
Cambridge	3.4	3.9	5.7	8.3	11.6	14.7
Sheffield	3.8	3.9	5.4	7.8	10.9	14.1
Durham	2.8	3.2	4.6	6.8	9.6	12.9

2. Create a new column named **Average** and enter a formula to work out the average temperature for **Brize Norton** over the six months. Copy this formula down the column to work out averages for the other locations.

3. Format all numerical data to two decimal places.

4. Centre the main heading across the top of the spreadsheet data and format to bold and italic.

5. Save as **Temperature** and print a copy.

6. Now delete the details for **Brize Norton** and make sure no empty cells remain.

7. Insert a new row for **Lyneham** between **Oxford** and **Cambridge** and enter the following data:

Jan	Feb	Mar	Apr	May	Jun
3.9	3.5	6.0	7.7	11.1	14.1

8. Work out the average temperature in **Lyneham** during the six months.

9. Head a new row **AVERAGE** and work out the average temperature in all the locations during January. Copy this formula along the row to work out averages for all the months and ensure they are formatted to two decimal places.

10. Apply borders and shading and realign or format any headings as you like and then print a copy of the spreadsheet to fit one page.

11. Update and close the file.

 Module 4 sections 4.3, 5.3 and 7.1

You need to know how to:

▶ Modify margins

▶ Use the **Edit | Replace** menu to search and amend cell entries

1. Create the following spreadsheet showing costs for boat hire and save as Boats.

BOAT HIRE					
No. of people	1 Day	2 Day	3 Day	Weekly	Average
2 – standard boat	80	120	180	240	
2 – superior boat	100	130	250	280	
4 – standard boat	125	155	210	295	
4 – superior boat	150	180	225	300	
6 – luxury	200	225	250	320	
8 – standard	210	300	330	360	

2. Use a formula to work out the average daily rate for the two-person standard boat hired for a week (i.e. *Weekly rate divided by 7*).

3. Replicate this formula to work out average daily rates for all other boats.

4. Save and print a copy of the worksheet.

5. Centre the heading across the width of the spreadsheet.

6. The four-person standard boat is no longer available, so delete this entry completely.

7. The weekly cost for a six-person luxury boat should be changed to £375.

8. Insert a new row between the 2 – superior and 4 – superior boats for a special offer. The row heading should be Autumn special – 2-superior. Rates are as follows: 1 Day – £90; 2 Day – £125; 3 Day – £200 and Weekly – £265.

9. Widen columns as necessary to display all data fully and work out the average daily rate for the new entry.

10. Format the Average column to currency and no decimal places, but all other prices should be formatted to two decimal places. Realign any headings as preferred.

11. Using the **Edit** menu, replace each mention of **boat** with **class**, except in the spreadsheet title.

12. Ensure in Print Preview that the data are centred vertically on the page. Increase the left margin to 2 cm and make sure the spreadsheet will print on a single page.

13. Print the spreadsheet and close the file.

 Module 4 sections 2.6 and 7.1

EXERCISES 5 AND 6

You will need to know how to:

▸ Create a database

▸ Sort records

Exercise 5 1. Set up a spreadsheet to display information about homes for sale using the following column headings: Type, Bedrooms, Garage, Garden, Price, Location

Enter the following data:

Flat 4 bedrooms garage no garden £100,000 York

Bungalow 3 bedrooms garage garden £175,000 Selby

Flat 3 bedrooms no garage garden £97,000 York

Semidetached 4 bedrooms garage paddock £217,950 Derby

Detached 5 bedrooms garage garden £345,750 Nottingham

Bungalow 2 bedrooms garage patio garden £75,799 Selby

Flat 1 bedroom no garage no garden £115,000 Sheffield

Semidetached 3 bedrooms garage garden £200,450 York

2. Format the numerical data appropriately and add a border round the column headings before printing a copy. Save as **Homes**.

3. Sort the records by price in ascending order (from lowest to highest) and print a copy of the reordered spreadsheet.

4. Now carry out a first- and second-order sort: alphabetically by location and then by number of bedrooms in descending order. Save this change and print a copy.

5. Add the following record:

   Detached house in Selby, price £300,990, 5 bedrooms, double garage, marina.

6. Sort first alphabetically by type and then by ascending order of price.

7. Delete the entire record for Nottingham and print a final copy of the spreadsheet before saving and closing the file.

 Module 4 section 2.7

Exercise 6   1. You have bought a range of tins and packets and want to work out which is the healthiest food. Set up a database with the title Healthy Eating and the following five field names (category headings):

   Item Weight (g) Kcals Fat Protein

2. Enter the data as follows:

Item	Weight (g)	Kcals	Fat	Protein
Baked beans	420	260	1.20	19.4
Sardines	90	156	8.1	20.7
Dried apricots	500	800	3	20.70
Peanut butter	340	2023	172.72	83.64
Tuna	132	120	0.28	28
Almonds	300	1842	150	63.3

3. Add a new column headed Kcals per 100 g and enter a formula to work out the figure for baked beans (i.e. *Kcals/weight × 100*).

4. Copy this formula down the column to work out Kcals per 100 g for all the items.

5. Now add two new columns headed Fat per 100 g and Protein per 100 g. Work out the amounts for baked beans (i.e. *Protein/weight × 100* and *Fat/weight × 100*) and then copy these formulae down the columns to calculate fat and protein content for 100 g of all the other food items.

6. Right align all column headings except Item and apply your own choice of AutoFormat.

7. Format the **Weight** and **Kcal** columns to Integer (no decimal places) and all other numerical data to two decimal places before printing a copy of the database.

8. Sort the records in ascending order of Kcals per 100 g to find the least fattening food.

9. Underneath the data, type and complete the following sentence formatted in bold: **The item of food with the least Kcals per 100 g is … .**

10. After saving the file, add the text **Healthy Eating** as a footer and insert the filename as a field into the header.

11. Save and print a copy of the worksheet displaying the data centred vertically and horizontally and fitting on a single page.

12. Sort the database to see which food items have the most protein per 100 g and least fat per 100 g before closing the file.

 Module 4 section 2.7

You will need to know how to:

◆ Create a simple chart

◆ Resize and move charts

◆ Print charts alone or with spreadsheet data

Exercise 7   1.   Create the following spreadsheet and save as Results:

Name	Score
Smith	245
Green	199
White	278
Burton	362
Wooleroote	299
Sims	375
Haversham	204

2.   Sort the records in alphabetical order.

3. Create a 2D column chart to display the scores and place it on the same sheet as the data. The title should be **Final Results in 1999**, the axes should be labelled **Names** and **Scores** and there should be no legend.

4. Resize the chart to display all the data fully and move it so that it does not obscure the spreadsheet data.

5. Print a copy of the chart together with the spreadsheet data and save and close the file.

6. Reopen **Shares** and create a simple line chart with the title **Share Prices January – May** to display share prices for the five-month period. The x-axis should be labelled **Months**, the y-axis labelled **Price** and the legend should show the different companies.

7. Place the chart on the same sheet, resize if necessary and print a copy of the chart only.

8. Update the file before closing.

 Module 4 section 6.1 and 7.3

Exercise 8 1. The following pens are available through mail order:

Ballpoint pens	Number in pack	Cost
Zebra	10	6.70
Berol pen set	12	24.51
Punchline	50	5.75
Zebra Jimnie Classic	2	1.78
Pilot rubber grip	12	12.25
Pentel superb	12	9.72
Papermate stick	50	8.09
Uni	12	7.20
Staedtler stick	10	1.70
Bic crystal	20	3.57

2. Create a spreadsheet and enter these details. Make sure the columns are wide enough to display the full entries.

3. Format the **Cost** column to currency and print a copy.

4. Insert a new column between **Ballpoint pens** and **Number in pack** headed **Cost of 1 pen**. Enter a formula to work out the cost of one **Zebra** ballpoint (i.e. *Cost/Number in pack*) and copy it down the column to find the cost of each type of pen.

5. Delete the entry for the **Berol pen set**, making sure you don't leave an empty row.

6. Add a footer showing your name and the date.

7. Use an AutoFormat or add borders and shading from the **Format** menu to improve the appearance of the spreadsheet, and print a copy.

8. Now create a pie chart on the same sheet showing the cost of one pen of each type. Resize if necessary, add a suitable title, include data labels and print a copy of the chart on its own.

9. Update and close the file.

 Module 4 sections 6.1 and 7.3

EXERCISES 9, 10, 11 AND 12

4

You will need to know how to:

▶ Format chart elements

▶ Change chart type

▶ Select non-adjacent cell ranges

Exercise 9 1. Create the following spreadsheet and save as Rugby:

Roverton Rugby Club			
First Quarter Income			
Description	January	February	March
Joining fees	4000	2000	1950
Club House	3700	5500	5500
Donations	350	0	275
Other	275	136	400
Monthly totals			

2. Enter a formula to work out the total income for January.

3. Copy this across the row to work out totals for the other months.

4. Add a new column headed Total and enter a formula to work out the total joining fees received during the quarter. Copy this formula down the column to work out totals for the other sources.

5. Create a bar chart showing the sources of income for January. Give the chart the title January Income, and label the vertical axis Source of income and horizontal axis Income (£).

6. Format the axis labels to italic. Realign the y-axis labels, e.g. from horizontal to a slant.

7. Select an alternative chart title font and move the title to a new position within the chart area.

8. Add your name as a footer and print a copy.

9. Change the chart to a pie chart, add a legend and label the sectors with the % income. Print a copy of the amended chart.

10. Now create a chart of any type on the same sheet to show only the source of income and the quarterly total. Format attractively and save and print just the chart.

11. Finally, on a separate sheet, create a comparative column chart showing the income for all three months. Format attractively and print a copy before saving and closing the file.

 Module 4 sections 2.2 and 6.1

Exercise 10 1. Create a spreadsheet based on the following data showing the audience share of different terrestrial television channels.

CHANNEL	%AUDIENCE
BBC 1	28
BBC 2	18
ITV	30
Channel 4	14
Channel 5	10

2. Use the data to produce a column chart with the title Television Share of Viewers, the x-axis labelled TV Channels and the y-axis labelled %Audience.

3. Print a copy of the chart only and save the file as TV.

4. Reformat the title to bold, underlined and the axes labels to italic.

5. Move the legend to the top, left-hand corner of the chart.

6. Save these changes and print a copy of the amended chart.

7. Now change the chart type to a pie chart. Format the data series to show both percentages and labels and delete the legend.

8. Make other changes to colours and labels as required to make the chart clearer.

9. Print a copy of the pie chart and update and close the file.

 Module 4 sections 2.2 and 6.1

Exercise 11 1. Open the file Temperature and create a line graph on the same sheet as the spreadsheet to display the overall average temperature for each of the months.

2. Make sure that the x-axis displays the names of the months, and the y-axis shows the temperatures. Label the x-axis **Months** and the y-axis **Temperature °C**.

3. Format the y-axis labels to show zero decimal places, and remove the legend.

4. Resize the chart and any fonts to display the data clearly.

5. Give the chart the title **Average Temperatures**.

6. Change the colour of the plot area and select an alternative marker style on the line.

7. Save and print a copy of the chart together with the spreadsheet data.

8. Now create a comparative chart of any type to show the January to June temperatures for all the locations. Format any elements to improve the appearance of the chart and print a copy without the spreadsheet data visible.

9. Update and close the file.

 Module 4 sections 2.2 and 6.1

4

Exercise 12

1. Create the following spreadsheet showing examination passes and save it as Exams:

Name	English	French	Mathematics	Total	Overall %
Jameson	34	18	26		
Renshaw	26	15	31		
Fuller	25	16	23		
George	31	19	28		
Hardacre	29	21	23		
Smithson	35	20	33		

2. Enter a formula to work out the Total score achieved by Jameson and copy this down the column to work out totals for all students.

3. The maximum marks available in each subject are as follows: English – 38; French – 25; and Mathematics – 35. In cell *A11* enter a formula to add these figures and work out the maximum score possible.

4. Now find Jameson's overall percentage, using the formula: *Total/Maximum score* × *100*. Make sure you refer to cell *A11* in the formula and *not* the actual figure. Copy this formula down the column to work out everyone's overall percentage. Format the results to one decimal place.

5. Create a pie chart on the same worksheet entitled **Class Marks 2002** showing just the students' names and their overall percentage results. Ensure that the data is clearly labelled and displayed and print a copy.

6. Change to a bar chart. On the **Scale** tab in the *Format* dialog box; change the minimum for the *y* axis to 50. Realign, resize, remove unnecessary labels and format as necessary to display the data effectively.

7. Print a copy of the chart before saving and closing.

 Module 4 sections 2.2 and 6.1

You will need to know how to:

▶ Copy spreadsheets or charts between worksheets

▶ Copy spreadsheets or charts into a separate application

▶ Rename worksheets

Exercise 13 **1.** Open **Exams** and change the name of the sheet holding the spreadsheet data to **Exam Results**. Copy the chart onto a new worksheet and rename the sheet **Exam Chart**.

2. Minimize Excel and open Word. Write the following letter:

Chalfont Senior School
West Widnes
Harnaton
HA15 3XP

(today's date)

Dear Parent

You will be pleased to learn that our 6th Form boys have done very well this term. They all sat their English, French and Mathematics examinations and have gained higher marks than the same set last year.

You may like to see the full details of their results and so these are set out below:

3. Now return to Excel and copy across the spreadsheet data.

4. Add the following sentence to your letter:

As you can see from the chart, Nigel Smithson fully justifies the prize for academic success and we look forward to seeing you at the award ceremony on the last day of term.

5. Return to Excel, click the **Exam Chart** sheet and copy the chart across. Finally, sign the letter:

Yours faithfully

Charles Belham

Headmaster

6. Save the file as **Chalfont** and print a copy before closing both Excel and Word.

 Module 4 sections 2.5, 3.1 and 6.1

Exercise 14 **1.** In Word, type the following text:

NEW AMERICAN-STYLE SPORTS SCHOOL IN BOGNOR REGIS

OUR MISSION

To provide high quality customized education within a caring and flexible environment in support of sport. Customized education is the process by which learning takes place.

We believe that learning should be:
personalized where curriculum more closely reflects the real world;
relevant with connections to real life;
cross-curricular to more closely reflect the real world;
flexible to accommodate the unique learning needs of students; and
multi-dimensional to involve more than skills and content

These students did particularly well last year:

2. Save the file as Sports.

3. Now minimize Word, open Excel and create the following spreadsheet:

Student	Cricket	Football	Tennis	Swimming	Total Score
James	45	27	55	14	
Peter	37	49	68	24	
Derek	49	34	49	28	
Samantha	33	28	78	18	
Noel	42	39	33	29	
Anne	29	14	67	35	

4. Enter a formula to total James' score and copy this formula down the column. Now add an extra column headed Average and work out the average score for all the students.

5. Create a stacked comparative chart showing the student names and sports data for tennis and football only. Alter the scale so the maximum is 120 and add appropriate chart and axes labels. Retain a legend.

6. Save and print a copy of the chart alone.

7. Now select the Student and Average columns only and use these details to create a new chart. Delete the legend, give the chart the title Student Scores 2002, and format it as attractively as possible.

8. Copy the chart onto a new worksheet and name this Sports Chart. Save this change.

9. Now paste the chart into your Sports document.

10. Update the document and print a copy before closing both applications.

EXERCISE 15

You will need to know how to:

- Use the IF, MAX and MIN functions
- Wrap text
- Apply font colour

1. Create the following spreadsheet and save as **Food Preferences**:

ITEM	TEST 1 %	TEST 2 %	TEST 3 %
Cheese	56	45	71
Pork sausage	67	93	87
Chocolate	78	61	67
Dried fruit	34	54	23
Steak	82	87	73
Tomato	54	65	38
Red wine	78	76	65

4

2. Add a column headed **Average Overall Score** and enter average results for all items. Format these to show no decimal places.

3. Add a final column headed **Final Result** and use an IF statement to enter the appropriate text. Those items gaining an average % of over 60 should show the word **liked**, and those under 60 should show the word **disliked**.

4. Wrap any heading text to show full entries, but keep columns narrow.

5. Format all headings to bold, font size 14 and right-align the entries in the **Final Result** column and all headings except **Item**.

6. Reformat the main text to font size 12. Colour entries in the final column red.

7. Save and print a final copy of the spreadsheet.

8. To practice using other functions, change the entries in the **Average Overall Score** column to display the maximum and then minimum test scores for each item of food.

 Module 4 sections 4.3 and 5.2

MODULE

Databases

In this module you can practise setting up databases, creating tables with appropriate datatypes and adding and amending records. You will be tested on your ability to sort your database and search for records meeting a range of criteria. The module also tests your knowledge of creating forms and reports and customizing them in different ways.

Subjects covered in this section:

Introductory exercises		ECDL module
1–2	Creating a database file; designing and saving a table	**5.1.1 and 5.2.1**
3–5	Opening a database; entering, editing and deleting data; changing the width of a column; printing a landscape page	**5.1.2, 5.2.1, 5.2.3, 5.6.1 and 5.6.2**
6–7	Sorting records; using **Edit | Find** and **Edit | Replace**; amending field names	**5.2.3, 5.4.1 and 5.4.3**
8–9	Changing field properties; adding a primary key	**5.2.2 and 5.2.3**
10–13	Filtering data	**5.4.1**
14–16	Creating and using queries	**5.4.2**
Advanced exercises		**ECDL module**
1	Setting up an index; creating a validation rule	**5.2.2 and 5.2.3**
2	Amending the design of a query	**5.4.2**
3–5	Creating a form using AutoForm; using the Wizard to design a form; using a form; printing selected records	**5.3.1 and 5.6.2**
6–8	Creating a report using AutoReport; designing a report using the Wizard	**5.5.1**

Advanced exercises   **ECDL module**

  9–10 Using grouping and summary options in   **5.5.1**
            a report

 11–13 Customizing forms and reports   **5.3.1 and 5.5.1**

    14 Creating a relationship between tables;   **5.2.4 and 5.4.2**
            designing a two-table query

EXERCISES 1 AND 2

You will need to know how to:

- Create a database file
- Design a table with appropriate field names and datatypes
- Save a table

Exercise 1

1. Open Access and create a database file named Food.
2. Design a new table with the following field names and datatypes:

Field Name	Data Type
Main food	Text
Title	Text
Cooking (mins)	Number
Portions	Number
Calories	Number

3. Save the table as Recipes but don't set a primary key.
4. Close the table.
5. Close the file but not Access.
6. Create a new database file named Furniture.

Field Name	Data Types
Name	Text
Price	Currency
Discount offered	Yes/No
Colours available	Number
Code	Text

7. Design a new table with the following field names and datatypes:
8. Save the table as Chairs but don't set a primary key.
9. Close the table.
10. Close the file.

 Module 5, sections 1.1 and 2.1

Exercise 2 1. Create a new database file named **Sailings**.

2. Design a table with the following field names and datatypes:

Field Name	Data Type
Dates	Text
UK port	Text
French port	Text
Short stay (£)	Currency
Long stay (£)	Currency
Weekend extra (£)	Currency

3. Save as **sailing costs** but don't set a primary key.

4. Close the table and then reopen it in Design view.

5. Add two further field names: **Bicycle supplement** and **Fast supplement** and set both datatypes as Currency.

6. Now save and close the table and close the file.

 Module 5, sections 1.1 and 2.1

EXERCISES 3, 4 AND 5

You will need to know how to:

 ◗ Open a database saved previously

 ◗ Open a table and enter records

 ◗ Amend entries

 ◗ Delete records

 ◗ Widen columns

 ◗ Print a table in landscape orientation

Exercise 3 1. Open the Food database.

2. Open the Recipes table and enter the following records:

Main food	Title	Cooking (mins)	Portions	Calories
Cod	Cod with herbs	40	4	193
Lentils	Lentil chilli	30	6	170
Tuna	Tuna bean salad	12	4	185
Aubergine	Roast vegetable soup	90	8	150
Pasta	Pasta with pesto sauce	30	4	538
Banana	Banana ice-cream	10	4	176
Eggs	Chocolate soufflé	30	8	204

3. Make sure all details are fully displayed.

4. Print a copy of the table in landscape orientation.

5. Now make the following amendments: Cod with herbs takes 50 minutes to cook; a portion of Banana ice-cream provides 250 calories; and the main food in the soup is Red pepper.

6. Delete the entire record for Lentil chilli and print a copy of the amended table.

7. Close the table and then close Food.

 Module 5, sections 1.2, 2.1, 2.3, 6.1 and 6.2

Exercise 4 1. Open the Furniture database and then open the Chairs table.

2. Enter the following records:

Name	Price	Discount	Colours	Code
Adjustable typist	19.99	Yes	4	TEK
Gas-lift typist	26.99	Yes	4	TCGL
Delux gas-lift typist	39.99	Yes	5	1116
Bentwood operator	69.99	No	1	WDOPR
Contemporary operator	69.99	No	2	AGNELLO
Modern operator	59.99	Yes	4	BETA
Ergonomic	149.99	Yes	5	VKHBA
Multifunctional	119.99	Yes	5	1228
Continuous use	179.99	No	3	HCT

5

1. Widen columns to display all the data fully and then print a copy of the table in landscape orientation.

2. Now make the following changes: the Delux gas-lift typist chair costs £43.99; the Ergonomic chair comes in seven colours and there is no discount on the Multifunctional chair.

3. Delete the entire record for the Gas-lift typist chair.

4. Print a copy of the amended records and then close the table.

5. Close Furniture.

 Module 5, sections 1.2, 2.1, 2.3, 6.1 and 6.2

Exercise 5 1. Create a new database called For Sale and then design a table to hold the following records. Decide appropriate datatypes (keeping Year as Number) but do not set a primary key, and save the table as Bikes:

Make	Price (£)	Type	CC	Year	Details
AJS	5999	Big port	350	1927	Black finish
Ariel	1750	Leader	250	1973	Clock
BSA	5250	DB34	500	1954	TLS front brake
BSA	8500	Rocket Goldie	650	1963	Single owner 30 yrs
AJS	2350	185	500	1957	Chrome tank panels
Ariel	3750	VH Red Hunter	500	1954	Excellent condition
Ariel	1950	Leader	250	1961	Blue finish

2. Print a copy of the table.

3. Now make the following amendments: the Ariel Leader priced at £1750 was produced in 1963; The Ariel Leader priced at £1950 has a red finish; and the BSA DB34 is for sale at £5999.

4. Delete the complete record for the Rocket Goldie bike.

5. Print a copy of the amended records and then close the table.

6. Close the For Sale file.

 Module 5, sections 1.2, 2.1, 2.3, 6.1 and 6.2

You will need to know how to:

- Sort records

- Use **Edit | Find** and **Edit | Replace**

- Amend field names

Exercise 6

1. Open the Food database and then the Recipes table.

2. In design view, change the field name Portions to Portion number.

3. Sort the records in alphabetical order of Main food and print a copy of the reordered table.

4. Now sort the records in descending order of Calories.

5. Find the first record where the cooking time is 30 minutes and change this to 35 minutes. Find the next record for a 30 minute recipe and change the cooking time to 40 minutes.

6. Print a copy of the amended records.

7. Close the Food database.

8. Open the Furniture database and display details of all the chairs.

9. Sort the records in descending order of price.

10. Print a copy of the reordered records.

11. Using **Edit | Replace**, amend all records showing chairs available in five colours to now offer six colours.

12. Sort the records in alphabetical order of chair Names and print a copy of the amended table.

13. Close the Furniture database.

 Module 5, sections 2.3, 4.1 and 4.3

Exercise 7 1. Open Sailings and the Sailing costs table in design view and change the Fieldname **Dates** to **Month**.

2. Now enter the following records:

Month	UK Port	French port	Short stay	Long stay	Weekend	Bikes	Fast
Spt	Portsmouth	Caen	£62.00	£87.00	£8.00	£0.00	£7.50
March	Portsmouth	Caen	£110.00	£146.00	£13.50	£5.00	£0.00
Spt	Plymouth	Roscoff	£65.00	£90.00	£8.00	£0.00	£7.50
July	Portsmouth	St. Malo	£145.00	£189.00	£16.00	£5.00	£7.50
Aug	Portsmouth	St. Malo	£126.00	£166.00	£13.50	£5.00	£7.50
Aug	Plymouth	Roscoff	£115.00	£152.00	£13.50	£5.00	£7.50

3. Widen the columns to display the data fully and print a copy in landscape orientation.

4. Delete the entire record for Portsmouth – St. Malo in August.

5. Add two new records:

Month	UK Port	French port	Short stay	Long stay	Weekend	Bikes	Fast
July	Plymouth	Roscoff	£133.00	£173.00	£16.00	£5.00	£7.50
March	Portsmouth	St. Malo	£126.00	£166.00	£13.50	£5.00	£0.00

6. Bike supplements in July are now £9. Using **Edit | Find**, find the first July record and then tab across to change the appropriate **Bicycle** entry. Find the next July record and repeat the amendment.

7. Using the **Edit | Replace** menu, increase the short stay cost of sailing from Plymouth to Roscoff in August from £115 to £121.

8. Sort the records in alphabetical order of French ports and print a copy of the table.

9. Now sort the records in descending order of the long stay cost and print a copy of the reordered records.

10. Close the file.

 Module 5, sections 2.3, 4.1 and 4.3

You will need to know how to:

◗ Change field properties

◗ Add a primary key

Exercise 8   1.   Create a new database file named **College**.

2.   Design a table with the following field names and datatypes:

Field Name	Data Type
Subject	Text
Room	Text
Tutor ID	Text
Start time	Number
End time	Number
Day	Text
Class code	Text
Price	Currency

1.   Set a primary key on the **Class code** field.

2.   Change the field properties for **Start time** and **End times** to show numbers to two decimal places.

3.   Change the **Price** field properties to show currency with 0 decimal places.

4.   Save the table as **Classes** and enter the following records:

Subject	Room	Tutor ID	Start time	End time	Day	Class code	Price
English	B7	H31	2	4	Tues	E142	£32
French	C9	W38	7	9	Wed	F43	£25
Watercolour	H5	J12	7	9	Tues	P712	£45
Sculpture	H5	M20	6.30	8.30	Th	P714	£85
IT	B7	M43	9.30	11.30	Mon	C24	£35
Spanish	C9	W38	7	9	Mon	S21	£25
Yoga	A15	M20	2.30	4.30	Th	Y2	£32
Business	B7	M43	2	4.30	Fr	B19	£25

5.   Sort the records in alphabetical order of subject.

6. Amend the records so that Watercolour classes start at 6.30, and Spanish is on Fridays and not Mondays and then print a copy in landscape orientation.

7. Close the table but not the file.

8. Now design a new table showing details of tutors with the following field names and data types:

Field Name	Data Type
First name	Text
Surname	Text
Subject 1	Text
Subject 2	Text
Telephone	Text
Tutor ID	Text

9. Set the primary key on Tutor ID.

10. Change the field size for the Telephone field to 7.

11. Save the table as Tutors and enter the following records:

First name	Surname	Subject 1	Subject 2	Telephone	Tutor ID
Mary	Harris	English	Business	0154752	H31
Diana	West	French	Spanish	0154851	W38
Peter	Jenkins	Painting	Collage	0154781	J12
Harry	Monks	Sculpture	Yoga	0154858	M20
Janet	Morrison	Computing	Business	0154732	M43

11. Sort the records in alphabetical order of surname and print a copy of the table.

12. Using **Edit | Replace**, make the following changes: Ms Morrison's first name is Jean; Peter Jenkins' ID should be J23; and Diana West's telephone number has changed to 0154233.

13. Close the table and then close the College database file.

 Module 5, sections 2.2 and 2.3

Exercise 9 1. Create a database named **Music** and design a table with the following structure:

Field Name	Data Type	Properties
Composer	Text	
Initials	Text	Field size 8
Title	Text	
Key	Text	Field size 15
Year born	Number	
Nationality	Text	
Price of CD (£)	Number	2 decimal places
Code	Text	

2. Set a primary key on **Code** and save the table as **Composers**.

3. Enter the following records:

Composer	Initials	Title	Key	Year born	Nationality	Price of CD (£)	Code
Beethoven	L. Van	Choral Symphony	D minor	1770	German	2.50	B5
Grieg	E	Peer Gynt Suite	N/A	1834	Norwegian	3.75	G3
Vivaldi	A	Spring	E major	1675	Italian	2.49	V2
Chopin	F	Piano Concerto no. 3	E minor	1810	Polish	3.99	C7
Bach	J.S	Brandenburg Concerto no. 1	F major	1685	German	7.50	B9
Schubert	F	Unfinished Symphony	B minor	1797	Austrian	2.95	S3

4. Print a copy of the records in landscape orientation.

5. Now make the following amendments using the **Edit | Replace** menu:

- The Bach CD costs £8.99.
- The Chopin Concerto should be no. 1.

6. Delete the entire record for **Grieg** and add a new record:

Mozart	W.A	Salzburg Symphony no. 2	B flat major	1756	Austrian	5.35	M6

5

7. Sort the records in alphabetical order of composer and print a copy of the table.

8. Using the **Edit** menu, find the first record for a **German** composer, and then find the second record.

9. Sort the records in descending order of year in which they were born and print a copy of the table before closing the file.

 Module 5, sections 2.2 and 2.3

EXERCISES 10, 11, 12 AND 13

You will need to know how to:

◗ Filter by selection to find records meeting one criterion

◗ Filter by form to find records meeting more than one criteria

◗ Use a range of expressions when filtering

Exercise 10 1. Create a database named **Children** and design a suitable table to display the following records. Save the table as CD-ROMs:

Title	Price (£)	Minimum age	Website	Rating
Games 3	10	7	www.tivola.co.uk	4
Identikit	10	7	www.planetdist.co.uk	2
Scrabble	13	12	www.johnlewis.com	3
Photo Expert	25	10	www.sierrahome.co.uk	3
Pop-up Dictionary	30	7	www.oup.co.uk	4
Card Studio	23	12	www.hallmark.co.uk	3
Heist	30	15	http://heist.vie.co.uk	2
Physicus	18	8	www.tivola.co.uk	4

2. Sort in ascending order of **Minimum age** and then print a copy of the table in landscape orientation.

3. Use a filter to find only those records with a rating of 4. Print a copy of the records and then remove the filter.

4. Sort the records in ascending order of price.

5. Now use a filter to find only those CD-ROMs that cost under £20 and are suitable for children under 9.

6. Print the records and then remove the filter and close the file.

 Module 5, section 4.1

Exercise 11
1. Open the College database and use a filter to find all the classes held on Tuesday.

2. Print a copy of the records and then remove the filter.

3. Sort the records in ascending order of Start times.

4. Now use a filter to find any classes being held in room B7 that start at 2 p.m.

5. Print a copy of the records displayed and then close the Classes table.

6. Open the Tutors table and use a filter to find any tutors who can teach Yoga. Print a copy of the records and then remove the filter.

7. Now sort the table in alphabetical order of Subject 1.

8. Use a filter to find the tutor whose ID begins with M and whose second subject is Business.

9. Print a copy of the record and then close the College file.

 Module 5, section 4.1

Exercise 12
1. Open the Sailings file and then the sailing costs table.

2. Use a filter to display all sailings to Roscoff and print a copy of the records.

3. Now find all sailings from Portsmouth that cost £90–£130 for a short stay. Print a copy of the records.

4. Finally, search for any sailings to St. Malo in March and print a copy before closing the file.

 Module 5, section 4.1

5

Exercise 13 1. Open **Music** and use a filter to search for any pieces of music in the key of E. Print a copy of the records.

2. Find any recordings that cost less than £5 and were written by a **German** or **Austrian** composer, and print the records.

3. Finally, print out details of any composers born after **1700** whose names begin with **B.**

4. Close the table and the file.

 Module 5, section 4.1

EXERCISES 14, 15 AND 16

You will need to know how to:

◗ Use a query to search for records

◗ Use a range of expressions when querying

◗ Save a query

◗ Hide fields in a query

Exercise 14 1. Create a database named **Outings** and then design a table to hold the following details of various activities taking place in the summer. Make sure the dates are **Date** datatypes (they can be displayed with the year or customized to show only days and months). Save the table as **Activities**.

Activity	Place	Start date	Duration (days)	Adult price (£)	Child price (£)	Family ticket
Flower show	Hampton Park Palace	9 July	3	17	5	Yes
Open day	Ramsgate Harbour	30 July	1	0	0	No
Creatures of the Night	Leighton Moss Nature Reserve	25 June	1	3	1	No
Arthurian antics	Pickering Castle	4 August	2	3.60	1.80	Yes
King for a day	Legoland	25 July	2	16	13	Yes
Puppet picnic	Grey's Court, Henley	30 July	1	5	0	No
Tortoises and turtles	Rescue Centre, Highbridge	18 June	2	4.75	3.50	No

2. Sort the records in alphabetical order of Activity and print a copy in landscape orientation, first making sure all data is fully displayed.

3. Now use a query to find all the activities taking place after 15 July. Display the Activity, Place and Start date only.

4. Print a copy of the records and save the query as Late summer.

5. Now search for all activities where a Family ticket is available. Show all the fields except Family ticket and Duration.

6. Print the results of the search and save the query as Family tickets.

7. Make the following changes to the table: the Puppet picnic is cancelled so the record needs to be removed completely; and add the Teddy Bears' Parade taking place in Richmond Park on 1 August. It costs £2.50 for adults, £1.50 for children, lasts a single day and a family ticket is available.

8. Close the table.

9. Now open the Family tickets query and check that it includes the Teddy Bears' Parade.

10. Print the query and then close the Outings file.

 Module 5, section 4.2

Exercise 15 1. Open the Furniture database.

2. Use a filter to find all chairs that cost more than £120 and print a copy of the records.

3. Sort the table alphabetically by Name and save this change.

4. Close the table and design a query to find all chairs offering a discount that come in more than 2 colours. Display only the Name and Price fields and save the query as Colourful.

5. Return to the design of the query and add the Code field. Then sort the records in descending order of Price before printing a copy.

6. Now use the * symbol to search for all chairs with a code beginning with the number 1 and display just the Name, Colours available and Price fields.

7. Save as Numerical Codes and print a copy.

5

8. Open the table and enter the following four new records:

   Comfort, £189.99, no discount, 4 colours, code COMFORT; Ultimate Executive, £229.99, no discount, 4 colours, code BBAS; Chrome Managers, £79.99, discount available, 5 colours, code CHRM; and Wood Executive, price £169.99, 1 colour, no discount and code 1314A5.

9. Design a new query to find all chairs costing more than £120 that are available in 4 or more colours. Display the name, price and code fields only and save the query as Chairs over £120.

10. Finally reopen the Numerical Codes query and check that the Wood Executive chair is now listed. Print a copy and then close the file.

 Module 5, section 4.2

Exercise 16
1. Open the Food database and search for all recipes that take less than 15 minutes to cook. Print a copy of the records showing only the Main food, Title and Cooking time. Save the query as Quick recipes.

2. Now add the following recipes to the table:

   - Rhubarb is the main food in a Crumble recipe that takes 40 minutes to cook, provides 8 portions and 192 calories per portion.
   - Flour is the main ingredient for Pizza that takes 20 minutes to cook, provides 4 portions and 375 calories in each portion.

3. Sort the table in ascending order of Calories per portion.

4. Search for all recipes for four or more people at less than 200 calories per portion. Sort alphabetically by Title, display just the Title, Cooking time and Calories and save as Under 200 calories.

5. Print a copy of the query and then close the file.

 Module 5, section 4.2

ADVANCED EXERCISES

EXERCISE 1

You will need to know how to:

▶ Create a validation rule

▶ Set up an index

1. Create a new file named Tennis and design the following table:

Field Name	Data Type	Properties
Membership No	AutoNumber	
Category	Text	
Surname	Text	
Firstname	Text	
Joining date	Date	Medium date
Female	Yes/No	

2. Set up an index on the Surname field, and allow duplicates.

3. The Category field should only accept the text Senior, Junior or Concession. Set this for the Validation Rules field and enter appropriate validation text to appear if the rule is not met.

4. Save the table as Members and enter the following records. Try to enter the Category of Diane Brown as 'Temporary' before typing the correct entry.

Membership No	Category	Surname	Firstname	Joining Date	Female
1	Senior	Brown	Joan	22-May-01	Yes
2	Junior	Brown	Terry	22-May-01	No
3	Junior	Brown	Madge	22-May-01	Yes
4	Senior	Bergot	Francis	18-June-01	Yes
5	Senior	Wilson	Harold	22-June-01	No
6	Senior	Brown	Peter	28-June-01	No
7	Junior	Brown	Diane	28-June-01	Yes
8	Concession	Hill	Susan	01-July-01	Yes
9	Senior	Harper	Graeham	04-July-01	No
10	Junior	Harper	Sally	04-July-01	Yes

5. Search the database for Madge Brown and display her full name, Category and Joining Date only. Print out the details.

6. Now search the database for anyone named Brown who joined before 1st June, sort alphabetically by first name and display only their Firstname, Joining Date and Membership No. Save the query as Brown in May.

7. Print a copy of the query displaying its name on the printout.

8. Finally, search for any male members in the **Senior** category and display only **Firstname**, **Surname** and **Joining Date**. Sort alphabetically by Surname and save as **Senior Males**.

9. Print a copy of the records and then close the file.

 Module 5, sections 2.2 and 2.3

EXERCISE 2

You will need to know how to:

◆ Amend the design of a query

1. Open the **College** file and then search the **Tutor** table to find which tutors teach **Business**. Display their Firstnames and Surnames only.

2. Save the query as **Business Tutors** and print a copy.

3. Using the same query, amend it so that you search for tutors who teach **Business** or **Computing**. Display *all* their **Subjects**, their **Surnames**, and add their **Telephone Numbers**.

4. Print a copy of the amended query and save the changes.

5. Now search for any classes that cost between **£20** and **£30** and print details of the **Subject**, **Room** and **Day** only. Save as **Classes from £20 – £30**.

6. Amend the query to display the same price range of classes but remove the **Room** field and add **Start** and **End** times. Save the changes and print a copy before closing the file.

 Module 5, section 4.2

You will need to know how to:

▸ Create a form using the AutoForm function

▸ Design a form using the Wizard

▸ Use a form for entering and amending records

▸ Print selected records

Exercise 3 1. Open the Children database and design a new table named Books to hold the following records:

Title	Author	Publisher	Price	Recommended age
Terrific I'm a Tarantula	Bradman	Bloomsbury	6.75	7
Public Enemy No. 2	Horowitz	Walker	3.99	12
I don't like Space Glop	Matthews	Bloomsbury	4.50	5
The Five Sisters	Mahy	Scholastic	4.99	8
Storm	Fisher	Collins	9.99	11
When the Forest meets the Sea	Baker	Walker	4.99	4

2. Sort the records alphabetically by Author and print a copy of the table.

3. Now create a Columnar AutoForm based on this table.

4. Use the form to add the following records:

  ● Scary Stories by Helen Paiba, aimed at 9 year olds and published by Macmillan at £6.99
  ● Star Wars Episode 1 by George Lucas, published by Scholastic at £4.99 aimed at children at least 7 years old.

5. Use the form to display the record for Storm and print a copy of this record only.

6. Use the form to make the following amendments:

  ● Public Enemy No. 2 is suitable for 9 year olds
  ● The Five Sisters is published by Puffin
  ● Bradman's book costs £3.99.

7. Close the form and save it as Books AutoForm.

8. Open the table and print a copy of the amended records.

9. Now design a new form using the Wizard with only the following fields selected in order: Author, Title, Price and Publisher.

10. Save as Wizard Books Form, open the form and print one record.

11. Close the Children file.

Exercise 4
1. Open the Food file and design an AutoForm based on the Recipes table. Save it as Recipe form.

2. Use the form to add the following recipes:
   - Macaroni Cheese, main food pasta, takes 25 minutes to cook, enough for 6 people and provides 280 calories per portion.
   - Borscht, main food beetroot, feeds 10 people at 102 calories per portion, and takes 30 minutes to cook.

3. With the form open, delete the record for Banana Ice-cream.

4. Use the form to make the following changes:
   - Cod with herbs takes 60 minutes to cook;
   - there are 410 calories in each portion of chocolate soufflé;
   - change pesto sauce to tomato sauce.

5. Design a new form using the Wizard that has a different layout and background to the AutoForm you produced, and save it as Wizard recipe form.

6. Go to the recipe for Tuna salad and print a copy of the form displaying only this record.

7. Close the form and the database file.

 Module 5, sections 3.1 and 6.2

Exercise 5
1. Open the Tennis database and create a form of your choice using the Form Wizard.

2. Use it to add the following new members:

   Shirley Webb, Concession, Female, Joined 3 August
   Martin Piller, Senior, Male, Joined 15 August.

3. Print a copy of the form showing one of the new records only.

4. Use the form to make the following amendments:
   - Graeham spells his name Graham
   - Joan Brown joined on 24 May
   - Francis Brown is male.

5. Close the form and check that the new records and amendments have been added to the table.

6. Design a query to find out joining dates of all senior members. Include only the dates, surnames and membership numbers.

7. Save as Seniors and print a copy before closing the file.

 Module 5, sections 3.1 and 6.2

EXERCISES 6, 7 AND 8

You will need to know how to:

▶ Create a report using the AutoReport function

▶ Design a report using the Wizard

Exercise 6
1. Open the Furniture database and create an AutoReport in table format based on the Chairs over £120 query. Give it the same name as the query.

2. Save the report and print a copy.

3. Open the table and sort the records in ascending order of price.

4. Design a report in table format using the wizard which is based on the table and where only the following fields are displayed: Name, Price and Code. Name the report Chairs 2002 and print a copy.

5. Use a query to find all chairs aimed at executives or operators that cost between £70 and £200. Decide which fields to display and save as Op or Exec chairs.

6. Create a report based on this query and print a copy.

7. Close the Furniture database.

 Module 5, section 5.1

Exercise 7
1. Open the database holding information about motorbikes.

2. Search for all bikes that are under £5000 built before 1962 and display all the fields except the Year.

3. Save the query as Pre-1962 Bikes.

4. Now create a report based on this query using the Wizard. Place the fields in the following order: Make, Price, Type, CC and then Details and give it the same name as the query.

5. Print a copy of the report.

6. Close the report and design a new table named Cars to hold the following records:

   £11800 97 R Saab 4 door, midnight blue, climate control from Oxford Saab
   £6695 98 S Rover 5 door, Oxford blue, alloys from Kernahan MG
   £15850 99 T Saab 4 door, black, CD player from Oxford Saab
   £7995 98 R Vauxhall Vectra 5 door, red, air conditioning from Autopark
   £8995 94 M Corrado 3 door, metallic red, full leather from Autopark
   £6990 97 R Honda Civic 5 door, silver, twin airbags from Kernahan MG
   £5995 98 R Peugeot 5 door, cherry red, tinted glass from Autopark
   £14995 99 V Mazda 5 door, black, only 2000 miles from Motorworld

7. Sort in ascending order of Price and print a copy of the records.

8. Search for all black or red cars that are post-1997 and display their Price, Make, Colour, Rgistration letter, Special features and Dealer name only. Save the query as Newer Cars and print a copy.

9. Finally, produce a report based on this query and print a copy before closing the For Sale database file.

 Module 5, section 5.1

Exercise 8 1. Open the Tennis database and create a query to display only the female members of the club.

2. Save as Female members.

3. Using the Wizard, create a report based on this query. The fields should be displayed in the following order, and you should not include Membership No or Female:

   Firstname   Surname   Joining Date   Category

4. Save and print a copy of the report.

5. Now create an AutoReport – Tabular report based on the complete table.

6. Save as Membership Details and print a copy before closing the file.

 Module 5, section 5.1

You will need to know how to:

▶ Design a report that uses grouping or summary options

Exercise 9   1.   Open **Outings** and design a report showing the various activities grouped by date (you may want to see the effect of changing the grouping options so that they are by day and not month). Give it the name **Activities Over the Summer**.

2.   Print a copy of the report and then close the file.

3.   Now open **Children** and design a query based on the **CD-ROMs** table to show all fields except **Rating**.

4.   Design a report based on this query that groups the records by **Minimum age** and then print a copy of the report before closing the file.

5.   Finally, open any other database and create a report that groups the records in some way, e.g. books by publisher, bikes by make or classes by day.

6.   Save and print a copy of the report before closing the file.

 Module 5, section 5.1

Exercise 10   1.   Create a new **Jobs** database and design the following table saved as **Job Details**:

Field Names	Data Types
Employer	Text
Job	Text
Salary	Currency
Location	Text
Contact	Text
Closing date	Date

5

2. Enter the following details into the table:

Employer	Job	Salary	Location	Contact	Closing date
Connell	Sales	£18,000.00	Oxford	01865 76333	20/02/02
St. Mary's	RE teacher	£23,000.00	Milton Keynes	01844 22366	15/02/02
Hedges	Secretary	£16,500.00	Oxford	01865 56699	01/03/02
Mango	Administrator	£17,500.00	Oxford	01865 44455	20/02/02
Buildbase	Sales	£24,000.00	Witney	01993 23111	03/03/02
Garsington	Education Officer	£14,000.00	Abingdon	01235 22288	14/02/02

3. Design a query to display only Oxford jobs, and show all fields except Location, Closing date and Contact.

4. Save and print a copy of the query.

5. Return to the table and delete the Milton Keynes record entirely and increase the salary for Hedges to £17,950.

6. Add the following two records:

    Beaumont House, Care Assistant, £12,500, Abingdon, 01235 44777, 14/2/02
    Gateway Hotel, 2nd Chef, £19,000, Witney, 01993 22134, 5/3/02.

7. Design a report to show all fields except Contact and group data by Location. Use the summary option to include the average salaries for each location and save as Average.

8. Print a copy of the report and close the file.

 Module 5, section 5.1

EXERCISES 11, 12 AND 13

You will need to know how to:

▶ Customize forms and reports

Exercise 11 1. Open your Recipe AutoForm.

2. In design view, add a large form heading label, type in RECIPES and make the font bold, 14 point.

3. Change the fill colour of the controls.

4. Format the text labels to italic.

5. Resize any of the controls to display the entry more clearly.

6. Print a copy of one record in form view and then close the file.

 Module 5, sections 3.1 and 5.1

Exercise 12 1. Open the report Membership Details.

2. In design view, reposition any headings so that they sit more clearly over the data, and resize if necessary to display the complete entry.

3. Change the title to Tennis Club Members and reformat the font type and size.

4. Change the Membership No. label to Number.

5. Add your name to the page footer.

6. Print a copy of the report and close the file.

 Module 5, sections 3.1 and 5.1

Exercise 13 1. Open the Average report in the Jobs database in Design view.

2. Delete the extra wording beginning summary for location ... .

3. Amend the Avg label to read Average salaries and format to italic.

4. Ensure that all column headings are clearly visible.

5. Reformat any headings, e.g. change the report label font or give it initial capital letters.

6. Print a copy of the report before saving and closing the file.

5

 Module 5, sections 3.1 and 5.1

You will need to know how to:

◗ Create a relationship between tables

◗ Design a two-table query

1. Create a database with the name **Sunsoak Holidays**. Design a table saved as **Villas**, setting a primary key on Code. (The data type should be Text to display zeros.) Enter the records as shown:

Name	Code	Country	Price (£)	Maximum No.
Nachtag	0011	Germany	276	5
Der Haus	0015	Germany	223	6
La Musique	0022	France	114	2
Flowers	0023	France	150	6
La Girande	0027	France	286	6
Le Pont	0046	France	245	8
High House	0062	Ireland	125	3
The Mill	0065	Ireland	134	4

2. Now create a second table, **Bookings**, with a primary key on Booking Number. This should have an AutoNumber data type.

Booking Number	Date taken	Name	Contact	Code	Month required
1	02/02/03	Marlow	01235 67584	0011	October
2	22/02/03	Johnson	01491 39987	0046	September
3	13/03/03	Hepple	01865 22114	0065	August
4	02/04/03	Smith	01865 33445	0011	July
5	03/04/03	Binns	01865 54838	0062	August
6	04/04/03	Paterson	01865 47738	0046	May
7	12/05/03	Black	01235 19876	0023	July
8	21/05/03	Thomson	01235 67584	0027	June

3. Sort the Villas table in ascending order of Country and print a copy.

4. Search for all French villas, then save and print a copy of the query.

5. Print a copy of all bookings taken before May, showing only the date, name and contact number.

6. Now create a relationship between the two tables, linking the Villa code in each table.

7. Create a query based on fields from both tables to show details of all bookings in France for summer holidays, i.e. June, July or August. Display only the client's name, contact numbers, month required, villa name and price.

8. First save as **Summer French Villas** and then print a copy that will now show the query name.

9. Close the database.

 Module 5, sections 2.4 and 4.2

5

MODULE

Presentation

This module includes exercises covering the main features of the presentation package PowerPoint. You need to be able to add text, images and objects to slides; customize backgrounds, and include transitions and animations when running a presentation on the computer. You can also test your knowledge of how to create organization or numerical charts and print a range of objects including notes pages and handouts.

Subjects covered in this section:

Advanced exercises		ECDL module
1–2	Adding a background to a slide; creating and printing a notes page; grouping drawings	**6.2.2, 6.3.1, 6.6.1 and 6.6.2**
3–4	Applying a design template; printing handouts	**6.2.3 and 6.6.2**
5–6	Customizing a design template	**6.2.2**
7–8	Using Slide Master; adding headers and footers	**6.2.4**
9–10	Creating and formatting an organization chart	**6.4.2**
11	Adding and formatting a numerical chart	**6.4.1**
12	Copying and resizing objects	**6.3.3**
13–14	Adding slide transitions and running a slideshow; hiding slides	**6.5.2 and 6.6.3**
15–16	Animating slides	**6.5.1**

You need to know how to:

- ▸ Start a new presentation
- ▸ Work in different views
- ▸ Use placeholders or text boxes to insert text
- ▸ Save and print slides
- ▸ Close a presentation

Exercise 1
1. Open PowerPoint and start a new presentation.
2. Select a bulleted list or title slide layout.
3. In Slide view enter the following title: Transport.
4. Click in the list box and add the following text as a list: Cars, Buses, Walking, Bicycles.
5. Go to Outline view and insert the word Trains after Cars.
6. Change to Normal view and use a text box to add the following text above the title: My first talk.
7. Add a further text box above the list and type: Topics that will be covered.
8. Save the presentation as Transport and print a copy of the slide before closing the file.

 Module 6, sections 1.1 and 6.1

Exercise 2
1. Start a new presentation and select a blank slide layout.
2. In Normal view, insert a text box and enter the text: Beware of the Dog.
3. Change to Slide view and add a second text box. Type the following:

   No hawkers, circulars or free newspapers, please. We only read material we buy ourselves and it is not environmentally friendly to waste paper.
4. Save as Notice and print a copy of the slide before closing the presentation.

 Module 6, sections 1.1 and 6.1

6

EXERCISE 3

You will need to know how to:

- Move text boxes
- Format text
- Change to portrait orientation

1. Start a new presentation. Select a blank slide layout.

2. Add the following title: Car Boot Sale

3. Below this, add the text: Come to 14 Greenacres and find a bargain!

4. Centre both entries.

5. Move the title below the address.

6. Change the text to Brilliant Car Boot Sale formatted to font size 40 point, and format the address to italic, 32 point.

7. Change to portrait orientation and reposition and re-size the text boxes if necessary so that they are centrally placed in the top half of the slide.

8. Save as Car Boot and print a copy of the slide before closing the file.

 Module 6, section 3.1, 3.3 and 6.1

EXERCISE 4

You need to know how to:

- Change line spacing

1. Reopen Transport.

2. Select the main title and format it to bold and underlined with a shaded effect.

3. Select the list and format this to italic.

4. Increase the line spacing within the list.

5. Centre My first talk and increase the font so that it is slightly larger than the title text.

6. Make Topics that will be covered bold and font size 18 point.

7. Save these changes and print an amended copy of the slide before closing the presentation.

 Module 6, section 3.1

You will need to know how to:

▶ Add images to a slide

▶ Move and resize images

Exercise 5 1. Start a new presentation and select a slide with Clip Art and text place-holders.

2. Make the title of the slide Gardens and format it attractively.

3. Double-click the Clip Art placeholder and find and insert an image of a plant.

4. Add the following text as a list:

   Plan carefully, Provide seats, Add fragrant and colourful flowers, Include a water feature.

5. Save as Gardens and print a copy of the slide.

6. Now reduce the size of the image by half and move it to a different position on the slide.

7. Insert a second gardening image, resized so that it matches the size of the first image, and position it somewhere on the slide.

8. Make any further changes to text or images as you like and then save and print a copy of the updated slide.

9. Close the presentation.

 Module 6, sections 3.2 and 3.3

Exercise 6 1. Reopen Notice.

2. Format the main heading in bold and increase the font size.

3. Apply a dark colour to the text.

4. Select the main text and format to italics.

5. Insert an image of a dog or newspaper, and print a copy of the slide.

6. Resize the image and position it in the top, right-hand corner of the slide. If necessary, resize or move text boxes so that all text is clearly displayed.

7. Save this change and print a revised version of the slide before saving and closing.

 Module 6, sections 3.2 and 3.3

EXERCISE 7

You will need to know how to:

▶ Add WordArt to a slide*

▶ Make changes to a WordArt object

▶ Format text boxes

1. Start a new presentation, select a blank slide layout and change to portrait orientation.

2. You are going to produce a poster advertising a concert. Insert a musical Clip Art image and the text Schubert's Symphony No. 8 in B minor anywhere on the slide, and then save as Concert.

3. Add two further text boxes that will display details of the date/time – Saturday, 23 May at 8.00 p.m. – and venue – The Hopkins Great Hall – in differently formatted text.

4. Select and insert an appropriate WordArt title: Concert Series. Move it so that it appears at the top of the slide, and resize or format the colours and shape to your liking.

5. Move the Clip Art image so that it appears at the bottom of the slide and re-arrange the text boxes so that all the details are attractively arranged.

6. Add borders and background colours to some of the text boxes.

7. Now edit the WordArt so that it reads: Opening Concert.

8. Update the presentation and print a copy of the slide before closing the file.

   * Please note that WordArt is not a requirement of (or included in) the ECDL syllabus and can be replaced with text boxes.

 Module 6, section 4.3

EXERCISE 8

You will need to know how to:

▶ Copy and paste objects within a slide

1. Reopen Car Boot.

2. Insert and format the following WordArt object: **Come Along on Saturday.** Place it under the text.

3. Copy the WordArt and paste it several times so that four or five sets of words fill the bottom half of the slide.

4. Insert an image of a chair or other item that might be found at a car boot sale. Resize it to fit in the top, right-hand corner of the slide.

5. Add a thick, coloured border to the image.

6. Edit one WordArt object so that it now reads: **You won't be sorry** and reformat it to contrast with those saying **Come Along on Saturday.**

7. Remove the border if it is showing round the address, but add a thick, coloured border and contrasting coloured background to the **Car Boot Sale** title.

8. Update the file and print a copy of the slide before closing.

 Module 6, section 4.4

EXERCISES 9 AND 10

You will need to know how to:

▶ Add new slides

▶ Move between slides

▶ Reorder slides

▶ Change slide layout

▶ Work with bullets

Exercise 9
1. Open your Transport presentation.

2. Add a new slide with placeholders for one left-hand text column and one Clip Art image.

3. Enter the title BUSES.

4. Click in the text column and type the following:

   Advantages of buses:

   Reading or sleeping as you travel
   Less pollution
   Season tickets can make this economical

5. Remove the subheading bullet point but retain bullets for the listed items.

6. Insert an image of a bus by double-clicking the placeholder.

7. Save the changes and print a copy of the slide.

8. Now change the slide layout to two text columns.

9. Move the image above the title and add this text in the right-hand column, formatted to match the first column:

   Disadvantages of buses:

   Waiting at bus stops
   Expensive for families
   Restricted times to travel

10. Add a third slide of any layout that has the title Walking in either normal text or WordArt.

11. Add three enjoyable reasons for taking walks and then insert a suitable Clip Art image.

12. Go back to the first slide and then add a new slide, slide 2, which will have the title CARS. Select any slide layout and just add the title.

13. Now move to Walking and insert a new slide 5 of any layout with the title Trains.

14. Change the slide order so that Trains appears between Cars and Buses.

15. Finally, add a slide 6 entitled Cycling and insert a suitable image. Save and close the file.

 Module 6, sections 2.2, 6.1 and 6.3

Exercise 10

1. Start a new presentation and insert three slides: two blank and the third with placeholders for text and Clip Art. Save as Nature.

2. Go to the first blank slide and insert an animal image.

3. Insert a WordArt object: Birds and other Animals above the image and add the following text:

   Presentation by Jane Wyckham, Milton Park Nature Reserve

4. Add a text box containing the following words:

   Friday 8.30–10.00 p.m. at Clarendon College, Brackley

5. Reformat the main and subheading text and add borders or shading to the text boxes.

6. Move through the slides until you reach slide 3.

7. Insert a flower picture, colour it yellow and add the title Telling Flowers apart followed by the following list of names:

   Coltsfoot, Ragworts, Hawkbits, Common fleabane and Sowthistle

8. Add a new slide 4 in two-column layout. Then enter the title Pollution Signs and, in one column, type:

   The Lichen Test

   None – bad air
   Small amounts – slightly better
   Long and shrubby – clean country air

9. In the other column, type the following list:

   Lifeless Water

   Sewage
   Oil
   Rubbish

10. Reorder the slides so that the flower slide is slide 4.

11. Go back to the blank slide and change the layout to display a title place-holder. Add a bird picture and the title: Birds around Britain.

12. Add further text boxes containing the names of different birds, such as peregrine falcon, swallow, swan, and golden eagle. Arrange these in a random fashion on the slide.

13. Format each text box and entry completely differently by using different font types and sizes and adding coloured backgrounds and borders.

14. Print a copy of all four slides and then save and close the presentation.

 Module 6, sections 2.2 and 6.1

EXERCISE 11

You will need to know how to:

▶ Duplicate slides

▶ Copy and paste images between slides

1. Start a new presentation and select a blank slide layout.

2. Insert the text *Decisions to Make* centrally on the slide, formatted to Arial, 44 point, bold.

3. Underneath, add the text: *What do you like to do?* Increase the font size and format in italic.

4. Now duplicate the slide twice to create two extra slides.

5. Go to slide 2 and change the question to *What are you good at?*

6. Go to slide 3 and change the question to *Will you fit in?*

7. Return to the first slide and add a Clip Art image of shaking hands (or other picture suitable for a presentation on getting a job). Resize if necessary and move it to the bottom, centre of the slide.

8. Copy this image onto the other slides.

9. Add a new slide to become slide 1, in title slide layout.

10. Enter the following text: *Tips on Job Interviews* and apply appropriate formatting.

11. Save as **Jobs** and print a copy of the presentation before closing the file.

 Module 6, sections 3.3 and 6.1

EXERCISES 12 AND 13

You will need to know how to:

▶ Insert and format AutoShapes

▶ Rotate, flip and layer objects

▶ Print selected slides

▶ Use guidelines

Exercise 12 1. You are going to start preparing a presentation on The History of Britain. Select a title slide, a slide with an organization chart placeholder and a blank slide.

2. Return to the title slide and type The History of Britain as the main title and your name and today's month and year as a subtitle.

3. Insert an enlarged image of a clock or historical character and place it centrally on the slide, but *behind* the text. You may need to change the text colour to white or yellow so that it shows up clearly.

4. Near the bottom of the slide, add a block arrow AutoShape pointing to the left, with text above it that says Come this way through time.

5. Save as History and print one copy of the slide.

6. Now rotate or flip the arrow to point to the right.

7. Insert WordArt with the text History Comes Alive and place this at the top of the slide. Border it with an oval AutoShape filled with a contrasting colour, making sure the words are displayed clearly.

8. Save and print a copy of the title slide only before closing the file.

 Module 6, sections 4.3 and 6.2

Exercise 13 1. You are going to design a get well card. Start a new presentation, select the blank slide layout and change to portrait orientation.

2. Add guidelines using the **View** menu, if they are not already visible.

3. In the top, left-hand quarter (to become the inside of the card) insert the following in a text box:

With Very Best Wishes from Everyone in the Office

4. Realign the text and format the text size so that it fills most of the message area. Add colours and borders as you like.

5. Rotate or flip the box so that the wording is upside down.

6. In the bottom, right-hand quarter (the front of the card) add a picture on the theme of illness or injury.

7. Now add an arched WordArt object above the picture that says Sorry and a horizontal object below it that says You are ill.

8. Border the front of the card by adding a rectangular AutoShape with a colour fill. Make sure the text and picture are still clearly visible.

9. Save as Sorry.

6

10. Add the words Get well soon in the bottom left quarter of the slide and rotate it so that it will appear at a 45° angle across the back of the card.

11. Save this change and print a copy of the card before closing the file.

 Module 6, sections 4.3 and 6.2

EXERCISE 14

You will need to know how to:

▶ Apply different line weights and styles to text boxes

1. Create a four-slide presentation and save as Villa. Select a title slide and three blank slide layouts.

2. On the title slide, enter the following heading: Villa For Sale

3. Add a thick, black border.

4. Add the following subtitle text: Sea Views and Luxury Fittings

5. Border this text box in green, selecting a double or triple line style.

6. Format the text in both boxes so that it fills most of the main slide area.

7. Move to slide 2 and add the title Location. Underneath, add the following bulleted list:

   ● Close to the seafront in sunny Portsmouth
   ● Near the shops and local schools
   ● Good road and rail links to London or the South West
   ● Ferries to the Isle of Wight or France always available.

8. Format the bullets in an alternative style and border and shade the text box containing the list in dark red, dashed lines and weight 6 point.

9. Print a copy of slide 2 only.

10. Go to Slide 3 and change the slide layout to text plus Clip Art.

11. Insert a seaside-related image and border with a thick, coloured border.

12. Add the following text:

   The Villa has a large sitting room with south-facing balcony, two bedrooms with en suite shower room and pine fitted kitchen

13. Add a title: Villa Details as WordArt and position this centrally at the top of the slide.

14. Reorder slides 2 and 3.

15. Change the layout of slide 4 to a title only slide and add the title: Contact Information

16. Add a separate text box containing the address:

    Wilmotts Estate Agent, 23 Harrington Road, Portsmouth, Tel: 01705 666777

17. Border the address with an oval border and fill with colour, making sure the text is still clearly visible.

18. Reformat any text or objects to ensure each slide is attractively laid out, and then print a copy of the complete presentation.

19. Save and close the file.

 Module 6, section 4.3

ADVANCED EXERCISES

EXERCISES 1 AND 2

You will need to know how to:

▶ Add slide backgrounds

▶ Create and print a notes page

▶ Goup drawings

Exercise 1 1. Open Gardens.

2. Add a second slide with just a title placeholder and enter the following words:

   View from your Window.

3. Underneath, draw a simple picture of a window with the sun and some flowers inside. Use the rectangle, oval, etc., AutoShapes – Stars and Banners, or Flowchart shapes can provide flower heads – and colour them as appropriate. The following shows an example:

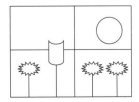

6

4. Select a green or brown background colour that either has an attractive pattern or other fill effect and apply it to both the slides in your presentation.

5. Reverse the order of your slides and amend the title text of slide 2 to Garden Planning.

6. Now create a Notes page for this slide and type the following notes:

College course starts 19 September
Address for enrolment forms
Book to read: 'Planning Your Garden' by Deirdre Wiseman

7. Print a copy of the Notes page and both slides.

8. Group your drawing, resize and move it to another part of the slide.

9. Save and close the presentation.

 Module 6, sections 2.2, 3.1 and 6.1

Exercise 2 1. Re-open Villa and apply a pale blue, graded colour background to all the slides.

2. Create a Notes page for the last slide and type the following:

Mention we are closed on Mondays.

Give out flyer on sister offices in Plymouth and Exeter.

Ask for names and addresses of anyone interested in viewing this or similar properties.

3. Print a copy of the Notes page only.

4. Duplicate the first slide and move the extra slide so that it become the last slide.

5. Change the background colour of this slide only to yellow, retaining the gradient.

6. Add a picture of a beach ball by using one crescent AutoShape, copying and flipping it horizontally and placing the two shapes together.

7. Colour two of the segments.

8. Group the shapes and move the ball to the top left of the slide.

9. Print a copy of the last slide only and then save and close the presentation.

 Module 6, sections 2.2, 3.1 and 6.1

EXERCISES 3 AND 4

You will need to know how to:

▶ Apply a design template

▶ Print handouts

Exercise 3
1. Open Nature.

2. Select a suitable design template with a brown or green main colour and apply to all the slides.

3. Go to the Birds around Britain slide and create a Notes page that includes reminders about an Owl Sighting evening; a conference on rare birds next Autumn in Inverness; and that cheap binoculars are available from Keswick Camera Stores.

4. Print just the Notes page.

5. Change the design template applied to the presentation.

6. Print a handout with all slides on one page.

7. Save and close the file.

 Module 6, sections 2.3 and 6.2

Exercise 4
1. Start a new presentation and select a slide layout with Clip Art and bulleted list placeholders.

2. Insert a picture relevant to holidays, e.g. suitcases, beach, aeroplane, etc.

3. Give the slide the title Holidays in India and save the file as Holiday.

4. Add the following list:

   Vaccinations; Tickets; Packing for hot countries; Things to see

5. Add four new slides and insert one WordArt object on each slide as a title, with the wording taken from the list.

6

6. On the Vaccinations slide, find or draw a picture of a hypodermic needle similar to the one below and partly fill with colour. (Use Basic or Flowchart shapes as well as lines.)

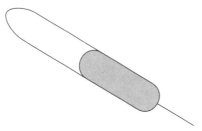

7. Group the drawing and rotate it so that it is at an angle.

8. On the *Things to See* slide, add the following text in separate text boxes, formatted differently and including borders and shading:

   Goa, Bombay, Madras, New Delhi

9. On the *Packing* slide, insert a picture of clothing, copy it three times and create a design of the picture in four different sizes, e.g. slanted across the slide or arranged round the edge. Make sure all text is clearly visible.

10. Now apply a suitable design template and print a handout displaying all the slides before saving and closing.

 Module 6, sections 2.3 and 6.2

EXERCISES 5 AND 6

You will need to know how to:

▶ Customize design templates

Exercise 5 1. Reopen Nature.

2. Add a final slide that will have the title: Looking after the Environment.

3. Add text boxes to contain some of the following phrases: Collect up rubbish; Shut gates; Grow plants to attract insects; Keep away from nesting birds. (You may prefer to include your own choice of topics.)

4. Format the colour scheme to change the main background colour for this slide only, so that it stands out from the rest of the presentation but is still in the same style. If necessary, make changes to text colours so that they are still clearly visible.

5. Add a suitable image, e.g. a gate, bottle, rubbish bags, etc., either from the Clip Art gallery or drawn by hand, and give it a coloured border.

6. Print a handout displaying all the slides on one page.

7. Save the changes and close the file.

 Module 6, section 2.2

Exercise 6
1. Reopen Holiday and insert a second slide that includes text and pictures related to food and drink. Make sure the same design template is applied.

2. In Outline view, add the words Food & Drink to the list on the first slide.

3. In slide view, customize the background for this slide in different ways, e.g. by selecting different shades or colour combinations whilst staying with the same basic design.

4. Print a copy of the complete presentation and then update and close the file.

 Module 6, section 2.2

EXERCISES 7 AND 8

You will need to know how to:

▶ Use the Slide or Title Master to change your presentation

▶ Add footers and slide numbers

6

Exercise 7
1. Open History.

2. Apply a suitable design template to the presentation and customize it to your liking.

3. Using the Title Master, change the main title font on the title slide to Algerian. The title slide is not affected by altering the Slide Master, so you must alter the title slide manually or go to **View > Master > Title Master**.

4. Using the Slide Master, add a small WordArt object, **Time**, to every slide, positioned in the top, right-hand corner, and re-format all titles to Algerian.

5. Add slide numbers and the date as a footer.

6. Check that these objects appear on all the slides.

7. Go to the blank slide and change it to one with a numerical chart place-holder.

8. Add a main title – *Kings and Queens* – and then save and close the presentation.

 Module 6, section 2.4

Exercise 8   1. Open Transport.

2. Use the Slide Master to reformat the bullet points throughout your presentation.

3. Find a very small cartoon character illustrating a transport theme and add it to every slide.

4. Add your name in a very small font to the bottom left-hand corner of every slide.

5. Number all the slides.

6. Go to the Trains slide and, if necessary, change the slide layout to one that includes a placeholder for a bulleted list. Enter the following as a list headed by the subtitle What You Will Need:

    Tickets, Passport, Luggage, Reading matter and Guidebook

7. Position the following three WordArt objects on the Trains slide, angled and formatted to look different:

    Timetables; Across continents; Through the night

8. Check that the transport cartoon is still visible and print a copy of this slide only.

9. Update and close the presentation.

 Module 6, section 2.4

You will need to know how to:

▸ Create and format organization charts

Exercise 9 1. Open **History** and go to the slide with the organization chart placeholder.

2. Create the following chart with the title **Kings and Queens of England:**

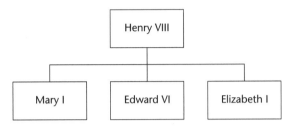

3. Save the amendments to the slide and then print one copy.

4. Now return to the chart and add the following descendants in a direct line from Mary: son **James I**, grandson **Charles I** and great grandsons **Charles II** and **James II**.

5. Add different borders and colours to the boxes.

6. Change the title font to bold and underlined and the names in the boxes to italic.

7. Save these changes and update the slide before printing a copy.

8. Close the file.

 Module 6, section 4.2

Exercise 10 1. Start a new presentation, select a blank slide layout or one with an organization chart placeholder and save the file as **Filing.**

2. Create an organization chart that shows the following:

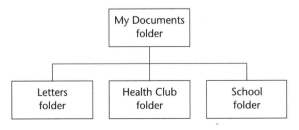

3. Update your slide and print a copy.

4. Return to the chart and add the files as set out below:

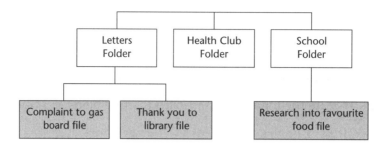

5. Make the folders yellow and the files green.

6. Change the title to: A Folders and Files Hierarchy

7. Reformat the text in your preferred style, and add borders or make any other changes you feel would improve the look of your chart.

8. Update your slide and print a copy of the amended chart.

9. Close the file.

 Module 6, section 4.2

EXERCISE 11

You will need to know how to:

▸ Add and format numerical charts

1. Open **History** and go to the slide with the numerical chart placeholder.

2. Insert a 2D column chart based on the following data and include titles for the main axes:

Monarch	Henry VII	Henry VIII	Edward	Mary	Elizabeth
Reign	24	38	6	5	45

3. Remove the legend and make sure the monarchs' names appear as x-axis labels.

4. Amend the slide title to read: **Royal Reigns**.

5. Print a copy of this slide alone.

6. Now change the chart type to a pie chart, add labels that show the years and include a legend.

7. On the slide, move both chart and main title higher up to make room for the following text:

   The average length of time on the throne in the 16th or 17th century was 21 years.

8. Save these changes and print a copy of the amended slide.

9. Close the file.

 Module 6, section 4.1

EXERCISE 12

You will need to know how to:

▶ Copy and resize objects

1. Open **Transport** and add a new blank slide.

2. Add the title: **Sailing to France**

3. Minimize your presentation.

4. Create the following spreadsheet using Excel or another spreadsheet package:

Dates	B and B	Standard Hotel	Premium Hotel
Nov–March	£219	£274	£374
March–May	£250	£305	£405
May–July	£280	£335	£490
Jul –Aug	£294	£349	£504
Sept	£250	£305	£405

6

5. Copy the data, and then minimize the spreadsheet package.

6. Paste the data on to your slide, and reposition and resize as necessary to display the data clearly.

7. Add the following text underneath the spreadsheet:

Cost of accommodation for 5 nights.

8. Print a copy of this slide only, and then save and close the presentation.

 Module 6, section 3.3

EXERCISES 13 AND 14

You will need to know how to:

- Add slide transitions

- Run a slide show automatically

- Hide slides during a slide show

Exercise 13 1. Create a new presentation to be called Cup of Tea (or choose a similar topic that can be set out in steps). Save as Tea.

2. Add the following five slides – feel free to vary the exact content of each slide – format backgrounds and borders and add images or WordArt where appropriate:

   a) Slide 1: Title – How to make a cup of tea; subtitle – your name and the date.

   b) Slide 2: Title – What you will need. List – tea leaves; teapot; kettle; water; spoon; cups and saucers; and possibly milk and sugar or slices of lemon.

   c) Slide 3: Different types of tea, e.g. Earl Grey, Assam, Darjeeling, Green, and where tea comes from, e.g. India, Ceylon, China.

   d) Slide 4: Title – Main Steps: shortened notes covering: Boil water; amount of tea in the pot – I spoonful per person; fill teapot with boiling water, leave 3 minutes (if preferred, have the milk ready in the cups), pour on the tea and add sugar/lemon.

   e) Slide 5: Title – End Result – a refreshing cup of tea.

3. Run the presentation as a slide show and make any changes to slide order, pictures, design template, etc., if you think these are needed.

4. Run the show with slide 3 hidden.

5. Unhide this slide and run the show again.

6. Apply the same transition to all the slides and run the show. Change the type of transition until you are happy with it.

7. Now vary the transition for the first and/or last slide.

8. Update the presentation, and then print a six-slide handout page.

 Module 6, sections 5.2 and 6.3

Exercise 14 1. Open Transport.

2. Run the slide show and then add suitable backgrounds or apply an overall design template.

3. Change the slide order if necessary, and complete any slides that need extra text or images.

4. Set transitions for each slide and run the show automatically.

5. Make any changes to type and speed until you feel you have chosen the best combination of transitions.

6. Save the changes, print copies of any *two* slides only and then close the file.

 Module 6, sections 5.2 and 6.3

You will need to know how to:

♦ Animate slides

Exercise 15   1.   Imagine you have been asked to give a talk on buying a house. You will need the following six slides:

Introduction (1)
Finding the right property (2)
Purchasing (3)
Moving in (4)
Gardening (5)
Conclusion (6)

2.   Create an introductory first slide with the title of the talk, your name and a suitable picture. All the other slides should have a title taken from the above list.

3.   On slide 2, add a bulleted list of different types of housing, e.g. bungalows, flats, semi-detached or detached houses, with a note about any pros and cons, e.g. no stairs, if this type of property is cheap or not, any gardens to maintain, the view, etc.

4.   On slide 3, include the following data as a chart titled **Average Costs:**

Year	Solicitors	Surveyors	Banks
1980	£300	£80	£450
1990	£440	£186	£680
2000	£578	£245	£890

5.   On slide 4, add suitable drawings or pictures to illustrate the topic, and include relevantly worded text boxes or WordArt objects, e.g. tiring, cups of tea, where's the dog? new neighbours, etc.

6.   On slide 5, bullet points about gardens – where to buy plants, digging a pond, keeping the front tidy, weeding, etc., with illustrations.

7.   On slide 6, summarize the contents of the talk and perhaps wish your audience good luck.

8. For each slide, experiment with animating objects and adding transitions.

9. Print a copy of all the slides, e.g. as a single handout or complete print-out. Save and close the presentation.

 Module 6, section 5.1

Exercise 16 1. Create a presentation (real or imaginary) about yourself that you will run as a slide show on the computer. You can include any aspect, e.g. family, home, work, leisure, pets, etc. (Naturally, if working with others, only disclose information you are happy to share.)

2. There should be six slides in the presentation which should include the following:

   a) an organization chart, e.g. showing a family tree, College staff or company management structure, etc.

   b) at least two examples of Clip Art and two of WordArt;

   c) one drawing produced either using the Drawing toolbar or within a separate drawing package;

   d) an overall colour scheme so that every slide has a similar 'look';

   e) transitions between slides;

   f) timing set so that the slides appear automatically;

   g) some pre-set animations.

3. Print the slides in the form of a single-page handout.

4. Save as Myself and close the file.

 Module 6, section 5.1

Information and communication

This final module tests your knowledge of the Internet. You need to be able to use a browser to visit Websites or search for information on the Word Wide Web, as well as store favourite Web page addresses. You will also need to be able to use an e-mail system to send and receive messages, attach files, maintain an address book and organize your messages in named folders.

Subjects covered in this section:

EXERCISES 1, 2 AND 3

You will need to know how to:

▶ Use the browser navigation buttons

▶ Use URLs to open Web pages

▶ Use hyperlinks to open new pages

▶ Work with more than one application at a time

▶ Save files into folders

Exercise 1

1. Open your browser and connect to the Internet.

2. Note down the full URL of your home page, or copy it into a new Word document that you can save as **Web Addresses.**

3. Click a hyperlink text entry (it will probably be blue and underlined) to go to a new page. Make a note of the URL now showing in the address box and check the information on your screen. Finally open another page and note its URL and contents in the same way.

4. Return to your home page using the Back button.

5. Move backwards and forwards through the three pages you have opened and, if you can, find an image that you can click. Note the URL for the page that opens.

6. Type the following URL in the address box: **www.bbc.co.uk** and go to the BBC Website.

7. Use the index and hyperlinks on the page to find out the following:

   ● what the weather will be like in your nearest main town tomorrow;

   ● what is on television tonight;

   ● background information about a programme or personality of interest;

   ● how to contact someone at the BBC.

8. Close the browser window and disconnect if preferred.

 Module 7, sections 1.3 and 2.1

Exercise 2 1. You are going to find out what information is available on Websites created specifically for older Web surfers.

2. Open www.laterlife.com and use the index hyperlinks to explore their leisure pages, e.g. look at holidays, events, etc.

3. Repeat this activity on www.lifes4living.co.uk, www.50connect.com and www.retirement-matters.co.uk. Look particularly for leisure and travel information.

4. Close your browser.

5. You may like to think about which of the four sites you preferred and why.

 Module 7, sections 1.3 and 2.1

Exercise 3 1. Go to Tesco's main site, www.tesco.co.uk, and explore their index page. Click some of the hyperlinks to find out what the site has to offer.

2. Repeat this exercise by visiting two other supermarket sites – e.g. www.waitrose.com, www.safeway.co.uk or www.iceland.co.uk – and compare their attractiveness and ease of use.

3. Minimize your browser window (disconnect if you want to) and open a word-processing application.

4. Give three reasons why one of the sites you visited would be your favourite to recommend to first-time Web users wanting to find out about online shopping.

5. Give one reason why one of the sites was your least favourite.

6. Save the document as Shops into a new folder labelled Web Research.

7. Close the browser and disconnect if preferred.

 Module 7, sections 1.3 and 2.1

You will need to know how to:

▶ Use a directory

1. Connect to the Internet and open www.excite.com, www.yahoo.co.uk or any other directory site you have been recommended.

2. You are going to search for information on ice rinks in your area. Find a top-level category related to leisure or recreation and click it.

3. Find a sport and then ice skating sub-category and, in a new Word document, saved as **Skating**, note down the directory site and how many 'hits' (Websites listed) there are.

4. Search for any sites related to ice rinks – you may need to type the phrase into a search box.

5. Select two or three sites from the top five in the list and check if they identify a rink near you. If they do, make a note of the URL of the site in your Word document.

6. Now repeat the exercise using another directory and note the hits and useful sites.

7. Decide which was the best directory and which was the best Website for locating the information you were seeking and note their names in Skating.

 Module 7, section 3.1

EXERCISES 5 AND 6

You will need to know how to:

▶ Use a search engine for locating information

▶ Use key words

▶ Define search requirements

7

Exercise 5 1. Open www.google.com, www.altavista.com or any other search engine site recommended to you.

2. Type in *skating rinks*.

3. Note down the search engine you are using and number of 'hits' in your Skating file. The list should be far longer than when you used a directory.

4. Explore the top three sites on the list – do they provide useful information about local skating rinks?

5. Go back to the search engine page, add the word UK inside the query box and search again. Are the top three sites more relevant and useful?

6. Now put quotation marks round the phrase *"skating rinks"* and search again. How has the resultant list of sites changed?

7. Can you refine the search criteria even further? (Try using AND or +, or adding your county as well as UK.)

8. Now repeat the exercise using a different search engine and compare the results.

9. Finally, go to www.ask.co.uk and type in the question: Where is the nearest skating rink to [*add the name of your nearest main town*]? Decide if the results are better or worse than using key words.

10. In Skating, make a few notes about the success of your search, then save and close the file.

 Module 7, section 3.1

Exercise 6 1. Open your browser. You are going to find shops or garden centres in the UK where you can buy tropical fish and accessories for your aquarium.

2. Use a directory site to see if you can find the information using just the categories that are offered, e.g. leisure, pets, fish, etc. You do NOT want to locate sites for Aquariums and Sea Life Centres to visit.

3. Change to a second directory and follow their links to see if the information is easier to find on this site.

4. Open some of the Websites you are offered.

5. Use your **Back** button to return to the best Website and then type the full URL showing in the **Address** box into a new word processing document.

6. Underneath the URL, type: *this was the best site located for buying tropical fish that I found using* [*name of directory Website*] and save as Fish before minimizing the file.

7. Now go to a search engine Website and type Aquariums into the search box. Look at the types of site located by your search.

8. Use a variety of key words and search criteria – e.g. include UK, use NOT or AND, use + or –, or put some text in quotation marks, etc. – to narrow down the list to places in the UK where you can buy your aquarium requirements.

9. Visit several of the sites resulting from your search and then copy your preferred URL into Fish and type underneath: *this was the best site for buying fish located by using [name of search engine] and keying in [the key words you eventually used]*

10. Save and close the file and close your browser.

 Module 7, section 3.1

EXERCISE 7

You will need to know how to:

▶ Print a Web page

---

1. Use a variety of directories or search engines and experiment with key words or search criteria to locate the information below.

2. In all cases you may like to use a Word document for noting down the number of hits; whether the eventual site that had the information was one of the first five on a search list or was located further down the page; and if you encountered any problems during your search with any of the search engines.

   a) Find the names and addresses of three estate agents in your local area who sell flats. Go to the sites before noting down the details, to check that they are relevant (i.e. not selling commercial properties only, or out-of-date Websites, etc.).

   b) Now find a good UK site where you can buy fruit trees on-line.

   c) Discover the opening hours for either the Tate Modern in London or National Railway Museum in York.

   d) Finally, find out the price of a return ticket from Heathrow to Athens if you fly one day next month.

3. For each of the four searches, print *one* page from the Website that contains the most relevant information. Then close your browser.

 Module 7, section 3.3

7

You will need to know how to:

▶ Save a Web page

▶ Save an image from the Web

▶ Add a Web image to a document

---

1. In this exercise you will be sending a letter to a friend telling them about an area of mutual interest and using information you have found on the Web.

2. First locate some useful information about one of your hobbies, e.g. breeding goldfish, playing golf, collecting stamps, etc.

3. Save the most relevant Web page onto your computer or on disk as an HTML file where it should be saved into a new folder labelled **Web Information**. Give the file a name related to the hobby, e.g. **Golf1**.

4. Locate a relevant image and save it with a suitable name into a new folder labelled **Web Images**.

5. Go back to the first page you saved and then minimize the browser window, as you will need to return to the page to note its URL.

6. Open Word and write the following letter, first adding the address **43 Firtree Road, Beckwith, Derbyshire, DB5 1JT** and today's date:

    Dear Harvey

    Searching the Web today I found the most brilliant information on [*name of hobby*]. The URL is [*full address of the Website*] but I've saved the information and will send it to you by e-mail once I get myself registered.

    What do you think of this picture for our newsletter?

    All the best

    Jan

7. Now insert the image you saved into your document below the line **What do you think ...**, format and save the letter and print a copy.

8. Close Word and your browser.

 Module 7, section 3.1

You will need to know how to:

▶ Save a Web page as a text file

1. Use a directory or search engine to find a site offering you guidance on watercolour painting. You may like to include key words such as **tutorial** or **tips**.

2. Look at several of the sites resulting from your search and find the most helpful one.

3. Save the Web page as **Colour1** and print a copy.

4. Now save the page as a text file named **Colour2** and then close your browser.

5. Using Windows Explorer or the Desktop, locate the file **Colour2** and print a copy.

6. Compare the two printouts and then close all files.

 Module 7, section 3.1

You will need to know how to:

▶ Copy text from a Web page

▶ Copy images from a Web page

1. Go to a toyshop site – e.g. ToysRUs (www.toysrus.co.uk) or Hamleys (www.hamleys.co.uk) – and use the index or form provided on the site to find a doll that costs under £50. Then minimize your browser.

2. Open Word, start a new document and type the following:

   DOLLS FROM THE INTERNET

   There are many products you can find by using the Web. Here is a doll I found at [name of shop.]

3. Copy information about the product, including the price, from the Web page into your word-processed document. (It may appear as a table or in a different format.)

4. Return to the site and copy across a picture of the doll below the text in your document.

5. Save the document as Doll and print a copy.

6. Close your word processing application and browser.

 Module 7, section 3.1

EXERCISE 11

You will need to know how to:

▶ Bookmark a Web page (add to **Favorites** menu)

▶ Go to a bookmarked site

1. Return to the page you located on your hobby for Exercise 8 by typing the full URL into the **Address** box in your browser window.

2. So that it is quicker to return here in future, bookmark this site, changing the name if necessary to a shorter one. At this stage, do not choose any particular location for the bookmark, but just add it to your **Favorites** menu in the default position.

3. Try to find two other sites on a related topic – either click a hyperlink within the first site or use a search engine to locate them. In each case, bookmark the sites with relevant page names.

4. For one of these new sites, highlight the URL in the **Address** box and copy it into the clipboard.

5. Minimize the browser and open the letter you wrote in Exercise 8.

6. Add the following sentence to paragraph 1, paste in the URL copied to the clipboard and then update and close the file:

   There was also some useful information at [*address of one other site*] but not such good pictures.

7. Back in your browser, use your bookmark to go to the new site mentioned in your letter. Save the most useful page into your **Web information** folder with a name that distinguishes it from the first saved page, e.g. Golf2.

8. Close your browser.

 Module 7, section 2.2

You will need to know how to:

▶ Organize bookmarks

Exercise 12
1. Open your browser window, but work offline if preferred.

2. Open the **Favorites** menu and go to **Organize favorites**.

3. Create a new folder where you will store bookmarks to Websites about your hobby: label it suitably, e.g. Golf.

4. Locate and move two of your three bookmarked sites into this new folder.

5. Locate and delete the third bookmarked page.

6. Close **Favorites**.

7. Connect to the Internet, open the **Favorites** menu and use it to visit one of your hobby sites.

8. Click a hyperlink that you have not opened before and bookmark the new page you visit, adding it to your hobby folder.

9. Close your browser.

 Module 7, section 2.3

Exercise 13
1. Open your browser and find one newspaper Website, e.g. The *Guardian*, The *Observer*, The *Sunday Times*, The *Daily Mirror*, etc.

2. Bookmark the page and add it to a new **Favorites** folder you will create named Newspapers.

3. Find two more newspaper sites and add these to the Newspapers folder.

4. Now use a search engine to locate a weather report Website. Add this to a new Weather folder.

5. Finally, find a second weather Website but this time add it to the Newspapers folder.

6. Organize your bookmarks as follows:
   a) Move the second weather Website bookmark out of the Newspapers folder and into the Weather folder.
   b) Delete one of the three newspaper bookmarks.
   c) Rename the Newspaper folder as News.

7

7. Use the **Favorites** menu to go to one newspaper Website.

8. Select the text of a short news report and copy it into a new word-processed document saved as **Paper**.

9. Copy an image from the page into the same document.

10. Print a copy of the document and update and close the file and your browser.

 Module 7, section 2.3

EXERCISE 14

You will need to know how to:

▶ Buy goods or services online

1. You have decided to buy a book as a present for a young nephew or niece. Go to an online book shop, e.g. www.amazon.co.uk; www.blackwells.co.uk or www.bol.co.uk

2. Search for **Alice in Wonderland** (if not available, find another well-known children's book, e.g. *Treasure Island* or *Just William*).

3. Follow the steps to add this book to your trolley or shopping cart and go through the process until you are asked to enter your credit card details. STOP at this point! (You may be asked to register with the site, but as this is free and could be useful for real purchases later, do so if you want to.)

4. Print a copy of the last page you reach that shows details of your proposed purchase.

5. Now go to any tour company site – e.g. www.markwarner.com, www.thomascook.co.uk or www.firstchoice.co.uk – and go through the process of buying any holiday, e.g. a one-week family holiday in Spain next month.

6. Check available accommodation/packages, select your preferred option and follow the purchasing procedure until asked for payment details.

7. Print a copy of the last page you reach that details the holiday you have chosen.

 Module 7, section 2.1

You will need to know how to:

▶ Open an e-mail system

▶ Compose and send an e-mail

Exercise 1

1. You are going to send an e-mail to John at Pearson Education.

2. Open your e-mail system and then the new message/composing box, staying offline if you can, and enter the following e-mail address: in the **To** box: john@pearsoned-ema.com

3. The subject of the message is Invitation to a Party.

4. Now type the following message in the main window:

   Hi John

   I have just moved house and want to invite you over for a house-warming party. Are you free next Saturday, 25th at 8.30?

   The address is 24 Mead Close, Warrington – just past the station on the left.

   Let me know if you can come. Hope to see you.

   Cheers

   [your first name]

5. Send your message, disconnect and close the e-mail system.

 Module 7, sections 4.3 and 5.3

Exercise 2

1. You are going to write to an imaginary television company commenting on a recent programme that you enjoyed or disliked.

2. In the **To** box enter the following TV company e-mail address: TVcomments@pearsoned-ema.com

3. The subject of the message is any real or imaginary programme title, e.g. Nine O-Clock News.

7

4. Write a short message mentioning something you enjoyed, or suggesting improvements. This is an example:

I am just writing to let you know that I am delighted to see that you now feature regional news quite strongly. In particular I am glad that the areas you cover have been reorganized so that people in the Berkshire/Oxfordshire area do not keep seeing repeats of London-based news items.

Many thanks for your excellent coverage.

[your name]

5. Send the message.

 Module 7, sections 4.3 and 5.3

EXERCISE 3

You will need to know how to:

▶ Use the spell-checker

▶ Set a priority on your message

1. You are going to send an e-mail to the Marketing Department at Pearson Education enquiring about books suitable for new computer owners.

2. If closed, open your e-mail system and then a new message window.

3. In the **To** box type: marketing@pearsoned-ema.com

4. The message subject is Computing for Beginners Books

5. Type the following message in the main window, RETAINING spelling mistakes to the words grateful and publications:

I would be gretful if you could send me the titles of 3 of your most recent pubblicatons that would be suitable for people like myself who have just bought a computer.

Many thanks

[Your name]

5. Now use the spell-checker to help you correct any mistakes.

6. Give your message a high priority.

7. Send the message.

 Module 7, section 5.3

You will need to know how to:

▶ Receive e-mails

▶ Reply to messages

▶ Forward messages

▶ Send copies

▶ Delete message text

Exercise 4
1. Open your Inbox and check that an automated response to your party invitation e-mail has arrived.

2. Open it and prepare the following reply:

Hello John

Glad to hear you can come. Vivien and I will look forward to showing you the new house. Wine to lubricate the proceedings will be gratefully received.

Best wishes

[Your name]

3. Delete your original message text showing in the main window.

4. Before sending, make sure you copy the reply to **yasmin@pearsoned-ema.com** and include a blind copy to yourself.

5. Forward a copy of the response you received to **sarah@pearsoned-ema.com**. Retain the original text and add this additional comment above it:

Sarah

Just heard John can come to my party. Are you free as well? You know where we live and it's on Saturday 25th at 8.30.

Bye

[Your name]

 Module 7, sections 5.2, 5.3 and 5.4

Exercise 5 1. Check your Inbox for an automated response from the message you sent in Exercise 17 to the Pearson Marketing Department.

2. Send the following reply, copying the message to yourself as a blind copy and leaving the original text in place as a reminder:

Thank you for the information you sent me. It will be most helpful.

With kind regards

[Your name]

3. Now forward the response from Marketing to John at Pearson Education, adding the following message:

As you were thinking of buying a computer I thought you might like the following information I have been sent by Marketing.

If you find out about any other books I might find useful, please let me know.

Best wishes

[Your name]

4. Check a little later to see if you have received the copy of your replies to John and Marketing that you sent yourself.

 Module 7, sections 5.2, 5.3 and 5.4

EXERCISES 6 AND 7

You will need to know how to:

▶ Print e-mails

▶ Copy text between messages or between applications

▶ Close messages without sending or saving (i.e. aborting e-mails)

Exercise 6 1. You have decided to send a late party invitation to Jack Spring.

2. Compose a new message with the Subject **House Warming** and enter the following e-mail address in the **To** box: jack.spring@webster.com

3. Open the original invitation you sent to John and copy the main text across into Jack's new message. Make sure you change **John** to **Jack** in the main message window.

4. Print a copy of the message and then cancel the e-mail.

 Module 7, sections 5.4 and 6.4

Exercise 7 1. Open your word processing application and create the following document:

Our house is on a new estate and can be quite confusing to find. Numbers 1 – 23 run parallel to Queen's Drive, but you have to turn right at the end of Charity Close before you start Numbers 24 – 42. Ours is the one with a red door and large conifer in the front garden.

2. Save as **House** and then minimize the file.

3. Open your e-mail system and compose a new message to Deidre Smith. Her e-mail address is d_smith@webster.com.

4. You are inviting her to tea next week. Enter the subject of the message as **Tea** and write the following:

Hello Deidre

So glad you can come over next Sunday.

5. Now restore your **House** document and copy the text across into the e-mail main message window.

6. Complete the message as follows:

Look forward to hearing about your holiday.

Best wishes

[your name]

7. Print a copy of the message and then close without saving.

 Module 7, sections 5.4 and 6.4

EXERCISE 8

You will need to know how to:

- ♦ Add e-mail details to an address book
- ♦ Insert addresses automatically into new messages
- ♦ Save messages in draft format

1. A number of examination bodies have Websites and offer an e-mail information service.

2. Add the e-mail addresses of the following three such organizations to your Address Book:

- City and Guilds: 1 Giltspur Street, London EC1A 9DD; enquiry@cityandguilds.com

- Oxford Cambridge and RSA Examinations (OCR): tel.: 01223 553998; helpdesk@ocr.org.uk

- Edexcel: tel.: 0870 240 9800; enquiries@edexcel.org.uk

3. Add the other information provided in appropriate places within your Address Book.

4. Open a new message window and automatically insert the e-mail address for OCR stored in your Address Book into the **To** box.

5. Type the following message:

   I am interested in taking a City and Guilds Business studies course next year. Please would you send me details of Centres where I could study the subject locally.

6. Add the subject of the message: Business studies courses in (*your county or main town*).

7. Save the message in your **Drafts** folder.

8. Close and then re-open your e-mail system. Open your draft message to OCR and amend it to read:

   ... taking an OCR Business studies course ...

9. Now print a copy of the message, save the changes and then close so that it remains in your **Drafts** folder.

 Module 7, sections 6.1, 6.2 and 6.4

You will need to know how to:

▸ Create a group e-mail address

▸ Send messages to everyone on a mailing list

▸ Delete an address

▸ Edit an address

1. You have entered the City and Guilds e-mail address incorrectly. Open your e-mail system and Address Book and change it to: **enquiry@city-and-guilds.co.uk**

2. Add the following e-mail addresses to your Address Book:

   ● The British Tourist Authority: **enquiries@bta.org.uk**

   ● The Heart of England Tourist Board: **htinfo@bta.org.uk**

3. Create a group e-mail address labelled **Tourist Boards** and add the Heart of England Tourist Board and BTA addresses.

4. Now create a group e-mail address labelled **Exam Bodies** to include City and Guilds, Edexcel and OCR. Add to it the e-mail address for the British Computer Society (**bcshq@bcs.org.uk**), which should *not* have its own entry in your Address Book.

5. Compose the following message to **Exam Bodies** with the subject **IT Training** and print a copy:

   Do you offer any qualifications in IT training for people who have an ECDL certificate? If so, please would you send me details.

   Many thanks

   [Your name].

6. Save the message into your **Drafts** folder.

7. Finally, locate and delete the individual entry for **Edexcel** in your Address Book.

 Module 7, section 6.2

7

You will need to know how to:

▶ Restore deleted messages

▶ Mark messages as unread

1.   Imagine you are writing from an advertising company, *Selling UK*. You are going to send the following message to John at Pearson Education.

2.   The subject of the message is Distance Learning Advertisement.

3.   This is the message:

John

It was good to meet you last week. I have had a think about the campaign and want to confirm my view that we should take a more negative approach. Negative campaigning is the IN thing, and I'm sure we will sell far more courses if we drop the final part of your presentation.

Do you still disagree?

Look forward to your views.

4.   Add the following:

Jay McWhortle
Managing Director and Campaign Designer
Selling UK
Tel: 0108 4321000
http://www.sellinguk.co.uk

5.   Send the message.

6.   When the automated reply arrives, read it and then mark it as unread.

7.   Delete the message.

8.   Open the Deleted Items folder, locate and restore the reply, and return it to your Inbox.

 Module 7, sections 5.1 and 6.3

You will need to know how to:

▶ Attach files to e-mail messages

Exercise 11 1. Open a word processing application and create the following document:

From: Head Office

To: All Heads of Department

Date: (today's)

Subject: Car Parks

You will be glad to learn that the new car park is now available alongside Block D. Any member of staff who would like to use it should complete the tear-off slip at the bottom of this memo and send it to Security. I hope this will put an end to lateness of staff due to car parking difficulties in the City.

....

To: Security

From: ....   Department: ....

Please issue me with a car sticker so that I can use the new car park. My car

registration number is ....

Signed ....

Date ....

2. Save as **Car Parking** and close the file.

3. Now open your e-mail system and write the following message to send to Yasmin at Pearson Education. Copy it to Sarah with a blind copy to yourself. The subject is **Parking**.

Dear Colleagues

I have just received the attached memo from HQ. Please print out and reply so that we can sort out this wretched parking problem once and for all.

Deirdre Wessex
Head of Finance

4. Attach the document **Car Parking** and print a copy of the message showing the contents of the attachment box.

5. Send the message.

 Module 7, section 5.3

Exercise 12 1. John at Pearson Education wants to find out more about the ECDL.

2. Write the following e-mail. The subject of the message is Computer Training.

ECDL covers seven aspects of computers: general theory about its use; filing and file management; word processing, databases; spreadsheets; presentations and the Internet. You can take the modules in any order and eventually will receive a certificate recognized world-wide.

3. Copy the text into a new word processed document, save as ECDL text and then close the file.

4. Back in your message, attach the file ECDL text to your e-mail. Now add the following text to your message:

I attach a copy of my words to check that attaching files is working properly.

5. Send the message with the attachment.

 Module 7, section 5.3

Exercise 13

You will need to know how to:

▶ Open attachments

▶ Delete attachments

1. Start a new Word document and insert a picture of a car, e.g. from Clip Art. Save as Car Picture and close the file.

2. Check your e-mail system and when the response to your parking message sent in Exercise 25 arrives in your Inbox, open the attachment and complete the reply slip with the following information:

Name: David Holmes

Department: Arts and Media

Car registration number: V980 MUI

3. Save the amended document as My Car and print a copy before closing the file.

4. Now open a new message window addressed to yourself and write the following message that has the subject Car Park Permit:

Dear Security Officer Biggins

Just in case the internal post plays up again, I am e-mailing my car details so that my parking permit can be forwarded as soon as possible.

Many thanks

Dave

5. Attach both the My Car and Car Picture files and save the message in your drafts folder.

6. Print a copy of the message showing the attachments in the attachment box.

7. Now delete the Car Picture attachment and send the message.

8. When it arrives in your Inbox, check that only one file is attached.

 Module 7, section 5.4

EXERCISE 14

You will need to know how to:

▶ Create folders for storing messages

▶ Copy, move or delete messages

1. Open your e-mail system and Inbox.

2. Create a subfolder within the Inbox folder labelled In-Exercises.

3. Move at least three of the messages you have received working through this section into the folder.

4. Locate and delete the Selling UK message.

5. Now create a subfolder within your Sent Messages folder labelled Out-Exercises and move at least two messages you have sent into it.

6. Find a third message and save a copy into your new folder.

7. Delete the reply you sent to Marketing thanking them for their information, and check that it is in the **Deleted Items** folder.

 Module 7, section 6.3

7

EXERCISE 15

You will need to know how to:

▸ Sort messages

▸ Find messages

1. Open your Inbox and sort the messages in date order – the most recent messages at the top. Repeat the sort so the messages are in the opposite order.

2. Now open the Sent folder and sort messages by subject in alphabetical order.

3. Using the Find facility, locate the message to the OCR concerning Business studies courses, making sure you look in all your folders. When it has been located, move it to the **Deleted items** folder.

4. Address a new message to yourself and then find all your messages to John at Pearson Education. Open two different messages and copy the main text into your new message window. Add the following text at the top of the message:

    The following text was sent to John in 2 different messages.

5. Send the message.

6. When it arrives in your Inbox, print a copy, and then delete the message and close your e-mail system.

 Module 7, section 6.3

Test your information and communication knowledge with this crossword.

ACROSS

1 Part of a Web page (5)
3 If you see this, you are over a hyperlink (4)
6, 14 Go here to save telephone charges (3, 4)
8 Needed to use the Internet (5)
10 Connects two Web pages (4)
12 Abbreviation for all those pages (3)
13 Starting page (4)
15 The Web address (3)
16 Box showing where your files are (6)
19 Keep the address handy (8)
20 Who are you? (2)
21 Click this to return (4)
22 Start the search (2)
23 Talking over the Internet (4)
28 Using technology to communicate (3)
29, 40 Help you find information (6, 6)
30 Do this to start searching (7)
31 Nasty germ (5)
32 Well known search engine (9)
35 Get rid of something (6)
41 Do this if downloading is too slow (4)
42 Example of a directory (5)
44 Post an e-mail (4)
46 Words to type in before searching (3)
47 Important consideration when buying on the Internet (8)
48 Needed to view Web pages (7)

DOWN

2 Do this to reload the page (7)
3 Code (4)
4 Send it to someone else (7)
5 Move through the list (6)
7 Place to revisit (8)
9 List of what's on the site (5)
11 It appears when you reply (2)
17 Sort things out (8)
18 Useful Website (6)
20 Use it for information and communication (8)
24 Results of a search (4)
25 @ (2)
26 Your machine may be one (2)
27 The opposite of 6 Across (6)
29 New sport (7)
33 Send files with your message (6)
34 Keep your friends safely stored here (7,4)
36 See stars when you type this (8)
37 Hundreds of multimedia documents (3)
38 Unwanted mail (4)
39 Make one to keep things tidy (6)
43 Visit the sites and view the details (6)
45 Could be a hard one (4)

2

Model answers

This part of the book contains model answers that show you what your finished work might look like, or what you should see on screen if you have performed the tasks correctly. Although your answers and computer screens may be quite different from the following examples, these will give you an idea of what you should be aiming for.

Part 2 is also broken down into sections that relate to each of the seven ECDL modules:

Module number

1. Concepts of information technology
2. Using the computer and managing files
3. Word processing
4. Spreadsheets
5. Databases
6. Presentation
7. Information and communication

Concepts of information technology

ANSWERS TO INTRODUCTORY QUESTIONS

1. You might mention Microsoft Publisher™ and explain that it is used to produce publications such as brochures, business cards or leaflets.

2. Networked computers can share expensive hardware such as printers; can share files so that different departments can access the same information; and can encourage collaborative working, e.g. contributing different information that will be brought together in a single publication.

3. Passwords prevent unauthorized people from accessing computer systems or stored information such as personnel records. The ***** stop people seeing your password if they are standing close to you when you type it in.

4. You could have mentioned any of the following ways that hospitals might use computers: to store patient information such as names and addresses, contact numbers, etc.; to keep details of a patient's medical history and current medication; a national database to help hospitals find empty beds; and a register of donors for organ transplants. In addition, computers are used for medical research.

5. You need to be aware that computer files can be lost or corrupted so that keeping backups means you will always have a reasonably recent copy of the information.

6. Viruses are commonly transferred by e-mail or when downloading programs from the Internet, or from using an infected floppy diskette. Safety measures include installing and regularly updating anti-virus software, and never installing programs or borrowing disks from an unknown source.

7. This Act is your safeguard against other people using your private information stored on computer. Organizations keeping personal records must be registered and abide by the law. Banks may hold your current or deposit

account details or information on loans; a school or college will have your personal contact details and information on qualifications; and a doctor will keep your full medical history.

8. System software, such as the operating system of your computer, is needed to maintain the efficient operation of your computer or peripherals such as printers. Application software allows you to perform specific tasks, e.g. word processors enable you to write letters, and browsers allow you to view Web pages.

9. The Internet is the name given to the networks of computers that are linked around the world and that enable you to send information from one computer to another. The World Wide Web is made up of thousands of multimedia pages containing text, pictures, sounds and moving images that are stored on computers and that each have a unique address, the URL. This allows you to locate any page and download it on to your computer.

10. GUI stands for Graphical User Interface and is easy to use as you work from menus and labelled buttons rather than having to type in code, and can have several applications running inside windows that are open on screen at the same time.

11. The telephone system allows you to speak to someone, or send fax, e-mail or telex messages. All except e-mail can be used without a computer.

12. You normally find a floppy diskette in the A: drive, the hard disk in the C: drive, and CD-ROM disks in the D: drive.

13. Systems development usually involves research, analysis, programming, and then testing and implementation. The programmer is involved in writing the software and documentation for the system.

14. E-commerce is the use of the Internet for business. Shopping online can save time as you won't need to visit a shop, save effort in carrying goods home and allows you to find the cheapest items, as you can compare prices very easily from your home. Disadvantages include not being able to see and handle the goods, it is difficult to take advantage of special offers that may be very local to an individual outlet, and the system may breakdown and prevent you placing your order.

15. Storing copies of files on floppy diskettes means you will still have your work even if something happens to the originals on the computer. You can also carry floppy diskettes around so that you can easily transfer files to different machines.

ANSWERS TO ADVANCED QUESTIONS

1. Working safely with a computer should involve taking regular breaks, sitting in a chair that encourages a good posture, keeping everything within easy reach to avoid stretching, cutting down on glare from the screen, holding the mouse lightly and supporting wrists with a wrist rest.

2. The CPU is the central processing unit and is the 'brains' of your computer as it determines everything it does. Its speed is measured in megahertz (MHz).

3. Customers are able to view statements and details of recent transactions in any of their bank accounts; they can pay bills by transferring money electronically to another account; and they can transfer money between accounts, such as current and savings accounts, held with the same bank.

4. Laser printers work by building up an image on an electrically charged drum. Pigment-loaded resin is attracted to the charged areas and heat is then used to melt and bond the resin to paper. Inkjet printers spray droplets of ink onto the paper from rows of nozzles.

5. The advantages of e-mail include no need to use stamps or go to the postbox, sending messages across the world very quickly, and being able to send large numbers of messages for the cost of a local phonecall.

6. Unlike ClipArt, pictures with © next to them are not free for you to use, and the copyright symbol is there to protect the rights of the owner. You must seek permission from the artist or photographer who created them before you can copy or use them, e.g. for cards or in publications.

7. Portable computers are called laptops or notebooks. They use batteries rather than mains power, have a built-in pointing device such as a touch pad, and have flat, liquid-crystal display screens inside the case.

8. Input devices include mouse, keyboard, scanner, digital camera and microphone. Output devices are monitor, speakers and printers. Printers are described in answer 19, so you might describe how the mouse works. It contains a ball that is free to roll. As the mouse is moved over a flat surface the ball rotates, and sensors send digital information to the computer regarding its position. This is translated into an arrow or other shape that moves around the screen.

9. RAM stands for Random Access Memory. It differs from ROM as it is lost when the computer is turned off, and it can have new data written into it.

10. Formatting a floppy diskette involves organizing the magnetic material into tracks and sectors that have a unique address, so that information stored there can be located easily. The answer to formatting a hard disk is (c) – only on special occasions. This is because formatting destroys all the information stored on the disk, and the hard disk houses important information such as your application software and files.

11. Shareware is the term applied to versions of software such as desktop publishing or zipping programs that are made available on the Internet and can be downloaded and used without an initial purchase. They normally have an expiry date, after which you must send a small fee to the program author. They differ from freeware, as these programs are entirely free to use.

12. Pointing devices are input devices that usually control an arrow used in GUI systems to select the menus and icons and carry out tasks such as moving text. You may come across joysticks, touch screens, track balls, mice or light pens. Mice have been described in answer 23, but touch screens are different as users use a finger to touch the screen when they want to choose from a series of options.

13. A modem is needed if you want to communicate with other computers on a network that uses the telephone cable system, such as the Internet. A modem (the name stands for *modulator–demodulator*) converts the digital information used by your computer into an analogue signal that can be sent down a telephone cable. The current top speed of a modem is 56kbps.

14. Zipping is the process of compressing large files so that they take up far less space.

15. Hard disks are usually measured in GB, but RAM, CD-ROMs and floppy diskettes are all measured in MB.

Using the computer and managing files

ANSWERS TO INTRODUCTORY QUESTIONS

1. To shut down properly, click the **Start** button, select **Shut Down** and check the *Shut down* option before clicking **OK**. You must do this so that temporary files or unsaved work are organized properly before your next session.

2. **a)** Image files may be bitmap (BMP), jpeg (JPG) or gif (GIF)
   b) Text files are .txt, Web pages are .htm, Excel spreadsheets are .xls and Word documents are .doc.

3. My **Help** menu indicated that you can open the calculator by clicking **Start**, then choosing **Programs**, **Accessories**, and finally **Calculator**.

4. To resize a window, first click its **Restore** button, then move the mouse pointer over any boundary and drag the edge in or out with the two-way arrow that will be displayed.

5. To find your default printer, you can select **Start | Settings | Printers** and check which icon has a tick above it. To change the default, click an alternative printer icon and go to **File | Set as default**.

6. Try holding down **Ctrl** and **Alt** and then clicking **Delete** to unfreeze a computer. In the window that appears, click **End Task**. You can repeat pressing **Ctrl + Alt + Delete** to restart the computer completely, or follow the shut down procedure described in answer 1, but check **Restart** in the Shut down window.

7. I am working with a computer operating Windows 98 on an AMD-K6™ 3D processor, with 128MB RAM

8. My Recycle Bin shows the following details:

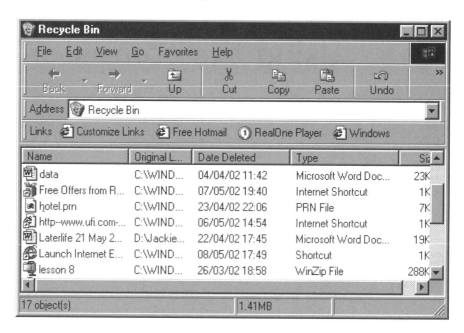

9. My search located six files or folders, shown below.

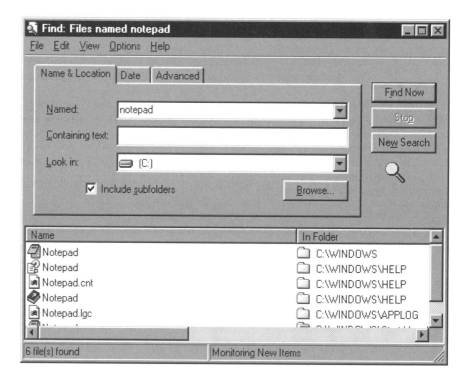

10. The steps are as follows:
    1. Open a zipping program such as Winzip
    2. Create an archive in which to compress the files by clicking **New**. Save and name this as normal.
    3. Browse your files and click by name any that you want to compress. Then click **Add**. The files will appear in the archive window.
    4. Close the archive and treat it just like a normal file.

ANSWERS TO EXERCISES

Exercise 1 Creating new folders on the desktop.

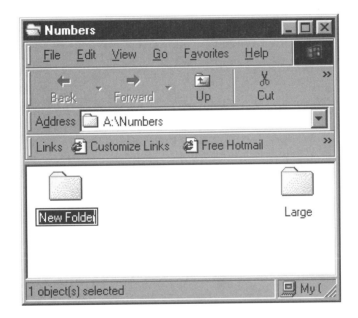

Exercise 2   Changing the name of the folder Veg to Vegetables.

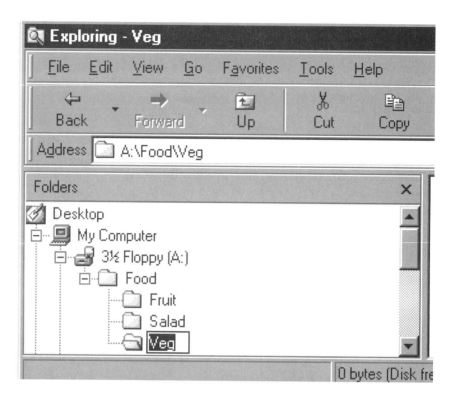

Exercise 3   Deleting a file should result in a request for confirmation.

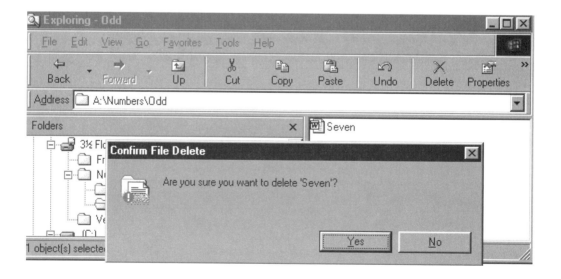

Exercise 4   Moving files in Windows Explorer.

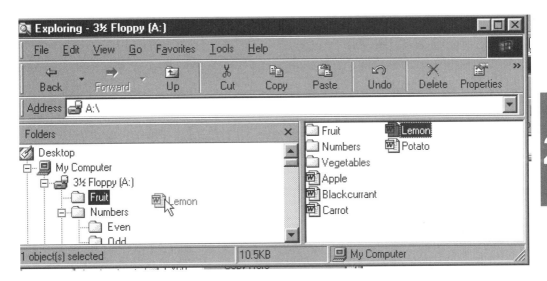

Exercise 6   Finding the details for 'Potato'. (Exercise 5 will produce a similar result.)

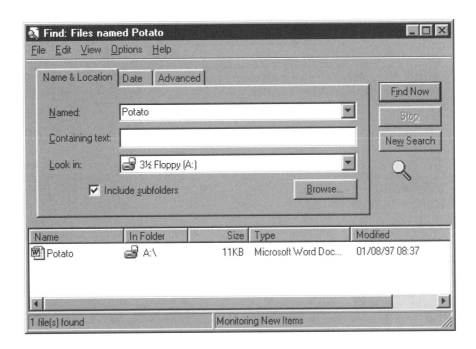

Moving more than one file at the same time.

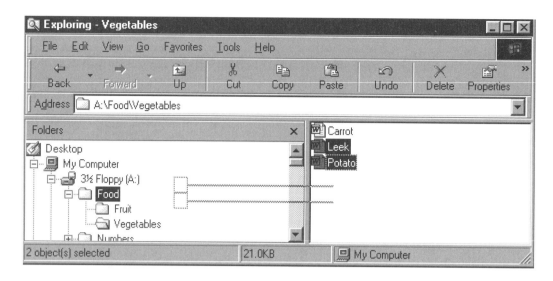

Exercise 7   Saving a file into a named folder. (Exercise 8 will produce a similar result.)

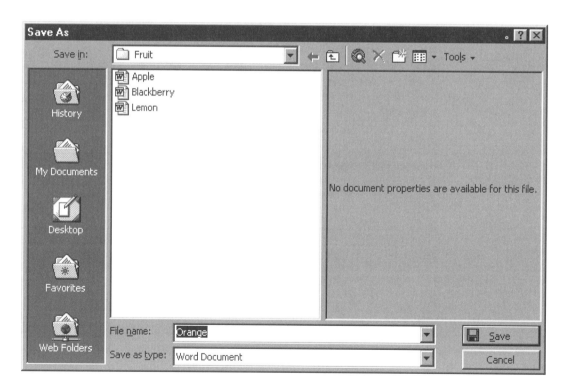

Exercise 9   Showing the contents of a folder.

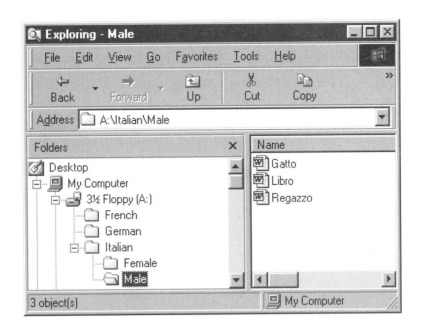

MODEL ANSWERS **3**

Word processing

ANSWERS TO INTRODUCTORY EXERCISES

Exercise 1 SURFACE FEEDERS

All the fish found 'just under the surface' have a perfectly straight back, which allows their upturned mouths (ideal for scooping up floating foods, usually insects) to get right up to the surface. Foods which float for some time are ideal for these fish.

A common surface feeder is the Zebra Danio. This fish is a native of India and is very active and lively. It can reach a size of about 5 cm and is best kept in shoals.

[My Name]

Exercise 2 THE POTENTIAL OF MUSIC

Teachers generally provide a stimulating environment for children in their classes, with respect to sight and touch. Other experiences may be overlooked. One of the senses which can be educated quite easily is hearing. Sounds are all around us in the infants and with careful structuring they can even become organized sounds – music.

Children make sounds all the time – they talk, shout, cry, scream or sing. A good way to focus on sounds is to use rhymes and poems and to tell stories needing 'sound effects', such as those of police cars, ambulances, trains or ghosts.

[My Name]

Exercise 3

FIGHTING FISH

All the fish found 'just under the surface' have a perfectly straight back, which allows their upturned mouths (ideal for scooping up floating foods, usually insects) to get right up to the surface. Foods which float for some time are ideal for these fish.

A common surface feeder is the Zebra Danio. This fish is a native of India and is very active and lively. It can reach a size of about 5 cm and is best kept in shoals.

The Siamese Fighting Fish is hardy, but you can only have one male in a tank otherwise fighting will break out. If you want to see it display, put a mirror at the side of the tank. Aquarium-cultivated strains usually have bodies and fins of one colour, apart from the Cambodia Fighter that has a cream body and coloured fins.

[My Name]

MUSIC GAMES

Teachers generally provide a stimulating environment for children in their classes, with respect to sight and touch. Other experiences may be overlooked. One of the senses which can be educated quite easily is hearing. Sounds are all around us in the infants and with careful structuring they can even become organized sounds – music.

Children make sounds all the time – they talk, shout, cry, scream or sing. A good way to focus on sounds is to use rhymes and poems and to tell stories needing 'sound effects', such as those of police cars, ambulances, trains or ghosts.

One activity teachers can try is to sit the group in a circle. Everyone claps three times, then leaves a space equivalent to three more claps, and then everyone claps three times again. How the gap is filled is up to the teacher, but you could alternate between 'oohs' and 'aahs'.

[My Name]

Exercise 4

The Problems of Heart Disease

Heart disease causes a quarter of all deaths in Britain. It is the biggest killer of middle-aged men in the developed world.

You need a healthy heart to pump blood around your body, and heart muscle needs food and oxygen for it to keep contracting. These are carried in the coronary arteries. If the arteries get blocked, then it can cause heart disease.

The artery wall can become rough and this can cause the blood to clot and block the vessel. A total blockage or thrombosis can cause a heart attack. Here the supply of oxygen is cut off, there are severe pains in the chest and the affected part of the heart is damaged.

Exercise 5   Using the spell-checker:

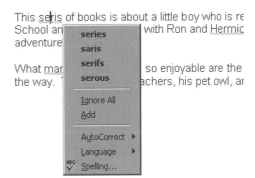

Harry Potter – Uncorrected

This se|ris of books is about a little boy who is re
School an[   ]with Ron and Hermic
adventure

series
saris
serifs
serous

Ignore All
Add

AutoCorrect ▶
Language ▶
Spelling…

What mar[   ]so enjoyable are the
the way. [   ]achers, his pet owl, ar

Exercise 6   ## The Problems of Heart Disease

Heart disease causes a quarter of all deaths in Britain. It is the biggest killer of middle-aged men in the developed world.

You need a healthy heart to pump blood around your body, and heart muscle needs food and oxygen for it to keep contracting. These are carried in the coronary arteries. If the arteries get blocked, then it can cause heart disease.

The artery wall can become rough and this can cause the blood to clot and block the vessel. A total blockage or thrombosis can cause a heart attack. Here the supply of oxygen is cut off, there are severe pains in the chest and the affected part of the heart is damaged.

You can take care of your heart by eating more poultry and fish. Cut down on fried foods and red meat and always eat plenty of fruit and vegetables.

Exercise 7   ## ONE POT WONDER
(Serves 2–3)

4 lamb chops
700g peeled and diced carrots, potatoes and swedes
pinch of dried oregano
15ml tomato puree

Preheat the oven to gas mark 7. Tip vegetables into a shallow ovenproof dish and arrange the lamb chops over the top. Sprinkle over the herbs, season then roast in the oven for 15 minutes.

Mix the tomato puree with a cupful of hot water and pour over the chops and vegetables. Continue cooking for another 20 minutes.

Exercise 8   15 October 2002

Breakfast at Hotel Belle Vue

fruit juice or cereal

++++++

fried egg, sausage, bacon, fried tomatoes, fried bread

+++++++++

grilled kippers

+++++++

toast and marmalade

+++++++++

tea, hot chocolate or coffee.

Breakfast will be served from 7.30–9.00 a.m. Please note that some items on the menu may change according to availability as we like to offer the freshest ingredients in our meals.

Exercise 9   # Catching the Fever

Viruses are an unpleasant fact of computing life we could all do without. However, by being aware of the nature of the problem you can guard against the risk of PC infections.

If you've yet to be infected by a computer virus, you're in a dwindling minority. There are now so many viruses in circulation that it's almost impossible to use a PC for any length of time and not encounter one. Cutting through the hype about viruses isn't easy though, particularly when some computer users add to it by forwarding bogus virus alerts to all and sundry.

15/10/2002

Exercise 10   IT'S <u>OK</u> TO GIVE ORDERS

Good behaviour in children is required not as a whim of parents but to make practical living easier. Unlike parents of the Victorian era, we do not need pointless obedience, such as brushing one's hair before tea, but we do ask children to co-operate to make life easier.

When children don't co-operate, the parents find their life inconvenienced. Soft parents will soon find they are being given the run-around. However much they want to give in and not inhibit their children's creativity, these parents find they are very angry and tired of the troubles this causes, and attempt to restore order. Feeling steamed up, they may lash out and discipline their children in a way that they and the child know is somewhat out of control. This is bad for everyone concerned and there are more successful ways to give orders.

Be clear in your own mind: It's not a request or open to debate, it's a demand which you have a right to make.

Make good contact: Stop what you are doing, go up close to the child and get her to look at you.

Be direct: Say, "I want you to ... now. Do you understand?" Make sure you get a "yes" or "no" answer.

3

Exercise 11

Mr & Mrs S.M. Tyler
Green Acres
17 Bathurst Close
Bath, Avon
BT3 7PY

The Editor
Greenfingers Magazine
44 Old Station Yard
Kingley
Wellington
WT5 7LL

22 May 2002

Dear Sir

Early Hellebores

You may like to know that I followed the advice in last month's edition of your magazine and ordered 26 Hellebores.

When they arrived, they were planted under a fir tree at the bottom of the garden, which you indicated in your article was an ideal spot.

According to your column, the plants would flower profusely from January until late April, and would give my garden much needed colour at this damp and dank time of year.

Unfortunately, I have wasted £35!

Only three of the plants have flowered, and these were a sickly sight. The rest provided a feeble show of leaf and then gave up and dropped all their foliage.

Frost damage was clearly visible on many of the plants and they obviously needed far more light and water.

I am very disappointed at the poor advice I received and have cancelled my subscription to your magazine forthwith.

Yours with regret

S. M. Tyler

Exercise 12

Come to a *House Warming* Party!

Jane & Rick
Invite .... to their
House Warming
at
12 Rymans Road, Reading
on
Saturday, 22 June

Exercise 13   15 October 2002

Breakfast at Hotel Belle Vue

fruit juice or stewed prunes

(choice of tomato, orange or pineapple juice)

++++++

Porridge, Muesli or Cornflakes

+++++

grilled kippers

+++++

fried, boiled or scrambled egg, sausage, bacon, fried tomatoes, fried bread

+++++++

toast and marmalade

++++++++

tea, hot chocolate or coffee.

Breakfast at Hotel Belle Vue

Breakfast will be served from 7.30 – 9.00 a.m. Please note that some items on the menu may change according to availability as we like to offer the freshest ingredients in our meals.

Exercise 14   15/10/2002

THE VERY BEST OF FRANCE

1. <u>**Normandy:**</u>
   - alluring medieval villages,
   - upmarket 19th-century seaside resorts,
   - the island-abbey of Mont St Michael
   - endless windswept beaches on the Cotentin peninsula.

2. <u>**Brittany:**</u>
   - magnificent beaches lining the north coast,
   - dramatically wind-battered west coast,
   - gentler bays in the south
   - rolling countryside inland.

3. <u>**Burgundy:**</u>
   - a wealthy region of forests, meadows, magnificent ancient cities
   - some of the world's great vineyards.

   4. <u>**The Alps:**</u>
   - holidays in the mountains,
   - less crowded than the Mediterranean coast,
   - ski lifts to take you up to the peaks for long hikes
   - après-ski haunts for morning coffee.

Exercise 15   *Flats*

Plumbing

Living in a flat means plumbing and drainage emergencies can cause problems above and beyond those experienced by house owners. After all, leaking water wherever it comes from won't just cause damage to your own property. It can also cause considerable distress to neighbours and can have potentially disastrous results if you are away for a while.

Here are some of the emergencies that can happen to flat owners:

- Burst pipes
- Leaking washing machine
- Nail through heating pipe
- Blocked kitchen sink
- Blocked toilet
- Leaking radiator valve

Views

However, there are also great advantages to flats. For example, if you are on a fifth floor or above, the views can be fantastic, and burglars are less likely to carry your heavy furniture or electric goods down many flights of stairs or in full view of other residents if they are brazen enough to use the lifts. This makes flats a good choice for those who are away for a good part of their working day.

3

Exercise 1   Inserting a page break:

Printing current page only:

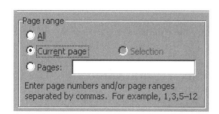

Using headers:

Exercise 2   Page 1 should look as shown below:

<u>Watercolour Painting</u>

Size

The size of a painting is very much a matter of personal preference. There are no rules, but if working small, say 6 × 4in., gives you confidence, that's fine. On the other hand, it can be exciting to work large and it can increase your enthusiasm. If you ever feel you are getting stale or need a change, try working in a different size and you might be amazed at the different work you create.

Page 2 showing footer at bottom of page 1:

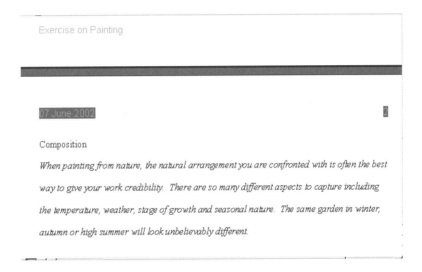

Exercise 3   <u>Special Characters</u>

Word processing packages often allow you to use symbols or special characters to liven up your documents.

A good use for these pictorial symbols is for children's games. For example, if you typed a message in a normal font and then applied Wingdings to the text, it would be impossible to read. Offering the alphabet code for each symbol would then allow a child to decipher the message. You should be able to find a book 📖, telephone, ☎, pair of scissors ✂ or smiley face ☺ when using Wingdings fonts, or insert symbols for hearts ♥, diamonds ♦, spades ♠ and clubs ♣ when searching the gallery of Symbols.

Exercise 4

FOR SALE

Flat 49, Seaview Road, Southbourne

Estate Agents: Grimble & Denton, estate agents of 22 Wattis Road, Boscombe, Bournemouth BN5 2AA.

Price: £250,000

Summary: A beautifully appointed ground floor 3-bed property with excellent sea views and balcony, situated close to the picturesque beaches of Southbourne. Included in the price are fitted cupboards, electric hob, carpets and barbecue. There is a garage behind the property which is in a well-kept block built around 1950. Internal inspection highly recommended.

Hall: Carpet, entryphone, radiator.

Sitting room: Large French windows to balcony, seaviews, fireplace, radiator, TV point, telephone point, shelving, Venetian blinds.

Dining Room: Wood floor, radiator, window to rear.

Bedroom 1: Seaviews, fitted cupboards, carpet, radiator.

Bedroom 2: Window to rear, radiator.

Bedroom 3: Window to side, fitted cupboards, radiator.

Kitchen: Breakfast bar, tiled floor, fitted cupboards, sink unit, electric hob, wall-mounted electric oven, plumbing for washing machine, door to communal gardens.

Bathroom: Gold taps, shower unit, green suite, glazed window to rear.

Study: Glass chandelier, wooden floor.

Exercise 5   The estate agent's property description using Clip Art:

<u>FOR SALE</u>

Flat 49, Seaview Road, Southbourne

Estate Agents: Grimble & Denton, estate agents of 22 Wattis Road, Boscombe, Bournemouth BN5 2AA.

Price: £250,000

Summary: A beautifully appointed ground floor 3-bed property with excellent sea views and balcony, situated close to the picturesque beaches of Southbourne. Included in the price are fitted cupboards, electric hob, carpets and barbecue. There is a garage behind the property which is in a well-kept block built around 1950. Internal inspection highly recommended.

Hall: Carpet, entryphone, radiator

Sitting room: Large French windows to balcony, seaviews, fireplace, radiator, TV point, telephone point, shelving, Venetian blinds.

Dining Room: Wood floor, radiator, window to rear.

Bedroom 1: Seaviews, fitted cupboards, carpet, radiator

Bedroom 2: Window to rear, radiator

Bedroom 3: Window to side, fitted cupboards, radiator

Kitchen: Breakfast bar, tiled floor, fitted cupboards, sink unit, electric hob, wall-mounted electric oven, plumbing for washing machine, door to communal gardens.

Bathroom: Gold taps, shower unit, green suite, glazed window to rear.

Study: Glass chandelier, wooden floor.

Exercise 6

Welcome to Boscombe Zoo

- Circus spectacular show twice a day
- See the animals being fed
- Cuddle baby lambs and goats
- Restaurant and cafe open all day
- Take a train ride round the zoo

Open every day except Christmas Day

Exercise 7

Stanley Road Hospital Trust

The following opportunity has arisen for a clear thinking, caring individual to join our acclaimed Trust as a full-time assistant.

For the post, we are looking for an exceptional person. You will help trained nurses assess need and deliver care to the many older patients at our brand new Saltwood Annexe. You must have first-aid training, good communication skills, be patient and caring and enjoy working flexibly.

To apply, please send us a full C.V. together with the names of two referees.

For further information, write to Marion Hobbs, Saltwood Annexe, Webleton Hospital, Grundy Close, Chesterham. Or phone her on 0166778 2349.

Exercise 8

SEE-RIGHT-THROUGH DOUBLE GLAZING

Who can you trust to install double glazing?

Few people are experts in double glazing, So if you're looking to improve your home with PVC-U windows, doors or a conservatory – and don't fancy entrusting such a major decision to a possible cowboy – use SEE-RIGHT-THROUGH.

We use only the best materials, and there's a free 20-year guarantee.

1. We are fast
2. We are careful
3. We leave the site tidy
4. We are the best.

Call now on Freephone 0800 444555 for a no-strings quotation.

One call and you will be in touch with a nationwide network of approved, fully trained installers who are monitored regularly by a team of inspectors.

> SEE-RIGHT-THROUGH
> The name to trust

3

Exercise 9   Landscombe College Evening Classes

Title	Day	Tutor	Time	Room
Bee-keeping	Monday	Jamie Green	7 – 9 p.m.	B3
Yoga for Beginners	Tuesday	Pat Hurt	6.30 – 8.00 p.m.	Hall
Computing for Beginners	Thursday	Howard Maynard	3 – 5 p.m.	C14
Advanced Yoga	Wednesday	Pat Hurt	7 – 9 p.m.	Hall
Car Mechanics	Wednesday	Jack Byrne	6 – 8 p.m.	Workshop
Watercolour painting	Tuesday	Nancy Smythe	2 – 4 p.m.	B9

New students may like to know that the following videos acquired by the College are relevant to this term's classes and may be available for hire.

Title	Presenter	Hire charge	Length	Available
Yoga For All	The Graceful Goddess	£1.50	110 mins	On loan
Know Your Car	Ray B. Wise	£3.00	90 mins	Yes
Bees For Life	William & Sarah Price	£2.50	150 mins	Yes
Keeping Bees	Walter Mitts	£1.50	90 mins	On loan

Exercise 10   A table listing PC software might look as shown:

Name	Publisher	Description	Age Range	Date
Encarta	Microsoft	Encyclopaedia	5+	1998
Body Works	PC Advisor	3D journey through the body	7+	2000
Age of Empires	Microsoft	Strategy game	7+	1999
Zoombinis	Broderbund	Maths games	8+	1999
Cartoon Studio	Softkey	Cartoon making kit	6+	1997
Voicepad	Softkey	Voice-enabling word processing	10+	1997

Exercise 11

Make	Type	Price	Colour
Miele	oven	£153.99	black
Electrolux	fridge-freezer	£245.00	white
Tricity	cooker hood	£76.99	silver
Servis	dishwasher	£196.50	brown
Philips	washing machine	£279.99	white
Hoover	upright vacuum cleaner	£89.00	red

Exercise 12

CLASS MARKS 2000

First Name	Surname	Maths	Science	English	Per cent	Total
Janet	Brown-Smythe	40	35	38	75.33	113
Peter	Smith	23	38	46	71.33	107
Richard	Wellington	31	48	40	79.33	119
Danielle-Celeste	Courvoisier	23	44	19	57.33	86
Harry	Longbottom	15	23	37	50.00	75
John	Baker	38	26	22	57.33	86
Mary	French	50	50	50	100.00	150

Exercise 13   Applying styles (your machine may have quite different style formats).

Home Decorating Ltd

To: *Denise Watermill, Marketing Manager*

From: *Arnold Morton, Ceramics Department*

Copied to: *Head of Purchasing*

Subject: <u>*Bali and Hong Kong*</u>

Date: (today's)

With regard to the recent sales, I am writing to let you know that there was a huge demand for the new lines we purchased from Bali and Hong Kong. Many customers asked when we would be stocking smaller items such as soup bowls, spoons and tea cups, and I feel such items would almost walk off the shelves if we had them in stock.

I suggest we have a meeting as soon as is practicable to discuss purchasing more items from the Far East, and a possible television advertising campaign to accompany these new goods.

Exercise 14   Your merged memo might look like this:

To: David Holmes, IT Department

From: My Name

Date: 2 July 2002

Subject: End of Year Party

As spokesperson for the course, I am writing to ask you to come to our final session in the Staff Room on Friday at 2.00 p.m. We would like to hold a party as a fun way to end the course, and would like you to bring some pizza as a small contribution.

Please let me know if you are unable to attend.

Exercise 15   Your letters should look something like this:

Mr James Smith
York

Date: (today's)

Dear Mr Smith

<u>Extra payment</u>

As a resident of York who has reached the age of 62 and who has been living in the city for 2 years, we have the power to pay you an extra £2,400.

This will be sent in the form of a cheque to your home address at the end of the month.

Yours sincerely

Gordon Best
On behalf of the Inland Revenue

Spreadsheets

ANSWERS TO INTRODUCTORY EXERCISES

Exercise 1

DARTS				
Name	Score 1	Score 2	Score 3	Final score
Marigold	8	11	3	22
Harry	12	22	6	40
Steve	3	9	18	30
David	18	16	5	39
Joan	9	12	11	32
Elizabeth-Jane	11	15	20	46

Exercise 2

SHOPPING			
Item	Cost (£)	Number bought	Final price (£)
Catfood	0.4	10	4
Milk	0.38	6	2.28
Loaf	0.87	2	1.74
Marmalade	1.15	1	1.15
Pasta	0.49	3	1.47
Melon	1.3	2	2.6
Lemonade	0.89	3	2.67

Exercise 3

SHOPPING AT SUPERMART			
Item	Cost (£)	Number bought	Final price (£)
Catfood	£0.40	10	£4.00
Milk	£0.38	6	£2.28
Loaf	£0.93	2	£1.86
Marmalade	£1.35	1	£1.35
Pasta	£0.49	3	£1.47
Melon	£1.30	2	£2.60
Lemonade	£0.89	3	£2.67
Total			£16.23

Exercise 4

Shares					
Months	Bellings	Thatchers	Gordington	Lowden	Morgan
Jan	£2.40	£12.60	£24.00	£0.50	£18.00
Feb	£3.70	£13.20	£14.60	£0.96	£16.50
Mar	£1.60	£7.90	£18.00	£1.30	£17.00
Apr	£0.75	£6.40	£30.30	£4.10	£17.80
May	£4.90	£14.10	£31.70	£3.70	£16.40
Total	£13.35	£54.20	£118.60	£10.56	£85.70
Average	£2.7	£10.8	£23.7	£2.1	£17.1

Exercise 5

Restaurant		
Item	**ME**	FRIEND
Melon	£1.25	
Soup		£1.00
Steak & kidney pie	£4.50	£4.50
Chips	£0.80	
Jacket potato		£0.75
Salad	£1.25	£1.25
Ice-cream	£0.95	
Fruit salad		£0.90
Coffee	£1.70	£0.85
TOTAL	£10.45	£9.25

Exercise 6

Own Brand Cereal Prices					
Comparison					
SHOP	*Gateway*	*Tesco*	*Asda*	*Co-op*	*Safeway*
Size of pack (gm)	500	450	1000	1000	1500
Price per pack	£2.50	£2.00	£3.50	£4.50	£3.75
Cost per 100 gm	£0.50	£0.44	£0.35	£0.45	£0.25

Exercise 7

PETTY CASH EXPENSES					
Dates	**Postage**	**Coffee/Tea**	**Cleaning**	**Furniture**	**Stationery/Disks**
January	£13.50	£11.00	£14.00		£15.75
February	£7.65	£3.50	£14.00		£17.38
March	£19.38	£3.45	£14.00	£385.00	£20.75
April	£9.23	£4.15	£14.00		£9.50
May	£11.68	£2.17	£17.00	£37.99	£12.45
Totals	£61.44	£24.27	£73.00	£422.99	£75.83

4

Exercise 8

Holiday Bookings							
Date of Booking	**Surname**	**Villa**	**Start date**	**End date**	**Max. number**	**Price**	**Price per person**
2/2/02	Browning	Caprice	01-Jun	08-Jun	5	£209	£41.80
25/2/02	Derbyshire	Miramar	15-Jun	22-Jun	4	£354	£88.50
3/3/02	Winslow	Capri	25-May	01-Jun	6	£567	£94.50
15/3/02	Harris	Nuit	15-Jun	22-Jun	3	£295	£98.33
16/4/02	Pentford	Soleil	18-May	25-Jun	4	£680	£170.00
TOTAL						£2,105	
Holiday Bookings							

Exercise 9

Pizza				
Item	Quantity for 2	Quantity for 30	Cost per item	Final Price for 2
Strong flour (lb)	1.50	22.50	£0.70	£1.05
Yeast (sachet)	1.00	15.00	£0.20	£0.20
Fat (oz)	2.00	30.00	£0.40	£0.80
Olive oil (tbs)	3.00	45.00	£0.30	£0.90
Tomatoes	2.00	30.00	£0.25	£0.50
Mozzarella (oz)	6.00	90.00	£0.80	£4.80
Spicy sausage (oz)	4.00	60.00	£0.85	£3.40
Onion	1.00	15.00	£0.30	£0.30
Total				£11.95

Exercise 10   TVs

Make	Price	Size of screen (ins)	Teletext	Features	No. in Stock
Westwood	£159.99	20	Yes	Stereo	20
Jacksons	£198.75	14	Yes	Televideo	14
Merit	£229.99	14	Yes	DVD-player	2
Piccolo	£99.99	14	Yes	Silver	12
Bradleys	£179.00	17	Yes	Silver	5
Clerical	£79.99	2.3	No	Pocket-size	8
Total	£947.71				
Average	£157.95				

Exercise 11   Writer's Costs

MONTH	PENS	PAPER	TRAVEL	DISKS	COFFEE	TOTAL
JAN	£2.50	£3.70	£15.34	£1.80	£0.65	£24
FEB	£3.67	£9.50	£7.78	£3.50	£2.40	£27
MAR	£1.80	£2.70	£12.90	£4.85	£2.50	£25
APR	£5.50	£0.00	£22.50	£2.70	£0.90	£32
MAY	£2.00	£3.45	£5.00	£1.10	£2.45	£14
Overall Total						£121
Average						£24

Exercise 12

Food	Price(£)	Discount offered
Omelette	£4.50	£0.23
Salad	£2.00	£0.10
Chips	£1.50	£0.08
Fudge cake	£2.75	£0.14
Tea	£0.85	£0.04
Total	£11.60	£0.58
Final Price	£11.02	
Discount is:		
5%		

Exercise 13   **Sale of Tiles for January**

Code number	Colour	Price of pack	Cost of 1 tile	Packs sold	Final price
005	Red	£6.50	£0.13	20	£130.00
026	Yellow	£12.45	£0.25	14	£174.30
041	Black	£8.75	£0.18	35	£306.25
018	Green	£7.95	£0.16	30	£238.50
019	Green	£18.45	£0.37	10	£184.50
006	Patterned-Brown	£3.25	£0.07	25	£81.25
TOTAL				134	£1,114.80
No. tiles per pack	50				

Exercise 14   New Carpets

Room	Length (ft)	Width (ft)	Area (sq ft)	Area (sq metres)	Cost (sq metres)	Final Price
Sitting	14.00	10.50	147.00	13.66	£22.85	£311.36
Bed	9.00	8.25	74.25	6.90	£19.25	£132.78
Bath	6.00	7.00	42.00	3.90	£8.00	£31.21
Total						£475.36

Exercise 1

Charity Contributions								
Charity	Percent	Jan	Feb	March	April	May	June	Average
RNIB	50%	£1,000	£1,840	£645	£2,500	£2,340	£1,158	£1,581
Birds	12%	£240	£442	£155	£600	£562	£278	£379
Lifeboats	5%	£100	£184	£64	£250	£234	£116	£158
Sue Ryder	25%	£500	£920	£322	£1,250	£1,170	£579	£790
Oxfam	8%	£160	£294	£103	£400	£374	£185	£253
Total	100%	£2,000	£3,680	£1,289	£5,000	£4,680	£2,315	

Exercise 2

Expenditure over four months					
	1st month	2nd month	3rd month	4th month	Average
Holidays	£0.00	£0.00	£350.00	£0.00	£87.50
Heating	£25.00	£25.00	£25.00	£25.00	£25.00
Food	£75.00	£30.00	£60.00	£45.00	£52.50
Travel	£5.00	£12.50	£5.00	£2.50	£6.25
Newspapers and magazines	£0.75	£0.75	£0.75	£0.75	£0.75
Clothes	£65.00	£13.45	£48.00	£7.00	£33.36
Total	£170.75	£81.50	£138.75	£80.25	
Income	£200.00	£245.00	£200.00	£200.00	
Remaining money	£29.25	£163.30	£61.25	£119.75	

Exercise 3

Temperature °C							
	Jan	Feb	Mar	Apr	May	Jun	Average
Oxford	3.70	4.20	5.80	8.40	11.70	14.90	8.12
Lyneham	3.90	3.50	6.00	7.70	11.10	14.10	7.72
Cambridge	3.40	3.90	5.70	8.30	11.60	14.70	7.93
Sheffield	3.80	3.90	5.40	7.80	10.90	14.10	7.65
Durham	2.80	3.20	4.60	6.80	9.60	12.90	6.65
AVERAGE	3.52	3.74	5.50	7.80	10.98	14.14	7.61

Exercise 4

BOAT HIRE					
No. of people	1 Day	2 Day	3 Day	Weekly	Average
2 – standard class	£80.00	£120.00	£180.00	£240.00	£34
2 – superior class	£100.00	£130.00	£250.00	£280.00	£40
Autumn special – 2 superior	£90.00	£125.00	£200.00	£265.00	£38
4 – superior class	£150.00	£180.00	£225.00	£300.00	£43
6 – luxury	£200.00	£225.00	£250.00	£375.00	£54
8 – standard	£210.00	£300.00	£330.00	£360.00	£51

Exercise 5
Data sorted alphabetically by type, then by ascending order of price.

	A	B	C	D	E	F
1	Type	Bedrooms	Garage	Garden	Price	Location
2	Bungalow	2	Yes	Patio garde	£75,799	Selby
3	Bungalow	3	Yes	Yes	£175,000	Selby
4	Detached	5	Double	Marina	£300,990	Selby
5	Flat	3	No	Yes	£97,000	York
6	Flat	4	Yes	No	£100,000	York
7	Flat	1	No	No	£115,000	Sheffield
8	Semidetached	3	Yes	Yes	£200,450	York
9	Semidetached	4	Yes	Paddock	£217,950	Derby

Exercise 6
Database sorted in ascending order of Kcals per 100g.

Item	Weight (g)	Kcals	Fat	Protein	Kcals per 100 g	Fat per 100 g	Protein per 100 g
Baked beans	420	260	1.20	19.40	61.90	0.29	4.62
Tuna	132	120	0.28	28.00	90.91	0.21	21.21
Dried apricots	500	800	3.00	20.70	160.00	0.60	4.14
Sardines	90	156	8.10	20.70	173.33	9.00	23.00
Peanut butter	340	2023	172.72	83.64	595.00	50.80	24.60
Almonds	300	1842	150.00	63.30	614.00	50.00	21.10
The item of food with the least Kcals per 100 g is baked beans.							

4

Exercise 7   The 2D column chart 'Final results in 1999':

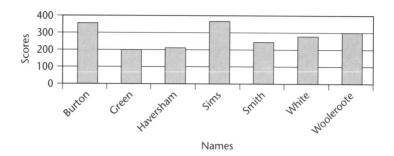

Exercise 8   The pie chart showing comparative pen costs for one pen:

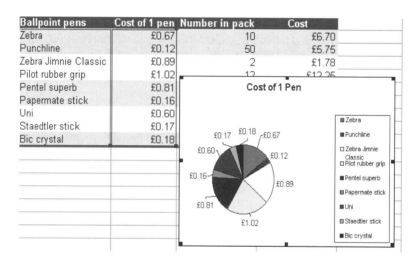

Ballpoint pens	Cost of 1 pen	Number in pack	Cost
Zebra	£0.67	10	£6.70
Punchline	£0.12	50	£5.75
Zebra Jimnie Classic	£0.89	2	£1.78
Pilot rubber grip	£1.02	12	£12.25
Pentel superb	£0.81		
Papermate stick	£0.16		
Uni	£0.60		
Staedtler stick	£0.17		
Bic crystal	£0.18		

Exercise 9   The original chart (step 6):

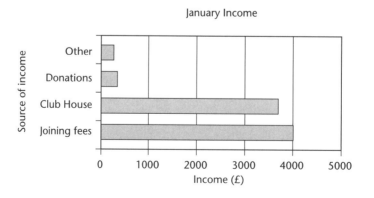

After amending (step 8):

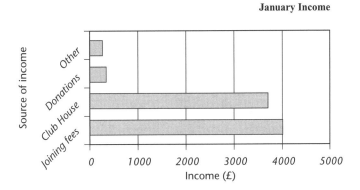

As a pie chart (step 9):

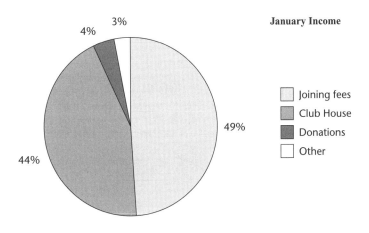

Comparative chart (step 11):

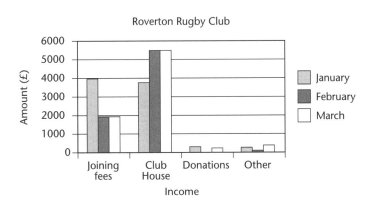

Exercise 10   The final version of the column chart (step 5):

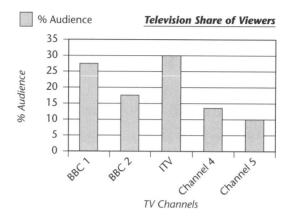

Exercise 11   The original line graph (step 6):

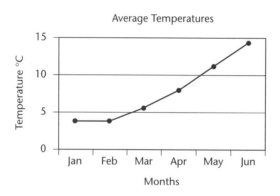

Comparative column chart showing the temperatures for January to June (step 8):

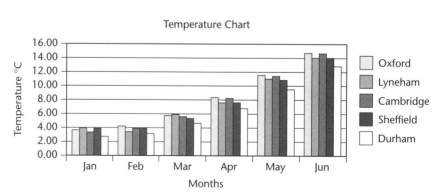

Exercise 12   Pie chart showing students' overall percentage marks (step 5):

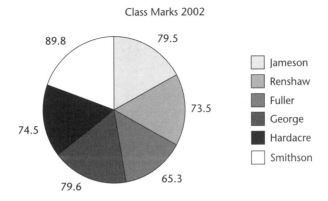

Class Marks 2002

Bar chart with scale adjusted (step 6):

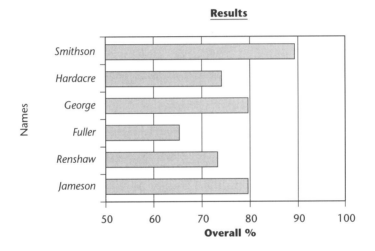

Exercise 13

Chalfont Senior School
West Widnes
Harnaton
HA15 3XP

[today's date]

Dear Parent

You will be pleased to learn that our 6th Form boys have done very well this term. They all sat their English, French and Mathematics examinations and have gained higher marks than the same set last year.

You may like to see the full details of their results and so these are set out below:

Name	English	French	Mathematics	Total	Overall %
Jameson	34	18	26	78	79.6
Renshaw	26	15	31	72	73.5
Fuller	25	16	23	64	65.3
George	31	19	28	78	79.6
Hardacre	29	21	23	73	74.5
Smithson	35	20	33	88	89.8

As you can see from the chart, Nigel Smithson fully justifies the prize for academic success and we look forward to seeing you at the award ceremony on the last day of term.

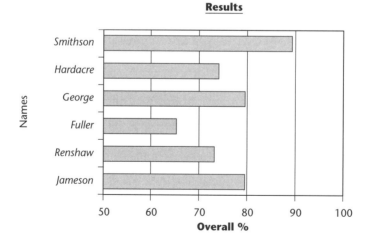

Yours faithfully

Charles Belham
Headmaster

Exercise 14   Stacked comparative chart showing tennis and football only (step 5):

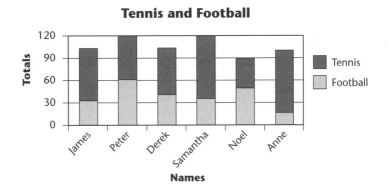

Chart showing the average scores for all sports (step 7):

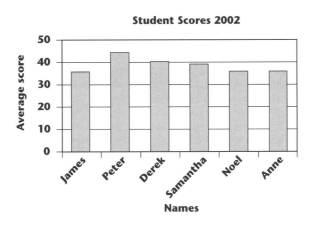

Exercise 15

ITEM	TEST 1 %	TEST 2 %	TEST 3 %	AVERAGE OVERALL SCORE	FINAL RESULT
Cheese	56	45	71	57	disliked
Pork sausage	67	93	87	82	liked
Chocolate	78	61	67	69	liked
Dried fruit	34	54	23	37	disliked
Steak	82	87	73	81	liked
Tomato	54	65	38	52	disliked
Red wine	78	76	65	73	liked

Databases

ANSWERS TO INTRODUCTORY EXERCISES

Exercise 1   The Food database:

⊞ Recipes : Table	
Field Name	Data Type
▶ Main food	Text
Title	Text
Cooking (mins)	Number
Portions	Number
Calories	Number

Exercise 2   The Sailings database, with the field names Bicycle supplement and Fast supplement added:

⊞ sailing costs : Table	
Field Name	Data Type
Dates	Text
UK Port	Text
French port	Text
Short stay (£)	Currency
Long stay (£)	Currency
Weekend extra (£)	Currency
Bicycle supplement	Currency
▶ Fast supplement	Currency

Exercise 3   The Recipes table of records:

Main food	Title	Cooking (mins)	Portions	Calories
Cod	Cod with herbs	50	4	193
Tuna	Tuna bean salad	12	4	185
Red pepper	Roast vegetable soup	90	8	150
Pasta	Pasta with pesto sauce	30	4	538
Eggs	Chocolate souffle	30	8	204
Banana	Banana ice-cream	10	4	250
*		0	0	0

Record: 6 of 6

Exercise 4   The Chairs table:

Microsoft Access - [Chairs : Table]

File Edit View Insert Format Records Tools Window Help

Name	Price	Discount offered	Colours available	Code
Adjustable typist	£19.99	☑	4	TEK
Delux gas-lift typist	£43.99	☑	6	1116
Bentwood operator	£69.99	☐	1	WDOPR
Contemporary operator	£69.99	☐	2	AGNELLO
Modern operator	£59.99	☑	4	BETA
Ergonomic	£149.99	☑	7	VKHBA
Multifunctional	£119.99	☐	5	1228
Continuous use	£179.99	☐	3	HCT

Exercise 5   The Bikes table after deleting the Rocket Goldie entry:

Make	Price (£)	Type	CC	Year	Details
AJS	5999	Big port	350	1927	Black finish
Ariel	1750	Leader	250	1963	Clock
BSA	5999	DB34	500	1954	TLS front brake
AJS	2350	185	500	1957	Crhome tank panels
Ariel	3750	VH Red Hunter	500	1954	Excellent condition
Ariel	1950	Leader	250	1961	red finish
*	0		0	0	

Exercise 6   The Furniture database sorted in alphabetical order of name:

	Name	Price	Discount offered	Colours available	Code
	Adjustable typist	£19.99	☑	4	TEK
	Bentwood operator	£69.99	☐	1	WDOPR
	Contemporary operator	£69.99	☐	2	AGNELLO
	Continuous use	£179.99	☐	3	HCT
	Delux gas-lift typist	£43.99	☑	6	1116
	Ergonomic	£149.99	☑	7	VKHBA
	Modern operator	£59.99	☑	4	BETA
✎	Multifunctional	£0.00	☐	6	1228
✱		£0.00	☐	0	

⊞ Chairs : Table

Exercise 7   The Sailing costs table sorted alphabetically by French port:

⊞ sailing costs : Table

	month	UK Port	French port	Short stay (£)	Long stay (£)	Weekend extr.	Bicycle supple
▶	March	Portsmouth	Caen	£110.00	£146.00	£13.50	£5.00
	Spt	Portsmouth	Caen	£62.00	£87.00	£8.00	£0.00
	July	Plymouth	Roscoff	£133.00	£173.00	£16.00	£9.00
	Aug	Plymouth	Roscoff	£121.00	£152.00	£13.50	£5.00
	Spt	Plymouth	Roscoff	£65.00	£90.00	£8.00	£0.00
	March	Portsmouth	St. Malo	£126.00	£166.00	£13.50	£5.00
	July	Portsmouth	St. Malo	£145.00	£189.00	£16.00	£9.00

Record: ◄◄ ◄ 1 ► ►► ►✱ of 7

Exercise 8   Primary key set on Class code and properties of Start time amended:

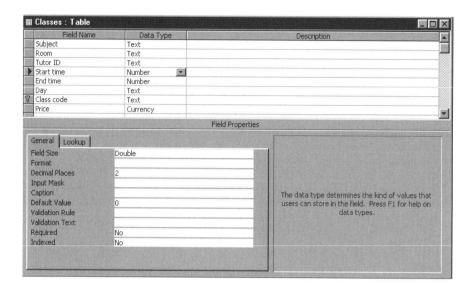

Exercise 9   Composers table sorted on descending order of year born:

Composer	Initials	Title	Key	Year born	Nationality	Price of CD	Code
Chopin	F	Piano concerto no. 1	E minor	1810	Polish	3.99	C7
Schubert	F	Unfinished Symphony	B minor	1797	Austrian	2.95	S3
Beethoven	L. Van	Choral Symphony	D minor	1770	German	2.5	B5
Mozart	W.A.	Salzburg Symphony no. 2	B flat major	1756	Austrian	5.35	M6
Bach	J.S.	Brandenburg Concerto no 1	F major	1685	German	8.99	B9
Vivaldi	A	Spring	E major	1675	Italian	2.49	V2
				0		0	

Exercise 10   Records filtered to find only those rated 4:

CD-ROMS : Table

Title	Price (£)	Minimum age	Website	Rating
Games 3	10	7	www.tivola.co.uk	4
Pop-up Dictionary	30	7	www.oup.co.uk	4
Physicus	18	8	www.tivola.co.uk	4
*	0	0		0

Record: 1 of 3 (Filtered)

Results of filtering to find CD-ROMs for the under nines costing less than £20:

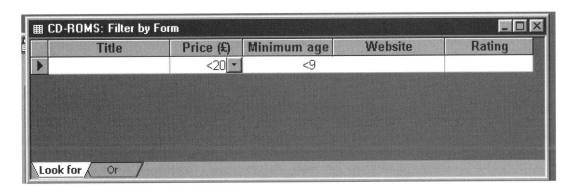

Exercise 11   Filter by Form:

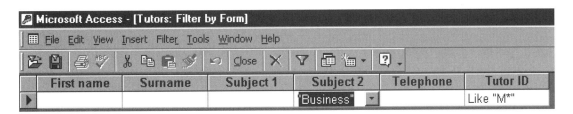

Exercise 12   The Sailing costs table filtered to find short stays from Portsmouth costing £90–£130:

Exercise 13   The Composers table sorted to find recordings costing less than £5 that were written by a German or Austrian composer:

Composer	Initials	Title	Key	Year born	Nationality	Price of CD	
Schubert	F	Unfinished Symphony	B minor	1797	Austrian	2.95	S3
Beethoven	L. Van	Choral Symphony	D minor	1770	German	2.5	B5

Composers : Table

Exercise 14   Query to find late summer activities:

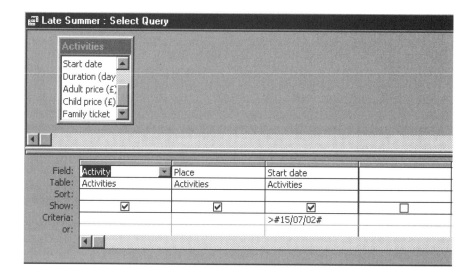

The results:

	Activity	Place	Start date
▶	Open day	Ramsgate Harbour	30/07
	Arthurian antics	Pickering Castle	04/08
	King for a day	Legoland	25/07
	Puppet Picnic	Grey's Court, Henley	30/07
*			

Late Summer : Select Query

Record: ◄◄ ◄ 1 ► ►► ►* of 4

Exercise 15   Query to find chairs costing more than £120:

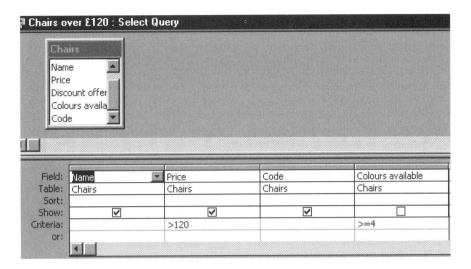

The results:

Name	Price	Code
▶ Ergonomic	£149.99	VKHBA
Comfort	£189.99	COMFORT
Ultimate Executive	£229.99	BBAS
∗	£0.00	

Chairs over £120 : Select Query

Exercise 16   Recipes that take less than 15 minutes to cook:

Quick recipes : Select Query

Main food	Title	Cooking (mins)
▶ Tuna	Tuna bean salad	12
Banana	Banana ice-cream	10
∗		0

5

Exercise 1   Table searched for senior males:

Senior Males : Select Query		
Firstname	**Surname**	**Joining Date**
Francis	Bergot	18-Jun-01
Peter	Brown	28-Jun-01
Graham	Harper	04-Jul-01
Martin	Piller	15-Aug-01
Harold	Wilson	22-Jun-01
*		

Exercise 2   There are three classes that cost between £20 and £30:

Classes from £20 to £30 : Select Query			
Subject	**Day**	**Start time**	**End time**
French	Wed	7	9
Spanish	Fri	7	9
Business	Fri	2	4.3
*		0	0

Exercise 3   AutoForm for the Books table

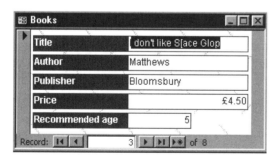

Exercise 4   Deleting a record:

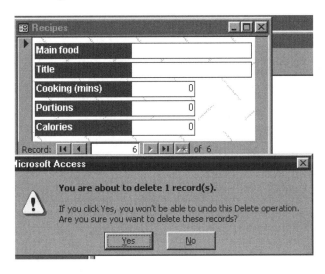

Wizard recipe form:

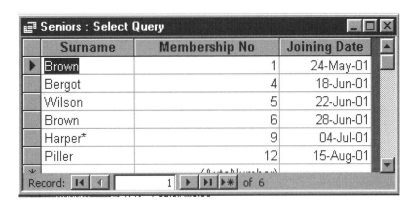

Exercise 5   Result of Query to find joining date of all seniors:

Surname	Membership No	Joining Date
Brown	1	24-May-01
Bergot	4	18-Jun-01
Wilson	5	22-Jun-01
Brown	6	28-Jun-01
Harper*	9	04-Jul-01
Piller	12	15-Aug-01

Seniors : Select Query

Record: 1 of 6

Exercise 6   Designing a query to find all chairs aimed at executives or operators:

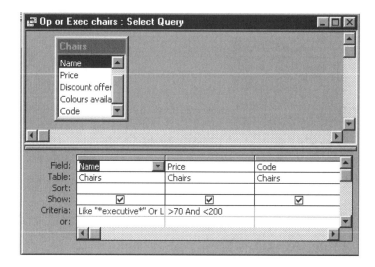

The result:

Op or Exec chairs

Name	Price	Code
Wood Executive	£169.99	1314A5

Exercise 7   Pre-1962 bike report (step 4):

pre-1962 bikes

Make	Price (£)	Type	CC	Details
AJS	2350	185	500	Chrome tank panels
Ariel	3750	VH Red Hunter	500	Excellent condition
Ariel	1950	Leader	250	red finish

Exercise 8   Report based on a query for female club members

Female members

Firstname	Surname	Joining Date	Category
Joan	Brown	24-May-01	Senior
Madge	Brown	22-May-01	Junior
Diane	Brown	28-Jun-01	Junior
Susan	Hill	01-Jul-01	Concession
Sally	Harper	04-Jul-01	Junior
Shirley	Webb	03-Aug-01	Concession

Exercise 9   Report grouped by age:

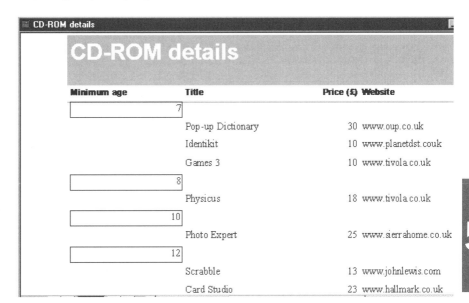

Minimum age	Title	Price (£)	Website
7			
	Pop-up Dictionary	30	www.oup.co.uk
	Identikit	10	www.planetdst.couk
	Games 3	10	www.tivola.co.uk
8			
	Physicus	18	www.tivola.co.uk
10			
	Photo Expert	25	www.sierrahome.co.uk
12			
	Scrabble	13	www.johnlewis.com
	Card Studio	23	www.hallmark.co.uk

Exercise 10   Grouped report showing average salaries:

job details

Location	Employer	Job	Salary	Closing date
Abingdon				
	Beaumont House	Care Assistant	£12,500.00	14/02/02
	Garsington	Education Officer	£14,000.00	14/02/02

Summary for 'Location' = Abingdon (2 detail records)
Avg   £13,250.00

Oxford				
	Mango	Administrator	£17,500.00	20/02/02
	Hedges	Secretary	£17,950.00	01/03/02
	Connell	Sales	£18,000.00	20/02/02

Summary for 'Location' = Oxford (3 detail records)
Avg   £17,816.67

Witney				
	Gateway Hotel	2nd chef	£19,000.00	05/03/02

Exercise 11   The reformatted Recipe AutoForm:

Exercise 12

Exercise 13   Average report customized:

Exercise 14

a) Creating a relationship.

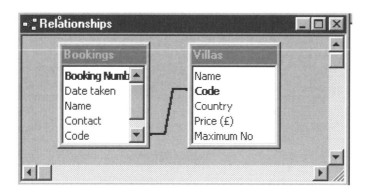

b) The Summer French Villas query.

Bookings.Name	Contact	Month required	Villas.Name	Price (£)
Black	01235 19876	July	Flowers	150
Thomson	01235 67584	June	La Girande	286

MODEL ANSWERS **6**

Presentation

ANSWERS TO INTRODUCTORY EXERCISES

Exercise 1

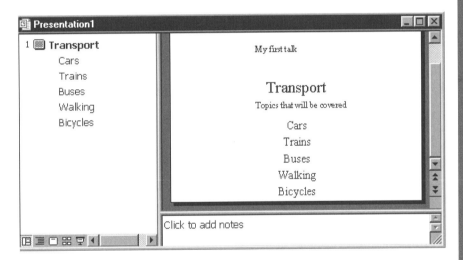

Exercise 2

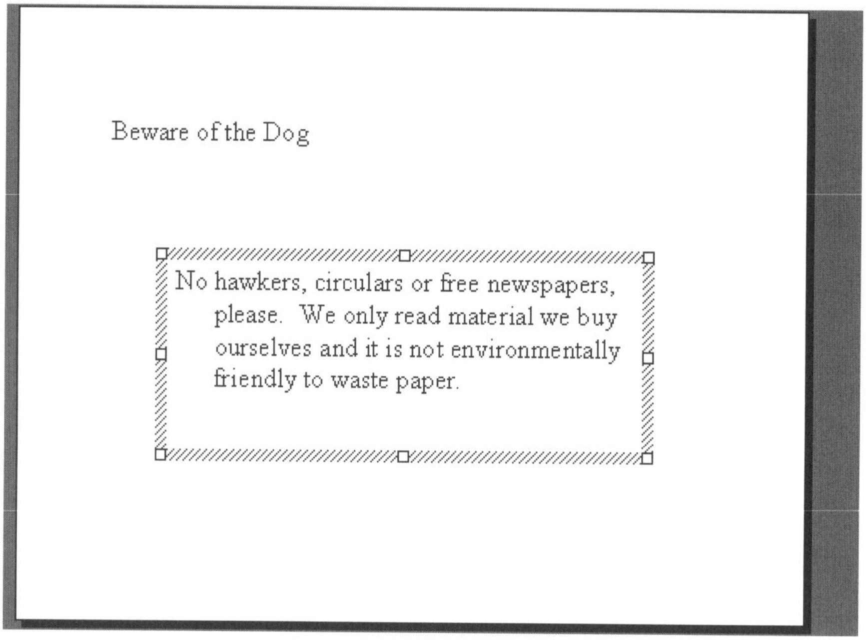

Beware of the Dog

No hawkers, circulars or free newspapers, please. We only read material we buy ourselves and it is not environmentally friendly to waste paper.

Exercise 3

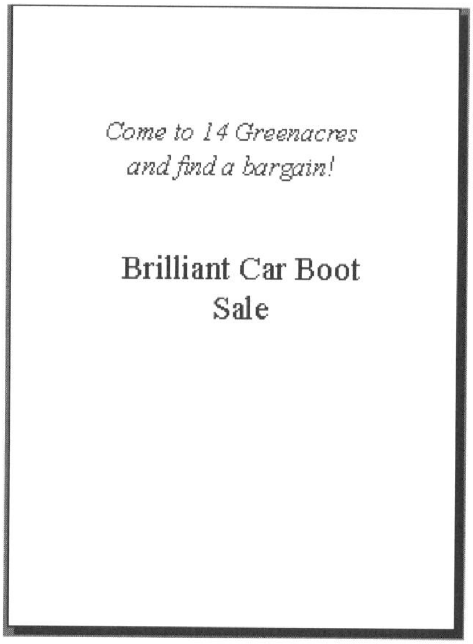

*Come to 14 Greenacres
and find a bargain!*

**Brilliant Car Boot
Sale**

Exercise 4

My first talk

<u>Transport</u>

Topics that will be covered

Cars

Trains

Buses

Walking

Bicycles

Exercise 5

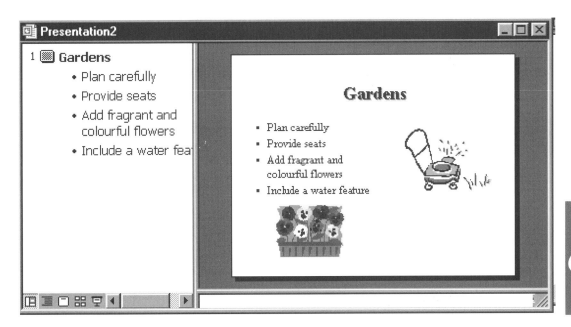

Exercise 6

Beware of the Dog

*No hawkers, circulars or free newspapers,
please. We only read material we buy
ourselves and it is not environmentally
friendly to waste paper.*

Exercise 7

Exercise 8

Exercise 9

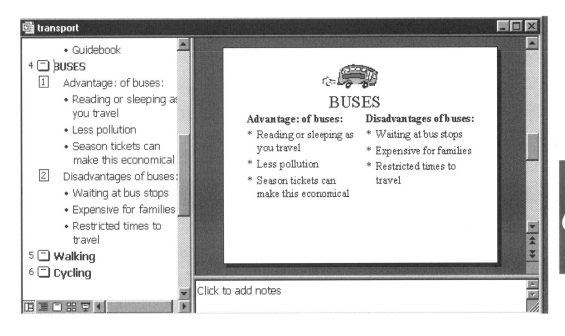

Exercise 10   The flowers slide (step 7):

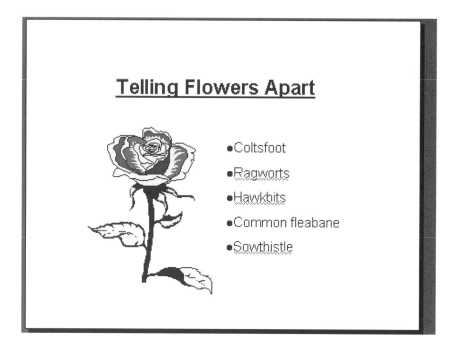

Exercise 11   Changing the text in a slide (step 5)

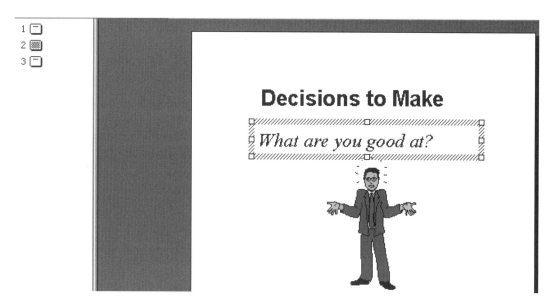

Exercise 12

Exercise 13   Creating a 'get well soon' card.

Exercise 14

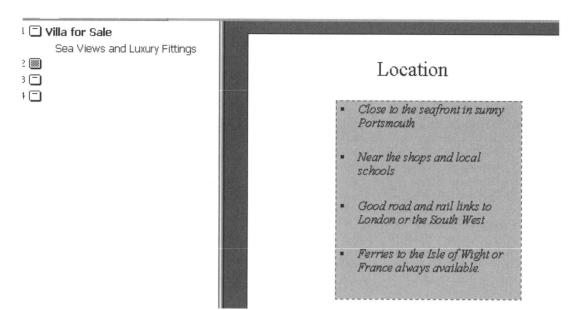

ANSWERS TO ADVANCED EXERCISES

Exercise 1   The notes page:

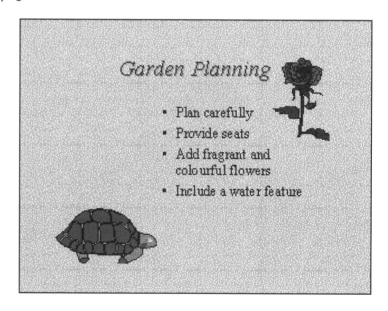

College course starts 19 September

Address for enrolment forms

Book to read: Planning your garden by Deirdre Wiseman

Exercise 2   Adding a picture using AutoShapes:

Exercise 3

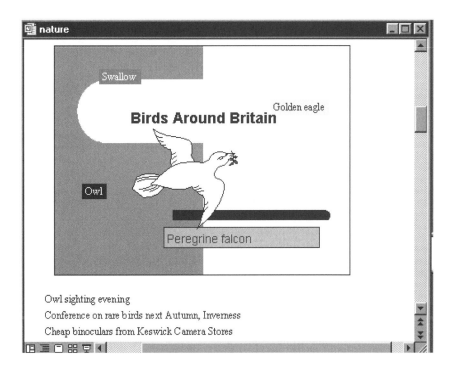

Exercise 4   Applying design templates:

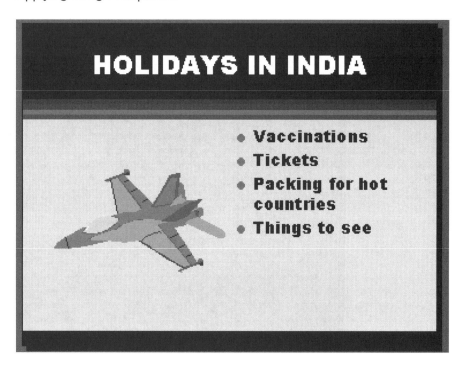

Exercise 5   Customizing design templates:

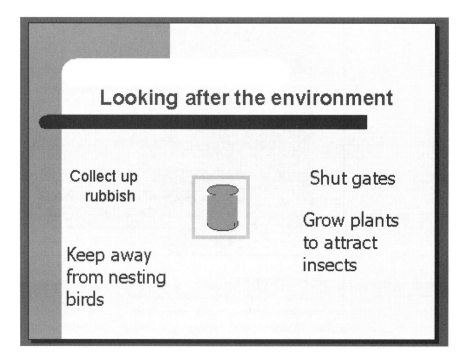

Exercise 6

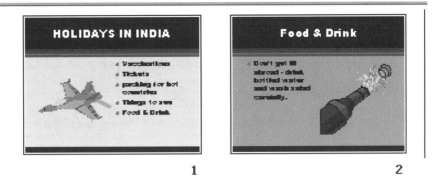

1   2

Exercise 7   Changing the title style using Slide Master:

Exercise 8

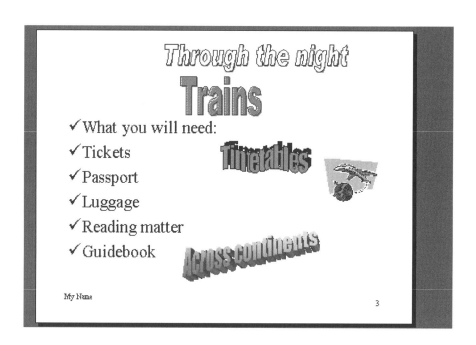

Exercise 9

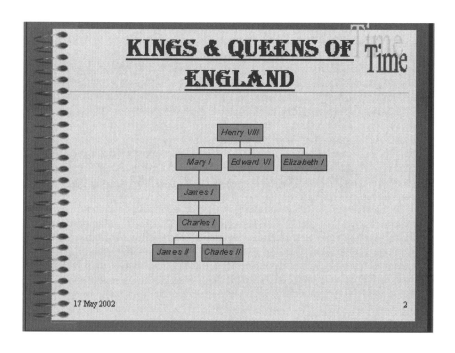

Exercise 10

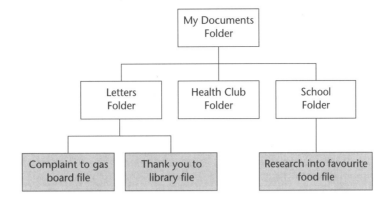

Exercise 11   Creating a column chart:

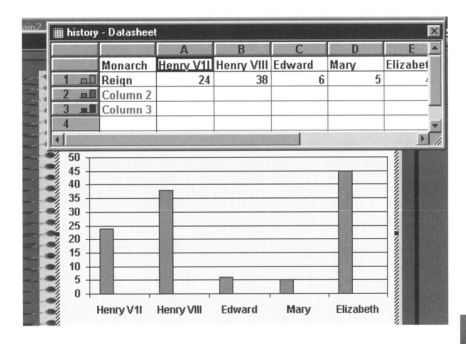

6

Creating a pie chart:

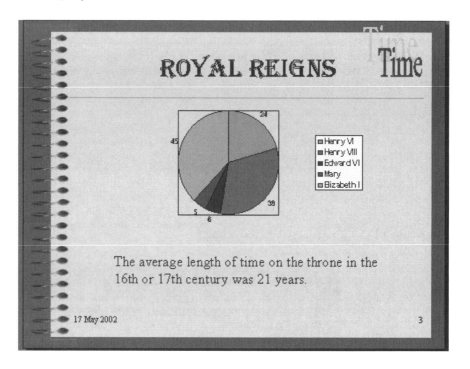

Exercise 12

Sailing to France

Dates	B & B	Standard Hotel	Premium Hotel
Nov - March	£219	£274	£374
March - May	£250	£305	£405
May - July	£280	£335	£490
July - Aug	£294	£349	£504
Sept	£250	£305	£405

Cost of accommodation for 5 nights.

Exercise 14   Setting a transition (Exercise 13 will require a similar process):

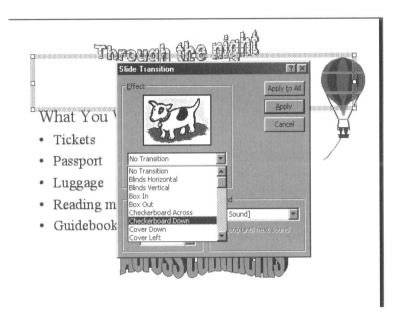

Exercise 15   Animating slides:

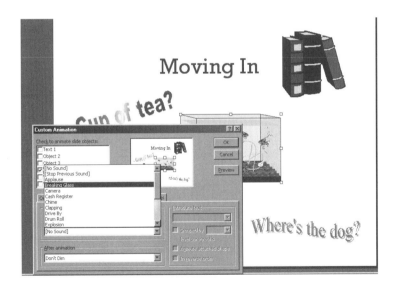

Exercise 16   Creating the presentation outline:

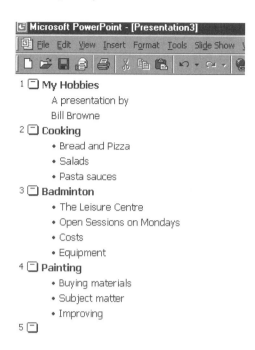

MODEL ANSWERS

7

Information and communication

ANSWERS TO INTRODUCTORY EXERCISES

Exercise 1   Finding what the weather will be like in Sheffield using the BBC Web site:

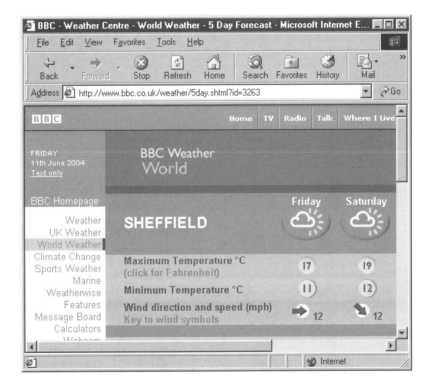

© BBC

Exercise 2   www.laterlife.com holiday page:

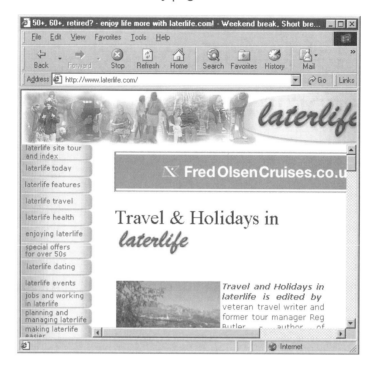

www.lifes4living.co.uk holiday page for comparison:

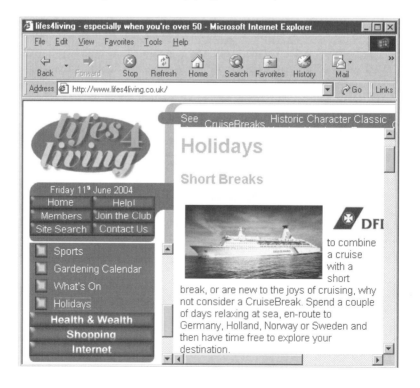

Exercise 3   Online shopping at www.waitrose.com:

Shopping at www.iceland.co.uk:

Exercise 4   A place to skate in Milton Keynes was found by going to
www.excite.co.uk>directory>Sports>Skating>Ice Skating>Skating Clubs
and Rinks:

Reproduced by courtesy of Roy Stubbs and Milton Keynes Ice Skating Club

Exercise 5   Use www.google.com to search for skating rinks:

Exercise 6   Following the directory listings on Altavista: Recreation>Pets>Fish and Aquaria> we discovered the Drumanee Aquatics site at www.drumaneeaquatics.co.uk:

Exercise 7   Details of the opening times of the National Railway Museum, York from www.nrm.org.uk:

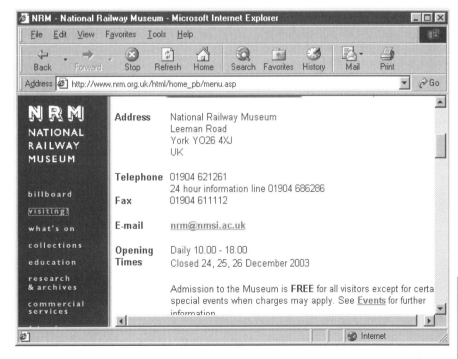

Reproduced courtesy of the National Railway Museum. © Trustees of the Science Museum, 2004

Exercise 8   Adding a Web image to a document:

43 Firtree Road
Beckwith
Derbyshire
DB5 1JT

15 July 2002

Dear Harvey

Searching the Web today I found the most brilliant information on breeding goldfish. The URL is http://members.aol.com/sirchin/gold-fish.htm but I've saved the information and will send it to you by e-mail once I get myself registered.

What do you think of this picture for our newsletter?

All the best

Jan

(Artwork supplied by Lyn Duedall).

Exercise 9   A Website on watercolour painting:

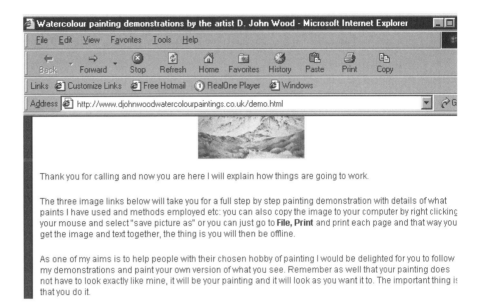

(Artwork supplied by D. John Wood).

Saving the page as a text file:

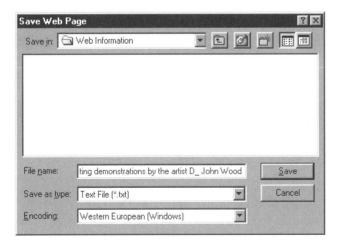

Opened as a text file:

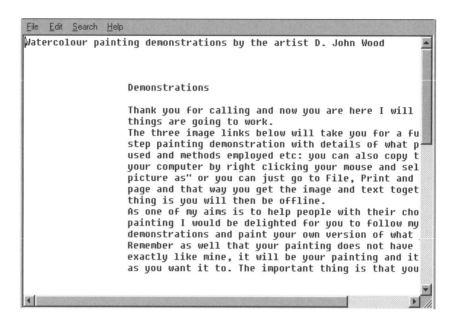

Exercise 10   Pasting information from www.toysrus.co.uk into Word:

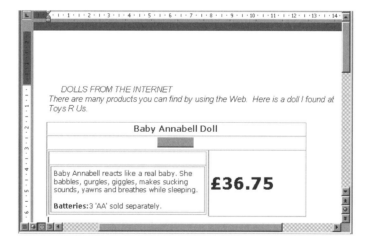

Exercise 11   Saving Web pages:

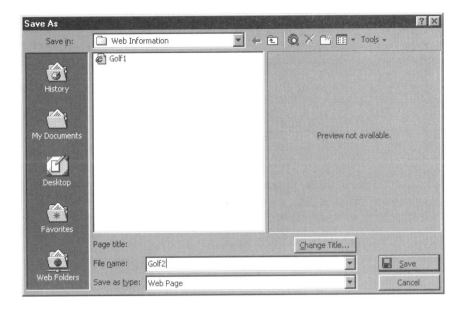

Exercise 12   Organizing favourite Web pages:

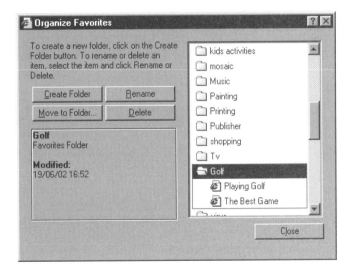

Exercise 13   Selecting the text of a news report:

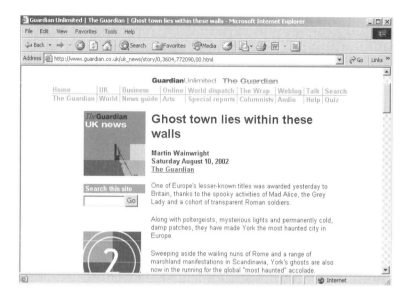

© The Guardian. www.guardian.co.uk

Pasting into Word:

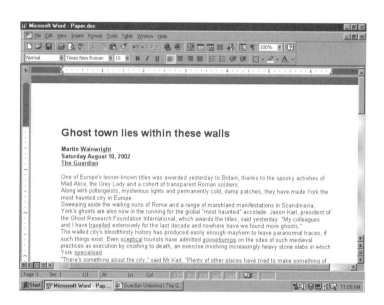

Exercise 14   Results of holiday search on www.firstchoice.co.uk:

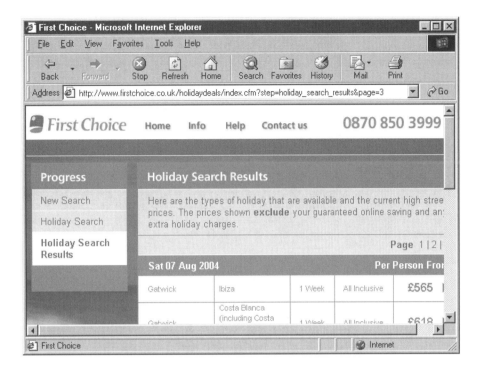

ANSWERS TO ADVANCED EXERCISES

Exercise 1   Writing an e-mail to a friend:

Exercise 2 Writing an e-mail to a TV company:

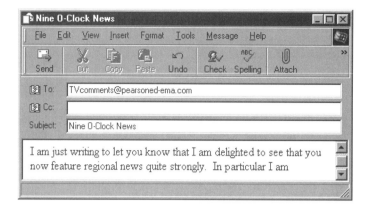

Exercise 3 Using the spell-checker:

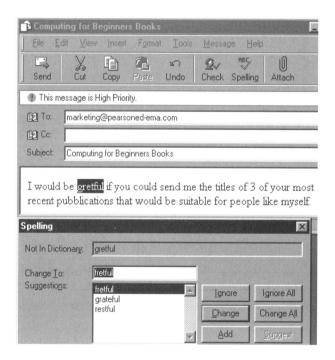

Exercise 4   Forwarding an e-mail:

Exercise 5   Replying to an e-mail:

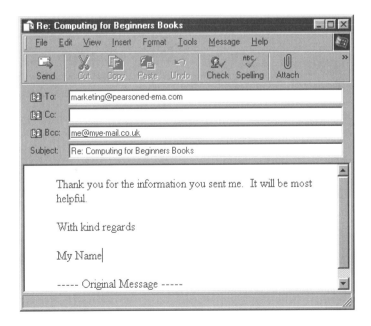

Exercise 6   Copying text between e-mail messages:

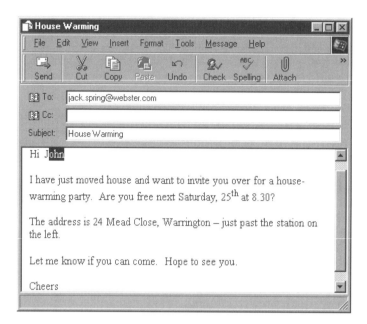

Exercise 7   Copying text between applications:

Exercise 8   Entering e-mail addresses in your Address Book:

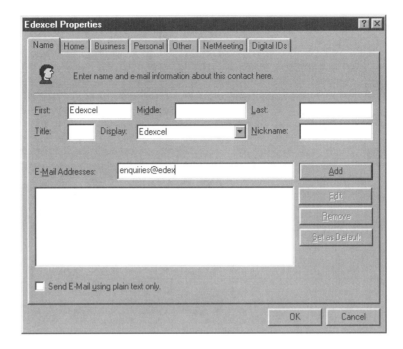

Exercise 9   Creating a group e-mail address:

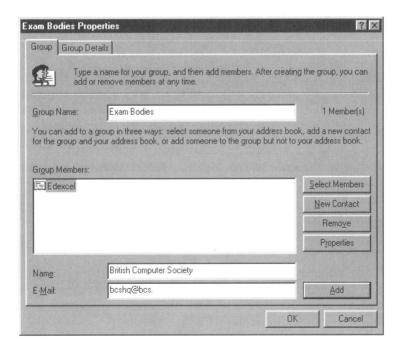

7

Exercise 10   Marking a message as unread:

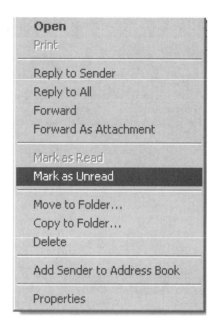

Exercise 11   Attaching a file to an e-mail:

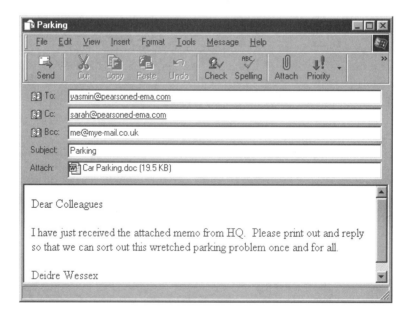

Exercise 12   Attaching another file to an e-mail:

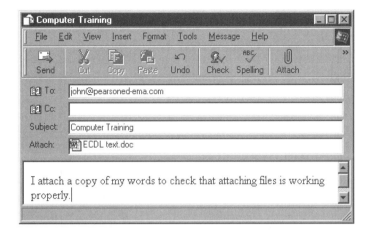

Exercise 13

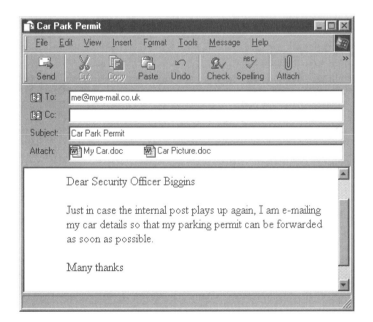

7

Exercise 14   Creating a new e-mail folder:

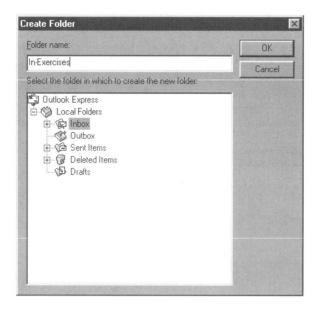

Exercise 15   Finding an e-mail:

Exercise 16   Crossword solutions:

7

Ideal books to accompany your Practical Exercises text:

Complete Coursebooks

Complete coverage of the syllabus, with lots of detail, examples, exercises, background information, hints and tips from experts, and much more! Ideal both for self-study and for tutor-led courses, the Complete Coursebooks will answer every question you could possibly have on the ECDL syllabus.

For Office 2003: 0131964313 (new for Dec 2004)
For Office 2000: 0130399159
For Office XP: 0130399175
For Office 97: 0131248421
Price: £19.99 – £21.99

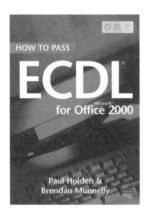

'How to Pass' Workbooks

Especially created for tutor-led courses, these workbooks will take you step-by-step through every part of the syllabus, using many worked examples to make sure you have fully understood each section. Check out the great four colour 'cut-out-and-keep' module reference guides – all the key information on each module, carefully laid out on these handy pull-outs.

For Office 2003: 0131964305 (new for Dec 2004)
For Office 2000: 0131130129
For Office XP: 0131130137
For Office 97: 0131130137
Price: £15.99 – £17.99

*Our books are written and designed to help you **study** for the ECDL, **remember** what you have learned – and **pass** the exams with confidence!*

To order or for more information, visit **www.pearson-books.com**